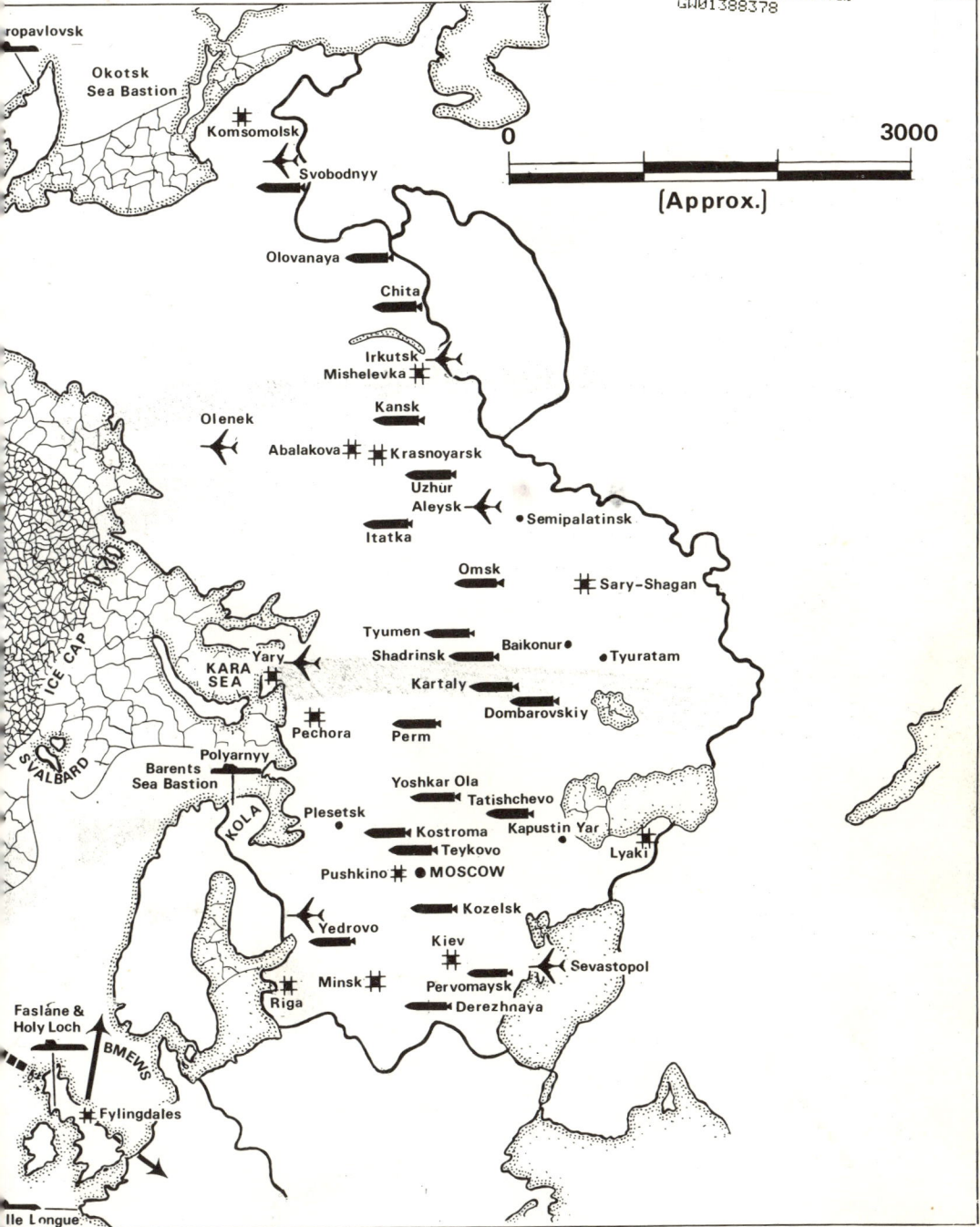

ropavlovsk

Okotsk
Sea Bastion

Komsomolsk

Svobodnyy

Olovanaya

Chita

Irkutsk
Mishelevka

Kansk

Olenek

Abalakova Krasnoyarsk

Uzhur
Aleysk

Itatka

Omsk

Semipalatinsk

Sary-Shagan

Tyumen

Baikonur

Shadrinsk

Tyuratam

KARA
SEA   Yary

Kartaly

Dombarovskiy

Pechora   Perm

Polyarnyy

Barents
Sea Bastion   Yoshkar Ola

KOLA   Tatishchevo

Plesetsk   Kapustin Yar

Kostroma   Lyaki

Teykovo

Pushkino   MOSCOW

SVALBARD

ICE CAP

Kozelsk

Yedrovo

Kiev   Sevastopol

Minsk

Pervomaysk

Riga   Derezhnaya

Faslane &
Holy Loch

BMEWS

Fylingdales

Ile Longue

0   3000

[Approx.]

GW01388378

HUGH FARINGDON

CONFRONTATION

The Strategic Geography of NATO and the Warsaw Pact

ROUTLEDGE & KEGAN PAUL

London and New York

First published in 1986
by Routledge & Kegan Paul plc
11 New Fetter Lane, London EC4P 4EE

Published in the USA by
Routledge & Kegan Paul Inc.
in association with Methuen Inc.
29 West 35th Street, New York, NY 10001

Set in Imprint
by Inforum Ltd, Portsmouth
and printed in Great Britain
by T J Press (Padstow) Ltd
Padstow, Cornwall

Library of Congress Cataloging in Publication Data

Faringdon, Hugh.

Confrontation: the strategic geography of NATO
and the Warsaw Pact.

Bibliography: p.
Includes index.
1. Europe—Defences. 2. North Atlantic Treaty Organization.
3. Warsaw Treaty Organization.
I. Title.
UA646.F37   1986   355'.03304   85–28123

British Library CIP data available

ISBN 0–7102–0676–3

Contents

Maps

Introduction

I can trace the immediate inspiration for this book to a hot day in midsummer. The location was an historic hall in central London. The speaker hailed from an anglophone foreign country, and he was discoursing on current issues of strategy (he pronounced it 'stradegy'). The audience was composed of typical representatives of the British upper class, or those who aspired thereto, and with few exceptions they displayed the correct tribal markings – dark suits, blue-striped collars, and hair curling at the nape of the neck. The ruddy complexions could have derived equally well from hours spent under a tropical sun or in expensive restaurants.

Every now and then a phrase from the rostrum cut through my reverie . . . 'attritional degradation of C³I'. That sounded good. . . . 'Capital units on the air/surface interface'. 'What are they?' I whispered to a neighbour. 'Aircraft carriers'.

A projection of South-West Asia flashed on the screen, and the speaker's hand glided from somewhere in Soviet Central Asia to the Arabian Sea, passing in one swift movement over those tracts of rocky ridges and desert which, doubtless for the sake of convenience, had been omitted from the map. There came upon me a realisation that I had once experienced during a talk by a celebrated American astronomer – THIS MAN DOESN'T KNOW WHAT HE IS TALKING ABOUT!

What was wrong? I was in no position to put our strategist right at the time, and I doubt whether I could do so now, but there welled up in me the conviction that much modern 'defence' debate is at fault when it ignores the deeper geographical and historical perspectives. There is something else, I am now reasonably certain. This is the enormous gulf which yawns between academic strategic studies on the one side, and the detail of weapons and military operations, which is the realm of the scientists and the serving officers.

Confrontation was born of these assorted frustrations. It focuses on the Soviet Union and the United States, and the zone where their geopolitical systems come into contact in Europe. It would have been foolish to have tried to compile a world strategic geography, and I hope I have resisted the temptation. You will find little or nothing here about the international arms trade, the work of the United Nations, the Arab-Israeli dispute or the injustices that reign in parts of Africa and Latin America. I accept the fact that nuclear weapons exist, but except in a narrow operational context I do not debate their rights or wrongs. At the same time I am aware that what matters to the Soviet Union and the United States on a global scale must matter indirectly to their European allies, and I have taken brief note of the out-of-area interests of these two superpowers.

I am not at all surprised that nobody has so far ventured to put together a geographical and historical survey of this kind. The great problem is how to reduce the subject matter to some kind of sense, without pretending that it is tidier than it really is. In outline the 'methodology' of *Confrontation* is straightforward. At the risk of appearing pompous, Part I, 'The Basics of Security and War', attempts to set forth the fundamental principles of policy-making, strategy and combat. We cannot progress very far in our enquiries before we have established, for example, the character of alliance systems, or whether hills and rivers are still important in warfare. Part II, 'The Map of Confrontation', applies the same process on a smaller scale to individual countries and the two alliances.

For up-to-date details of 'force levels' I refer readers to *The Military Balance* and *Strategic Survey*, both published annually by the International Institute for Strategic Studies, London, and to John Keegan's *World Armies*, the second edition of which appeared in 1983. A wealth of relevant information is also encapsulated in *The Europa Year Book* (Europa Publications, London), *The Statesman's Year-Book* (Macmillan Press, London) and *The World Almanac and Book of Facts* (Enterprise Newspaper Association Inc., New York).

This book was compiled without the benefit of access to any kind of privileged information, and is derived solely from a reading of history, recently published literature, maps and the ground.

Distances are given in kilometres, and elevations in metres. The 'billion' used here signifies one thousand million.

PART I

THE BASICS OF SECURITY AND WAR

CHAPTER 1

Political Considerations

THE IRON TRIANGLE

Words like 'patriotism', 'nation' and the Russian *rodina* derive from birth and relationships, and perhaps the old political philosophers were not so far astray when they compared states with extended families. The instinct to safeguard or extend the family property, and the family way of doing things, has led in its turn to the acquisition of weapons and the threat or reality of war.

The security policies of most developed states are the product of three main influences:

- interests
- resources
- commitments

INTERESTS

The most obvious danger to national security is posed by outright invasion. Britain was threatened in this way in 1588, 1805 and 1940, and the experience has been commonplace in continental Europe, with its land borders. At such times the issues are clear-cut, and there is an urgent incentive to build up armed forces and cast around for friends.

It is less easy to know what to do when the peril happens to be distant or indirect. A seemingly trivial incident might trigger off a major war if a government deems that the time has come to ward off an impending attack, or that something must be done to uphold the credibility of its pledged word.

A great deal of modern strategic calculation revolves around making sure that the nation continues to enjoy access to the resources that it needs for its survival. These natural commodities fall into two principal groups, namely sources of energy and metals.

Energy

The first oil well in history was drilled at Titusville, Pennsylvania, in 1859, and this date serves as well as any for the start of the second phase of the Industrial Revolution. Petroleum is the base material of many industrial processes, and a compact and very potent source of power for vehicle and aircraft. Here petroleum is likely to maintain its commanding lead into the foreseeable future over natural gas, coal, and nuclear and hydroelectric power, whose contribution is mainly or exclusively that of generating energy in static installations.

Strategic analysts rack their brains to work out how much individual states depend on imported oil. Countries like Japan and West Germany produce virtually nothing, but the simple division between 'producers' and 'non-producers' does not take us very far. The United States is anxious to conserve its native deposits of oil for strategic and economic reasons, and imports of oil account for about half the American consumption. The picture is further complicated by the fact that crude oil is not a uniform substance throughout the world. Some of the crudes are glutinous substances which yield a high proposition of heavy fuel oil and asphalt, while others are more productive of higher fractions like petrol and kerosene. Unless a country is very large it is unlikely to be able to produce a sufficient variety of crudes for all its needs, which accounts for the paradox that most net exporters of oil are also importers.

Chemically and geographically natural gas is the commodity most closely allied with oil. From the strategic point of view, however, the most important difference is probably that most natural gas is transported across frontiers by means of pipelines, which are vulnerable to sabotage, and which leave the consumers entirely at the mercy of the suppliers, who may so easily turn off the tap at source.

By way of contrast coal is relatively invulnerable. National reserves are measured in centuries, and about nine-tenths of the world's coal is consumed inside the very many countries where it is mined, which diminishes the danger of economic blackmail accordingly.

The principal 'Free World' sources of uranium are Canada, Australia and South Africa/Namibia. The volume of uranium is infinitesimally small compared with that of coal or oil, but it is a substance of unique strategic interest, being at once a source of energy and the raw material of nuclear weapons. The dangers of uranium's being misappropriated for military ends was shown in 1974, when uranium from Canada enabled the Indians to test their first nuclear device. The use of uranium for the generation of energy is very attractive to France, West Germany and other counties which are technically advanced but dependent on imported oil. In this respect too the middle 1970s happened to be a period of some importance, for the deposits of high-grade ore in the United States had become heavily depleted, and national economies were shaken by the twin oil crises of 1973 and 1978. Supplies of ore and processed yellowcake were now extremely difficult to obtain on the world market.

Metals

Depending on their use, metals may be divided into three main categories:

- The most basic are iron and the important non-ferrous metals copper, aluminium (from bauxite), lead and zinc.
- Ferro alloys form a second group. They are added to steel to give it toughness, hardness, resistance to corrosion or other special qualities. Tungsten, which is used in the production of armour plate, is a leading strategic member of this family, which also embraces chromium, cobalt, manganese, molybdenum, nickel and vanadium.
- Finally there are many industrial and military uses for 'exotic' ores like beryllium, columbium, gold, graphite, niobium, palladium, silver, tantalum and titanium.

Much of this assorted wealth is deposited in some of the most awkward locations it is possible to imagine. The world's cheapest and most physically accessible oil is found in the Middle East, and stands at the mercy of the notorious instabilities of that region. South Africa and the Soviet Union share probably the most significant reserves of gold, vanadium, platinum and natural diamonds, and tiny and eccentric Albania accounts for about one-third of the global production of chrome.

RESOURCES

The military power of a state is not just the product of measurable assets like industries, raw materials, population and so forth. It also results from the priority which the government awards to military spending, over and above the other very proper calls on its bounty, like education and health.

In peacetime the two elements – the physical resources and the actual military effort – usually come closest together in totalitarian states. The democratic countries tend to be slow off the mark in time of crisis, but if they are given the opportunity to organise themselves they will sometimes surprise their militaristic rivals by outdoing them in energy, efficiency and ruthlessness. This is what Soviet geopoliticians have in mind when they remark:

> when we come to determine the economic potential of capitalist countries we must take into account their inactive manufacturing power, their reserves of workers, and the extent of the national wealth. In the case of necessity all of this might serve to expand the volume of industrial production. (Ministry of Defence [Soviet], 1974, 7)

COMMITMENTS

Alliances

In an ideal world states will be able to safeguard all their vital interests without overstretching their resources. In reality there are limits to what an individual country can do, and throughout history many governments have found that they can provide themselves with adequate security only with the help of allies.

The grand treaties of alliance are no more than founding charters, and they are underwritten by a great number of smaller understandings which usually escape the public attention. Bi-lateral defence agreements are treaties concluded between pairs of nations within the alliance. There are documents providing for the exchange of equipment, technology and military intelligence. Status of Forces treaties govern the legal standing of troops on foreign soils, while Host Nation Support agreements arrange for help with transport and supplies. The Americans hold their base on Diego Garcia island in virtue of three oddly named 'Exchanges of Notes', which took place with Britain in 1966, 1972 and 1976. All the time the work of the civil servants and the military men helps to provide the alliances with a core of continuity and professionalism. Thus in the second half of the twentieth century 'while the public image of Anglo-American relations has been one of 'fading cooperation', the defence establishments of both countries have generally got on with the task of quietly but effectively coordinating their policies in various (often vital) areas of the defence field' (Baylis, 1984, 207).

An enemy will seek to undermine the unity of the alliance in various ways. In peacetime he exploits the fears and resentments of the weaker members. During hostilities he will be tempted to direct his blows along the boundary lines between national military contingents – the equivalent of slamming a ball directly between the partners in a match of tennis doubles.

Conversely, it becomes important for members of a league to uphold the unity of the alliance as an object in its own right. The risks must be shared out, as well as the benefits, and this important principle leads to some apparent military absurdities. The large American and British military establishment in West Germany, with its complement of families, housing and schools, is viewed by Germans not just as a strategic contribution but a pledge to defend German soil. In the same way cruise missiles have been apportioned to the territory of more NATO allies than is strictly necessary, just from the military point of view. It is also accepted that an outbreak of hostilities in a particular location must involve a response from as many different allies as is physically possible. This is the thinking behind the 'layer cake' deployment of national contingents along the NATO Central Front, with its multitude of vulnerable boundaries, and the same doctrine accounts for the variegated composition of NATO's strategic fire brigade, the ACE Mobile Force, which will be rushed to crisis points on the flanks of the alliance. Countries like Norway and Italy therefore have an assurance that they will not be left to face a threat without support from their friends.

At the same time no state can sacrifice itself unreservedly for the common good. Towards one extreme some of the members will earn their keep by a very feeble commitment. These uncharitable comments apply to Romania in the Warsaw Pact, and to Canada, Belgium, the Netherlands, Denmark and Norway in NATO. They know that in the last resort their more active partners would much rather have them in the league than out of it, and that by offering the use of their territory, for example for completing a chain of air defence radars, they do more for the alliance than by maintaining a few under-strength divisions. Iceland, which makes no direct military contribution to NATO whatsoever, is invaluable to the West for the bases which help to secure the Transatlantic passage.

Less obviously selfish, at first sight, is the notion that individual nations of an alliance ought to specialise in what they are best fitted to do by their geography, economy and traditions. Britain, for example, could withdraw its army from Germany and build up its naval and amphibious power. West Germany, on the other hand, could put on its Rommel goggles and expand its already impressive armoured forces, following its landbound destiny. Such arrangements would give a better return on military expenditure, but they could well lead to an ally facing a local crisis without support, which runs counter to the principle of risk-sharing. Also an alliance of specialists will find itself in a sorry state if one or more of the members drop out, leaving the others very weak in some essential military dimension.

The United States, as a centrally placed global power, cannot ignore the attractions of airborne mobility. This enables the Americans to stand by their pledge of support to European NATO, while retaining a powerful reserve in the United States, ready to fly or steam across the Atlantic when it is needed. There are some obvious risks. When defending troops are already in place on a potential theatre of war they contribute to stability, but when they are rushed in from outside they might heighten tension just when the diplomats are calling for an atmosphere of calm. The reinforcements and material, and especially those going by sea, are exposed to the possibility of attack on their passage, and there is a very real risk that before they can reach their destination their ports, airfields, and stocks of pre-positioned supplies and heavy equipment will have been overrun by the enemy, or rendered unusable by sabotage, aerial bombing, missile strikes or persistent chemical agents.

Non-aligned ('neutral') states

Ireland is a free-riding neutral, whose security depends on the fact that NATO forces stand between the Emerald Isle and the Warsaw Pact. More forthright is the posture of the armed neutrals Sweden, Switzerland, Austria and Yugoslavia, whose declared intention is to maintain a 'defence against help', holding their territory against all comers, at least in the early stages of an invasion. Finland stands in a special relationship to the Soviet Union, though in all other respects she is a fully qualified member of the group. The armed neutrals have a number of characteristics:

- Their national territory includes large areas of rocks, woods or other easily defensible ground.
- Their regular forces are small, but they have an impressive capacity for calling up trained reserves which are very suitable for purposes of local defence.

– They fear that the forces of the alliances, and especially the Warsaw Pact, might try to barge their way through the national territory, but they believe that the destruction of their state or independence will not be the primary objective of such an invasion.

NATO has a great deal to learn from the example of the armed neutrals in the way of organising reserves and civil defence, but in the last resort the preservation of neutral independence rests on the probability that the main forces of the two alliances will be at grips outside the national territory, and that they will not be able to spare many troops to bother the neutrals. It follows that armed neutrality is not a choice which is readily open to front-line European states.

GEOPOLITICS

Geopolitics is the study of the 'influence of geography on the political character of states, their history, institutions, and especially relations with other states' (*Supplement to the Oxford English Dictionary*).

The continental European style of geopolitics derives ultimately from Friedrich Ratzel (1844–1907), who was a pharmacist, geographer, naturalist, journalist and many other things besides. Ratzel, in a particularly influential article of 1896 ('The Laws of the Spatial Growth of States'), promoted the idea of the state as a living entity, whose limits were determined not by permanent treaty frontiers, but by its quasi-biological vigour.

Under the influence of Ratzel the Swedish political scientist Rudolf Kjellén (1864–1922) defined the 'geopolitical instinct' in more detail. In the process he actually coined the word *Geopolitik*, and he contributed further to our impression that a bleak, Nordic-sounding name is a prerequisite for those who wish to involve themselves in those arts.

The most important of the English-speaking geopoliticians was Sir Halford Mackinder (1861–1947), who was the author of the celebrated paper 'The Geographical Pivot of History' (1904). Mackinder's message was an uncomfortable one for the maritime powers, for he maintained that seaborne mobility was losing its historic advantages, and that the arrival of railways had given new potential to whatever state could dominate the land mass of Euro-Asia, a 'pivot area' which was rich in resources and lay beyond the reach of seapower. A similar theme was voiced by the once highly regarded German geopolitician Karl Haushofer (1869–1946), who argued that Germany and Russia, as the two great powers of Euro-Asia, must establish an 'absolutely unassailable' community of interest – an arrangement that would give the Germans the chance of grasping world domination.

Mackinder refined his own ideas with the passage of time, and in the middle of the twentieth century some interesting new directions in geopolitics were explored by American writers like Nicholas Spykman and Saul B. Cohen. In later years the British-born Colin S. Gray emerged as the most perceptive of the interpreters of Mackinder. Gray found that the basic teachings of the great man still stood up well, and that they illuminated the way in which the Soviet Union was acquiring world-wide naval power (*The Geopolitics of the Nuclear Era*, New York, 1977).

It is difficult to contemplate all of this without mixed feelings. Geopolitics is dangerously seductive, for a well-argued theory couched in geopolitical terms will correspond only too well to the kind of message which busy politicians and military men like to hear from the academic world, namely something which is simple, which explains everything, and which has never been thought of before. Geopolitics is not so much a science as a pseudo-science, hovering somewhere between the sinister and the ludicrous. It passes over significant detail, it underestimates the role of accident and personality, it is given to seeing patterns where they do not exist, and it is very bad at explaining why states which exist in similar environments fail to develop along the same lines.

The great virtues of geopolitics are the incentive it gives to form pictures beyond the confines of immediate time and space, and its rich storehouse of vocabulary and images. The word 'geopolitics' is very useful in itself, and much terminology of a more or less geopolitical nature has entered the language of geopolitical debate. Here are some of the most common terms:

- core regions (Derwent S. Whittlesey, 1939). These are the areas of good communications and economic development around which modern states have grown. Peter Vigor (*Soviet Blitzkrieg Theory*, 1983) applies the description 'chewable' to core areas which stand within easy reach of an aggressive neighbour, and we shall return to this productive notion on several occasions.
- heartland (Sir James Fairgrieve, 1915). The word was adopted by Mackinder in place of his own less euphonious 'pivot area', and it has remained in currency ever since.

– *Lebensraum*. In this emotion-laden term Haushofer and his school referred to directly ruled territory in which the German nation could find 'living space' for its expansion. Modern *Lebensraum* takes the form of freedom of access to natural resources in foreign countries, and it has more to do with political influence and economic domination.
– rimland (Nicholas Spykman, 1944). A word now used instead of Mackinder's 'inner crescent' to define countries located vulnerably around the fringes of the heartland.
– superpower (William Fox, 1944). This term was originally employed in relation to the Allied 'Big Three' in the Second World War. Since then, by common consent, only the United States and the Soviet Union deserve to qualify, in virtue of their technical development, the size of their territories, population and resources, the strength of their nuclear and conventional arsenals, and their ability to reach out to the world.
– Third World. This shadowy entity first came into being in the 1950s, when a French journalist hit on a phrase that he could apply to the nations which stood outside the two great power blocs. It has now acquired connotations of hot climates and post-colonial deprivation. The Japanese, South Koreans and Taiwanese were rapidly banished from the club, if indeed they were ever members, and the literature of current affairs also tends to exclude the oil-rich Middle Eastern states.

CHAPTER 2

Military Considerations

THE GEOPOLITICS OF NUCLEAR WAR

TARGETS

In their nuclear targeting, which is surely the blackest of all black arts, the main nuclear powers have distinguished between two types of objects. If the intention is to achieve a 'first strike' (a knockout blow against the victim's means of nuclear retaliation), then powerful and accurate warheads will be directed against 'counter force' targets like missile silos, strategic nuclear airfields and submarine bases, with their relevant command systems. There are about 1,700 such targets in the Soviet Union and 1,300 in the United States, as well as the high-priority military objectives which in theory can be destroyed without causing undue 'collateral damage' (i.e. killing civilians and wrecking property).

Nuclear deterrence rests upon the supposition that the aggressor will in his turn be at the receiving end of a 'second strike', delivered by the surviving launchers of the offended party. This blow will be aimed at the first party's cities, whose wretched populations are considered as hostages to the nuclear peace.

In an intercontinental nuclear exchange the societies of the two superpowers appear to be almost equally at risk, though in different ways. The United States is the more obviously vulnerable, since the national territory measures under half that of the Soviet Union, and it contains great cities like Los Angeles, Chicago and New York, which are bigger than anything in the Soviet Union. Russia, on the other hand, is vast, and the fifty largest Soviet cities contain only about 50,000,000 people, which is less than one-fifth of the whole. The Soviet political order is, however, much more highly centralised than that of the United States, and it might not survive an intercontinental exchange.

It is notoriously difficult to calculate possible fatalities, since so much depends on the warning time and shelter available, and whether the immediate targets are military or civilian. Estimates of the numbers of dead range from 5,000,000 to 165,000,000 Americans, and 3,700,000 to 100,000,000 citizens of the Soviet Union.

Western Europe will suffer badly in a nuclear war pitched at any level, for she has half a dozen megapoli like the British urban spine, which stretches down a corridor about sixty-five kilometres wide from Liverpool to London. Both of the superpowers stock thousands of nuclear warheads beyond their borders, and especially in the two Germanies, which accommodate the largest concentration of nuclear forces in the world.

The United States and the Soviet Union are approximately even as regards strategic nuclear power. They can devastate one another so completely that it is easy to forget that the nuclear arsenals of the secondary nuclear power, though puny in comparative terms, still have an immensely destructive capacity on any absolute reckoning. The Polaris A-3 missiles of the British strategic submarines are considered to be relatively inaccurate second-strike weapons of last resort. All the same they have a range of 4,600 kilometres, which is more than enough to destroy Moscow and its neighbourhood, inflicting between fifteen and twenty million casualties. The French strategic nuclear force is also a very deadly machine.

From the east, the Soviet Union is threatened by the land-based missiles and manned bombers of the People's Republic of China. Moscow must also be aware that, with the exception of India and Libya, the potential or emerging third-rate nuclear powers are unsympathetic to the Soviet Union, and that five of them (Israel, Iran, Pakistan, Taiwan and South Korea) are arranged around or close to its southern perimeter. Not only does 'proliferation' accentuate the gravest single strategic weakness of the Soviet Union, which is the threat of nuclear attack from many different directions, but it presents the Soviet leadership with the problem of calculating the response of a number of independent centres of nuclear decision-making.

STRATEGIC DELIVERY SYSTEMS

The nuclear superpowers repose their trust in a spread of weapons systems, a 'Triad' of forces consisting of:

- Land-based long-range rockets (Intercontinental Ballistic Missiles, ICBMs)
- Nuclear missile submarines (SSBNs)
- Manned bombers, or the 'air-breathing leg' of the Triad in the barbaric jargon of this barbaric business

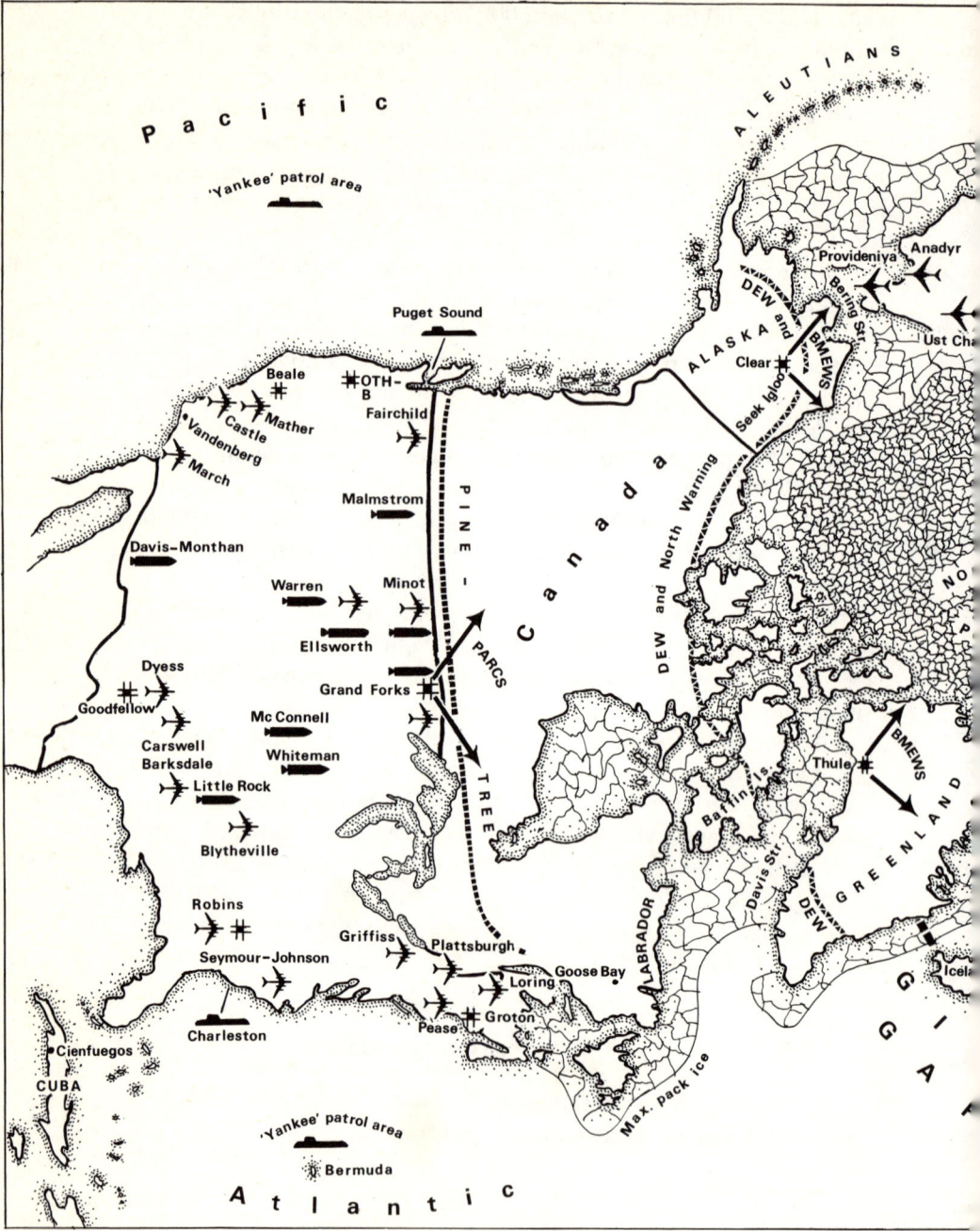

MAP 1   The Nuclear Superpowers

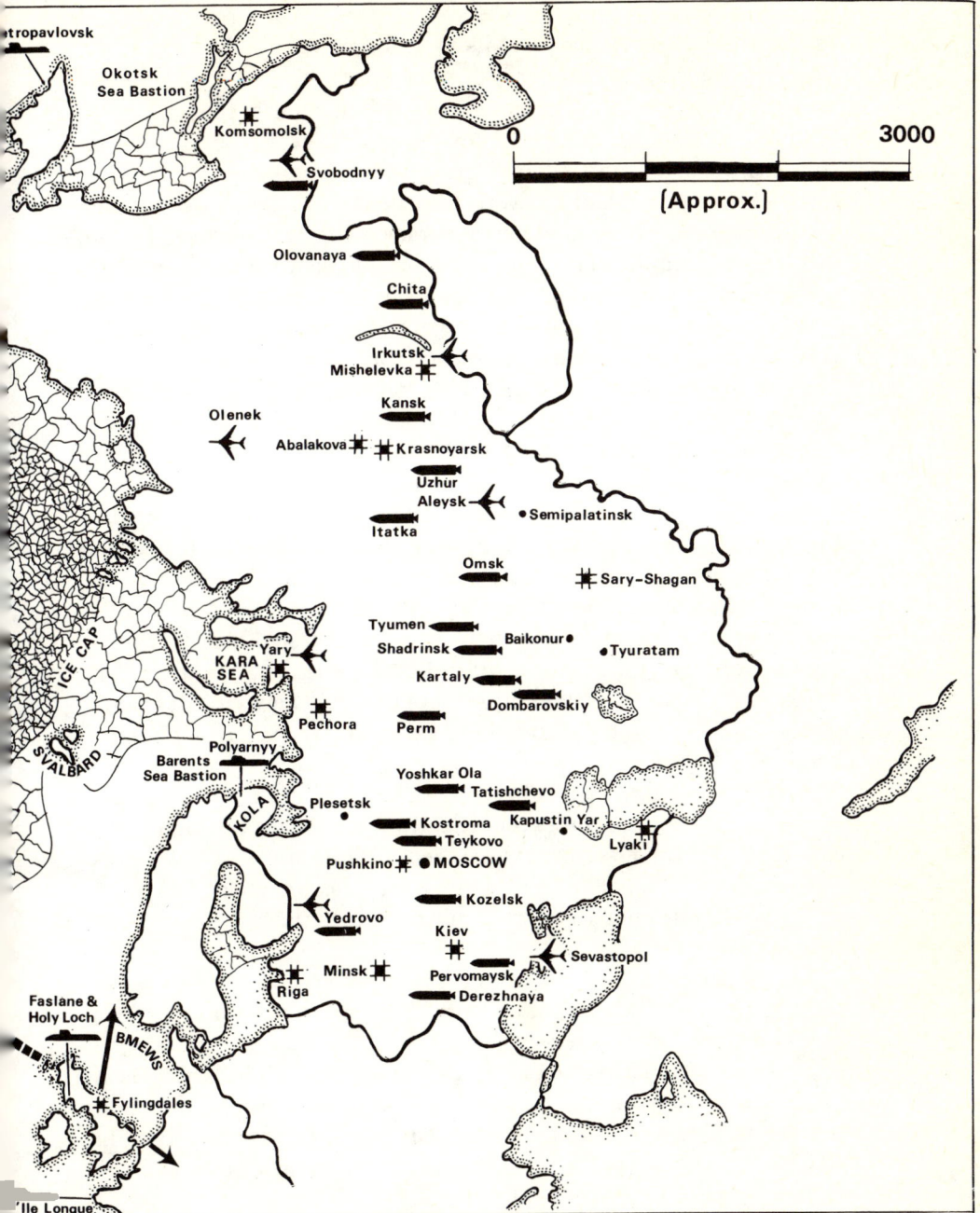

Petropavlovsk

Okotsk
Sea Bastion

Komsomolsk

Svobodnyy

0   3000

(Approx.)

Olovanaya

Chita

Irkutsk
Mishelevka

Kansk

Olenek

Abalakova   Krasnoyarsk

Uzhur
Aleysk   • Semipalatinsk
Itatka

Omsk   Sary-Shagan

Tyumen
Shadrinsk   Baikonur•   • Tyuratam

Kartaly
Dombarovskiy

Yary
KARA
SEA
Pechora   Perm

Polyarnyy
Barents   Yoshkar Ola
Sea Bastion   Tatishchevo
Plesetsk •
KOLA   Kostroma   Kapustin Yar
Teykovo   Lyaki
Pushkino • MOSCOW

ICE CAP

SVALBARD

Yedrovo   Kozelsk

Kiev
Faslane &
Holy Loch   Minsk   Pervomaysk   Sevastopol
Riga   Derezhnaya
BMEWS

Fylingdales

Ile Longue

Individually, each type of weapon suffers from important dis-advantages which detract from its overall capability; taken together, the elements of the Triad are formidable.

Land-based intercontinental nuclear missiles suffer the least from limitations on size, because they do not have to be carried in submarines or aircraft. These great tubes are stuffed with large quantities of propellant, powerful warheads and elaborate systems for guidance and evasion. Their accuracy is further improved by the fact that the location of the parent silo (underground launching tube) is known with near-absolute exactitude – something which is virtual-ly impossible for nuclear-armed vessels or aircraft. Finally the launching crews enjoy direct and easy contact with their command centres. On the other hand the large land-based systems offer static targets to an enemy first strike, and the silos cannot be guaranteed against destruction, in spite of all the steel and concrete 'hardening' which might be built into them.

As a general rule the Soviets and Americans locate their intercon-tinental missiles in the bleak interiors of their land masses. However, the situation of the superpowers does not match exactly. The Soviets have a vast national territory but only short stretches of usable coastline, and for that reason they have invested nearly three-quarters of their nuclear force in land-based missiles. At the time of writing they possess 1,398 silos, most of them clustered in sites along a belt about 1,500 kilometres wide, extending from the neighbour-hood of Moscow to that of Lake Baikal along the axis of the Trans-Siberian Railway. The path of nuclear exchange with the United States does not cross the Atlantic or Pacific, as we might have expected, but traverses the Arctic, and a flight of 6,000 kilometres (well within the range of modern missiles), lasting about forty-five minutes, is quite enough to bring destruction to the core areas of the two nations.

The Americans have explored a variety of eccentric schemes for putting their rockets in mobile launchers, but in the middle 1980s their deterrent is still housed in oldish sites scattered across the central states from Montana south-east to Arkansas. The Titan IIs at Davis Monthan Air Force Base in Arizona stand to the south-west of the main alignment. Another odd man out is Vandenberg base in California, which has become important for missile tests and the launching of military space shuttles.

The peculiar characteristics of nuclear missile submarines are just as strongly pronounced. Their 'shooting', though much improved, is still relatively inaccurate, and communication with command centres is beset with great problems, since radio waves do not readily penetrates the sea (see p. 40). In compensation the water gives the submarines a high degree of concealment.

The ideal home base for a nuclear missile submarine will have unobstructed access to the chosen patrol area. The Americans have the advantage in this respect, with their long and open sea coasts, and the United States has placed nearly half of its deterrent on board submarines, leaving the silos and aircraft with about one-quarter each. The Americans also benefit from their wide and well-established network of bases and facilities overseas. The Soviet control systems are largely confined to the Russian land mass, and the unfavourable maritime geography of the Soviet Union (see p. 76) means that the Soviets find it roughly twice as difficult as the Americans to keep a given number of submarines on station.

The missiles of the strategic submarines have acquired progressively greater range ever since these craft made their appearance in the early 1960s. The first American Polaris submarines, armed with the 2,200-kilometre A-1 missile, were forced to cruise close to Soviet shores in the Arctic. Advances in range generated interest in the Mediterranean, and then in the northern Indian Ocean. From 1980 the 7,400-kilometre range of the Trident I (C-4) missile opened further vast tracts of the world's oceans to the patrolling American craft, and the advent of the Trident II (D-5), which has a range of about 11,000 kilometres, has given the Americans almost unlimited freedom of deployment.

The home ports of the American strategic missile submarines are Charleston (South Carolina) and King's Bay (Georgia) on the Atlantic coast and Puget Sound on the Pacific, and there are forward bases at Holy Loch in Scotland and on the island of Guam in the Pacific, to save the long and potentially dangerous transits from the United States. The old base at Rota in Spain is no longer used.

Like all large nuclear-missile submarines, the American SSBNs keep sedulously clear of hostile forces. However, the arrival of long-range and accurate cruise missiles has caused as much confusion of roles at sea as on land. Many of the American attack submarines, whose primary duty is to seek out the enemy at sea, have now been equipped with Tomahawks to be fired from their torpedo tubes.

A different pattern may be observed in the deployment of the Soviet strategic submarines. An older generation of vessel, the Yankee class, still patrols off the east and west coasts of North America, in order to bring targets within reach of its stubby missiles.

The newer weapons have a longer reach, and the submarines of the modern Delta classes are able to stand back in home waters and still strike at America without having to make the passage through choke-points like the celebrated Greenland–Iceland–United Kingdom (GIUK) Gap. The domestic patrol areas, or 'sea bastions', are fairly small, but they allow the submarines to operate under close air and naval protection. The Sea of Okhotsk offers a zone of this kind for the Soviet Pacific Fleet, and the Barents Sea does the same for the Northern Fleet.

The first double-hulled Typhoon class submarine has gained a further dimension for the Soviet force of strategic vessels. At 30,000 tons the displacement of this monster is greater than that of some battleships of the First World War. The Typhoon is armed with SS-N-20 missiles, which have a range of 8,300 kilometres, and the peculiar construction of the hull enables the craft to operate under the cover of the Arctic ice cap.

It used to be fashionable to write off the manned bomber as a hopelessly vulnerable element of the Triad. Strategists opened the figurative dustbin lid with some regret, for they valued aircraft for their unique responsiveness and flexibility. No other nuclear weapons system could be so easily recalled, diverted to alternative targets or adapted for a conventional role.

In the 1970s and 1980s the manned bomber sprang into new and vigorous life. The aged American B-52 has a large and strong airframe, which can be gutted and filled up again with new equipment, and this remarkable machine is likely to see service into the next century as a cruise missile carrier. Craft like the American F-111 and B-1, and the Soviet Fencer, Backfire and Blackjack, have swing wings and advanced radar, and can fly fast and low under the radar horizon. Another principle, that of 'stealth' technology, is being exploited by the Americans to build bombers which are well-nigh invisible to radar.

The manned bomber poses a greater threat to the Soviet Union than to the United States, which is more geographically isolated, and the Soviets therefore devote considerable resources to the air defence of their homeland. The Americans have F-111 bases in Britain (see p. 217), though the main tasks of the aircraft are tactical nuclear and conventional strikes. In peacetime most of the B-52s are deployed in the mainland United States, and there are significant concentrations in California and the north-east.

STRATEGIC EARLY WARNING SYSTEMS

Anti-ballistic missiles (ABMs) are ground-based defensive missiles which have the very difficult task of destroying the incoming strategic nuclear warheads. The relevant technology must always be very costly and complicated, and for many years the only operational system of the kind has been the double ring of Galosh installations around Moscow. Early in 1985, however, the Americans declared their intention of developing a 'star wars' defence system, designed to destroy missiles by laser beams directed from or by way of space satellites (see p. 24).

Otherwise the main defensive effort of the superpowers has gone into building up early warning systems, through which they hope to identify missile or bomber attack in time to alert their civil defence, and activate their anti-aircraft missiles and interceptor aircraft. A hostile missile launch might be identified in as little as ninety seconds by satellite – for example an American machine stationed over the Indian Ocean and looking into Siberia.

The Anti-Ballistic Missile Treaty of 1972 permits the two super-powers to establish ballistic missile early warning radars on the peripheries of their national territories. Some of the most powerful machines currently available for this purpose are the phased array radars, which are massive static structures, looking like a giant fence, which manoeuvre their beams electronically, unlike the conventional radars with their rotating antennae.

The largest radars 'acquire' the incoming missiles at great ranges, and pass them on to supplementary radars in the interiors, which identify the nature of the threat with greater precision. Com-plementary radars give notice of attack by aircraft or cruise missiles.

Moscow and European Russia are cushioned by early warning stations at Kiev, Minsk and Riga near the western borders, Yary and Pechora near the northern end of the Urals, and Lyaki in the south near the Caspian Sea. The Soviets are also on their guard against missile attack from China in the south-east, though at the time of writing it is difficult to gain information on the status of their radars on this flank.

The principal nuclear threats to the United States come from missiles and manned aircraft arriving from the direction of the Arctic, and from shorter-ranged missiles launched from submarines lurking offshore. The Americans are vulnerable to this second form of attack, for most of their population is located within 320 kilometres of the coasts.

Responsibility for the strategic nuclear readiness of North America lies primarily with the US-Canadian NORAD (North American Air Defense) Command, which was set up in 1958. The headquarters is sited about 300 metres inside Cheyenne Mountain, Colorado, and monitors nearly eighteen million square kilometres of airspace between the Arctic and the Mexican border. NORAD controls early warning satellites, satellite- and space object-detecting systems, and a great battery of radar systems (some of them surprisingly old) which give a coverage of sorts around the perimeter of the North American land mass.

Northward-looking systems

BMEWS

The Ballistic Missile Early Warning System is designed to detect nuclear missile attack up to a range of 4,800 kilometres, and it represents the outermost and the longest-seeing of the ground-based systems. The first of the stations became operational in 1960, and its twelve great radars are now installed in three locations in the wilds of Clear (Alaska), Thule (Greenland) and Fylingdales Moor (Yorkshire, England).

PARCS (PERIMETER ACQUISITION RADAR ATTACK CHARACTERIZATION SYSTEM)

Near Grand Forks, North Dakota, stands a solitary phased-array radar, representing the last element of a now dismantled active anti-ballistic missile system. The PARCS has a range of 2,800 kilometres and an arc of 130 degrees, and it provides a useful backup for the thinly spread BMEWS line.

PINETREE LINE

This is the oldest of the anti-aircraft radar systems. Its remaining twenty-four sites stretch across southern Canada from Vancouver Island to Goose Bay in Labrador, and they are being allowed to sink into obsolescence.

DEW LINE

The Distant Early Warning Line was built in the later 1950s. It lies much further north than the Pinetree Line, stretching along the Arctic shore of the Canadian mainland, and prolonged by two stations in Iceland and one in Scotland. The range of the individual radars is 320 kilometres. DEW was built to give warning of attack by manned aircraft, like the Pinetree, but it also has the capacity of detecting the new threat of cruise missiles, which has helped to extend the life of its surviving thirty-one stations.

Eastward- and westward-looking systems

OTH-B

Over-the-horizon-backscatter radars are powerful new devices which bounce their pulses off the ionosphere. They are effective up to 3,350 kilometres, and provide good coverage against aircraft and cruise missiles when these objects are still below the direct line of sight. The system is still under development, but one station will be installed on the east coast (Bangor, Maine), another on the west coast, and possibly a third looking south from the interior. OTH-Bs have a minimum range of 900 kilometres, and they cannot be pointed towards the north, on account of interference caused by the aurora borealis.

PAVE PAWS

These are modern phased-array radars, which have the ability to detect submarine-launched missile attack up to a range of 5,500 kilometres. Stations have been built in Massachusetts (Otis Air Force Base) and California (Beale AFB). A third site is under construction in Georgia (Robins AFB), and a fourth is planned for Texas (Goodfellow AFB).

Patrolling AWACS aircraft (see p. 26) help to cover some of the gaps left by the ground systems. Active defence against manned aircraft is the business of fighters and a number of batteries of elderly Nike missiles.

In 1982 an Air Defence Master Plan outlined programmes for updating the strategic nuclear defence of North America, and especially for giving improved warning of attack by cruise missles and manned bombers. In addition to the OTH-Bs mentioned above, the Plan suggested the construction of a new line of conventional radars across Alaska (Seek Igloo System), and a continuation along the coast of the Arctic Ocean to southern Greenland (North Warning System). The DEW line is to be deactivated, and the Pinetree Line gradually phased out.

THEATRE DELIVERY SYSTEMS

The all-round radar systems of the United States emphasise the fact that North America is a geopolitical island, and the arrival of an effective 'star wars' anti-ballistic missile system might decouple the United States still further from the defence of European NATO, which is distant and vulnerable. Already the introduction of so-called 'theatre' nuclear systems has reminded Western Europeans that they live on a small peninsula, tacked onto the great Euro-Asian land mass.

For many years, when strategists considered the purpose of nuclear weapons, they were able to identify two main categories which could be told apart without too much difficulty, on account of the ways they were made and deployed. These were long-range strategic systems, which were designed primarily for intercontinental nuclear destruction, and tactical nuclear forces (short-range missiles, aircraft bombs and large-calibre artillery shells), which were intended for use on or closely behind the battle field, and lacked range, accuracy and destructive power. Thus, while the Titan II rocket can strike to a distance of 15,000 kilometres, the nuclear shell of the American 203 mm can be lobbed only as far as 16.

From the middle 1970s, however, things have been complicated beyond measure by the advent of very effective middle-range weapons, whose baleful influence extends from the battlefield to the whole of the European continent, including western Russia. Medium bombers like the Soviet Backfire and some versions of the American F-111 can fit easily into this role, for they have unrefuelled combat ranges in excess of 3,000 kilometres. Among the land-based missiles the Soviet SS-20 was first deployed in 1977, and combines the compactness and mobility of the tactical systems with an entirely new order of destructive power, accuracy and range (5,000 kilometres). The SS-20 can be deployed as far back as the Urals, and still deposit its multiple warheads anywhere within an arc drawn from Greenland through North Africa to the Middle East.

NATO hesitated to respond in kind, hoping that this new dimension in the arms race might be curtailed by talks, but at the end of 1983 the alliance began to deploy two new American theatre nuclear systems in Western Europe. The weapons in question were the mobile Pershing II rocket (with a total of 108 launchers), and the low-flying Tomahawk cruise missile: 464 Tomahawks were to be deployed in Europe altogether, made up of 160 in Britain, 112 in Italy, 96 in West Germany and 48 each in the Netherlands and Belgium.

The declared range of the Pershing II is 1,800 kilometres, which indicates that missiles launched from West Germany would cover Eastern Europe but fall short of Moscow. The range of the Tomahawk is given as 2,400 kilometres, which extends over Moscow but not as far as the Urals.

There is nothing new about cruise missiles as such, for they are descended from the German V-1s of 1944. The core of the American models is their guidance system, which depends on very accurate mapping. Whereas the other long-range missiles sail through the ether with lordly indifference to the ground beneath, the Tomahawk is sub-sonic and low-flying, and grubs its way forward over a pre-planned and circuitous route by means of a terrain contour-matching guidance system (TERCOM), which every now and then corrects its complementary inertial guidance system by 'reading' a selected block of land over which it has just flown and comparing it with an electronic map that is stored in its primitive brain.

Individual cruise missiles are vulnerable to interception, and not just by the enemy, but by outraged neutrals whose national airspace they violate on the way to the target. However, cruise missiles are very cheap devices, by the standards of modern weaponry, and they will probably be launched *en masse* with the intention of saturating the defensive systems. The fact that cruise missiles are capable of being intercepted is something which turns in one respect to the advantage of the West, for a relatively small investment in these weapons will force the Soviets to divert further costly resources to their national air defence.

Western European countries were plunged into what Dr Henry Kissinger calls a state of 'schizophrenia' by the theatre nuclear weapons. In the late 1970s leaders like Helmut Schmidt of West Germany feared that the United States would become 'decoupled' from the defence of Western Europe unless the Americans answered the SS-20 by installing effective devices of their own on European soil. In the 1980s, however, the slow deployment of cruise missiles in Europe took place in the teeth of vocal opposition from an 'anti-cruise' movement in public opinion, which argued that the Americans might employ Europe as a weapons platform for a 'stand-off' nuclear war against the Soviet Union. The effect would be to leave Europe in ruins, while the United States (which lies beyond the reach of theatre nuclear weapons) survived the passage of arms unscathed.

SPACE

There is no hard and fast rule defining the border between air and space. In fact the American space shuttles (which to outward appearances have the aerodynamics of a brick) represent a hybrid between space vehicle and aircraft. For practical purposes, however, the dividing line comes at an altitude of about 100 kilometres, where the atmospheric gases attenuate into nothingness.

The main object of space rockets and shuttles is to throw satellites into orbit. Satellites have a number of real or potential military purposes:

- early warning and high orbital surveillance
- intelligence gathering on low orbit
- relaying signals
- meteorology
- providing accurate navigational fixes
- destroying enemy satellites
- destroying strategic missiles in a 'star wars scenario'

A few brief details are called for. Communications and early warning satellites are positioned in high orbit of about 36,000 kilometres and they stand 'geosynchronously' above the equator – in other words, they keep pace with the rotation of the earth and are therefore stationary in relation to objects on the surface. Intelligence-gathering satellites loop the earth at high velocity and at low orbits of about 200 kilometres. They pass over the target areas, and then over receiving stations where they can 'dump' their electronic intelligence and television pictures in quick bursts of transmissions.

The development, testing and deployment of space-based defensive systems and their components are banned under Article 5 of the American and Soviet Anti-Ballistic Missile Treaty of 1972. On 23 March 1983, however, President Reagan made his 'Star Wars' speech foreshadowing a Strategic Defense Initiative – a programme of research into the interception of strategic missiles from ground and space. A system based on satellites will probably be targeted against Soviet missiles in their 'boost phase' – the four or five minutes after takeoff – and before the release of multiple warheads and decoys. The cheapest solution seems to be to put reflecting mirrors into orbit, and use them as relay points for laser beams fired from the ground. A full orbiting battle station will probably have to be a substantial piece of hardware, capable not only of directing particle or laser beams against the earth, but of surviving hostile attack in space.

The ends of this book do not extend into space voyages or artistic perceptions, but as people of the later twentieth century we cannot banish from our minds the image of the spaceman's view of the earth as a glowing orb, fixed in the blackness of the universe. Amid all the blue and the swirling white, the predominant golden-brown hue of the land masses offers a reminder of how vulnerable mankind is to physical changes which are, in cosmic terms, minute. Countries like Russia and Canada might benefit in the long term from any general warming of the climate, but drought and the unshielded brassy sun have already helped to devastate a broad belt of the subtropical world. The effect has been to give new relevance to Mackinder's statement that 'the southern border of Europe was and is the Sahara rather than the Mediterranean, for it is the desert which divides the black man from the white' (reprinted in Kasperson and Minghi, 1970, 164).

AIR WAR

CHARACTERISTICS OF AIR WAR

Machines like the American F-15 Eagle fighter are capable of tearing through the air as fast as 2,600 kilometres per hour, and speed is certainly of the very essence of aircraft. When, however, we look at aircraft in the mass, or air power in general, then flexibility is the quality which springs most readily to mind.

In-flight refuelling makes it practicable for normally short-ranged aircraft to span the oceans. Within the European theatre NATO aircraft are able to transfer concentrations of striking power between the Central Front, to delay a Warsaw Pact assault while the friendly ground forces are still moving into position, or to attack local break-throughs. The Soviets might find it equally expedient to move large quantities of Backfire bombers to airfields in the Kola peninsula, from where these aircraft can strike at shipping in the middle of the Atlantic. Individual types of aircraft are by no means confined to the roles for which they were specifically designed. For example, in case of emergency almost anything that flies might be called on to help in ground attack.

Much of this flexibility will derive into the foreseeable future from the combination of machine with pilot or aircrew. Manned aircraft are capable of responding to a uniquely wide range of challenges, and human flying and combat skills are still a deciding factor in aerial warfare. The work of missiles, pilotless drones and reconnaissance satellites is becoming more important, but the contributions of these devices are likely to remain highly specialised.

The speed and flexibility of aircraft might appear to be very responsive to centralised control. In reality the higher commanders are faced with great problems of 'airspace management' – that is, sorting out the multitudes of flying objects that will show themselves in European skies in wartime, and conveying the appropriate instructions to interested parties. Meanwhile the aircraft will go about in almost as much peril from friendly anti-aircraft defences as they do from those of the enemy.

There is an obvious need for unified air command. This has always been enjoyed by the Warsaw Pact, in virtue of the dominant role of the Soviet Union, and in 1977 NATO was impelled to set up the joint headquarters of the Allied Air Forces Central Europe (AAFCE), which controls air operations on the Central Front with the help of a Central Control and Information System.

It is scarcely possible to exaggerate the importance of NATO's next move, when twelve member nations combined to establish flying command and early warning posts. These are the E3-A Sentry aircraft of NATO's Airborne Warning and Control System (AWACS).

Adapted from the Boeing 707 civilian airliner, the E3-As are equipped with revolving radomes which enable the operators to detect and plot the movements of hundreds of aircraft, missiles and ships up to a range of about 400 kilometres. Thus a single aircraft, on orbit over the Rhine at 12,000 metres, acquires a picture of air movements well into East Germany and Czechoslovakia. The E3-As have the endurance to stay aloft for twelve hours at a time, and they give NATO a chance of warning against sudden attack, as well as a centralised but highly mobile means of directing aerial operations and anti-aircraft defence. The comparable Soviet aircraft (SUWACS) are by no means so well equipped.

The first of the eighteen NATO E3-As came into operation in 1982. Their main operating base is at Geilenkirchen, near Mönchengladbach in West Germany, and they have Forward Operating Bases at Oerland (Norway), Preveza (Italy), Trapani (Greece) and Konya (Turkey). The crews are fully integrated ones, drawn from several member nations at a time, and the AWACs would have been upheld as a shining example of inter-NATO co-operation if the British had not chosen to develop an early warning fleet of their own. The British systems communicated fully with those of their allies, but the British have encountered severe problems in developing adequate computers for their NIMWACS aircraft, and at the time of writing it is uncertain when these very expensive machines will enter service. For the time being Britain's airborne radar coverage is maintained by old Shackletons.

USES OF AIR POWER

Reconnaissance

Surveillance was historically the first role of military flying machines, and it dates from the balloons which the French employed at the battle of Fleurus in 1794. Many modern aircraft have been adapted for the reconnaissance role, in addition to specially designed high-altitude spyplanes of the U-2 type. Thus the reconnaissance version of the Soviet Bison bomber wings its lonely way over the oceans of the world, while the pilots of the American RF-4 Phantoms train for their desperate dash over the battle lines on the Central Front.

Transport

Airpower makes a unique contribution to long-distance strategic mobility. Three wide-bodied jets are sufficient to carry the 900 men of an American battalion across the Atlantic at a speed of up to about 800 kilometres per hour.

Inside a theatre of operations, medium-lift aircraft and helicopters are available to shift reinforcements and supplies, and thus contribute to the mobility of reserves. Airborne assault is a specialised form of aerial movement. Parachute drops of the classic kind are by no means outmoded, but helicopters have the advantage of being able to make use of troops who have undergone the ordinary infantry training.

Ground attack

Close air support (CAS) may be executed by attack helicopters as well as fixed-wing aircraft, and it extends over the battlefield and the immediate rear areas up to about twenty kilometres from the forward edge of the friendly troops.

Interdiction

Long-range attack, or 'interdiction', aims to knock out targets like airfields, tactical nuclear weapons, armoured columns, stores and bridges. The strike aircraft proper are usually supported by planes which have specific tasks against radar systems and anti-aircraft defences.

Air defence and air superiority

Aircraft are important for the defence of ground forces, rear areas, shipping and homelands. The ideal air-defence fighter, or interceptor, is a very high-performance aircraft, which has great agility, speed and rate of climb at a range of altitudes. Its elaborate radar equipment enables it to operate at night and in bad weather, and gives it a 'look down, shoot down' capability against low-flying aircraft and cruise missiles.

AIRCRAFT AND THEIR NEEDS

The military helicopter came to its own in the 1960s, utilising newly developed turbine engines which were much superior to their reciprocating predecessors. Since then the trend in helicopter design has favoured specialisation, and fairly clear distinctions have emerged between general transport helicopters, troop-carrying assault helicopters (e.g. the American Blackhawk; the Soviet Mi-8 Hip), and attack helicopters like the American AH-64 Apache or the Soviet Mi-24 Hind D, which are armoured helicopter gunships, capable of absorbing considerable punishment, and of dealing it out with their machine guns and missiles. The Soviet Hokum represents a further and inevitable development, that of a machine designed to engage enemy helicopters in combat.

In contrast it is by no means easy to pin down fixed-wing aircraft to a particular function. Only rarely do we encounter machines like spyplanes, which are designed just for surveillance at very high altitudes, or an aircraft like the American A-10 Thunderbolt whose every feature shows its dedication to close ground attack. Nevertheless aircraft are very sensitive to their surroundings, and climate and physical geography will often determine a nation's final choice of machine.

Even when they have the use of radar, experienced pilots are unhappy about taking to the skies when the cloud ceiling presses down to 100 metres, or the lateral visibility falls to below one and a half kilometres. It is highly relevant for NATO that the skies of Central Europe are very murky by world standards, and that in midwinter the sun rises only at about eight in the morning and sets at tea time. Here an investment in a very expensive aircraft like the multi-role Tornado will prove to be good economy if it results in good performance in all weathers. In a very different environment Canada and Australia have chosen to equip their air services with the American-made F-18 Hornet, which has the characteristics required for long flights over the Arctic and Pacific oceans.

Of all the kinds of major military vehicles, tactical aircraft are the ones with the shortest operational endurance. Within a matter of minutes or a very few hours they must come back to earth to be serviced and replenished with fuel and munitions. Theoretical combat ranges must be reduced by about two-thirds to yield the true combat radius, taking account of the outward and inward journeys, and the time spent over the target, and the figures will be cut further still if the pilot makes much use of his afterburner, which guzzles fuel at an astonishing rate. The location and characteristics of airfields therefore have great geopolitical significance.

All conventional aircraft require a longer run for take-off than for landing. As some indication of the distances concerned, we may mention that an advanced interceptor usually takes off in less than 800 metres and lands in under 400. Medium and heavy transport aircraft take off between 850 and 3,500 metres, and land in between 460 and 2,100. The requirements of individual models of aircraft differ greatly, however, and the distances are influenced by the load which is carried and the nature and altitude of the airfield. The standard NATO airfield was designed by the Americans in 1951. It has a large concrete apron, and a single runway measuring at least 8,000 feet (2,438 metres) in length.

On the whole the aircraft of the Warsaw Pact are better adapted for making use of poor runways. Thus the Soviet transport aircraft are furnished with strong undercarriages and many wheels, enabling them to cope with uneven ground, while the light MiG-21 Fishbed combat aircraft, which is still the mainstay of many Warsaw Pact airforces, is capable of taking off from grass airstrips. NATO pays a penalty for the generally superior range and payload of its machines, but the light F-16 Fighting Falcon interceptor is suited for operating from short and icy runways, and the demands of the Tornado are impressively modest. In tests near the Ahlhorn Woods in 1984 a west German aircraft of this kind showed that it could land, stop and take off from a single two-kilometre stretch of autobahn. The British Harrier has the unique advantage of being able to heave itself into the sky from very small patches of open ground like car parks and forest clearings.

Main Operating Bases (MOBs) are lavishly equipped airfields with a full complement of proper runways and taxiways, ground support and stores, and individual or two-machine Hardened Aircraft Shelters. MOBs make an important contribution to the effectiveness and survivability of air forces. Dispersed Operating Bases (DOBs) and standby bases are usually much less well furnished.

These two kinds of airfields represent the forms of passive protection available to air forces on the ground – the MOBs giving hardened cover, and the DOBs a measure of concealment. The principle of dispersal can be taken still further by utilising lengths of motorway as improvised airstrips, as has been explored by NATO, the Warsaw Pact, Sweden, South Korea and the air forces of the Middle Eastern powers. The chosen stretches of highway are flat and straight, and the surface must be strong enough to withstand the impact of an aircraft when it lands (which punishes the road much more severely than a truck of the same weight). The crash barriers are removed from the central reservation, which should be of concrete. Ground and anti-aircraft defence perimeters are set up, and arrangements are made to provide navigational, meteorological and servicing facilities.

In Europe NATO probably has the advantage in hardened aircraft shelters, but the Warsaw Pact has more MOBs (about forty on the Central Front) and a multitude of grass airstrips.

There is level ground in abundance in Central Europe. In Greece, however, airfields are concentrated in isolated plains like those of Macedonia and Thessaly, and in Norway it is difficult to find space for runways among the mountains and fjords.

Outside Europe, Soviet airfield-building may be taken as a rough guide to the direction of Moscow's ambitions. The heavily laden Soviet long-range bombers and reconnaissance aircraft demand a concrete runway about one metre thick and 3,200 metres long. Airfields of this description have been made at Cam Ranh Bay in Vietnam and at Puenta Huete in Nicaragua, and another field was being built on Grenada when the Americans landed in October 1983.

Runway denial is one of the most important tasks of aerial interdiction. Runways become at least temporarily unserviceable when the craters are two metres or less apart, and there is no single

clear strip measuring more than about 600 metres in length. Between fifty and one hundred craters will make most runways unusable. Standard bombs are not ideal for this work, and the British
have accordingly developed a JP 233 bomb which dispenses special
runway-cratering submunitions.

GROUND RADARS AND ANTI-AIRCRAFT DEFENCE

Radars are the 'eyes' by which commanders may detect and track
the movements of shipping, aircraft and missiles.

Small and mobile 'gap fillers' help to plug holes in radar coverage, or provide immediate protection for valuable installations or
formations of troops. Long-range surveillance radars are bigger
machines which have ranges of between 440 and 510 kilometres,
though even these examples of high technology are influenced by
atmospheric disturbance and cloud, and any obstructions to the line
of sight. Radars of all kinds are blind to objects travelling lower
than about fifty metres, on account of interference from the
ground. Hills have 'radar shadows' on their lee sides, which opens
up further possibilities for aircraft to penetrate radar defences, and
underlines what Clausewitz wrote about mountains being 'labor-
atories of hostile forces'.

The Soviets have more than 7,000 air surveillance radars in some
1,200 locations. The comparable Western network forms part of the
overall air defence system called the NATO Air Defence Ground
Environment (NADGE), which was founded in 1963. The radar
component originally consisted of a thin eastward-looking line of
stations, stretching from Norway to Turkey. The coverage began to
look distinctly thin when the Soviets acquired long-range aircraft
capable of exploiting gaps or turning the flanks, and programmes of
updating were undertaken from 1975 and again in the early 1980s,
to give a better all-round surveillance. The chain now consists of
about forty-seven long-range radar stations, together with the
necessary complement of gap-fillers and computerised control centres. NADGE forms an integrated whole with the British
UKADGE network, the Spanish Combate Grande system and the
French Strida II.

Active air defence comprises fighter aircraft, missiles, and highly
specialised artillery. Its effectiveness comes as much from disrupt-
ing air attack as from scoring actual kills.

Taken together, the anti-aircraft guided missiles (surface-to-air
missiles, or SAMs) are theoretically capable of scouring all height

bands from near the surface to about twenty-five kilometres. The old heavy anti-aircraft guns are obsolete, but there is still a very important place for light radar-guided rapid-firing cannon, heavy-calibre machine guns and even small arms. These are employed against helicopters, and ground-attack aircraft and other machines which fly low in order to avoid the attention of the missiles.

SEA WAR

USES OF THE SEA

The sea is the home of the nuclear missile submarine, as we have already remarked. The oceans are also very important in three further geopolitical dimensions:

The resources of the sea and the sea bed

In the second half of the twentieth century the wealth of the sea has acquired great significance on its own account. The Soviet admiral Gorshkov recognised as much in a geopolitically flavoured passage of his celebrated *Sea Power of the State*, in which he writes that 'the constantly growing maritime might of our country ensures our ability to enlarge our exploitation of the colossal natural resources of the World Ocean' (Gretton, 1979, 32).

Oil and natural gas are found in sedimentary rocks. Layers of this description extend across the continental shelves of south and south-east Asia, the Persian Gulf, north-west Europe, the Gulf of Mexico, and the Barents and Kara Seas of the Arctic. Technology is already extending recoverable depths below 200 metres, and one-half or more of the world's oil production might ultimately come from offshore rigs.

Undoubtedly the time will come when metals too will be extracted from the oceans on an industrial scale. The most immediately tempting deposits are those nodules of manganese which are scattered liberally over considerable areas of the sea bed, but especially at depths of between 3,500 and 6,000 metres. These represent a potentially rich source of copper, cobalt and nickel as well as of manganese itself.

Fish is at present fairly insignificant on the global scale as a source of food, but it figures largely in the diet of individual nations, accounting for 15 per cent of the protein intake of the Russians, and still more for the Japanese. Factory ships already range the oceans, receiving and processing billions of fish, and the fishing nations have yet to exploit (or devastate) the krill-rich waters of the southernmost Atlantic. 'Fish hunting' of this kind is admittedly a primitive and wasteful occupation, but scientific sea-farming is unlikely to overtake it in importance in the foreseeable future.

All of this helps to account for the urgent interest which the coastal states display in the seas off their shores, and explains why many a lonely atoll or guano-splashed rock now figures largely in the calculations of statesmen. The time has long passed since the oceans represented a symbol of freedom.

There exists no such thing as the Law of the Sea, in the sense of a book you can take down from the shelf. What we have instead is a body of case law, and a series of general principles that have been hammered out since 1958 at successive United Nations Law of the Sea Conferences (UNCLOS). The law of the sea now admits the right of a coastal state to establish safety zones immediately around offshore installations, and to exercise full sovereign territorial control out to twelve miles from the shoreline. National rights of economic exploration and exploitation extend to an Exclusive Economic Zone (EEZ) of 200 miles, with rather vague provision for the use of the continental shelf out to a depth of 200 metres, or more if 'the depth of the superjacent waters admits of the exploitation of the natural resources', whatever that is supposed to mean.

The navigation of straits is regulated by special arrangements and treaties, and by the old principle of the right of 'innocent passage', which gives free transit through channels which connect one body of open international water with another.

We are left with endless sources of conflict. For a start the world does not consist of islands which are equally spaced 400 miles apart. Thus the Irish do not dispute the British sovereignty over the barren rock of Rockall, but they do challenge the right to exploit the waters to the south. Thus the Turks demand that the Greeks must accept the principle of the median line, as the only fair way of determining the navigation and exploitation of the Aegean. A particularly contentious notion, the 'archipelagic principle', has been advanced by people like the Indonesians, who draw imaginary lines between their outermost islands, and claim sovereignty over the whole space enclosed within. Similarly the Libyan government has extended exclusive claims over the whole of the Gulf of Sirte, which forms a wide indentation in the national coastline.

In practice, the interpretation and enforcement of the law of the sea is a matter of geography, physical means and political climate. South-east Asia is clamorous with conflicting territorial claims which are the product of the multitude of islands and straits, the presence of off-shore oil and gas in many areas, and a general raising of the military stakes. If, however, a navy desires to send a warship or submarine through the sovereign straits of a friendly nation, then a low-level and unofficial approach is usually enough to secure the necessary permission.

Missiles, mines and aircraft give the regional powers of south-west Asia the ability to close off the narrow straits leading from the Persian Gulf and the Red Sea. At the other extreme, unmilitaristic countries like Ireland and Norway do not have the means of enforcing their control over the vast tracts of water that legally belong to them.

Projection of influence

The sea is a medium in which military and political power may be projected to critical areas of the world, without the cost and the degree of risk associated with engaging ground troops. This is an activity which is associated largely, but certainly not exclusively, with aircraft carriers and amphibious forces. The Second World War was fought out bitterly for seven months at sea before any serious clash occurred on land in Western Europe, and nowadays it is possible to envisage that the oceans might witness a prolonged war of blockade or even a limited nuclear conflict before the alliances grapple on the mainland, or the superpowers fire off their intercontinental nuclear weapons.

The word 'base' has lost something of the significance it held for Alfred Thayer Mahan and his generation, if by that term we understand a wholly owned naval port with an assured hinterland. The nearest modern equivalents are main home bases like those on the Kola peninsula, or at Pearl Harbor or Norfolk (Virginia), which are mighty establishments containing fleet anchorages, airfields, dockyards and a full industrial infrastructure. More relevant today, at least outside home waters, are foreign basing facilities, where visiting squadrons or individual warships may avail themselves of more or less elaborate support. Where such facilities are particularly generous, as at Yokosuka for the Americans in Japan, then it is practicable to arrange a system of 'home porting', whereby major refits may be carried out on the spot.

The most tenuous kind of base is an anchorage, where warships find good holding ground for their anchors in open waters of strategic interest. The Soviets have anchorages of this kind off Alboran Island in the far western Mediterranean, and off Pugad Island (in the Spratly group in the South China Sea), Socotra Island (South Yemen) and Perim Island (Ethiopia).

If they came to life again in the latter part of the twentieth century, the old-time naval strategists would be quick to point out that Providence is as unjust as ever in the way she grants access to the open seas. Britain is almost uniquely well placed, but the United States, Canada, and on a smaller scale Spain, France, West Germany and North Korea all have to make provision for bases, fleets or flotillas on either side of a land mass or peninsula. The Soviet Union is burdened with the greatest disadvantages of all, being forced to keep up four separate fleets, one of which is located in the Far East about 7,000 kilometres from the other three.

Showing the flag is an activity which has retained all its old relevance. It is still a matter of political and symbolic moment for a warship to visit a foreign port, and countries like Romania and Greece have not been above inviting calls from 'enemy' squadrons as a means of conveying a carefully calculated insult to their own nominal allies. Appearances count for a good deal on such occasions. Artists are allowed to have a hand in the final stages of Soviet ship design, which helps to give a lean and dangerous look to Admiral Chernavin's navy. Most American ships, even when they are heavily armed, look bland and inoffensive in comparison.

Peacetime expeditions to foreign waters become a question of immediate and deadly earnest when you wish to remind a potential enemy that the seas off his coasts are not a private lake. Forays by NATO warships into the Black Sea and the Barents Sea help to remind us of the chilling truth that peacetime naval activity is but a hair's-breadth removed from active hostilities.

Sea transport

A military transport of the largest kind, such as the American C-5A Galaxy, is capable of lifting one main battle tank at a time or a total maximum cargo of about ninety tons. The giant Soviet An-140 Condor does better still, with a reputed maximum payload of 150 tons. These figures sound impressive, but a small ocean-going freighter carries about ten times as much, and a supertanker one thousand times. The disproportion is huge, even when we take into account the far greater speed of the aircraft. At the lower end of the scale the C-130 Hercules remains the workhorse of the Western alliance, and even in its 'stretched' version it lifts only around twenty-one tons. The Soviet An-12 Cub has a comparable perform-ance. Arithmetic of this order explains why the sea is the most significant means of conveying material between countries and continents that are separated by water.

Without sea transport it would be almost impossible for the Americans to support a major operation overseas, bearing in mind that an American armoured division and its supplies weigh about 56,000 tons, and a mechanised infantry division 50,000 tons. The role of air transport must always be specialised – ferrying items of vital hardware across the seas, or rushing 'dual-based' troops to pre-positioned stores of equipment and supplies. The war in Viet-nam is usually taken as an example of high technology in action, and yet between 1965 and 1969 ships carried all the fuel and lubricants, about 95 per cent of the tonnage of all other materials, and a high proportion of the manpower which crossed to that theatre from the United States.

We have still to take account of the needs of industries and civilian populations. Strategists are acutely aware that shipping transports virtually all the oil, metal ores and other vital bulk commodities which the West derives from abroad, as well as the food and goods which are carried by way of trade.

The capacity of seaborne transport is more impressive than ever, but ships must still be routed around the land masses, and funnel-led through straits and canals. This is the origin of those maritime 'choke points' which will certainly figure largely in any general conflict between the superpowers. Channels which spring to mind are the Turkish, Danish, and Japanese and Mediterranean straits, the canals of Suez and Panama, the East Indian passages, the GIUK Gap (see p. 134), and the narrows at the entrances to the Red Sea and the Persian Gulf. 'Perhaps the most important military campaign that Britain has fought since 1945, far more vital than the battle for the Falklands, was the long guerrilla war between 1968 and 1977 in Oman, a war to keep a pro-western ruler in charge of the country which dominated the Straits of Hormuz' (Barnaby, 1984, 17).

THE WEAPONS OF NAVAL WAR

Surface ships

Among the instruments of naval warfare the surface ship retains its high importance for every power that wishes to use the sea for positive purposes, instead of just denying it to somebody else – a work which could be done at a pinch by submarines, aircraft or mines.

By far the greatest concentration of naval surface striking power is held in the carrier task forces of the United States. Each of these groups comprises one or two of the carriers proper, and at least six escorting surface ships together with smaller anti-submarine warfare (ASW) vessels and outlying attack submarines.

The carriers in question are what deserve to be called 'super-carriers'. These are huge nuclear – or conventionally powered vessels displacing 78,000–82,000 tons, and they are crammed with an armada of at least eighty aircraft. These are designed for a wide variety of roles, whether ASW (helicopters; the S-3 Viking), air-borne radar early warning, high-performance defensive intercep-tion (F-14 Tomcat), or long-range strikes which carry the offensive reach of the carriers beyond 900 kilometres (A-6 Intruder; A-7 Corsair and its replacement, the F/A-18 Hornet).

The supercarriers are an attribute of genuine global power, and they give the United States the means of exercising a highly selec-tive kind of force over all the land masses of the globe except the interior of the greatest continents. Admiral Gorshkov calls them the backbone of American imperialism.

The United States has a total of fifteen serviceable carriers (1985), out of which a dozen carrier groups might be formed. The only Soviet attempt to respond in kind is a single nuclear-powered craft of 65,000–75,000 tons, thought to be called the *Kremlin*, which is still a-building at Nikolayev on the river Bug. It will be impossible for the Soviets to rival the Americans in supercarrier force in the present century. Meanwhile the Soviets look to land-based aircraft to provide them with the necessary air cover at sea, utilising foreign clients and the huge extent of their own land mass to provide them with the necessary airfields.

All the other carriers of the world's navies are much smaller. As a general rule, the more diminutive the ship the more the ASW role is pronounced, and the more the fixed-wing aircraft gives way to the helicopter. There is a first pronounced drop in tonnage to medium-strike carriers like the Indian *Vikrant*, the French *Clemenceau* and *Foch*, and the Soviet *Kiev*-class anti-submarine carriers with their helicopters and dismal Forger aircraft. A further descent to around 16,000 tons brings us to the British *Invincibles* and the Italian *Giuseppe Garibaldi*.

Finally the specialised American amphibious assault carriers, their fleets of troop-carrying helicopters, are a category of vessel which shade into amphibious warfare ships proper, like the Soviet *Ivan Rogovs*, or the Americans' own *Tarawa* class.

At the other end of the amphibious scale a number of exotic machines have acquired some of the characteristics of aeroplanes. Hovercraft, like the Soviet *Lebeds* in the Barents Sea, are capable of transporting eighty tons of troops and equipment across a much greater variety of shorelines than is accessible to conventional landing craft. Heavier and faster still is the Soviet sea-skimming *ekranoplan*, a highly specialised amphibious aircraft which rides over a cushion of air that is trapped beneath the fuselage and wings.

The other major surface combat vessels – cruisers, destroyers and frigates – are distinguished more by capacity than armament. Nowadays almost every surface ship has weapons capable of attacking shipping, aircraft and submarines, as well as some provision to receive helicopters. Cruisers usually weigh in at more than 5,000 tons' displacement, destroyers between 3,000 and 5,000, and frigates between 1,000 and 3,000. Intelligence-gathering craft, mine countermeasures vessels, fleet auxiliaries, patrol boats and fast attack craft complete the catalogue of surface units.

In 1967 an Egyptian *Komar*-class patrol boat of Soviet manufacture caused something of a sensation by sinking the Israeli destroyer *Eilat* by means of a missile which she launched from within the safety of Alexandria harbour. However, the ship-killing midgets have not swept every other kind of craft from the seas. The range of a sea-launched missile is limited by the radar horizon of about twenty kilometres, unless the missile can be guided further on its way by friendly ships or aircraft, or is taken under control by a miniature radar installed in its nose. The larger warships not only accommodate greater quantities of missiles and other weapons, but they have larger, more elaborate and more highly placed radars, they are better suited to serve as command centres, they have much greater range and endurance, and much superior ability to cope with severe weather conditions. Western warships have significantly greater internal volume than their Soviet counterparts, and allow more space for stores and access.

It is true that seamanship in the pure Nelsonian sense is no longer a decisive advantage in naval warfare (something which has allowed the Soviets to build up their 'blue water' navy by a process resembling an industrialisation). However, old-fashioned enemies of the sailor like reefs, tides and bad weather still demand respect in these days of radar and echo sounders. Heavy seas have the power to hinder amphibious landings, render steering and station keeping difficult, and cause both immediate and long-term structural damage. The average life of a warship (very approximately twenty years) is extended by prolonged service in the Mediterranean, but shortened by a career in the North Atlantic.

The work of fast attack craft and patrol craft is still therefore confined to inshore waters, where speed and quick reaction are at a premium. Naval warfare still has an important place for surface warships as large as the 23,000-ton Soviet nuclear-powered *Kirov* cruiser, or the refurbished American battleships of the *Iowa* class.

Merchantmen have shared in the general advances in ship design. Many freighters are capable of travelling at up to forty or fifty kilometres per hour, which means that convoys (if indeed convoys are ever formed) will no longer have to creep along at the fifteen or so kilometres per hour of the Second World War. At a sustained speed of thirty-six kilometres per hour it takes a modern cargo ship about thirteen days to travel from the United States to Europe, eighteen to South Korea, and forty-four to the Persian Gulf by way of the Cape of Good Hope. Moreover, certain new types of ships, such as barge-carriers and roll-on roll-off (ro-ro) vehicle ferries are very well suited for supporting amphibious operations.

Submarines

Submarines have become most formidable instruments of war. They have acquired very high underwater speeds (a reported seventy-five kilometres per hour from the Soviet Alpha class), which gives them an advantage over conventionally hulled surface ships. They can dive to 600 or more metres without crumpling up. They detect and attack shipping and other submarines at unprecedented ranges, using sensitive sonars, wire-guided torpedoes and missiles. If they are equipped with nuclear propulsion, they can stay under water for as long as the crewmen can be fed and are capable of enduring their tomb-like existence.

This is not to suggest that submarines can go everywhere and do everything. As a species they suffer from the almost ridiculous shortcoming of being difficult to control by radio. Submarines usually establish contact with their masters by rising to near the surface and releasing an aerial buoy or a long wire antenna. Instructions may then be relayed by means of an aircraft, which itself trails a long aerial through the sky. Such a system is considered unduly haphazard and dangerous for nuclear missile submarines, and the Americans are in the process of developing extremely low-frequency transmitters which are designed to send signals to submarines cruising well below the surface. In 1984 the research transmitter at Clam Lake, Wisconsin, succeeded in projecting a signal to a submarine hiding 120 metres deep in the Mediterranean, and new stations will cover the Atlantic and the Pacific (see p. 121).

Precise navigation is another problem for submarines. They can obtain some of their most accurate fixes by taking bearings from shore transmitters, like those of the American Loran-C system.

Most nuclear-powered submarines (by no means all armed with nuclear missiles) are large and noisy animals. Their nuclear reactors are inherently bulky mechanisms, and the cooling pumps must be kept running in order to prevent fatal overheating. Nuclear-powered submarines are happiest when they have a relatively clear run to open waters, and the Soviets have accordingly attached all their vessels of this kind to their Pacific and Northern fleets. In fact the characteristics of nuclear-powered submarines fit them very well to operate in the Arctic Ocean, where the covering of ice helps to protect these vessels against surface-breaking sensors and weapons.

In most other respects the conventionally powered submarines give more freedom to the designer and tactician. The diesel-electric submarines make a lot of noise only when gulping air from the surface (snorkelling), which permits the diesel engines to recharge the batteries. They are much quieter when they cruise under electric power, and nearly silent when lurking in a choke point or some other well-chosen station. Coastal submarines are small and agile versions of the conventional attack submarines. They are designed to navigate confined or shallow waters, and they are in service with navies such as those of West Germany, Norway and Greece.

Anti-submarine warfare has been the object of huge investment, and navies call on the help of machines such as submarine-tracking satellites, sonobuoys, active on-board 'pinging' sonars, and long-range passive sonar arrays which are trailed astern of the parent vessel.

Among the static devices, the most elaborate is certainly NATO's Sound Surveillance System (SOSUS). Each SOSUS array consists of rows of hundreds of passive hydrophones which are laid or moored across likely submarine transit routes. The underwater noises are passed by means of cables to shore stations, where the data is processed, and from where information on the type, speed and bearing of any intruders is passed to the anti-submarine forces.

The first SOSUS lines were laid along the eastern and western coasts of the United States in the 1950s, when the practicable depth was probably limited to about 200 metres. Since then SOSUS has been deployed across the GIUK Gap (see p. 135), and appropriate shore stations established at Pitreavie in Scotland and Brawdy in south Wales. Further arrays are said to have been laid off Norway between the North Cape and Bear Island, in the Mediterranean, the Caribbean, off the Philippines, between Alaska and Japan, and in the Japanese straits. The maximum depth for deployment has probably been increased to about 2,000 metres.

In spite of all this immense effort, naval literature is replete with the woes of the anti-submariners. Water in a glass at table appears to belong to a transparent and uniform element, but at sea it is totally transformed. Deep waters are zoned in four shifting layers where the combinations of temperature, salinity and water pressure distort the speed of sound in different ways. Shallow waters offer no compensating advantage, for they are influenced by surface turbulence, daily variations in temperature, mixing of currents, and the way that sound bounces off the surface and bottom. Rocky bottoms are the worst of all, for there it is scarcely possible to distinguish a submarine from the craggy outcrops, or so the Swedes say.

It would certainly take an advance in anti-submarine warfare of quite unprecedented magnitude to cancel out another of the inherent advantages of underwater forces. 'Whereas on land the classic formula of a three-to-one advantage may be needed to launch a successful offensive, the same is not true at sea where one Russian raiding submarine has a numerical advantage akin to that of the terrorist in Northern Ireland' (Admiral Sir John Fieldhouse, reported in the *Daily Telegraph*, 20 January 1984).

Mines

For many years naval mine warfare was invested with an aura of the 1940s. Its renaissance owes something to the appreciation that mines can be laid very easily by many different types of craft, but something also to important technical advances in the science.

Most waters down to a depth of about seventy metres are suitable for emplacing ground mines, which are actuated by noise, or the magnetic or pressure 'signatures' that ships and submarines make when they pass overhead. On this principle ground mines could be profitably laid in wide areas of south-east Asian waters, and in the Gulf of Mexico, the Adriatic, the Baltic, the Danish straits and the approaches to Britain across the North Sea, the Channel and the eastern Atlantic.

Still greater areas are open to the deployment of self-propelled rising mines or captive torpedoes, like the American CAPTOR or the projected British Continental Shelf Mine. The greatest depth at which such mines might be laid is obviously a sensitive military secret, but published estimates vary between 600 and 1,000 metres. If applied to the Mediterranean, the latter depth suggests that almost all the Aegean and the Adriatic could be sown with rising mines, and that a mine barrier could be established across the Sicilian Channel, effectively dividing the Mediterranean into eastern and western basins.

Mine clearance is the responsibility of a variety of mine countermeasures (MCM) vessels or helicopter-towed sledges, which seek to establish 'swept channels' for the safe passage of shipping. Modern mines are not susceptible to being 'swept' in a literal sense, but must be located and then destroyed by explosives.

LAND WAR

The action of air forces and navies is usually indirect and cumulative. It is the ground forces which have to do the decisive work of winning ground and making a victory 'stick'.

THE INSTRUMENTS OF LAND WARFARE

Organisation

The fundamental strategic building brick of modern armies is the division. This is a balanced force of very approximately 12,000 men and 300 tanks, with artillery, engineering, mechanical repair, signals and logistical support. The size varies greatly from one army to another, and the proportion between infantry and tanks is determined by whether the formations are designated 'mechanised infantry divisions' or 'armoured divisions'.

Mechanised infantry divisions ('motor rifle divisions' in Soviet parlance) have a preponderance of infantry, and are usually deployed in the more broken and difficult terrain. Armoured divisions (the Soviet 'tank' divisions) are strong in tanks, and operate best where they can take advantage of relatively open and level ground. (A third kind of division, the light infantry division, has been introduced for American mobile reserves. It possesses 10,000 troops, but lacks heavy armour and is backed only by light artillery.)

The figures given in Table 2.1 provide a rough guide to the mix of forces in the two main categories of division.

TABLE 2.1

	Troops	*Tanks*	*Infantry fighting vehicles*
Soviet motor rifle	12,500	270	451
Soviet tank	10,500	322	243
US mechanised infantry	18,500	216	216
US armoured	18,300	324	180
West German mechanised	17,500	250	337
West German armoured	17,000	300	300

British and French armoured divisions are the equivalent of large brigades.

As a general rule, forces are much more heavily concentrated for purposes of attack than when they are on the defensive. Thus a Soviet division in the defence occupies a frontage of about 45 kilometres. On the attack the frontage shrinks to about 10–16 kilometres for the chief blow, or 20–30 for a secondary attack, and the depth extends to 30–5 kilometres.

Infantry

In modern land warfare a great deal still depends on a balanced effort by infantry, tanks, artillery and engineers. Service with the infantry is a most arduous and terrible experience, as Frederick the Great and Napoleon pointed out, but even now infantrymen are the only forces capable of holding ground for any length of time, controlling civilian populations, and giving armour the close support it needs against anti-tank weapons.

In order to survive in mechanised operations, the infantry must have protection and mechanised mobility. These are provided by light armoured carriers, which carry the troops through or close up to the point of contact with the enemy. Most of the modern carriers are 'infantry fighting vehicles', which are combat vehicles in their own right, furnished with light guns or missiles, and provided with portholes to enable the infantry to use their personal weapons. If the troops are ordered to 'debus', they leave the carrier with all possible speed and continue the advance on foot. Typical modern infantry fighting vehicles are the upgraded Soviet BMP, the American Bradley and the West German Marder. The classic American M-113, of which more than 70,000 have been built for various armies, is an obsolescent vehicle which represents the earlier generation of 'battle taxis'.

Both the British and the forces of the Warsaw Pact employ a mix of tracked and wheeled infantry carriers. The cross-country mobility of wheeled vehicles falls off sharply once the weight exceeds eighteen or twenty tons, but inside this limit there is still space for wheeled carriers like the British Saxon and the Soviet BTR-60, and for heavily gunned armoured cars of the kind which have been developed by the French. Wheeled vehicles give significant advantages in road speed, economy of fuel, reliability and ease of driver training. They are also suitable for use in delicate internal security operations, where tracked carriers will arouse outraged cries of 'Tank!'

Pistols are a kind of military jewellery, worn for reassurance and ornament as much as anything else. Rifles have effective combat ranges of some 450 metres, and machine guns of very approximately 1,000. The infantry are also equipped with anti-tank missiles and with mortars. The most common calibre of NATO mortars is 81 mm, and the British version lobs its shell to the phenomenal distance of 5,650 metres.

Many armies have forces of specialised paratroops, trained for parachute jumping and for aggressive action after they reach the ground. In addition the modern assault helicopter (see p. 28) carries parties of ordinary infantrymen to vital objectives behind enemy lines – important road junctions, for example, missile sites, or bridges across roads and canals.

These kinds of forces are most highly developed in the Soviet army. The airborne divisions proper are equipped with light, air-portable artillery and carriers, and the Soviet ground formations have a large complement of assault helicopters. The standard Mi-8 Hip has a maximum speed of 250 kilometres per hour, and a radius of action which is capable of transporting twenty-six fully equipped troops to a distance of 200 kilometres – or as far as the middle Rhine from the Thüringer Wald. The larger Mi-26 Halo can take on board about eighty-five troops, and fly to a radius of 370 kilometres.

Tanks

The tank must be supported by the other arms in order to be fully effective, and few other land weapons systems are so costly. At the same time it represents a unique combination of firepower, protection and mobility. It is the spearhead of the assault, and a mobile fortress on the defensive.

The main battle tank weighs between thirty-eight and fifty-five tons (Warsaw Pact tanks towards the bottom of the scale; NATO tanks towards the top). It measures about 3.5 metres wide, 3.5 metres high and 8 metres long. Its primary armament is a very long gun (of about 120 mm calibre in the newest tanks) which fires a high-explosive shell, or a solid armour-piercing dart that is effective against other tanks up to about 2,000 metres away.

We shall pause later on to see how the tank fares in particular environments. Naturally its general performance falls well short of the theoretical maxima. In Central Europe it is unusual to have a clear shot at an enemy out to the full range of the gun (see p. 59). Normally tanks move fastest along roads or when they are scuttling from one hull-down firing position to another. On level ground the attack speed across country is only around fifteen or twenty kilometres per hour, and it is reduced still further by uphill slopes. The Soviets have worked out the following effects of gradients:

Slope	*Speed of tank attainable*
3–6 degrees	15–12 kph
6–10 degrees	12–10 kph
10–15 degrees	10–6 kph
15–20 degrees	6–4 kph

Tanks are very vulnerable when they are being unloaded from wheeled tank transporters, and again when they are being refuelled, which can become necessary after as little as 240 kilometres of travelling.

The tank is a powerful anti-tank weapon in its own right, but the armoury of specific anti-tank weapons includes aircraft-bombs and long-range missiles (especially the newer designs, dispensing a spray of bomblets), guided shells and mortar bombs, and a very great variety of shorter-range guided and unguided missiles, some of which may be mounted on helicopters.

Many politicians, journalists and students of strategic affairs have been excited by the potential of the man-portable devices, which appear to have turned the balance of advantage away from the tank, the symbol of aggression, and towards light infantry and virtuous citizen militia, who are now supposed to have the means of putting up a powerful but 'non-provocative' defence. This attractive prospect is probably flawed:

- For technical and psychological reasons the performance of the penny packets of missile-armed infantry is not likely to be very effective.
- There is no such thing as a purely 'offensive' or 'defensive' weapon. Everything depends on the operational context. After attacking forces have made a breakthrough, it might well be to their advantage to consolidate behind a screen of missiles and mines.
- In any case the only way to evict an intruder is by counter-offensive action (Clausewitz's 'flashing sword of vengeance'), and history shows that counter-attacks have formed an essential part of most defensive campaigns and battles.

Artillery

The attribute of artillery, its great destructive power, is something that is rarely appreciated in times of peace. The gunners usually live and train by themselves, and in most NATO exercises the effect of artillery fire is simulated in a very feeble way. Once hostilities have begun, the artillery becomes more and more important as time goes on.

The gun or howitzer is still the weapon *par excellence* of the artillery. In any given period of modern history there appears to be a fairly narrow range of what might be called 'operative' calibres, which represent the best that technology can bring together in firepower and mobility. The 12-pounder cannon reigned supreme from 1756 to 1865. The prize in the Second World War was disputed between artillery of 88 and 105 mm calibre, and now anything below the 152 mm of the Warsaw Pact and the 155 mm of NATO must be counted as light. A 155 mm shell weighs about ninety-five pounds (forty-three kg), not including the propelling charge, which is on the very limit of what can be loaded by hand.

Motorised self-propelled guns give artillery the mobility to keep up with armoured formations. In many models the gun detachment is protected by an armoured turret, and the result looks very much like a tank. At the same time there is still an important place for towed artillery, like the FH-70 155 mm piece, which is a joint British, West German and Italian production. Guns of this kind are relatively cheap, and they are light enough to be slung from medium-lift helicopters and whisked away to new battery positions.

The work of the tubed artillery may be supplemented by unguided multi-launch rockets, or by long-range guided missiles like the American Lance (110 km), which is capable of being fitted with nuclear or conventional warheads, or the three modern Soviet tactical nuclear missiles, the SS-21, -22 and -23.

Engineers

Engineering support enables armies to clear routes across broken country, construct bridges over waterways, emplace or sweep away obstructions and minefields, and dig themselves into defensible positions. In other words, engineers determine to an important extent the use that an army may make of a theatre of war.

Bridge building is one of the prime responsibilities of the engineers, and the details of crossing rivers and canals are highly relevant to the topography of the Central Front (see pp. 52–3).

In land warfare mines are designed to nullify vehicles or personnel. The immediate object is not necessarily the total physical destruction of the victims. For tactical ends it might be enough to blow the tracks off a vehicle, or turn the infantry into injured casualties who will become a burden on the medical services. The general purpose of sowing mines is to deny areas of ground to the enemy, and the result corresponds very closely to the action of persistent chemical agents.

Mines may be emplaced by hand, or laid, dispensed or scattered by trailers, helicopters, missiles or artillery. It is technically possible to create aerial blast mines by detonating sprays or liquids. Further obstacles may be effected by conventional or nuclear 'blowdown' of trees, or by excavating anti-tank ditches by explosives or mechanical diggers.

A simple open trench will reduce the heat and blast effects of a nuclear explosion by about half. Properly prepared defences reduce casualties from all kinds of attack by some two-thirds, and increase the capability of direct-fire weapons by between five and ten times, benefiting from protection, stable weapons platforms and surveyed defensive fires.

Permanent fortifications are more impressive still. The effect of fortifications in the Second World War (including the much-maligned Maginot Line) is much better understood by analysts than it used to be. The Israelis, who certainly cannot be accused of excessive defensive-mindedness, set great store by their permanent defences, and the Soviets, Finns, Norwegians, Austrians and Italians have all deployed large numbers of obsolescent tank turrets in static positions.

Supply

The purpose of logistics, or military supply, is to make sure that the right material is delivered at the right place at the right time. This is a fundamental but easily overlooked consideration in warfare. Field-Marshal Montgomery remarked that 'during the last world war 80 per cent of our problems were of a logistical nature', and nowadays it is reasonable to suppose that they are not much nearer solution.

On NATO's Northern Flank the forces involved in operations will be comparatively small, but the distances are great and facilities of every kind are very meagre. Even after the stores have been emplaced, they must still be protected against the weather.

On the Central Front the spread of mechanisation and automatic weapons will cause the ground forces to gobble supplies at an unprecedented rate. It is calculated that a Soviet division on the attack will have a daily consumption of about 1,026 metric tons of stores, comprising 400 of ammunition, 530 of petrol, oil and lubricants (POL), 70 of spares, and 26 of rations. The division has an organic 'lift' of 3,700 tons, and replenishment is effected by every possible means – forward dumps, fuel pipelines, five-ton bowsers, and fleets of military and civilian trucks. The Soviet order of priorities is strictly established, and runs in descending sequence as follows:

1 missiles
2 ammunition
3 POL
4 spares
5 rations

Chemical and tactical nuclear weapons

Chemical and low-yield nuclear weapons are delivered by aircraft, missiles or artillery. These devices are very cheap, in comparison with their great destructive power, and NATO governments still rely on tactical nuclear warheads as a partial substitute for conventional forces.

This is not the place to debate whether chemical or tactical nuclear weapons ought ever to be employed in Europe, but the fear that they *might* be used will exercise a powerful influence on all kinds of operations. The mere threat of chemical attack will force armoured vehicles to operate with closed hatches, and make the troops put on their protective clothing, which is cumbersome, hot and smelly.

Similarly commanders will probably deploy their forces in a 'nuclear-scared' posture, lest they should offer large and slow-moving targets to nuclear strikes. Here we have an important link between effective conventional defence and NATO's threatened first use of tactical nuclear weapons. Without this cloud hanging over their heads the Soviets would be free to mass their forces, making NATO's task of conventional defence more difficult.

GROUND AND WEATHER

Prophecy is a hazardous business without the benefit of some kind of higher revelation, but it must be stated that this book is written on the assumption that well-tried principles of warfare are still valid, and that 'old-fashioned' considerations of terrain and climate must still bulk large in our calculations.

This is not to deny that man's brain has a powerful ally in computers, just as his sight has been extended and refined by radar, television, lasers, thermal imaging, infra-red illumination and by image intensification. Also military communications have reached a level which permits a President of the United States to follow the movements of an individual aircraft or a company of infantry.

However, technology can only do so much. Electronics help to inform the judgment, but they cannot make a bad decision into a good one. Men are not machines which operate with equal proficiency for twenty-four hours a day. Images, beams or waves are degraded by distance or interference. We know that the new gadgets are very expensive, but we cannot be certain how effectively they will work together in combat conditions. 'Airspace management' is a problem that awaits solution, as we have seen, and it is still difficult to bring together the processes of 'acquiring' a possible target, identifying and tracking it, and finally sending an appropriate weapon to the chosen destination.

WINTRY CONDITIONS

The coldest part of European NATO is in northern Norway, but 'there is an unfortunate tendency . . . to equate Arctic conditions to winter operations. The logical flaw here should be obvious. "Winter" is a climatic season; "Arctic" is a geographic region' (Eyre, 1981, 47).

Even the furthest north enjoys some relief in summer. Salla in Finland lies fifty kilometres north of the Arctic Circle, but when the Germans attacked the Soviets here on 1 July 1941 the temperature stood in the high eighties Fahrenheit.

Conversely Central Europe and the south can be very cold. In the depths of winter something like Arctic conditions prevails across the highland regions of continental NATO, from southern Scandinavia through central Germany to north-east Italy and Turkey. Erzurum in Asiatic Turkey lies under snow for about six months of the year, and the temperatures are low enough to kill entire battalions overnight, as happened in the neighborhood in the First World War.

Extreme cold and heavy snow impair the performance and mobility of all troops except trained skiers, and they injure men who are badly clothed or inadequately trained in the techniques of personal survival. Batteries and radios are affected by great cold, and in northern Scandinavia compass needles fail to point true during the invisible magnetic storms, just as high-frequency radio signals are liable to be halted by the Aurora Borealis (Northern Lights). There are resulting problems of communication and navigation for the small and scattered units which are characteristic of such theatres of war.

Logistics become something of a nightmare, especially in northern Scandinavia, where the distances are very great, roads, docks and airstrips are scanty, and the stores must be sheltered against the elements.

At very low temperatures many machines begin to suffer in bizarre ways, for oil becomes waxy and metals turn brittle. All types of vehicles slither on the snowy and icy roads, and even tanks are in danger of falling into roadside ditches if there is an accumulation of compacted snow on the crown. Off the road, wheeled vehicles are usually totally immobilised. On level ground a depth of snow of more than about eighty-five centimetres (thirty inches) will cause difficulties for tanks, and on a twenty-five-degree slope a mere fifty centimetres of snow produces the same effect. These figures are in turn modified by the type of snow. Powdery snow is the easiest to cross, though the driver may be blinded by a 'white out' when the surface is whipped up by the wind. Wet and dense snow is often found in Norway. It is much more difficult to pass, for it tends to pack together around wheels, tracks and mudguards.

In a broken and wintry landscape the artillery encounters additional embarrassments. The gun pits for the towed artillery must now be excavated in frozen ground. Mortars offer obvious advantages, but some fine judgment must be exercised to dig down to the right depth for the base plates – soft snow does not offer enough support, but hard snow may cause the plate to crack. White phosphorus shells (for artillery registration) are invisible against a white background, and deep snow absorbs some of the blast and splinters from shells and mortar bombs.

In clear winter weather suitably equipped aircraft and helicopter gunships can operate to devastating effect, for alien objects show up against the snow, and movement on the ground is often canalised along readily targetable tracks or valleys. However, the flying machines must contend with the frequent blizzards and fogs, as well as the frosts and the endless midwinter nights, and in certain conditions (minus fifteen degrees Centigrade and 85 per cent humidity) the Soviet Mi-24 Hind flies in the company of a self-generated snowstorm, due to the interaction of the exhaust gases with the downdraught from the rotors.

On the whole, 'Arctic' conditions favour the defenders. In a mountainous, rocky or heavily wooded terrain lightly equipped forces are usually well placed to frustrate their enemies by ambushes and flanking counter-attacks. Where the hill slopes are open, and incline at between thirty and forty degrees, avalanches may be usefully triggered by explosives or artillery. On the other hand it takes about four times longer than usual to construct field fortifications in hard-frozen ground, and mines are ineffective in deep snow unless they are packed artificially from beneath.

The days lengthen when the thaw approaches, and the combatants have a last chance to get in a stroke before the landscape dissolves in slush, mud and running water. In many southern regions the winter frequently blows itself out in heavy March or April blizzards, and these in turn give way to the spring rains. Thus in 1941 the Germans were forced to postpone the attack on Greece until April because their airfields in Bulgaria were swamped and unusable.

FOG, CLOUD AND WIND

Fog, smog and low cloud

- limit ground visibility
- bring down the operational ceilings of many aircraft
- intensify the local effect of chemical weapons
- facilitate surprise attacks.

A wind speed of no more than twenty-four kilometres per hour makes parachute drops hazardous, and above eighty kilometres per hour the wind uproots trees, and causes some damage to vehicles, ships, and aircraft on the ground. Shells and bullets are carried downwind; rockets, oddly enough, creep upwind as long as their propellant is burning. Chemical agents are dispersed and made rapidly ineffective on a gusty day, but a slow movement of air on a calm day might extend a lethal plume for tens of kilometres.

RIVERS AND CANALS

Waterways are very important in military calculations, and especially in flat country, where they are frequently the only natural obstacles of any value. The crossing of a major river or canal therefore becomes a set-piece operation. The first lodgment on the far bank is made by airborne forces, or troops crossing in carriers or assault boats. The follow-up forces, and especially the tanks, usually make the passage by military ferries or bridges.

Some measurements are significant. In order to qualify as an obstacle in the first place, the channel must compel the tanks to wait for engineering support. This happens when the gap is more than about three metres wide, and (depending on the model of tank) the depth of water exceeds 1.22 (M 48) – 2.44 (Leopards 1 and 2) metres. Soviet tanks are capable of being fitted with snorkelling tubes, but the crews must leave the vehicles in order to set these devices up, and snorkelling becomes impossible if the water is fast-flowing or more than 5.5 metres deep. The underwater voyage is at best a nerve-racking business, for the driver must navigate by compass, and the ground pressure of the tracks is so low that the tank easily wanders off course.

The most convenient form of bridge is a span laid by a tracked carrier. Single-span carriers can bridge a gap of about twelve metres. Folding scissors bridges extend between about eighteen and twenty-two metres, and can be laid in from two to five minutes. A gap of more than twenty-two metres forces the engineers to assemble girder bridges, or call up bulky and soft-skinned equipment like the Soviet GSP ferries or fast-laying pontoon bridges like the Soviet PMP and the American-built Ribbon Bridge.

The approaches to the chosen crossing point must be firm enough to prevent the vehicles becoming bogged down. The maximum angle of entry into the water is in the region of 47 degrees. Amphibious vehicles do not perform brilliantly as boats, and a current of any strength will sweep them well downstream, causing a greater or lesser misalignment between the points of entry and exit. The far bank of a waterway is often the greatest obstacle of all. The side of a river or canal is more difficult to climb than a comparable slope on dry land, for the tracks and wheels have less ground on which to take a grip, and a gradient of more than 27 degrees is usually prohibitive. When, at last, the tanks or carriers haul themselves over the crest, there is a dangerous moment when they present their soft underbellies to the enemy.

Waterways are strongly influenced by weather conditions. Floating ice appears on many German rivers in December, January and February, and in a hard season a crust of static ice will form and the canals are completely frozen over. The Norwegian fjords remain almost totally ice-free during the winter, thanks to the benign influence of the Gulf Stream, but lakes and rivers may solidify into the solid and air-free 'blue ice', which supports tanks when it is seventy centimetres in depth. Thick ice is difficult to break once it has been allowed to form. Artillery fire just forms a scattering of isolated holes, so you can make effective gaps only by laying rows of explosive charges.

River levels rise and fall according to season and weather. The volume of German rivers is mainly governed by the rate at which the snow melts on the higher ground. In southern Europe the level of the streams and shorter rivers is less predictable, for they are prone to flash floods after cloudbursts.

Waterways act to the disadvantage of the defenders where they intersect their communications. The American and British bombers waged a devastating campaign of interdiction against the river crossings in north-western France before the D-Day invasion in 1944, and at the present time the bridges across rivers like the Rhine, Ems, Weser, Elbe, Saale and Oder are prime targets for attacks by missiles, aircraft or airborne forces. In Exercise Lionheart in 1984 the British made the reasonable assumption that the Rhine bridges were out of action, and with German help they established ferry crossings at five points from Duisburg in the south to Xanten in the north.

MOUNTAIN AND HILLS

Full-scale mountains or very lofty hills make up many of the frontier regions of the first-line members of continental NATO – Norway, West Germany on its Alpine borders with Austria, north-east Italy, northern Greece and Asiatic Turkey.

This ground gives the defenders the advantages of wide fields of fire and observation. Well-prepared positions are strong, for they can be blasted or drilled out of the rock; improvised defences are usually much weaker, and normally consist of loose stones piled into sangars. As a general rule tactical strength is purchased at the price of mobility.

In mountainous terrain the progress of invaders is not so much halted as highly canalised. If they are lucky the grain of the country – the alignment of the ridges and valleys – will correspond with the way they want to go; on the other hand the most awkward conformation of the ground is a central massif with spurs running away in a variety of directions.

The classic form of attack in high mountains is to send light forces racing ahead to seize the peaks or ridges on either side of the chosen axis of advance, while the main force hammers its way along the valley floor. The helicopter has given new force to this mountain-hopping technique, but at high altitudes the ground vehicles emit highly visible clouds of exhaust, which detract from the surprise element in flanking movements.

Mountain roads are characteristically narrow and winding, and vulnerable to artificial landslides and avalanches. The thinning of the atmosphere brings an 8–10 per cent reduction in engine perform-ance for every 1,000 metres of climb, and a three- to four-degree Centigrade drop in the temperature of boiling water, which produces labouring engines and teaming radiators. The corresponding drop in the ambient temperature is about five or six degrees.

Natural features have been classified in some detail by the Soviet military topographers, and their definitions of 'mountainous' terrain covers some quite low ground, as shown in Table 2.2.

It is sometimes overlooked that some of the best terrain for putting up a defence is encountered not only in Wagnerian mountain land-scapes but in 'rather undramatically rolling countryside, with plenty of folds in the ground and the occasional village or copse for protection. In most cases terrain of this type will offer good oppor-tunity for all three of the key defensive qualities, namely observation, concealment and cover, and for mobile reserves as much as for front line troops. It will also allow enemy assaults to be broken up and

TABLE 2.2

Type of terrain	Height above sea level in metres	Relative height of hills in metres	Gradient	Effects
Plain	up to 300	up to 25	1 degree	Easily passable
Hilly country	300–500	25–200	2–3 degrees	Passable for heavy vehicles in most places
Low mountains	500–1,000	200–500	5–10 degrees	Mass use of heavy vehicles difficult
Medium mountains	1,000–2,000	500–1,000	10–25 degrees	Use of heavy vehicles possible only in restricted directions
High mountains	Over 2,000	Over 1,000	Above 25 degrees	Movement of heavy vehicles almost impossible

Source: Watt, 1983, 98

separated from each other in a confusing patchwork of dips and low crestlines' (Dinter and Griffith, 1983, 130).

At all altitudes the slope of the ground has an appreciable effect on the cross-country mobility of vehicles. The Soviet *Military Topography Officers Handbook* (Moscow, 1980) yields the figures shown in Table 2.3. These calculations apply to firm surfaces with a normal humidity factor of 20 per cent. At 50 per cent the figures for mobility must be reduced by half (Watt, 1983, 101).

In mountainous and hilly terrain the effects of nuclear explosions are highly localised. Heat and blast are funnelled along the valleys, but steep reverse slopes reduce their magnitude by about 14 per cent.

TABLE 2.3

Gradient	Effect on tracked vehicles	Effect on wheeled vehicles
Up to 5 degrees	Easily passable	Passable
5–10 degrees	Passable	Passable with difficulty
10–20 degrees	Passable with difficulty	Passable with great difficulty and slow speeds
20–30 degrees	Passable with great difficulty and slow speeds	Practically impassable
Over 30 degrees	Practically impassable	Impassable

FORESTS

Wooded areas, which often coincide with the hilly ones, cover about
one-quarter of Norway and one-third of Central Europe, to wit
Czechoslovakia with 35 per cent, Poland with 27 per cent, and West
Germany with 29 per cent overall (and a good deal more along its
borders with the Warsaw Pact).

The older-established deciduous forests have tall trees and light
undergrowth, and favour the concealed concentration of forces.
Beechwoods are particularly suitable, though the floor is easily
churned up in wet weather. The younger, more thickly set plantations (almost invariably conifers) impose severe restrictions on
observation, movement, and ranges of direct-fire weapons, and they
are consequently not much use to anyone except as passive barriers.
Armoured vehicles can penetrate woodlands when the trees are set
more than eight metres apart, but they are stopped short when the
trunks stand closer than six metres and exceed twenty centimetres in
girth.

Woodland paths and roads are easily obstructed by felled trees,
and great areas of forest may be transformed into impassable chaos
by nuclear tree-blowdown. However, it may be difficult to construct
good field fortifications in forest clearings, since the rock often comes
close to the surface.

RAILWAYS AND ROADS

Effective overland communications are an important element in
warfare, as we have noted. Even the Transatlantic reinforcement of
European NATO depends heavily on such facilities, for the 'wet
time' spent in moving material across the ocean amounts to only
one-third of the journey, and all the rest is devoted to land transportation inside the United States and Europe.

Railways offer swift and unencumbered movement, and in wartime they are astonishingly resistant to aerial attack, provided efficient repair teams are at hand, and diesel or steam locomotives are
available to replace the inoperative electrically powered units. The
countries of the Warsaw Pact have sedulously maintained their
railways, but some of the networks in the West have been sadly run
down. The Dutch will have to borrow flatcars from the *Bundesbahn*
in order to move their tanks to the assigned sector in West Germany.
The British tracks have been severely pruned, and the American
roadbeds are in a deplorable condition.

Roads are at the same time lines of communication and avenues of military advance. Fighting across country is the predominant form of land warfare, but movement by road is far more speedy, far more economical of fuel and tracks, and much easier to control.

The greater the density of the road network, the more easy it is to pass through a particular area. Any remotely passable route might be exploited by the Soviet commanders, who are accustomed to moving on the primitive roads of Russia, but they will be attracted above all by the potential of highways like the German autobahns and the Italian autostradas. These roads favour mechanised breakthroughs and exploitations, as the Americans demonstrated a number of times during their campaign in Germany in 1945. In March of that year a detachment from the First Army drove down the autobahn from Limburg and helped to precipitate the collapse of the German LXXXIX Corps. In the next month forces from Patton's Third Army roared along the autobahns to execute their speedy turning movements to the south of Frankfurt and Erfurt.

Many of the smaller roads may be barricaded by felling trees or telegraph poles. The best way to cut autobahns is to blow up the bridges. This can be done speedily if the necessary demolition chambers have been prepared in advance.

CITIES AND TOWNS

Most modern cities have expanded well beyond the old town centres and 'smokestack' industrial zones which form the inner cores. In southern Europe, Africa, Asia and Latin America the flight from the land has produced endless reeking *bidonvilles, barrios* or *favelas*, and a nightmarish agglomeration like Mexico City, where the population has reached 16,000,000 and is still expanding fast. In more favoured societies the motive force derives from car transport and the spread of suburbs and light industries, which increases urban areas at a rate about two and a half times that of the rise in population. The expansion is usually along the main axes of communication, and frequently the suburbs and satellite towns of one urban core merge with those of the next. The result is shown in phenomena like the sprawling Dallas–Fort Worth 'metroplex', or the long-drawn-out Dutch *Randstad*.

Over the centuries war has gravitated to cities for much the same reason that people have come to live in them, namely that they occupy flat ground on nodal points of communication. One of the grimmest certainties of our subject must be that large-scale operations in Europe will bring war to many such centres of population. A tactical nuclear war is likely to kill eight civilians to every soldier, and a chemical war might dispose of twenty.

For the defenders of Western Europe, the control of civilian populations could well bring insuperable problems of treating casualties, maintaining public hygiene, directing refugees, and controlling riots among racial minorities. On his side, a Soviet commander must reckon with the danger of mass demoralisation among his troops, who will come face to face with a hostile population and see clear evidence of the West's superior standards of material life.

Towns, considered as objects, possess what Paul Bracken calls 'enormous defensive potential' (1977, 33). Recent history indicates that offensive operations have a way of coming to a halt when they reach an urban area, and that to get them going again requires enormous concentrations of force.

The tank does not show to its best advantage in such surroundings. It is a bulky vehicle, out of place in narrow streets. The turret is designed for action in the open field, and at short ranges it is physically impossible for the gunner to aim the main armament at cellars and upper storeys. For the same reason the upper armour is thin, especially over the engine compartment, and vulnerable to bombs or missiles coming from above. At close quarters the commander is often forced to operate with a closed hatch, which adds to the problems which tank crews encounter in orientating themselves in towns, and keeping open the communications with their supporting infantry, who must be their eyes and ears.

Air strikes and artillery have the notorious effect of creating mountains of wreckage, which afford a multitude of hiding places for the sitting tenants, while obstructing the advance of armour along the streets. These improvised fortifications might be usefully produced by controlled 'rubbling' on the part of the defender (Hammond, 1983, 46).

The expression 'urban area' covers a great range of environments. In older buildings, where the weight is carried by the walls, the interior is liable to catch fire and collapse, leaving the outer shell more or less intact. Modern tower blocks are vulnerable to powerful blast explosions. Sometimes a corner or the whole building collapses into a hideous concrete sandwich. More frequently the surface cladding (which is lightly attached) falls away in an avalanche of glass, while the skeleton of steel and ferro-concrete beams is left standing.

The tops of tower blocks command excellent fields of vision and fire, but they are exposed and vulnerable locations, usually suited only for observation posts. The best emplacements for active defence are probably on the lower floors, and it is a good idea to build *ad hoc* bunkers of furnishings and office equipment well in from the outer edges of the floors. The underground levels reach very deep into the earth, and may be used for shelters and command posts.

Suburbs and satellite towns radiate into the countryside like the spokes of a wheel, and they help to disrupt columns which might seek to bypass the urban hubs (see p. 54 for similar effects in mountainous topography). At the tactical level, however, the suburbs are a less favourable environment for the defence than are the inner cities. Rubble barriers are obviously less effective on wide roads, and when the buildings are low, far apart and flimsy. The length of the line of sight down most suburban roads is about 240 metres, which happens to be an awkward distance, for it is not enough to allow missiles like the Dragon or Sagger to be brought under control by the operator or guidance system. The Milan and TOW missiles can be 'gathered' over a much shorter distance, but like most of the other systems they have a powerful backblast which makes them unusable in confined spaces. The light West German Armbrust is a significant exception, and is very suitable for fighting in all kinds of built-up areas.

Many European towns have changed more in the last twenty years than in the previous two hundred. The influence of the past usually lingers longer in the countryside, where the patterns of settlement are the result of land usage and tradition. The massive farm buildings of the north Italian lowlands have done service as improvised fortresses in many a campaign. In the arable lands of Germany the villages are characteristically isolated and evenly spaced, for they serve as centres for the cultivation of the open fields. These places now offer strongpoints for anti-tank defence, and pivots for counter-attacks by armoured units.

THE CUMULATIVE EFFECTS OF OBSTRUCTED GROUND

The landscape of continental NATO is becoming more cluttered every year. Broken ground as a whole interferes with movement off the roads and complicates the problems of control and communications.

Combat ranges are significantly reduced. Topographical studies have shown that in typical West German terrain moving tanks at less than 500 metres are visible for 40 per cent of the time, and

at 500–1,000	for	20%
1,000–2,000	for	25%
above 2,000	for	15%

The Italian Geographic Institute has made calculations on a slightly different basis for the potential theatre of war in north-east Italy, and states that at ranges up to 700 metres 25 per cent of a given force will be visible, and that

at 700–1,000	16%
1,000–2,000	40%
2,000–3,000	14%
above 3,000	5%

(Verdecchia, 1983, 35)

Broken terrain increases the opportunities for camouflage and concealment. These are increased not only by 'dead ground' and the extent of natural and artificial cover, but by an element of variety in the landscape – mixed woodland, for example, is a more suitable environment than a uniformly coloured plantation, where intrusive objects stand out as anomalies. The Soviets estimate that one of their battalions can be concealed in 785 structures in a built-up area, a one-kilometre long ravine, a 0.4 square kilometre patch of woodland, or a three-kilometre long strip of plantation.

KNOWLEDGE OF THE GROUND

The defender, as the party in place, has always enjoyed the advantage of a superior knowledge of the scene of operations. This is a state of affairs which NATO is well placed to exploit.

At the most basic level the NATO territorial forces, and especially those of the Norwegians, know their country very well and know how to operate most effectively inside it.

The West's accomplishments in high technology also lie at the disposal of NATO. The cycle of the aerial reconnaissance, which at present is still based on photography, will be immensely speeded up by digital data links which transmit real-time 'pictures' direct to the surface. Maps of the ground, already logged in digital form (Digital Topographical Data), are now capable of being transmitted by data link, summoned up on television screens in a variety of scales, and persuaded to yield highly specific information. Finally satellite-assisted navigation helps in the not-unimportant business of finding out where you are on the ground.

The judgment and informed instincts of military men will, of course, still be required to turn this mass of information to operational advantage. It is unfortunate that modern military training finds so little time to sharpen the faculty of *coup d'oeil*, or the rapid grasp of the tactical potential of situations and ground. This quality was prized very highly in the eighteenth and nineteenth centuries, when it was developed by topographical rides, and the study of military history, military sketching and the classical principles of fortification. The modern sport of orienteering offers only a partial substitute.

To say that the Soviets cannot use maps would be to put ourselves in the same league as the people who, in the 1930s, claimed that the Japanese had such bad eyesight that they would never become formidable enemies. However, both as the attackers, and as products of an isolated and highly centralised society, the Soviets are faced with inherent problems of how to find their bearings in an unfamiliar and crowded environment.

Soviet military maps are excellent, but they are issued on a restricted scale, usually only to battalion and company commanders, and anybody who loses a map is liable to very severe punishment. Moreover, the conditions of civilian life in Eastern Europe give the soldiers of the Warsaw Pact little relevant experience. Very few citizens of the Soviet Union as yet own private cars, and in countries like Poland road maps have become difficult or impossible to obtain.

PART II

THE MAP OF CONFRONTATION

CHAPTER 3

The Soviet Superpower

Area:	22,402,000 square kilometres
Population:	277,000,000
Army:	193 divisions

SOURCES OF STRENGTH AND COHESION

THE SOVIET GIANT

The early Muscovites lived in a tract of level and exposed ground, and like the Brandenburg-Prussians they obeyed the grim imperative 'expand or go under'. The advance from the Moscow core region to the east was very fast and easy, when we consider the enormous distances that were involved. The Russians established the first border with China along the Stanovoy Mountains as early as 1689, and they continued their push across the Bering Strait and some distance down the Pacific coast of North America before they were persuaded that they had finally outrun their communications. Alaska was sold to the Americans in 1867.

The drive to the south was much more of a military operation, and brought the Russians into conflict with Tartars, Turks, khanates, tribesmen and brigands. It culminated in the nineteenth century in prolonged campaigns in the Caucasus Mountains and in Russian Central Asia – the bulge of land between the Caspian Sea and the Chinese border.

The advance to the west was the shortest and most bitterly contested of all. By the early eighteenth century the Russians finally broke through to the Baltic along a wide frontage, after generations of war against Lithuanians, Poles and Swedes. Brandenburg-Prussia and its progeny, united Germany, eventually emerged as Russia's most implacable enemy. The two states shared many military traditions, and they were competing in the same environment. The last and most bloody of their confrontations was in what the Soviets call their 'Great Patriotic War' (1941–5), in which the victorious Soviets

MAP 2   The Soviet Union

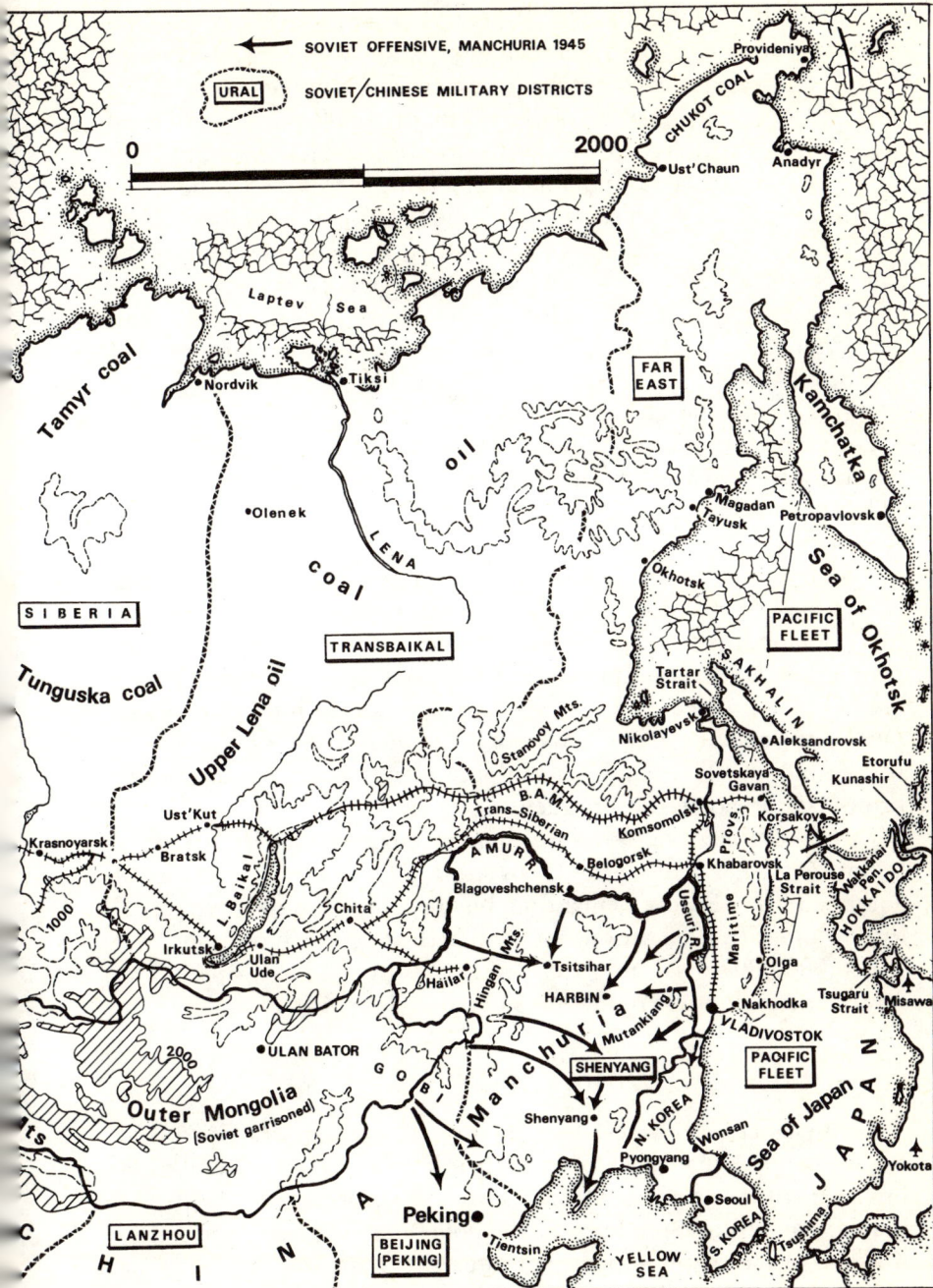

SOVIET OFFENSIVE, MANCHURIA 1945

URAL   SOVIET/CHINESE MILITARY DISTRICTS

0   2000

Providenya

CHUKOT COAL

Ust'Chaun   Anadyr

Laptev Sea

Nordvik   Tiksi

FAR
EAST

Kamchatka

oil

Magadan
Tayusk   Petropavlovsk

LENA

Olenek

coal   Okhotsk

Sea of Okhotsk

SIBERIA

TRANSBAIKAL

PACIFIC
FLEET

Tamyr coal

Tartar
Strait

SAKHALIN

Tunguska coal

Upper Lena oil

Stanovoy Mts.

Nikolayevsk   Aleksandrovsk

Etorufu
Kunashir

B.A.M.   Sovetskaya
                        Gavan

Trans-Siberian   Komsomolsk   Korsakov

Ust'Kut

Krasnoyarsk   AMUR   Belogorsk   Khabarovsk

Bratsk   La Perouse
                                                          Strait

Chita   Blagoveshchensk

HOKKAIDO

Irkutsk   Hingan Mts.

Ulan
Ude   Hailar   Tsitsihar

Olga

Maritime Prov.   Usuri R.

1000

L. Baikal

HARBIN   Nakhodka   Tsugaru
                                              Strait   Misawa

ULAN BATOR   Mutankiang   VLADIVOSTOK

200   SHENYANG   PACIFIC
                                              FLEET

Outer Mongolia   Shenyang

GOBI   Manchuria

(Soviet garrisoned)   N KOREA

JAPAN

Peking   Wonsan   Sea of Japan

LANZHOU   Pyongyang

BEIJING   Tientsin   Seoul   Yokota

(PEKING)   YELLOW   S. KOREA
                              SEA   Tsushima

CHINA

lost about 20,000,000 soldiers and civilians, or the equivalent of ten lives for every one of the metres that separate Moscow from Berlin.

The Soviet national territory is immense by any reckoning. At its maximum dimensions it measures about 4,500 kilometres from north to south, and 10,000 from east to west – which is roughly half way around the northern hemisphere. Thus the sun rises above the Bering Strait while Moscow is still about ten hours removed from daybreak. The area of Russia amounts to some 17 per cent of the world's land surface, or more than 40 per cent of Euro-Asia.

The Soviet Union comes closer to economic self-sufficiency than any other of the major powers. Its borders enclose about one-third of the world's forests, between 35 and 40 per cent of the global reserves of natural gas, and abundant ores of iron, copper, aluminium and very nearly all the more exotic minerals. The reserves of coal are for practical purposes unlimited, and the infinitely renewable resource of hydroelectric energy accounts for one-fifth of the power generated in Russia.

The Soviet Union is still the world's largest producer of oil, and Soviet exports of oil and natural gas help to hold the Warsaw Pact together and link the economies of Western Europe with the greater Euro-Asian land mass. It must be mentioned, however, that nothing has been discovered in recent years to compare with the supergiant oilfield at Samotlor in the district of Tyumen in West Siberia, which was found in 1969, and some doubt hangs over the long-term prospects for Soviet oil production.

Only a comparatively low level of investment was needed to tap the bountiful gusher wells of the 1960s and 1970s, and the Soviets are ill equipped for the more demanding business of secondary extraction by pumping. In 1983 the output of oil in the Soviet Union amounted to 616,000,000 tons, but in 1984 the figure dropped to 613,000,000, representing the first reduction since the Great Patriotic War.

CIVILIAN AND MILITARY ADMINISTRATION

The Soviet armed forces, merchant fleet, civil air transport and railways are the biggest systems of their kind in the world, and most Soviet institutions are built on a similarly heroic scale.

It is generally accepted that Soviet policy-making is determined by the interaction of three powerful interest groups, representing the great empires of the Red Army (i.e. the armed forces), the KGB and the Party. The leadership is a collective one, and the longer-serving members of the Politburo help to preserve continuities of purpose and direction.

The internal administration of the Soviet Union is highly central-ised, despite appearances to the contrary. The national territory is organised into a scattering of *okrugs* (circles), *oblasts* (districts), semi-autonomous Soviet Socialist Republics, and fifteen privileged Union Republics which have the theoretical right to secede from the union. Fourteen of the Union Republics are the homes of significant and recognisable minority groups – Georgians, Tadzhiks and so on – but a fifteenth, the Russian Soviet Federated Socialist Union Re-public (RSFSR) contains a population of 135,000,000 and sprawls for 17,000,000 square kilometres all the way across the country, which helps to promote national unity and Russification.

The Soviet body politic is racked by ills that might have destroyed another country long since – low productivity in consumer goods, persistent shortcomings in the harvest, widespread corruption, a cynicism about the professed ideology of the state, and the survival or resurgence of 'destructive' forces like religion and local national-isms.

A number of things hold Soviet society together. Conformity is encouraged by the all-pervading apparatus of the government and Party, which punishes (or at least withholds rewards from) dissent. Most Soviet citizens are in no position to compare their standard of life with that prevailing in the West. Their only indices are with their own experiences and those of their parents, and they know that what they have now is usually better than what they had then. They respect a regime which inspires fear at home and abroad, and for many of them the sacrifices made by their nation in the Great Patriotic War represent an alternative framework of spiritual refer-ence to a God-based religion.

It may seem odd that the Soviet Union can put forth such impressive armed forces when, by Western standards, everyday life in the Soviet Union is a chapter of deprivations and bizarre ineffi-ciencies. Here we must take into account the power of a totalitarian state to direct effort to specific ends – in the Soviet Union, just as in the Russia of the Tsars, it is the military priority which is given first place. Education, recreation, the economy and the means of trans-port all show a high interdependence of military and civilian control and purpose.

In the Warsaw Pact countries of Eastern Europe most of the Soviet troops come under the control of four Groups of Forces, covering East Germany, Czechoslovakia, Poland and Hungary respectively.

Inside the Soviet Union the units of military administration are the sixteen Military Districts. These also provide ready-made command structures, and enable the Soviets to put together 'force packages' for military interventions abroad. The Military Districts in the west are smaller in area but much more densely packed with forces than those in the east. Five of them have probably been incorporated into the order of battle of the Warsaw Pact, and the Carpathian Military District has a particularly important role as the policeman of South-Eastern Europe.

The Military District happens to be an institution which goes back to pre-Revolutionary times. Another legacy of the old Russia is the idea of organising wartime military effort in regional 'theatres'. This is the result of the sheer size of the national territory. Already in the seventeenth and eighteenth centuries the Russians began to appreciate that when they went campaigning in any single direction, against the Swedes in the north-east, for example, or against the Turks in the south, they would have to provide 'tailor-made' support in the way of supplies, armament and tactical guidelines, and make a commitment of force that might last for years or even a whole generation at a time.

The same thinking is shown in the way the Soviets plan to construct their wartime operational commands. At the highest level the activity of the forces will be co-ordinated by the headquarters of Theatres of War (TVs), 'the term given to vast areas of land, sea and air, prepared in a political, economic and military sense, on which bilateral hostilities are conducted between two states or coalitions, or several states or coalitions. The boundaries of the TVs are established in peacetime, but may be subject to adjustment in the course of hostilities' (Binieda, 1981, 2). If by 'vast areas' we understand the Far East, south-west Asia and Europe, then three such Theatres of War might spring into life.

In the more specific and local strategic directions the armed forces will be managed by the headquarters of Theatres of Military Operations (TVDs). About six or seven such TVDs would be created in the event of a general war, providing commands for the various Asian theatres, and at least three for operations against NATO – possibly a Northern TVD against Scandinavia, a Western one for the Central Front, and a South-Western one for the Balkans and southern Europe.

SOURCES OF WEAKNESS AND DIVISION

It is natural for many Westerners to make a straightforward equation between Russia's size and Soviet strength. The Soviets do not necessarily share the same viewpoint, and in the following pages we shall touch on some of the countervailing weaknesses that weigh heavily with the Soviet leadership.

DEMOGRAPHIC PROBLEMS

There are about 40,000,000 more Russians than Americans. When, however, we consider that the Soviet Union is nearly three times as big as the United States mainland (itself a very large country), then Russia begins to appear very thinly settled. Worse still, most of the population is still heaped up west of the Urals around the old Muscovite core area.

European Russia makes up only 25 per cent of the Soviet Union, but contains nearly 70 per cent of the population. The leading three cities, Moscow (8,301,000 people), Leningrad (4,520,000) and Kiev (2,300,000), are all located in Europe, and the pattern of urban settlement (and indeed of economic development as a whole) resembles a great triangle, with its wide base west of the Urals, and a thin tapering apex reaching eastwards into Siberia along the lines of communication to Omsk, Novosibirsk and Novokuznetsk. The emptiness of eastern Siberia is particularly embarrassing because this region lies close to the overcrowded home of the Chinese – those 'one billion yellow bastards' (Brezhnev). This is one of the reasons why the Soviets are putting so much effort into the economic and military development of their Far East.

The Soviet population is therefore small and very unevenly distributed. It is also racially mixed. During the expansion of Russia the state extended its rule over about 120 main groups of non-Russian peoples. The Slavs as a whole number about 190,000,000 souls, or more than 70 per cent of the total population of 274,300,000. Of these the Great Russians of the historic heartland represent 137,000,000, or only about half the total population of the Soviet Union. The 42,000,000 Ukrainians comprise the second largest Slavonic group, and they have no liking for their Russian cousins.

This leaves us with a non-Slavonic population which has already reached about 30 per cent of the whole and is still growing. Some of these folk are notoriously susceptible to ethnic or religious excitements and live on strategically interesting borderlands. In European Russia itself the Lithuanians, Latvians and Estonians are white but non-Slavonic peoples, who by race and culture belong to the West or to the Baltic world. Many of them now tune in to Polish or Finnish television transmissions, which helps to reinforce their feeling of separate identity. Likewise in the south the Moldavians, Armenians, Azerbaidzhanis, Turkmen, Uzbeks and Tadzhiks have ties across the frontiers with related groups in Romania, Turkey, Iran or Afghanistan.

When the Soviets look into the future they are not encouraged by what they see. Education will probably make inroads on the approximately one-quarter of Soviet citizens who still have only a sketchy acquaintance with the Russian language. However, Christianity and Islam are proving highly resistant to 'scientific atheism'. It is also evident that the Asiatics are breeding fast at a time when the ranks of Slavonic Russians are being thinned by abortion, tobacco, alcohol and fatty foods. Altogether regional nationalisms interfere with the effective day-to-day running of the state, and represent a long-term threat to the Soviet system. So seriously is the danger taken that the Soviet army goes to the trouble of dividing up the racial groups as evenly as possible among its sub-units, down to platoon and section level, out of fear that ethnically related soldiers might gang up against authority.

DISTANCE AND COMMUNICATIONS

The difficulties of settling and exploiting the Russian land mass begin to assume a more tangible form once we translate 'size' into 'distance'.

The old mining regions like the Urals and the Donbass–Dnieper bend fields are easy to reach and still productive. However, the West Siberian oilfields have outstripped the historic Caucasian wells in production, and it is estimated that almost 94 per cent of the reserves of coal are located beyond the Urals, in deposits such as those of the Tunguska and Lena fields and the Kuznetsk basin. The great Siberian rivers offer the best potential for hydroelectric power, and exports of Siberian natural gas already earn valuable hard currency from the West.

Unfortunately for the Soviets, much of the wealth of Siberia is locked up in places which are difficult to get at, for reasons of terrain, climate (see below) and distance. The communications across this great region are tenuous in the extreme, and depend principally on water transport and on just two railways – the original Trans-Siberian Railway (built 1891–5), and the new Baikal-Amur Mainline, which comes into full operation in the later 1980s (see p. 84). The sea route around the north of Russia is closed by ice for eight or nine months of the year (see p. 234), and the Siberian rivers flow to the north, or across the desirable axes of communication. No proper trunk road runs all the way across Russia, and the total length of hard-topped roads (about 750,000 kilometres) is exceeded by that in Britain, a country which occupies one-ninetieth of the space of the Soviet Union.

CLIMATE AND AGRICULTURE

Russia is a northern land and on the whole a very chilly one. The climate tends to continental extremes, and in winter a static 'cell' of cold air hangs over Siberia, producing very low temperatures in the east. Most of Russia lies under snow for between 100 and 180 days every year, and across the north the great cold has created extensive zones of permafrost, or permanently frozen ground. Construction costs in the permafrost are about double those in unfrozen areas. Foundations of buildings, roads and railways (being relatively warmer) are gradually engulfed by the soil, and tunnels in the permafrost are rendered unstable by exposure to warm air.

Russian summers are brief but characteristically hot, and a concerted effort is needed to exploit the time available for planting and harvesting. We have still not exhausted the attractions of the seasons. One of the best times for getting about happens to be early in the year, when most of the snows have already fallen, and the ground lies hard frozen under open skies. Spring is actually much more difficult for transportation, for the thaw transforms the countryside and the unmade roads into a morass of mud and slush. Much the same effect is sometimes experienced in western Russia in the autumn, during rainstorms of almost tropical intensity.

Climate and terrain conspire to render more than one-third of the surface of Russia totally unsuited for agriculture. As regards vegetation, we encounter a pronounced banding effect as we progress south from the Arctic Ocean. The cold and bare tundra supports scarcely any vegetable life except moss, lichen, heather and dwarf trees. These Arctic deserts give way to the deep belt of the coniferous *taiga* forests, and these in turn yield to mixed woodlands, and finally to the open plains and steppes. Great tracts of desert extend from the Caucasus to the Gobi, and every spring much of West Siberia is reduced to an inaccessible swamp, for the ice on the headwaters of the rivers begins to melt at a time when the lower reaches to the north are still hard frozen. The water is unable to escape downstream, and spreads over the countryside.

Three out of four Russian rivers are inconsiderate enough to flow to the north in this way, when their waters could be put to much better use in the main agricultural areas in the drier south, where it is calculated that proper irrigation brings about a five-fold increase in production. Russia has about 80,000,000 acres of adequately watered land, which make up only 12 per cent of the arable area but account for more than 35 per cent of the crops.

Around 75 per cent of the agricultural production of the Soviet Union is concentrated in European Russia, and more particularly in the fertile Black Earth regions of the south. Even here many of the potential riches are squandered. Rigid programmes like the Five Year Plans originated early in the history of the Soviet Union, when the priority was given to heavy industrial production, but they do not work very well when applied to agriculture. The Soviet Union has more than 35 per cent of its labour force employed on the land, and must still import great quantities of foreign grain. In Britain the agricultural workers amount to less than 3 per cent of the whole, and yet they produce about as much wheat as the whole of Kazahkstan, which is ten times the size of the United Kingdom.

Russians consume at least 220,000,000 tons of grain per year (much of it indirectly as cattle feed). The harvest exceeds this figure in bumper seasons like that of 1978, but in most years the Soviet Union must buy in grain from abroad.

SPECIFIC STRATEGIC PROBLEMS

Open borders

In the Soviet version of Russian history, the unoffending national territory has undergone repeated violations at the hands of malevolent forces which have struck across the open and defenceless borders of the motherland. The Ural Mountains (which are really no more than hills) give no protection in the east, and it is easy for the Soviets to cast the present-day Chinese in the historic role of the Mongol hordes who for a time held Muscovy under their sway.

Nothing much better can be expected from the West. Schoolbooks, films and museum displays hammer home the message that Russia has been the object of repeated assaults from this direction, of which the most celebrated authors are:

– King Charles XII of Sweden in 1708–9
– Napoleon in 1812
– The British and French in the Crimea and the Baltic in 1854–6

- The anti-Bolshevik contingents of the Allies in 1918–20
- Hitler in 1941

NATO and rearmed West Germany are placed in the direct line of descent.

The Soviet view of the art of war has been influenced profoundly by these experiences. About 95 per cent of the operations of the Great Patriotic War revolved about the great land battles that were fought on the plains stretching to the west of Moscow. Massed formations and superior numbers were the things that counted, not the qualities of flexibility and initiative, and Soviet officers were guided by the set rules they found in their regulations. The Soviet air and naval forces were, and still are, given an entirely subordinate place in the order of priorities.

The strategic hollow

The Soviet Union appears to have the great advantage of a central strategic position, and indeed roughly 85 per cent of the world's population lies within 5,000 kilometres of Soviet borders. It is equally true that Russia is strategically empty in the middle, and that vulnerable locations, and consequently many of the Soviet forces, are scattered around the rim of the national territory.

The eighty-odd divisions in European Russia are the nearest thing to a strategic reserve. Thirty divisions are stationed in the territory of East European satellites, another thirty in the southern Military Districts and Afghanistan, and fifty-two in the Far East.

If the SS-20 missile can reach the whole of European NATO, then American intermediate-range nuclear missiles could devastate the Soviet core area from forward sites in Europe, without the need to commit the American intercontinental nuclear forces (see p. 23). Continental NATO is a rimland of the Euro-Asian land mass, and therefore undeniably vulnerable to a Soviet overland attack. However, NATO as a whole is divided into segments by two grand strategic water barriers – the outer ditch of the North Sea and Channel, and the great moat of the Atlantic – and the Soviets' chance of a knockout victory over the West is reduced accordingly.

Scattered fleets

Russia has a very long coastline, but most of this extends along the Arctic Ocean, which is icebound for the greater part of the year, and the Soviet navy is forced to take to the water in four widely scattered locations.

- *The Northern Fleet* (see pp. 231–2) is based largely on the Kola peninsula, and has under command the greatest force of submarines of all kinds, and the second largest number of surface combatants. Not only do the icy Arctic waters offer cruising areas for their nuclear missile submarines, but the North Atlantic shipping lanes lie more accessible to attack than from any other base. In addition the Northern Fleet has the responsibility for furnishing the ten or so attack submarines which operate in the Mediterranean.
- *The Baltic Fleet* (see pp. 226–7) owns no strategic nuclear missile submarines at all, for these vessels would be too vulnerable in the Baltic. However, the Baltic bases lie close to the Soviet heartland, and their shipbuilding and repair facilities are of great importance (in the long term even for the Northern Fleet). Moreover, the Baltic Fleet comprises the Soviets' largest concentration of light surface craft and amphibious warfare vessels.
- *The Black Sea Fleet* (see p. 152) has no strategic nuclear missile submarines, but operates the second largest force of major surface combatants. In addition to its local role, it provides the surface element of the Mediterranean squadron, which must do battle on the far side of the Turkish straits against the American Sixth Fleet.
- *The Pacific Fleet* (see p. 85) is the largest as regards major surface combatants, and is the most balanced and self-sufficient of all the fleets, commanding nuclear missile submarines as well as respectable numbers of smaller surface craft and attack submarines, and a powerful naval aviation. The Soviet forces in the South China Sea and beyond come under the control of the Pacific Fleet.

The exchange of vessels between the Soviet fleets is a matter of peacetime routine, and forms an important component of some exercises. However, the vast geographical separation of the bases is a great inconvenience, and one which might well prove operationally fatal in wartime.

Nowhere, not even in northern waters, does the Soviet navy enjoy a free and unchallenged run from its home bases to the great oceans. Its navigation is everywhere obstructed by islands, shallows, capes or straits, as we shall have frequent occasion to remark. Among their foreign outstations Cam Ranh Bay (see p. 89) happens to be magnificently placed, but their establishments in the region of the north-west Indian Ocean are all imprisoned in narrow waters.

It might be possible for the Soviet navy to execute a 'surge deployment' and reach the open seas before the West could close the choke points, but this is a desperate measure that in peacetime would put NATO on a high state of alert. Meanwhile at any given time about 85 per cent of Soviet warships are to be found in port, which must detract from the cost-effectiveness of this expensive navy.

ASIAN FRONTIERS

The Soviet Union's dealings and interest in the Mediterranean, Scandinavia and on the Central Front will be reviewed in later chapters. It is perhaps easy to forget that in purely geographical terms Russia is more of an Eastern country than a European one. Seventy-five per cent of the national territory is in Asia, and the Asiatic borders are about seven times longer than those with European countries.

AFGHANISTAN

The Soviet intervention

The direct Soviet access to the Middle East is at present blocked by two states. Turkey (in spite of every discouragement) remains part of NATO, and provides the Americans with electronic outposts that see far into the Soviet Union (see p. 159). Iran has been in the grip of Shi'ite Islamic fundamentalism since 1979. The Iranian Communist party, the Tudeh, is a tiny and persecuted minority, and Iran became so impervious to Soviet influence that Moscow put its indirect support behind Iraq, which since 1980 has been engaged in the bloody Gulf War with the Iranians. A Soviet military push through Iran would be an immensely risky enterprise in international terms, but, if it was successful and unchallenged, it would open a very useful path to southern waters. In the Second World War the 'Persian Corridor' became the most important avenue of Western supplies to the Soviet Union, and demonstrated the practicability of overland transport between the Gulf and the Caucasus.

Further to the east the Soviet military intervention has been much more forthright.

On 27 December 1979 the first of successive waves of Soviet

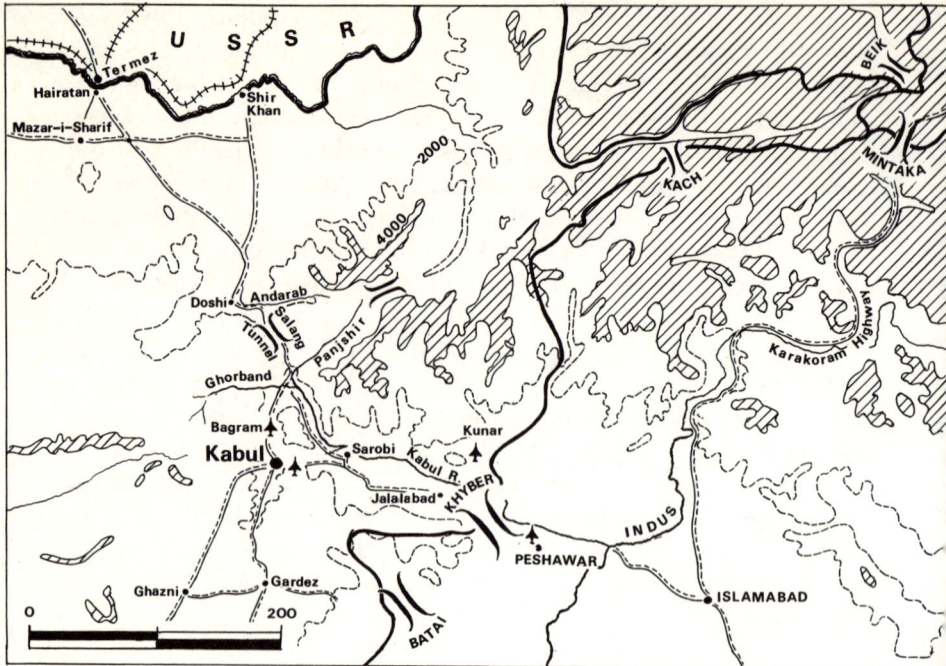

MAP 3   Kabul and Surroundings

transport aircraft delivered Soviet troops and air-portable armour
and assault artillery to Kabul International Airport and Bagram
airbase nearby. Within a few days a column of Soviet motor rifle
divisions had crossed the Afghan frontier at Hairatan and pushed on
to Kabul. To the west a further force was consolidating at Herat and
Shindand, having made an entry by way of Kushka.

   A fresh Marxist government was installed in Kabul under Babrak
Karmal, but the puppet Afghan regime and army failed to gain the
support of most Afghans, and before long the Soviets were faced
with full-scale guerrilla resistance. The Afghan rebel bands,
although very disorganised, were able to stage destructive ambushes
of Soviet convoys along routes as vital as the Herat–Kandahar
highway, and the roads leading to Kabul by way of Gardez, Jalalabad
and the Salang Tunnel. The last of these entries passes close to the
Andarab and Panjshir valleys, the lair of the celebrated guerrilla
fighter Ahmadshah Masud.

   For a long time the Soviet strategy in Afghanistan appeared
passive, being based on holding the main towns and the airfields, but
gradually the Soviets came to terms with the theatre of war. They

acquired excellent intelligence, they became more flexible in their ways, and they combined a ruthless application of air power with drives by ground forces and fast-moving helicopter-borne troops.

By 1985 up to 115,000 Soviet military personnel were present in Afghanistan. In no sense, however, could the Soviet military effort be called 'Russia's Vietnam'. It has absorbed very much fewer resources than the American intervention in south-east Asia, which weakened the United States in its confrontation with the Soviet Union in other theatres and dimensions. The Afghan scene of operations lies immediately next to Russia, not thousands of kilometres distant, and the Soviet forces and politicians (unlike the American ones) are not answerable to organised public opinion.

Possible Soviet motives

A number of theories have been advanced to explain what the Soviets are doing in Afghanistan. They are by no means exclusive of one another, nor must we discount the possibility that the Soviets have not always been clear and purposeful in their resolutions.

THE DRIVE TO THE ARABIAN SEA

It is conceivable that the Soviet intervention in Afghanistan was a purely defensive action, designed to emplace a more stable Marxist regime, and perhaps also to forestall the spread of unrest among the Tadzhik and Uzbek peoples of the neighbouring areas of the Soviet Union.

Other interpretations hark back to the 'Great Game' of the nineteenth century, and the Tsarist urge to push south to warm waters. It is physically difficult for the Soviets to advance straight overland to the Arabian Sea, for Afghanistan is separated from the water by the very inhospitable area of western Pakistan, where hill ridges alternate with deserts. However, the enterprise is more feasible if we imagine the Soviets taking a left turn through the Khyber, Gomal and Khojak Passes to the plain of the Indus, where they would have a clear run by way of Hyderabad to the sea. Here the port of Karachi is at their disposal, and they could reach out to the large airfield and partially completed naval base on the bay of Chah Bahar, just inside Iran. Such a clockwise circuit – by way of the south-east Afghan passes, the Indus lowlands and the Iranian coast – would correspond to the routes taken by the forces of Alexander the Great between 327 and 324 BC.

Pakistan is now beginning to look distinctly vulnerable. There is a breakaway nationalist movement in Baluchistan in the south, and another dedicated to creating a 'Pakhtunistan' in the north. Both of these lend themselves to Soviet exploitation. Islamabad, the Pakistan capital, is located only about 200 kilometres from the Khyber Pass, and northern Pakistan as a whole forms a corridor sandwiched between Afghanistan and India (which has claims to the areas of Baltistan and Gilgit). The airfield at Peshawar, where the Americans have some spyplanes, is completely untenable against attack from the Khyber.

Chinese interests are also heavily engaged. A short push from Afghanistan or India would be enough to sever the winding Karakoram Highway, which is the only communication between China and Pakistan. This route, which was completed in 1978, is 500 kilometres long and crosses the frontier from Sinkiang at the very vulnerable Mintaka Pass. The Indus actually rises in Chinese territory, and eighteenth-century strategists (who paid close attention to such things) would probably have told us that Russia clearly intended to bar China's way to the Indian Ocean.

The Chinese Institute of American Studies claims (1985) that the Indus valley could become the scene of a major showdown between the Soviet Union and America, and that the Soviets would be able to devote many more forces to operations in this direction than is generally appreciated in the West, calling on troops from the Moscow strategic reserve and the more distant Chinese frontiers, as well as the neighbouring Military Districts.

EXTENSION OF AIR POWER

Quite apart from opening up a possible avenue of overland advance, the Soviet presence in Afghanistan extends Soviet air power in the direction of the oil-rich Gulf region.

Already in the middle 1950s Soviet construction teams began to build airstrips and airfields inside Afghanistan in the interests of Soviet–Afghan friendship. The late 1970s witnessed the extension of air bases in Soviet Central Asia at Merv, Karshi and Chardzhou, and after the military intervention in 1979 the Soviets began a new programme of lengthening or building runways in Afghanistan. Faizabad, Bagram, Kabul, Jalalabad, and Kerala (in Kunar Province) lie on or around the shortest route between the Soviet Union and north-west Pakistan. The fields and bases beyond the turbulent air of the Hindu Kush are particularly valuable; Sardeh Band, Kandahar and Lashkar Gah are situated within short flying range of the southern border with Pakistan; Farah, Herat and the very

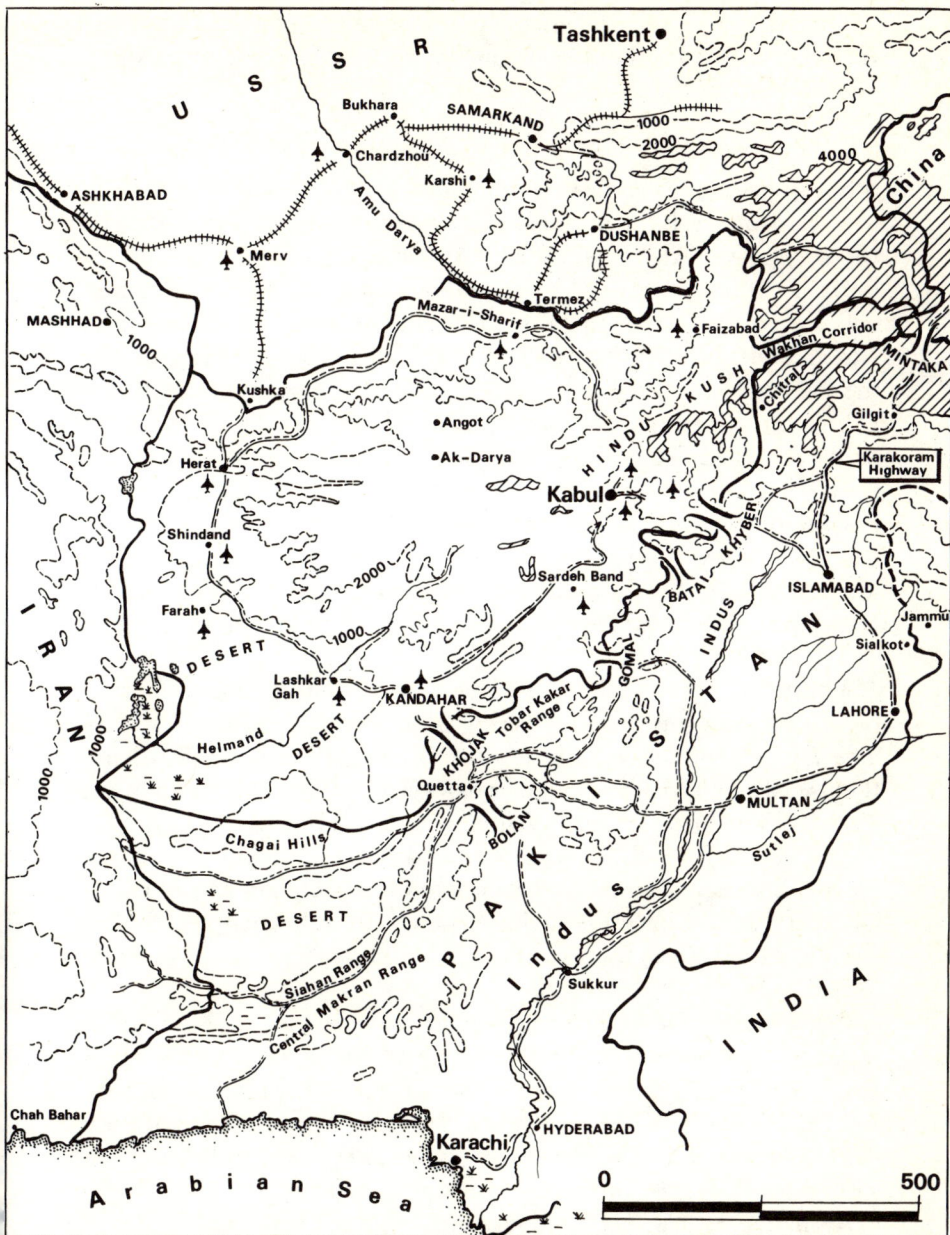

MAP 4   Afghanistan

important long-range reconnaissance base at Shindand look towards Iran, and provide the physical means for surveillance and military intervention in the Gulf.

COLONISATION

A body of evidence is starting to suggest that the Soviets might be up to a very old-fashioned venture in territorial expansion. Over the years northern Afghanistan has been integrated ever more closely into the communications and economic system of the Soviet Union, and it is by no means impossible that the invasion in 1979 was just a violent episode in a longer process. Once again the story begins with the work of Soviet engineers. The principal achievement has been to help to build the great circular highway which connects the principal towns of Afghanistan. The most important sector runs from Mazar-i-Sharif (the nearest point to the Soviet border) south to Kabul, passing the central ridge of the Hindu Kush by the Salang Tunnel, and vaulting over the valley of the Ghorband River by means of the Mattak Bridge. From Kabul the highway continues south-west to Kandahar, then loops back through Shindand and Herat to complete the circuit.

The Soviets have a back door to Herat from Kushka, but their main effort has gone into perfecting the communication with Kabul. The tap root of the supply line is the navigable river Amu Darya (Oxus), which is reached by the Soviet rail system at Chardzhou and Termez. The ports at Termez and upstream at Shir Khan have been expanded, and in May 1982 a road and rail 'friendship bridge' was opened between Termez and Hairatan on the Afghan shore. Hairatan will in turn become an important railhead when the Soviets complete the railway that is intended to run parallel with the highway to Kabul.

From the Pakistani point of view there are two dangerous spurs leading from the circular highway, the one being the reconditioned Khyber route, and the other the new Route 14 leading south-east from Kandahar to the Khojak Pass. Ironically enough both of these roads were built by the Americans when they were still competing with the Soviets for influence inside Afghanistan.

Afghanistan lies well to the south of the main axis of Soviet economic development, which is across Siberia. However, it is by no means impossible that we are witnessing the projection of a secondary axis through Soviet Central Asia to Afghanistan, where the resources of oil, natural gas, copper, iron and uranium might prove easier to extract than in Siberia. In 1967 the first natural gas was piped to the Soviet Union from the field at Shibarghan in northern Afghanistan, and now almost all of the Afghan production of natural gas is received by the Soviets. The oilfields at Angot and Ak Darya will be a welcome supplement to the depleting reserves of exploitable oil in the Soviet Union, and it is also significant that the Soviets have thought it worth their while to construct an electricity power line all the way from the Soviet frontier to Aynak, near Kabul, in order to open up the reserves of copper ore.

Soviet Central Asia is the link between the Soviet core area and what seems to be the expanding frontier in Afghanistan. This region is the only part of the Soviet Union with a rapidly expanding population, and Tashkent has already become the fourth largest city in the Soviet Union (population 1,900,000). The Aral Sea has been sucked almost dry by the demands of industry and the state farms, and the Soviets are considering the drastic expedient of digging a 2,000-kilometre canal to divert the course of the great Ob and Irtysh rivers from the Arctic Ocean to the Aral Sea.

THE CHINESE FRONTIER

NATO derives great indirect benefit from the diversion of force to the Chinese borders. Thus the Soviets have fifty-two divisions (nearly 700,000 troops) deployed within reach of China in the eastern Soviet Union and the People's Republic of Mongolia, in addition to the 80,000-odd men of the KGB Border Guards. The Soviet divisions facing China are more lightly equipped than those garrisoning Eastern Europe (forty-five motor rifle divisions and only seven tank divisions), and they stand at a lower category of readiness, but in absolute terms the Soviets have more troops facing China than looking west. Unless the Soviet Union is able to dispose of one enemy before turning against another (as actually happened in 1945), it is unlikely that the Soviets will have the freedom to transfer reinforcements between the two extremities of Euro-Asia.

The origins of the quarrel

In one perspective the Sino-Soviet dispute is a theological one, for the mantle of Marx has been tugged from opposite corners by the Soviets (with their industrial proletariat) and the Chinese (with their puritanical and peasant-based revolution, and their new experiments in a 'capitalist' Communism).

Power politics are another important ingredient. The Soviets fear the rise of China as a nuclear power, and it was the Soviet Union's unwillingness to help China to develop nuclear weapons that precipitated the breach between the two countries in 1960 and 1961. The issue of disputed borders goes well beyond the rather ridiculous series of frontier clashes which culminated in open hostilities along the Amur and Ussuri rivers in 1969. It has its roots in the Chinese desire to recover the ground lost to Russia over the generations, and in particular the Maritime Provinces, which extend between Manchuria and the Sea of Japan and contain the principal bases of the Soviet Pacific Fleet. More than one and a quarter million square kilometres of territory were annexed by Tsarist Russia in the era of the 'unequal treaties', and further land was filched by the Soviet regime.

The Chinese have a sense of being contained and bottled up, which at first seems strange in view of the great size of their country (9,597,000 square kilometres). Unfortunately the western part of China takes in large tracts of mountain and desert, quite unsuitable for cultivation, which has the effect of cramming nearly 40 per cent of the population on just 10 per cent of the territory, in the lower Yangtze core area and the northern plain. These claustrophobic feelings have been strengthened by the success of the Soviets in planting political and military outposts around the periphery of China. 'Take a look at the map', declared a Chinese strategist; 'north, west and south, the Russians are everywhere, on our borders in Mongolia, Afghanistan and Vietnam' (*Guardian*, 12 March 1984). On their side the Soviets are disturbed by the knowledge that China lies so close to underpopulated eastern Siberia.

There could be no more convincing evidence of the Soviets' interest in opening up their Far East than the stupendous effort which has gone into building a second railway across eastern Siberia, namely the Baikal–Amur Mainline (BAM). The historic Trans-Siberian Railway is a busy and successful line, but suffers from the disadvantages of running too close to the Chinese frontier (130 kilometres or less), yet too far from the zones of economic development in eastern Siberia. The new BAM follows a more northerly route. It branches from the Trans-Siberian Railway at Tayshet, and continues by way of Ust'Kut, the northern tip of Lake Baikal, Chara, Tynda and Komsomolsk to the Pacific at Sovetskaya Gavan.

The BAM was begun in 1974. The tracks were completed in 1985, and they are expected to become operational along all their length in about 1988. The length amounts to 4,340 kilometres, and the line passes over about 150 major bridges and through five principal

This effort will probably be repaid many times over. The BAM helps to open up hitherto inaccessible mineral deposits, and together with the Trans-Siberian Railway it will provide a speedy and competitive route for container traffic across the Euro-Asian land mass, accounting ultimately for perhaps as much as half of the cargo in transit between Western Europe and Japan.

The ports of the Soviet Pacific coast are likely to acquire increasing importance as outlets for bulk commodities from Siberia, and as points of departure for the short-haul cargo routes to Japan and the northern Pacific. These establishments already have great significance as the home of the Pacific Fleet (see p. 76).

The Soviet Pacific Fleet increased in size by about 80 per cent between 1965 and 1985, by which time it held half of the force of carriers, and 40 per cent of the entire navy. It supports the Soviet military and political presence in the Indian Ocean. Its nuclear missile submarines threaten the United States, and its attack submarines and reconnaissance and strike aircraft endanger the lines of communication of the Americans and their friends in the Pacific, the South China Sea and the straits of the East Indies.

If we count the Mongolian People's Republic (Outer Mongolia) as a strategic part of the Soviet Union, the border between the Soviets and the Chinese runs for about 10,000 kilometres, or across most of the width of Asia. Much of the frontier region consists of mountains, desert and steppe, and at first sight it is not easy to assess the balance of advantage. Excluding local forces, the Chinese have about seventy-six divisions deployed in the border Military Districts of Ürümqi, Lanzhou, Peking (Beijing) and Shenyang (Mukden), as well as a further forty-six divisions deployed in the Military Districts immediately to the rear. The Soviets are unable to match these numbers, and in order to eke out their forces they are said to be planning to make considerable use of helicopter gunships and airborne troops, and to grind down Chinese assaults in extensive Fortified Areas, where they have thousands of turrets from old tanks and warships emplaced in permanent defences (Suvorov, 1981, 75).

On balance, however, the Soviets seem to have the upper hand. They are superior in firepower and mobility, and they might be expected to employ nuclear and chemical weapons with fewer inhibitions against China than against the West. It is true that the Soviets have a number of sensitive targets on their side of the divide. Some of the bases of the Pacific Fleet are distinctly vulnerable to a push by the Chinese across the Ussuri. The Trans-Siberian Railway, if not the BAM, is at risk from raids across the border, and it is possible that the Soviets might experience some anxiety for their nuclear testing site at Semipalatinsk and their 'new industrial frontier' in Kazakhstan.

The Chinese nevertheless have very much more to lose, for the location of valuable installations close to the frontier makes their country a highly 'chewable' object in strategic terms. We may cite the nuclear testing site at Lop Nor, the oilfields around Ürümqi and Lanzhou, the political capital at Peking (Beijing), and the heavy industries in Manchuria. The Chinese keep their strategic nuclear missiles dispersed and concealed, not massed in 'farms' of silos on the open plain in American or Soviet style, but China is vulnerable in the nuclear dimension in view of the very heavy concentration of its population and industries.

The core area of the Soviet Union lies west of the Urals, and is invulnerable to all save strategic nuclear attack by the Chinese. The Soviets, on the other hand, do not need to strike deep into China in order to be able to set back the military and industrial progress of the Chinese for a generation or more.

If the Soviet Maritime Provinces could be pinched out by a Chinese thrust across the Ussuri, they might equally well serve as one of the bases for a pincer movement against Manchuria, on the model of the Soviet attack against the Japanese there in August 1945. The thrust from the Maritime Provinces was executed by the First Far East Front, commanded by Marshal Meretskov. Further north a Second Far East Front (General Purkayev) broke across the Manchurian border near Khabarovsk and advanced on Harbin. Marshal Malinovsky's offensive was the most spectacular of all. His Transbaikal Front anticipated the Japanese at the passes of the Great Hingan Mountains, and exploited into the industrial centre of Manchuria. A subordinate raiding force under General Pliev meanwhile executed a wide outflanking movement across the Gobi Desert and emerged in the neighbourhood of Peking, a stroke which demonstrates how a comparatively short advance from Mongolia to the Yellow Sea has the effect of severing the body of China from its industrial head in Manchuria.

Some highly relevant arrangements were made in 1978. Hitherto the Soviet military commands had been arranged in something like overlapping walls along Russia's Asian frontiers. Now the Military Districts were reassigned in such a way as to give the means of forming two coherent masses of forces. The eastern command structure lost the Central Asian MD but gained the Siberian one, giving a potential Far Eastern Theatre of Operations (TVD) depth and concentration for a stroke against Manchuria and Peking (Siberian, Transbaikal and Far Eastern MDs). The other likely TVD, the Central Asian or Southern, is likely to have the Central Asian, Turkestan and Transcaucasus MDs under command.

However, the difficulties of interpretation are still very great. In 1985 the Chinese strategic analyst Hua Di, of the Institute of American Studies (see p. 80), warned the West against assuming that Soviet forces were irretrievably committed in one or the other direction. Even divisions garrisoned as far east as those in the Transbaikal MD were capable of being switched to operations in the south (Erickson, 1983, 58).

FAR EASTERN WATERS AND JAPAN

In the 1960s and 1970s, when Sino-Soviet relations were deteriorating fast, it seemed that the Soviets were establishing a productive liaison with the Japanese, whose technology was well suited to unlock the wealth of Siberia. From 1965 areas of the Japanese economy were gripped by something of a 'Siberian fever', and Japanese companies helped to develop oilfields, mines and ports on the Russian mainland. If the impetus was later lost this was largely because the Soviets have put such a high priority on building up their military strength in the Far East.

The Soviets retain their hold on the Kurile Islands and southern Sakhalin, which they seized from Japan in 1945. The 30th Air Army is now a formidable force, along with the land-based aviation of the Soviet Pacific Fleet. Soviet aircraft frequently violate Japanese airspace, and Japanese fishing vessels in their hundreds have been confiscated by Soviet patrol boats. Soviet strategic missile submarines lurk in the Sea of Okhotsk, which has become an area defence zone or 'sea bastion', while the SS-20s deployed east of Irkutsk are able to hit Japan just as effectively as China.

In view of the importance the Soviets attach to their Pacific Fleet and its supporting aviation, it is perhaps surprising to discover how badly placed their military establishments turn out to be. The Far Eastern bases as a whole stand 7,000 or more kilometres remote from the heartland of Russia, and their intercommunication is poor and frequently dependent entirely on sea and air. There is no proper road along the Kamchatka peninsula, or between there and the Maritime Provinces. Almost all of the Soviet bases are afflicted to some degree by ice and fog, and those in the south have their egress restricted by Japanese or South Korean territorial waters. This is one theatre in which the Americans and their friends enjoy the advantage of interior lines.

We shall now undertake a brief journey from north to south, calling in at a few of the more interesting establishments on the way. Petropavlovsk on the remote Kamchatka peninsula has become the principal submarine base of the Pacific Fleet, and the home of about a quarter of the entire submarine force of the Soviet navy. The Delta nuclear missile submarines need to make just a short voyage around the tip of the peninsula to the Sea of Okhotsk, while the shorter-reaching Yankees have a clear run to their patrol areas off the western coast of the United States, and the attack submarines must travel only about 1,200 kilometres to the main shipping lanes between North America and Japan. The frequent fogs are the chief navigational hazard. However, the winter pack ice does not extend as far south as Petropavlovsk, and any light sheets of ice are easily cleared.

There are three main series of southerly bases:

The string of the Kuriles serves as an air defence and anti-submarine outpost line, and brings the Soviets to within literal sight of the Japanese island of Hokkaido. The military bases and the airfield constructions on the isles of Kunashir and Etorufu (Iturup) have caused particular offence to the Japanese.

The long Soviet island of Sakhalin lies closer inshore and reaches out to Hokkaido from the north-west. Sakhalin supports a number of military, air and naval bases, and might be employed as a jumping-off point for an invasion of Hokkaido across the La Perouse Strait. The Japanese seem to have concluded that it would be impossible to defend the narrow isolated tip of Hokkaido at Wakkanai, and they keep the main force of their Second Division in reserve at Asahigawa.

Finally a heavy concentration of air and naval bases is found in the Maritime Provinces, where the headquarters of the Pacific Fleet at historic Vladivostok (founded 1860), and the ports of Nakhodka, Vladimir, Olga and Sovetskaya Gavan, face the near-landlocked Sea of Japan. These establishments enjoy direct or indirect communications with the Trans-Siberian Railway and the BAM, but they become badly iced-up in winter, and in wartime vessels from here could reach the open Pacific only by steaming up the inner side of Sakhalin to the Tartar Strait, making hazardous dashes through the straits of La Perouse or Tsugaru, or passing to one side or another of the island of Tsushima – a place of unhappy associations for Russians.

The victory of the Communist forces in the Vietnam War enabled the Soviets to gain the use of some valuable warm-water outstations for the Pacific Fleet far beyond Soviet national territory. Most important of all is the access to Cam Ranh Bay, which is located about 3,500 kilometres from Vladivostok, and 6,000 from Petropavlovsk, representing immense gains in steaming time.

Cam Ranh Bay is one of the strategic pivots of south-east Asia. In French colonial days the Russian warships refuelled here on the way to their defeat at Tsushima in 1905. The importance of Cam Ranh Bay was further underlined in 1941 when it served as a base for the Japanese invasions of Thailand, Malaya and the Dutch East Indies. The facilities were greatly expanded by the Americans in the 1960s, and since 1978 the work has been continued by the Soviets, who have installed a floating pier and a 8,500-ton floating dry dock.

Based on here, Soviet attack submarines, Bear reconnaissance aircraft, Badger medium bombers and MiG-23 fighters now patrol the waters of south-east Asia. The arrival of the long-range Backfire bomber (5,500 km combat radius) would put all the straits of this region at risk.

THE SOVIET UNION'S GLOBAL REACH

MOTIVES

By the 1980s the Soviet Union had accomplished an historic breakout from its geopolitical boundaries as a land power, and acquired the capacity to challenge the interests of the West in every corner of the globe.

An investigation of the Soviet connections world-wide would far outrun the scope of this book. However, a brief review is in order. India, although a very useful check on China, should be counted as a Soviet client rather than an ally. The Soviet military ties with countries like North Korea, Vietnam, Syria and Libya are much closer. Iraq, South Yemen and Ethiopia give the Soviets naval or air bases in the north-west corner of the Indian Ocean, and Soviet warships are welcome at many ports of call around the coast of Africa. Finally Cuba has given the Soviets a military foothold in the New World, and sympathetic regimes and 'liberation movements' have declared themselves among the islands of the South Pacific.

These developments seem to represent a coming-together of principles, opportunities and physical means.

From an earlier generation the modern Soviet leadership inherits the mandate for world revolution, or as the new Constitution of 1977 put it, 'strengthening the position of world socialism; supporting the struggle of the nations for national liberty and social progress'. These outgoing instincts have been strengthened by the belief that it is necessary and fitting for a great power like the Soviet Union to exercise an influence on world affairs. The foreign minister Andrei Gromyko proudly asserted in 1972 that 'there is no question of any significance [i.e. on the international scene] . . . which can be decided without the Soviet Union or in opposition to it'.

The projection of world-wide power has been to a great extent the affair of the Soviet navy. Commentators therefore pay close attention to the strategic requirements of the modern Soviet naval forces, and the ideas of their founder, the veteran Admiral of the Fleet Sergei G. Gorshkov (articles 'Navies in War and Peace' in the *Morskoi Sbornik*, February 1972 – February 1973, trans. in *United States Naval Institute Proceedings*, January – November 1974; book *The Sea Power of the State*, 1976, English trans. 1979).

Gorshkov explains that the sea has gained vital new importance as a platform for nuclear weapons systems, and for this reason the acquisition of sea power is a matter of national survival. Thus we have seen how the need to counter American nuclear missile sub-marines helped to draw the Soviet navy into the Mediterranean and the Indian Ocean.

The Cuban missile crisis of 1962 turned to the immediate advan-tage of the Americans, for they were able to establish an effective naval blockade in the path of Soviet freighters. This episode helped Gorshkov to persuade his masters that sea power is an essential component of true global power, allowing a state to extend the range and freedom of its political and military action well beyond its boundaries. Such a state will also win a share in the dividing up of the potentially great material resources of the oceans (see p. 32).

In wartime the cutting of the West's maritime lines of communica-tion will be an important responsibility of the Soviet navy. This role commanded international attention in 1975, when the exercise *Okean-75* (or *Vesna-75* as the Soviets call it) simulated a co-ordinated assault on Western sea communications on a global scale. On that occasion the Backfire bomber flew from the Kola peninsula in its first sorties in its career as a naval aircraft, and Soviet air and naval forces carried out mock attacks on North Atlantic convoys and American carrier groups in the Mediterranean.

Eminent Western naval authorities have emphasised that the peaceful use of the sea is a matter of life and death for the NATO countries, but no more than a 'convenience' for the Soviet Union (Ratley, 1979, 62; Leach, 1982, 11; Train, 1982, 18). However, the more benefit the Soviets derive from the resources and uses of the sea, the more they stand to lose in the event of hostilities. The penalty to the Soviet Union would be a minor consideration in an all-out intercontinental war, in which the survival of the capitalist and socialist systems was at stake, but in any other framework the blow would be heavy.

The concern of the Western naval men reflects not only a proper vigilance against a very serious threat, but also an old assumption that certain states (i.e. ourselves) are 'entitled' to naval power, but other countries are not. Winston Churchill and Admiral Sir Herbert Richmond wrote in these terms about Kaiser Wilhelm's navy, and so did General Sir Howard Douglas about the rise of French naval power under Napoleon III: 'Preponderating naval power not being essential to the security of France, the effort to secure it can only be considered as a hostile measure towards Great Britain – to which naval supremacy is indispensable, and must be maintained at any cost' (*On the Defence of England*, London, 1860, 5).

Lastly it is impossible to ignore the element of opportunism in the extension of the Soviet reach. In the late 1960s and through the 1970s the state of the world was propitious for the Soviets to make the bid to move out of their continental fastness. This was the period when the British abandoned their 'East of Suez' role, when the United States lost its outright strategic nuclear domination, and the international crusading spirit of the Kennedy era ran into the sand. In 1975 South Vietnam was abandoned to the Communists, and in the same year the Portuguese at last let slip the burden of their African colonies. It was there in a condition of strategic vacuum that the Soviet long-range air transport fleet was able to carry out a number of celebrated *tours de force*, flying powerful contingents of Cubans to Angola in 1975–6 and Ethiopia in 1977–8, and ferrying about 85,000 Soviet troops to Kabul between December 1979 and February 1980.

MEANS AND LIMITATIONS

Airlift

The spectacular airlifts of forces to Angola, Ethiopia and Afghanistan were accomplished without any active opposition from the West. Indeed, the effectiveness of the Soviet airborne reach depends very closely on the state of the political climate.

The Soviets possess eight crack airborne divisions together with an impressive array of air-portable carriers and assault guns. However, the air transport capacity is very limited, even if we add the assets of Aeroflot (the 'civilian' airline), and the Soviets have no experience of carrying out large-scale 'hot' drops and landings against well-armed opposition on the ground, let alone in contested airspace. So far the Soviet strategic airborne operations have taken the form of long-term ferrying operations to secured airfields.

Seapower

The extent and impressive nature of Soviet naval powers are well known. Excluding strategic nuclear missile submarines, the Soviet navy comprises about 500 submarines and major surface combat ships, many of which are acknowledged to be among the most formidable of their classes in the world. The construction capacity of the Soviets is immense, being of an order which produces one nuclear-powered submarine about every six weeks. Their seaborne aviation is weak, for the *Kiev*-class carriers (37,000 tons) and the smaller *Moskva* class (17,000 tons) are not designed to compete with the mighty American supercarriers. In compensation the reach of their land-based naval aviation is very long, and their foreign airfields have become the strategic equivalent of the carrier groups of the United States. The Soviets are backward in the technology of anti-submarine warfare, but their minelaying capacity is very great.

The Soviet naval command structure takes under its wing the Soviet fishing vessels and the component shipping companies of the *Morflot*, or mercantile marine. The *Morflot* has military roles of intelligence-gathering and helping to provide logistical support for the warships, and its civilian tasks are to carry goods to and from the Soviet Union, and compete in the passenger cruise market and in the lucrative 'cross trade' (i.e. bearing cargoes between foreign ports). *Morflot* earns valuable hard currency for its masters, and although it still ranks low in the tonnage of world shipping, it has established a powerful presence on selected trade routes of strategic interest. In the course of a NATO exercise in 1967 the British Royal Marines were unable to effect a landing at the Danish port of Esbjerg, for every berth was found to be occupied by a Soviet merchant ship. Indirectly the competition from *Morflot* knocks out Western merchantmen as effectively as if they had been sunk by battleships. Like the Polish merchant marine, *Morflot* is not burdened by the costs of commercial insurance and high pay, and it is therefore in a position to quote some very attractive rates.

None of this should be taken to mean that the Soviet navy is omnipresent and all-conquering. NATO still possesses a naval tonnage one and a half times greater than that of the Soviet Union. Moreover, the Soviets must contend with the very great geopolitical disadvantage of having their navy dispersed in four fleets, operating from the peripheries of their land mass (see p. 76).

The Soviets have still failed to build up a firm infrastructure to support their worldwide sea and air forces over the long term. Their missile ships, although no longer 'one-shot' vessels, are still mostly smaller than their NATO counterparts and accordingly need to be rearmed more often. It is by no means easy for the Soviets to supply this and the other needs of their overseas flotillas, for their supply ships must make the *via dolorosa* of the choke points, and the Soviets do not have many properly stocked and fully equipped overseas bases.

The Soviet amphibious forces consist of about 16,000 Naval Infantry (marines), which is adequate to carry out short-range hooks in nearby theatres like northern Norway, the Baltic approaches and the Turkish and Japanese straits. As an instrument for grand strategic projection, however, it does not stand comparison with the US Marine Corps, a mighty establishment whose three active divisions and powerful 'organic' air forces take in 198,000 personnel.

Finally there is something of a contradiction between the strategy of long-range reach and the requirements of the 'sea bastions', which demand close-in naval and air protection for the nuclear missile submarines patrolling in inshore waters. According to press reports the case for the 'sea bastions' has been put with particular cogency by Admiral V.N. Chernavin, who in December 1985 succeeded the venerable Gorshkov as commander of the Soviet naval forces.

Economic limitations

The Soviets are able to sell military equipment to the Third World on good terms, simply by prolonging their already lengthy production runs. However, the Soviet exports of oil, which have lubricated their links with countries like India, will probably decline, and the Soviets do not have enough hard cash to be able to resolve the problems of vast distressed regions like sub-Saharan Africa. The West is often criticised for not doing enough in this field, but its help in the way of credits and non-military aid to foreign countries is still about twenty times that forthcoming from the Soviet Union.

Libya and Iraq are able to buy munitions from the product of their oil sales, but many of the other friends of the Soviet Union are a strain on Soviet pockets and patience. The burden of defence against China is a lonely one, because the fellow nations of the Warsaw Pact are unwilling to render fraternal assistance to the Soviets against the 'common enemy' in the Far East. This is a poor return for the indirect subsidies which the Soviet Union extends to Eastern Europe (see p. 97). The Soviets also carry the main responsibility for help to Cuba, which has cost the Soviet Union the equivalent of many billions of dollars in economic and military aid.

Many Soviet military men and advisers – nationalistic, racialist, hard-drinking and homesick – represent poor ambassadors of Marxism-Leninism in the Third World. This is a shortcoming which has probably played a part in enabling the West to regain the support of countries like Egypt and Somalia. We are left with the impression that, outside Europe, socialist gains are much less secure than in the states which lie close to the Soviet core area.

CHAPTER 4

The Warsaw Pact

STRATEGIC PURPOSES

The socialist states of Eastern Europe make up a region 800 or more kilometres in depth, which is tacitly admitted by NATO as falling within the Soviet sphere of influence. The satellites provide both a defensive buffer zone and an offensive launching platform for the Soviet Union. These two purposes are inseparable, for the Soviet view of defence wears a decidedly offensive aspect. The satellites are also supposed to form a socialist community, lending support and companionship to the Soviet Union. This means that the Warsaw Pact tries to do something that NATO does not attempt, namely to enforce an ideological uniformity, and the result is that the Warsaw Pact has a vulnerable psychological flank to compare with the vulnerable physical flanks of NATO.

The satellite nations make a contribution of about 1,140,300 regular military personnel to the Pact's force of 6,440,300. The Soviet contingent comes to about 5,300,000, or more than four-fifths of the total. The Soviets therefore make up a much higher proportion of the Pact's array than do the American forces in NATO, and they bear at least 80 per cent of the costs of the Warsaw Pact, as opposed to the American contribution of about 60 per cent to NATO. The strengths and weaknesses of the Warsaw Pact are therefore to a large extent those of the Soviet Union.

The military effectiveness of the satellites has very little to do with whether or not they 'like' the Soviets. Their initial enthusiasm for a combat would probably hang on the circumstances in which hostilities broke out, or the way in which the crisis was conveyed to them by the propaganda machines of the Warsaw Pact and NATO. Thus a hint of an aggressive move on the part of West Germany would be likely to bring the Poles and Czechs smartly into line. Much also depends on the speed of events: 'Given Soviet concerns about the reliability of the East Europeans, it would be to Soviet advantage to minimise consultation and preparation time and achieve quick multinational involvement of forces and early battlefield success'

(Johnson, Dean and Alexiev, 1980, 148).

The deployment of forces in Eastern Europe makes little sense unless we assume that the satellite contingents will form operational parts of Soviet armies, standing under wartime Soviet direction. This will obviously make it more difficult for individual satellites to offer armed resistance against the Soviets or their neighbours in the event of an internal crisis in the Warsaw Pact. However, the satellites would probably find that their immediate national interests were best served by putting all misgivings aside, and making a whole-hearted contribution to a Soviet offensive against NATO that would push the scene of the fighting away from their territories.

STRUCTURE, DIVERSITY AND INTERNAL DISCIPLINE

The fundamental Treaty of Friendship, Mutual Assistance and Co-operation was signed in Warsaw on 14 May 1955. Over six years had passed since the establishment of NATO, and the Soviets claimed that they had exercised admirable patience until they were at last spurred into action by the rearming of West Germany. More probably the Soviets were looking for a new legal basis for keeping their forces in Eastern Europe, and more particularly in Hungary and Romania, where up to then the garrisons had been retained on the grounds that they were needed to support the lines of communication to the Soviet zone of occupation in Austria. It is significant that the Austrian State Treaty, which set up the independent Austrian state, was signed just one day after the Warsaw Pact.

Albania left the Warsaw Pact in September 1968, but with this one exception the membership has been held in line, and includes the Soviet Union, Bulgaria, Czechoslovakia, East Germany, Hungary, Poland and Romania. The Soviet Union has established status-of-forces agreements with the individual satellites (though the agreement with Romania lapsed in June 1958), and Pact members are in addition linked by a complicated network of bi-lateral treaties.

On 26 April 1985 the partners met again in the same ornate hall in the Radziwill Palace in which the original treaty had been signed nearly thirty years before, and renewed the Pact for another two decades, with the option to add a further ten years on top.

The political structure of the Warsaw Pact consists of a Political Joint Consultative Committee, and two bureaux which live permanently in Moscow – a Joint Secretariat, and a Permanent Commission.

The Council for Mutual Economic Assistance (COMECON) was set up in 1949 as a showpiece counterweight to the Marshall Plan. Since then the organisation has developed into something much more than a propaganda front, and the membership now extends beyond Europe to Cuba, Mongolia and Vietnam, though Romania characteristically stays outside.

COMECON has nothing directly to do with the Warsaw Pact, but it provides an important economic connection between the partners of the military alliance. The most important business of COMECON is the exchange of Soviet energy (oil and natural gas) for East European manufactured goods. This essentially simple transaction has been attended with increasing complications. One difficulty comes from the fact that it is less profitable for the individual nations to have dealings with their COMECON partners than to sell their wares or commodities to the West for hard currency. In the case of the Soviet Union the sales of oil and gas to Eastern Europe are the equivalent of a very large indirect subsidy (even if Western analysts cannot agree as to the amount – see R. Marer, 'Intrabloc economic relations and prospects', in Holloway and Sharp, 1984, 220–1), and in 1982 the Soviets announced that they were cutting their oil deliveries by an immediate 10 per cent.

Inside the Warsaw Pact the military doctrine and equipment are standardised on the Soviet model. The Soviets supervise the national security and intelligence agencies, they work out all the contingency plans, and in wartime they will exercise all the important military commands. However, the countries of the Warsaw Pact do not make up a passive and uniform entity, and the Soviets condone or even encourage a degree of individuality and specialisation.

In this way the Hungarian economy acts as a testbed for experimentation. Likewise the Polish strategists have made varied and well-received contributions to Soviet military doctrine, and Polish amphibious troops and landing craft are assigned an important role in operations in the region of the Baltic Approaches. The Hungarians are renowned as builders of military bridging equipment. The Czechs, with their 'golden hands', inherit a tradition of weapons manufacture which goes back hundreds of years; they are significant suppliers of arms to foreign countries, and they have made some useful improvements to equipment of original Soviet design. Similarly the East Germans have furnished police, intelligence and security experts to Marxist regimes in Africa.

Old resentments retain a surprising force. The Balkans are the scene of ancient and unresolved feuds, as we shall have occasion to remark. Poland, which is universally cast by the West in the role of the 'good guy', is regarded with little sympathy by its neighbours, and not just in official circles. Conversely 'no Polish diplomat can watch, with any feeling of comfort, a military parade in East Berlin with German soldiers goose-stepping down the Unter den Linden to the tunes of the Kaiser's army' (Millar, 1981, 9). Such national tensions undeniably help the Soviet Union in its policy of divide and rule.

Toleration has its limits, and ideological deviation is something which unfailingly calls down armed invasion, or 'fraternal assistance' in the language of the Pact. The Soviet Union brought the Hungarians to heel in the bloody fighting of November 1956, and the Soviets joined other Warsaw Pact allies in the invasion which terminated the Dubcek regime in Czechoslovakia in August 1968. In September 1968 Moscow went on to proclaim what has become known as 'the Brezhnev doctrine', whereby the Soviet Union claims the right to intervene in a socialist country if the gains of socialism or the rights of other socialist countries come under threat. In all probability the Poles were spared from being fraternally assisted in their turn only by their internal military coup on 13 December 1981.

The 'Brezhnev doctrine' is just the latest expression of a kind of imperium which the Russians have long extended over central Europe. The origins may possibly be traced back to the reigns of the empresses Elizabeth and Catherine the Great in the eighteenth century. The ideological element was certainly present in the early decades of the nineteenth century, in the almost messianic crusades of Tsar Alexander I against Napoleon, and the fervour with which Nicholas I suppressed revolutionary movements outside Russia. Another theme is the notion that the military efforts of the Russian nation bring with them a claim to moral authority. A number of Russians were affronted by the opprobrium they drew down on their heads by suppressing the Polish revolution of 1830, and the poet and publicist Pushkin attacked the ingratitude of those foreigners who had forgotten that the Russians had rid Europe of Napoleon, and 'bought its freedom, honour and peace with our blood' (*Slanderers of Russia*). This sentiment was echoed 138 years later when the Czech leader Dubcek was summoned to Moscow. 'Brezhnev spoke at length about the sacrifices of the Soviet Union in the Second World War: the soldiers fallen in battle, the civilians slaughtered, the enormous material losses, the hardships suffered by the Soviet people. At such a cost the Soviet Union had gained security, and the guarantee of that security was the postwar division of Europe, and, specifically, the fact that Czechoslovakia was linked with the Soviet Union "forever" ' (Mlynar, 1980, 239–40).

It is now time to embark on a geopolitical tour through the satellites, describing a clockwise route from the Balkans to Poland, by way of Hungary, Czechoslovakia and East Germany. The relevant borderlands with NATO countries or Yugoslavia will be reviewed in later chapters.

ROMANIA

Area:	237,000 square kilometres
Population:	23,500,000
Army:	10 divisions, 3 mountain brigades

Romania is a medium-sized country in European terms. It has a Black Sea coastline of sand, estuary and marshes, and land frontiers with Bulgaria, Yugoslavia, Hungary and the Soviet Union. In south-east Europe the prefix 'Greater', when applied to the name of a country, signifies an intended or accomplished annexation of territory from a neighbour, and since 1947 Greater Romania has extended across the curve of the magnificently wooded Carpathians to the region of Transylvania, which was an historic principality of Hungary. Transylvania takes in about 300,000 ethnic Germans, and 1,700,000 – 2,000,000 people of Hungarian blood, which represents a source of potential instability.

The true core area lies in the plains of Wallachia and Moldavia, which are the home of a Latin culture which is unique in south-east Europe, and is a focus of national pride. Colonel Tatarinov, a Tsarist Russian liaison officer in the First World War, remarked that the Romanians combined the garrulity of the Latins with the lethargy of the Slavs, which seems rather rude. Others have pointed out that the Romanians are renowned in south-east Europe for their flexibility of conscience and alertness to material gain. This suggests something very highly flavoured indeed, when we consider that they share this part of the world with people like the Hungarians and the Greeks.

In 1944 a well-timed change of sides detached Romania from the sinking Axis cause, and allied her with the Soviets and the West. Romania was a signatory of the Warsaw Pact in 1955, but gradually drew apart from the rest of the Soviet bloc. Through a considerable effort (the 'industrialisation through starvation') Romania proceeded to build up independent steel-making and heavy engineering plants, resisting the pressure from COMECON that would have reduced her to the status of an agricultural colony. The Soviet troops

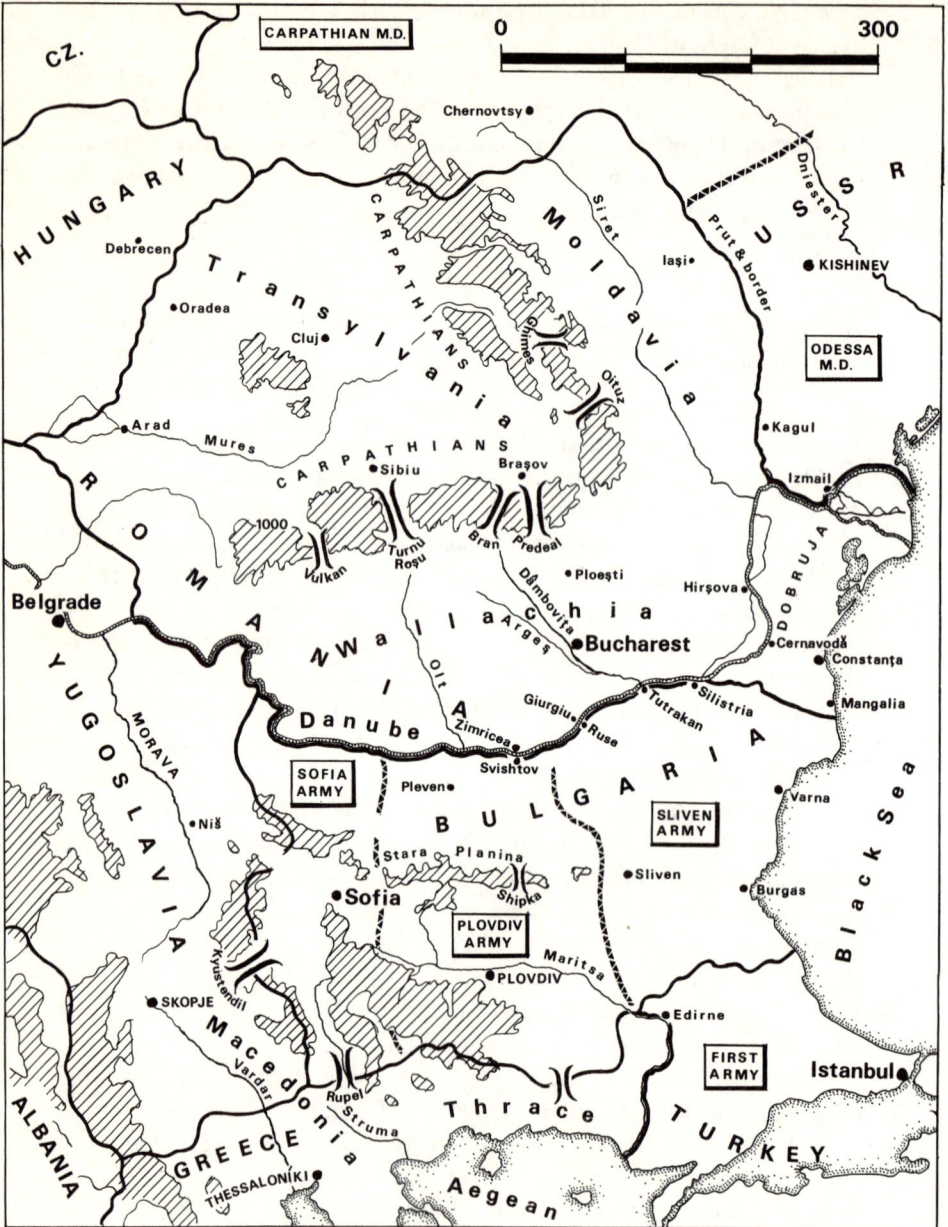

MAP 5   Romania and Bulgaria

left Romanian soil in 1958 and they have never been readmitted. The Soviet military advisers quit in 1960, and eventually Romania ceased to participate in joint Warsaw Pact exercises. All the time Bucharest has continued to make public announcements of a kind calculated to enrage the Soviet Union.

Why has Romania been allowed to become the licensed maverick of the Warsaw Pact? It can hardly be on account of the deterrent value of the Romanian armed forces. Nor does the strategic geography of Romania do much to impede a would-be attacker.

The nearest approach to a continuous and defensible barrier is in the south along the frontier with Bulgaria, which for the most part follows the line of the Danube. This river varies greatly in depth, but the width is seldom less than 900 metres, and extends up to two and a half kilometres or very much more if we take in the islands which are scattered along many stretches of this great stream. The Bulgarian or southern bank is almost everywhere higher than the Romanian bank, which is flat and muddy.

The most important Danube crossings are at Silistria, Tutrakan (Tutracaia, only about sixty-five kilometres from Bucharest) and the major road and rail passage between Ruse and Giurgiu. In past wars, however, many bridgeheads have been established in less obviously appealing locations, especially when the attacking army has been able to cross under the cover of fog or wooded islands. Thus on 23 November 1916 Field-Marshal Mackensen made the passage from Svishtov on the Bulgarian bank to Zimricea in Romania, and thereby unseated the whole Romanian strategy of national defence.

Downstream from Silistria the Danube turns slowly to the north, but instead of conforming with this new direction the frontier passes the river and strikes across country to the Black Sea, presenting Romania with what is virtually a maritime province on the southern side of the Danube estuary. This region, which makes up the greater part of the old Dobruja, contains the principal Romanian port of Constanţa and the Black Sea tourist resorts. Much of the terrain of the Dobruja is broken and wooded, and in 1916 the Romanians were able to put up a successful resistance against the Bulgarians along a line protecting the vital road and rail communications between Constanţa and Cernavodă on the Danube.

The same campaign of 1916 revealed that the most defensible ground inland is up in the Dracula country of the Carpathian Mountains. Even now the remains of trenches and thousands of shell holes testify to the ferocity with which these bosky heights were contested. The eastern and south-eastern passes (Ghimes, Oituz, etc.) are the more difficult by nature, but the Romanians also stood their ground well on southern passes like the Predeal, the Bran (Torzburg), the Turnu Roşu (Red Tower), the Surdec and the Vulkan.

It might be possible for the modern Romanians to offer a pro-longed Yugoslav-style resistance along the Carpathians, utilising their Patriotic Guard militia, but (supposing the main enemies to be Bulgaria and the Soviet Union) they would be seeking to hold Transylvania as a redoubt and fighting along a reversed front from 1916. In any case the loyalty of the Transylvanian Hungarians would be in doubt, and Transylvania is open to an invasion up the river valleys from Hungary in the west.

In the Wallachian lowlands the Ploieşti oilfields appear to be indefensible. The capital at Bucharest stands in the middle of one of the flattest plains in Europe, and the ring of detached forts, which were designed by the Belgian engineer Brialmont in 1882–3, have sunk into decay, being turned over to lemonade bottling plants and the like. The principal rivers of the plain (Olt, Arges, Dâmboviţa) are steeply banked in places, though very vulnerable to outflanking movements. Romania's ultimate refuge in 1916 was the line of the Siret in Moldavia, but this was an asylum which depended on the support of the Russians.

Altogether Romania seems to be incapable of defending her independence against 'fraternal assistance' even in the short term. Commentators agree that the main reason for the forbearance of the Soviet Union is an ideological one. Romania is run internally as a hardline Stalinist police state, which is certainly flawed by nepotism and corruption, but which offers no danger of doctrinal contamination inside the Warsaw Pact.

Moreover, Romania's geopolitical importance in the superpower confrontation is minimal, not to be compared with that of Bulgaria or Hungary, let alone Czechoslovakia or East Germany. The Soviets are annoyed, but not fatally embarrassed, by the denial of overland military communications between Russia and faithful Bulgaria, for these can be kept up by air and sea.

Even now Romania represents in some ways a flanking bastion of the Warsaw Pact. The Romanian services continue to receive mod-ern (if not the very newest) Soviet equipment, and the army has been reorganised on current Soviet lines. The air defence system is integrated into that of the alliance, and Romanian radar stations will help to give warning of any NATO air or cruise missile attack coming from the Mediterranean over Yugoslavia. It is perhaps significant that Romania's Danubian border with Yugoslavia is intensively patrolled by river craft and that the 200 or so kilometres of the land frontier are both fenced and heavily manned. In contrast the borders with Bulgaria and the Soviet Union are 'soft', being guarded only at the crossing points.

BULGARIA

Area:	110,911 square kilometres
Population:	8,970,000
Army:	8 divisions, 5 separate tank brigades

Bulgaria is a small country, which owns less than half the area and population of its northern neighbour, Romania. The capital, Sofia (population 946,000), and its industrial basin are located in the far west, close to Yugoslavia, and from there the ridges of the Stara Planina (Balkans) and the Rhodope Mountains extend eastwards on either side of the broad Maritsa valley. One-third of the country is covered by hilly and wooded terrain, and the principal cultivation is along the Danubian lowlands facing Romania, and in the region from the Maritsa valley to the Black Sea coast.

The economy of Bulgaria is varied, and closely integrated with the rest of COMECON and especially the Soviet Union. Travellers through Slavonic Europe will notice that bottles of Bulgarian jam compete with dead flies to be the sole occupants of shop shelves in countless small towns.

In south-east Europe the Bulgarians have earned the title of the 'Prussians of the Balkans', being credited with bellicose ways and the harsher virtues. All such national stereotypes are crude and dangerous, but the fact remains that Bulgaria is an expansionist state which has territorial or ideological quarrels with all its neighbours.

Bulgaria became an autonomous principality of the Turkish empire in 1878, and in 1908 the Bulgarians proclaimed their full independence of Ottoman rule. The Bulgarians went on to join enthusiastically in the carve-up of the old Turkish territories in the Balkans, but they ended up with the smallest share of all. Thus began a long chapter of frustrations, which results from the Bulgarians being militaristic by nature but unlucky in war – a most unhappy combination.

The two Balkan Wars (1912–13 and 1913), the alliances with Germany in two world wars, and the quasi-Romanian change of sides in 1944 all left the dreams of a Greater Bulgaria unaccomplished.

The Bulgarian coastline on the Black Sea is still narrow, and the exit is controlled by the Turks. In the south the last foothold on the Aegean was forfeited in 1919, and it is galling for the Bulgarians to know that the outlets of their two principal rivers, the Maritsa and the Struma, lie in foreign territory.

The present socialist regime looks hungrily on Yugoslav and Greek Macedonia, Greek Thrace, and the Romanian corridor of the Dobruja, which extends on the 'Bulgarian' side of the mouths of the Danube. Relations with Turkey are bad, and the Bulgarian government has waged a campaign of persecution against the one million ethnic Turks who live in the east of the Bulgarian national territory. It is by no means impossible that the time will come when the operational requirements of the Warsaw Pact coincide with the irredentist urges of the Bulgarian state.

The other driving force in Bulgarian geopolitics is the long-standing connection with Russia. The Bulgarian and Russian peoples are fellow Slavs, sharing the same alphabet and much the same language, and it was the Russians who first plucked Bulgaria, hot and steaming, from the melting pot that was the Turkish empire in its period of dissolution. For generations Tsarist armies fought their way south across the Danube and over the Stara Planina range in the direction of Constantinople, and bloody encounters on Bulgarian territory at places like Silistria, Ruse (Rushchuk), Pleven (Plevna) and the Shipka Pass have earned an honoured place in the annals of Russian military history. The alliances between Bulgaria and Germany are now dismissed as a passing aberration.

Modern Bulgaria is the Soviet Union's Trojan Horse in the Balkans. Logistically Bulgaria is stranded on the wrong side of Romania (see p. 102), but the port and railhead of Varna receives cargoes carried on freighters or hovercraft from the Soviet port of Odessa, and Bulgaria has become a useful channel for the transmission of Soviet arms to the Middle East. More importantly, Bulgaria gives a protection for the Warsaw Pact on its soft Balkan underbelly, and provides a launching platform for military actions against Yugoslavia and the thinnest and most vulnerable sectors of Mediterranean NATO.

Out of the three Military Regions of Bulgaria, that of the Sliven Army in the east has the role of supporting any Soviet amphibious actions against the Turkish Straits. The Plovdiv Army in the centre is likely to strike across the narrow coastal corridor of Greek and Turkish Thrace.

Together with Hungary, Bulgaria might become a jaw of a

strategic pincer movement against Yugoslavia. Here the Bulgarians would have the incentive of occupying Yugoslav Macedonia. Sofia lies fifty kilometres from the Yugoslav frontier, and the base facilities of the capital, together with its outer ring road, would give the Sofia Army and any Warsaw Pact allies the means of effecting rapid concentrations on the Kyustendil Pass and the corridors into Yugoslavia (see p. 182).

In 1981, however, Bulgaria took over the leadership of the movement for a 'nuclear-free' Balkans, and it is possible that even Bulgarian complaisance towards Moscow might reach an ultimate limit if the Soviets insisted on Bulgaria becoming a base for nuclear warfare against the West. The south-west corner of Bulgarian Thrace (Pirin Thrace) certainly offers itself as an excellent base for medium-range missiles like the accurate and powerful SS-22, whose range of 900 kilometres would embrace half Turkey, all of Greece, Sicily with its cruise missile base at Comiso, and mainland Italy up to the plain of Lombardy.

HUNGARY

Area:	93,032 square kilometres
Population:	10,800,000
Army:	6 divisions

Small, landlocked Hungary has borders with Austria, Yugoslavia and its Warsaw Pact partners Czechoslovakia, the Soviet Union and Romania. In geopolitical terms broad similarities exist between Hungary and Bulgaria. The Hungarian army is smaller, if somewhat better armed. Hungary's geographical situation, like Bulgaria's, is a pivotal one, but whereas the latter country is lodged in the heart of the Balkans, an area which is not necessarily of global importance, Hungary stands at the crossroads of Central Europe, the Balkans and the Mediterranean world, and owns good communications in all of these strategic directions.

In juxtaposition the names 'Hungary' and 'Warsaw Pact' call to mind the unhappy events of 1956 (see p. 98). Since then Hungary has been reincorporated in the Warsaw Pact to an extent which is not generally appreciated in the West. The party secretary Janos Kádár has managed to allay Soviet anxieties concerning Hungarian loyalty, while earning a degree of respect from his own high-spirited people and diverting their energies into economic experimentation. By encouraging managerial responsibilities and small-scale essays in private enterprise, the Hungarian regime has raised standards of living to an acceptable level, and persuaded many people in the West that it is still possible for a member of the Warsaw Pact to present a human face to the world. This state of affairs is threatened less by Soviet tanks than by inflation.

The Soviet garrison on Hungarian soil is called the 'Soviet Southern Group of Forces', and comprises two tank and two motor rifle divisions, which are grouped in a rough circle around Budapest. The Soviet and Hungarian forces are well integrated at both official and unofficial levels, and since at least 1966 the Hungarian army has taken part in joint Warsaw Pact exercises in a wide background of 'scenarios'.

Given the parlous state of brotherly love in Eastern Europe, the memories of 1956 are unlikely to deter the Hungarians from lending a hand in any Warsaw Pact ventures in 'fraternal assistance'. The Hungarians have long been unpopular with their neighbours on account of their alleged nationalism and arrogance. In the 1930s Czechoslovakia, Romania and Yugoslavia formed a Little Entente against the territorial ambitions of Hungary, and after the Munich agreement of 1938 Hungary exacted a revenge by annexing some of the Czech borderlands. The territorial dispute with Czechoslovakia has long been papered over, but many Hungarians now hanker after the privileged position which their country attained in the Habsburg Empire, and there is much resentment against Romania for its treatment of the Hungarian minority in Transylvania, which is regarded as the cradle of Hungarian culture.

The excellent communications radiating from Budapest lend themselves equally well to a Warsaw Pact offensive east into Romania, or south into northern Yugoslavia. For operations against NATO the geographical position of Hungary is of literally crucial importance. If the designated target is Mediterranean NATO, Soviet reinforcements might pour in from the Ukraine, and then, in association with the Southern Group of Forces and the Hungarians, advance by way of Szombathely and break into the north-western corridor of Yugoslavia. From there the spearheads could be sent into the plain of Lombardy, or across the Austrian Alps by the A10 autobahn to emerge into Bavaria near Salzburg.

The main operational axis of the Southern Group of Forces is more likely to be westwards up the Danube through Austria, from where, in association with a hook from Czechoslovakia, they would strive to unseat the southern flank of the NATO forces in West Germany.

In view of the importance of Hungary's geographical position, it is not easy to establish why NATO has accepted the Soviet claim to exclude the troops in Hungary from the long series of talks for Mutual Balanced Forces Reductions (MBFR) in Central Europe.

CZECHOSLOVAKIA

Area:	127,889 square kilometres
Population:	15,600,000
Army:	10 divisions

The 'Northern Tier' is the useful term for those three nations, Czechoslovakia, East Germany and Poland, which stand most directly in line with NATO's Central Front. Their combined population is about 27,000,000 greater than than of the Southern Tier, and their forces are likely to be employed in the first waves of any Warsaw Pact offensive, absorbing punishment from NATO, and being kept away from the rear areas (where they might cause trouble if the war went badly).

Czechoslovakia is a long, thin, sausage-shaped country which extends for 750 kilometres from the Russian Ukraine to West Germany. As a geopolitical phenomenon, Czechoslovakia along with East Germany therefore constitutes the Warsaw Pact's salient into Western Europe. Czechoslovakia's southern border with neutral Austria runs roughly parallel with the Danube at an average distance of about fifty kilometres, and the river valley can easily be reached across the open plain north of Vienna, and again by the corridor which runs through the hills from Česke Budějovice to Linz. The frontier with West Germany, the principal European partner of NATO, follows the wooded and nearly continuous ridge of the Böhmerwald (see p. 312).

In the 1970s and 1980s a considerable programme of road building opened up the interior of Czechoslovakia to fast motor transport. The Prague–Brno–Bratislava motorway provides good lateral communications, and the greatly improved branch road from Olomouc in the north-east enables the Soviet garrison there to move rapidly in a number of interesting directions.

There is good rail communication between Prague and East Germany, but the road access from the Democratic Republic and Poland is no more than adequate, and the frontier follows the highest and most difficult ground. The direct road from Russia extends from Lvov in the Ukraine and arrives in Czechoslovakia through the narrow corridor of Slovakia, which is wedged between Poland and Hungary. The reinforcement of the Soviet forces in Czechoslovakia is by no means physically difficult, but it might prove to be a crowded and highly visible affair in time of crisis.

The deployment of the Warsaw Pact forces in Czechoslovakia has long been a source of fascination for strategists. In Czechoslovakia, alone among the satellites, most of the native divisions are placed in front of their Soviet allies, in this case figuratively speaking shoulder-to-shoulder in a line of five divisions down western Bohemia, with two further divisions in close support. The five divisions of Soviet troops (the Soviet Central Group of Forces) are arranged in eastern and western commands.

These arrangements suggest that the Central Group might be regarded as a mobile reserve (roughly comparable in strategic terms with the French contingent in West Germany), and that the Czech divisions might be thrown forward to absorb the firepower of the American and West German forces.

The national aspirations of the Czechs do not extend much beyond physical survival. The terrible experiences of the 1930s and 1940s left them disillusioned with Britain and morally alienated from all their neighbours – Germans, Poles and Hungarians. The sentiment of Pan-Slavism, which had fired the nationalism of the Czechs in olden times, did not long survive an intimate acquaintance with the Soviets.

EAST GERMANY (GERMAN DEMOCRATIC REPUBLIC)

Area:	108,333 square kilometres
Population:	16,800,000
Army:	6 divisions

East Germany was constituted in 1949 out of the Soviet zone of occupation in Germany. This new German socialist state emerged into a distrustful world still clinging to the coat tails of its Soviet godfather. The armed services (the National People's Army, or NVA) stand under direct Soviet command, and the status-of-forces agreement allows the host nation no control over the positioning of the huge Soviet garrison of 380,000 troops. Gradually the power of the East German economy, and the dedication and professionalism of the NVA, earned East Germany a high place in the esteem, if not the affection, of the rest of the Warsaw Pact. The East German arms production is small, but East German economic, security and military experts play a disproportionately large part in the assistance which the alliance extends to its clients in Africa, the Middle East and the Far East (see p. 97).

The Soviets voiced no misgivings when the Democratic Republic began to develop a national pride, or rather state consciousness, based on economic and sporting achievements as well as the proficiency of the NVA. Nor was any protest uttered when the party secretary Erich Honecker embarked on a cautiously favourable 're-historisation' of figures like Luther, Frederick the Great and Bismarck. The silence was finally broken in 1984, when relations between the two Germanies began to improve and Honecker made plans to visit the Federal Republic. On 27 July a statement in *Pravda* bore a clear message of disapproval, and within a matter of days the meeting in West Germany was cancelled.

The aircraft of the NVA are of relatively short range, and similarly the naval forces are designed for inshore and amphibious operations in the nearby western Baltic. The three component flotillas are based at Peenemünde, Warnemünde and Sassnitz, and further harbours are available at Dranske-Bug, Wolgast, Tarnewitz and Barhöft.

In contrast the land forces of the NVA are very powerful, and in wartime they will have the privilege of fighting alongside their Soviet allies in the first echelon. The six East German divisions are deployed almost as far apart as is physically possible in this small country, and they are totally integrated into the Soviet peacetime and wartime commands.

POLAND

Area:	312,683 square kilometres
Population:	37,500,000
Army:	15 divisions

Poland is one of the larger European countries, and it has survived into the later twentieth century as the bearer of a defiantly distinctive national character, and with its identity with Western cultural traditions intact. Poland's industrial and agricultural shortcomings are a source of embarrassment to COMECON, and the Soviet leadership has almost ceased to believe that Poles can ever be proper Communists.

Poland extends for 600 kilometres from east to west and for 500 kilometres from north to south in the heart of the Warsaw Pact, and in December 1980 a feature in the Polish army newspaper drew attention to Poland's interesting position across 'the transit routes and lines of communication from the Soviet Union to the German Democratic Republic'. The Soviets took some offence, for at that time the resupply of the garrison in East Germany was largely effected overland across Poland, and especially by means of the good rail network. Since then the Soviets have taken care to reroute most of their communications around Poland. Thus the twice-yearly rotation of troops to the Group of Soviet Forces in Germany is accomplished almost entirely by air, and the improvement of the sea communications between the Soviet Union and East Germany gives a direct and reasonably rapid means of conveying heavy equipment. Between 28 July and 6 August 1984 the Soviets tested their new system of communications in an exercise which extended across East Germany and Poland to Liberec in Czechoslovakia. The exercise involved 60,000 Soviet troops but none of their Warsaw Pact comrades, which is unusual for an operation which covered the territory of different countries.

It would almost certainly be unjustified to draw the easy conclusion that Poland has ceased to be a net asset to the Warsaw Pact, or that the Poles have somehow become spiritual members of NATO. On the contrary every sign indicates that the Polish forces are a valued and highly integrated element of the Eastern alliance. They form the third largest military establishment in Europe (after the Soviet and the West German ones), and by far the largest armed body among the satellite states.

The Polish air forces are being brought up to date, after a long period in which they were sunk in obsolescence. It is also worth mentioning that amphibious warfare is a national speciality. The Polish shipyards build landing and support craft for the alliance, and the Poles are capable of employing up to two divisions in an amphibious role in the region of the Baltic Approaches. The navy is largely designed to support these amphibious *desants*. Its bases are strung along the estuaries and sandy coasts of Pomerania at Gydnia, Swinoujscie, Kolobrzeg and Ustka.

The main force of the army has probably been assigned an important role on the Central Front. Military service still commands respect in Poland, and, at a time when much of Europe is facing a demographic crisis, 52 per cent of Poles are aged less than thirty, which provides an ample population base for the armed services.

The Soviet military presence in Poland is surprisingly small. The Soviet Northern Group of Forces consists of two tank divisions, which are stationed at Legnica in Silesia and Borne in Pomerania.

Both of these garrisons are located in former German provinces in western Poland, according to a principle agreed by the Poles and Soviets in 1947.

CHAPTER 5

The American Superpower

Area:	9,369,885 square kilometres
	(8,431,629 excluding Alaska)
Population:	239,600,000
Army:	16 divisions
Marine Corps:	3 divisions

CONTINENTAL GEOPOLITICS

Russia was formed over a period of many centuries. By way of contrast the United States was rounded off in a comparatively short time. The War of Independence (1775–83) not only ended British rule over the Thirteen Colonies but removed the last legal barriers to expansion westwards beyond the Appalachians. The Mississippi valley region was purchased from the French in 1803, Texas entered the Union in 1845, and in 1848 Mexico was forced to yield extensive territories in the south-west and west. The 1860s proved to be particularly significant. In 1865 the North's victory in the Civil War upheld the integrity of the Union. Two years later the Alaska territories were purchased from Russia, and in 1869 the Americans completed their first railway across the continent. The development of the West went on apace, and in 1891 the Frontier was formally declared closed. When the Panama Canal was finished in 1914 America could aspire to be a power of world class.

The indigenous Red Indian population increased over the years, contrary to a general impression, but the peopling of America came above all through immigration from the Old World. In Russia, on the other hand, the subjugation of alien peoples was much more important to the national growth.

Remote, wild and cold Alaska is America's nearest approach to Siberia in every sense, and it extends American territory to within some 100 kilometres of the Soviet Union across the Bering Strait.

Mainland America measures about 4,000 by 2,000 kilometres, which is very impressive by European standards, but under half the dimensions of Russia. This is an important reason why the United

States is not as well provided with raw materials as the Soviet Union. In compensation the Americans have purchasing power and technical and financial skills which enable them to reach out much more easily to world markets. The old 'smokestack' industries are in decline in the United States as well as in Western Europe, but the underlying vitality of the American economy is impressive, and in the science of electronics the American lead over the rest of the world is great and still growing.

The internal geopolitical problems of the United States are much more manageable than those in the Soviet Union. The American population, although outnumbered by the Russians, fills out the national territory more evenly, and it is not engaged so heavily in basic and labour-intensive tasks. A smaller proportion of Americans labour in the older manufacturing industries, and less than 5 per cent of the workforce is committed to the land. American agriculture benefits from the southerly location of the national territory, and for this and other reasons the American Midwest is more productive than the comparable Russian Black Earth region. It takes a good harvest for the Russians to provide enough for their own needs, but the Americans feed themselves and much of the rest of the world besides.

The problems of minority civil rights were confronted and largely overcome in the 1960s, and although illegal immigration is swelling the numbers of the 'Hispanics', the ethnic issue does not pose a threat to the American body politic. In the Soviet Union racial consciousness has separatist and ideological overtones, and the worst of Russia's racial troubles are probably still to come.

Few Russians genuinely wish to live in Siberia, and the opening up of Russia east of the Urals is the result of state direction. Without deliberate guidance of this sort America has meanwhile grown away from the political and economic domination of the old northeastern core area, and the European-looking 'establishment' is yielding power to something more purely American – to people who owe their fortunes and values to the world of the western and southern states, with their high-technology 'sunrise' industries and their confidence in capitalist and patriotic virtues.

The move to the sunbelt owes much to effective communications, but a great deal also to a single technical device. Modern air conditioning was invented by Willis Carrier in 1902. These machines began to appear in large buildings in the 1920s, and now that they are a common feature in offices and homes they have created tolerable living and working conditions throughout the United States even in the most hideous months of summer. The air conditioner, as an agent of internal colonisation, is as important in its way to the United States as was the success of the Russians in eliminating the threat from the Crimean Tartars in 1774, which made the country as far as the Black Sea secure for intensive exploitation.

The United States is not well off for port facilities, which seems very odd at first sight, in view of the fact that the Americans have long coastlines on the Atlantic, the Pacific and the Gulf of Mexico. The Atlantic ports are to some degree cut off by the wooded inland ridges of the Appalachians. The Pacific coast is even more isolated, for it lies beyond the Rockies and other highland systems, which extend for a depth of 1,500 kilometres, or nearly half the continent. The Gulf shore is easier to reach from inland, for it receives the highly developed north–south communications of the Mississippi basin. This consideration helps to explain why there is such a heavy concentration of depots of the US Army in the Old South. However, the seaward approaches to the Gulf ports are shallow, and the means for receiving supertankers and other deep-draught vessels are limited (see p. 124).

We have already taken some note of America's strategic early warning systems, and of the air- and land-based nuclear forces (see p. 16). The nuclear missile submarine fleet takes full advantage of the fact that America has immediate access to the great oceans of the world, in contrast with the bottled-up Soviets. The home bases of the American 'SSBNs' are at Bangor in Washington State on the Pacific, and at Charleston on the Atlantic coast. Until the land-based extremely low-frequency systems of communication are perfected (see pp. 39–40) the instructions for the nuclear missile submarines will continue to be relayed through the C-130 Hercules aircraft of the TACAMO fleet, which are based at Patuxent River (Maryland) and on the islands of Bermuda and Guam.

INTERNATIONAL GEOPOLITICS

POLICIES

In the Soviet Union the making of foreign policy is very bureaucratic, and develops gradually over the generations. Things are managed differently in the United States. Here the power is concentrated in the person of the President, who is at once the ceremonial head of state, the chief executive, and the commander-in-chief of the armed forces. The influence of the State Department (Foreign Office) depends greatly on the credit which its Secretary happens to enjoy with the President at a particular moment. The Secretary of Defense has a say in foreign affairs, and all the while the President feels free to consult old political friends, or personally appointed advisers who hail from the academic world – the counterparts of the gurus and soothsayers of the fabled Orient.

Congress shows its power chiefly through its authority to ratify treaties, and its control of 'appropriations' (grants of money). Congress is in its turn the field of competing interests, such as the human rights lobby, the supporters of the 'military-industrial complex' (who are fond of elaborate and expensive weapons systems), and the representatives of ethnic groups like Jews, Greeks and the 20,000,000 (or is it 40,000,000?) folk who claim Irish descent.

All of this helps to produce cyclical changes between outgoing and isolationist moods in American public opinion and foreign policy. Scholars like Frank Klingsberg have identified about eight swings of the kind in the course of American history (Kupperman and Taylor, 1984, 28–9). America is surely too locked into the life of the outside world to turn in on itself as completely as in the 1920s, but modern isolationism of a persuasive and rational kind may be promoted by American faith in high technology and strategic mobility, and by the reluctance of allies to bear their proper share of the common burden of defence.

WORLD POWER AND STRATEGIC CHOICES

The United States is a world power, and the bulk of its resources must be held in a central reserve in North America ready for use in whatever directions may be required.

In 1984–5 the regular complement of the American forces stood at 2,136,000, and the principal concentrations were as follows:

United States	1,627,000	(76%)
Europe	35,000	(16%)
Pacific and Far East	139,000	(6.5%)
Caribbean and Latin America	20,200	(0.9%)

By Chinese estimates the Americans deploy about 16 per cent of their strength in Europe, and 9 per cent in Asia and the Pacific. The rest, 75 per cent, stays in the Americas.

The American forces amount to less than half the Soviet complement. The Americans are weak in ground formations. Their air forces are outnumbered, but are superior in technology and flying skills. The United States Marine Corps is far more powerful than the Soviet naval infantry, and the United States Navy has the upper hand with its carrier groups, and its means of sustaining warships in foreign waters.

How well do these forces lend themselves to being moved around? By the nature of things the air forces are the most mobile of the American strategic assets. Moreover, the US Marine Corps and specialised forces like the airborne, air cavalry (helicopter-borne) and 'high technology' formations and units are specially designed for speedy strategic and tactical movement. The Reagan Administration plans to increase the size of these and other 'rapidly deployable' forces from the 222,000 which existed in 1984 to 440,000 by 1989.

The Americans maintain four fleets:

- The Second Fleet (Atlantic) is the largest single concentration of naval force.
- The Sixth Fleet (Mediterranean) is the weakest and most exposed.
- The Third Fleet (eastern Pacific, nearest the United States).
- The Seventh Fleet (western Pacific).

In the 1970s the American government believed that it could pre-serve a certain freedom of choice through the 'swing strategy' whereby carrier groups could be switched from the Pacific to the Atlantic in case of need. In the 1980s, however, developments in Asia and the continuing build-up of Soviet power in the Far East made it unrealistic for the United States to consider its forces in the Pacific as a disposable reserve.

The difficulties with the navy help to underline the American dilemmas. The United States is a geopolitical island, which confers virtual immunity against overland invasion. On the other hand, it is not easy for the Americans to uphold their indirect interests across thousands of kilometres of ocean on the eastern and western rimlands of Euro-Asia, and the problem becomes all the more acute when more than one centre of tension is identified at the same time.

It is evident that the American forces, far more than those of the Soviets, are geared for overseas intervention. However, the size of the American armed services has not kept pace with the expanding commitments, and it is no help at all that the American units of force are so few and so clumsy.

Naval operations must revolve around the carrier groups, of which only about a dozen could be formed in wartime. In the middle 1980s the Reagan Administration announced its intention to build a '600-ship navy'. This sounds impressive until you recall that by the end of the Second World War the American navy had under command 78,000 vessels of all kinds, including 5,250 major combat units, of which 128 were aircraft carriers. The number of maritime aircraft came to 40,000, not including the machines of the Marine Corps. In comparison the modern naval forces are spread very thinly indeed across the face of the world.

In the same way the American Army and Marine divisions amount to only nineteen, as opposed to the 193 of the Soviets. Up to four of the army divisions are being converted to fast-moving 'Light Divisions', but there will be no real gain in strategic mobility if these formations arrive on theatres of war without adequate supporting artillery and armour. On the global scale, therefore, the Americans can emphasise one strategic direction only at the expense of others.

In the early 1960s the Kennedy Administration adopted a 'two-and-a-half war' strategy, allowing for a major war against the Soviets in Europe, another against the Chinese, and a smaller contingency elsewhere. The original calculations were thrown out when the contingency in Vietnam proceeded to gobble up very much more than a 'half war's' share of resources. From 1969 the Nixon Administration accordingly rearranged American commitments. In that year the Americans began to withdraw their forces from Vietnam, and President Nixon proclaimed a 'Guam Doctrine', telling Asian allies that they must look to themselves for their first line of defence. 1970 gave birth to a 'one-and-a-half war' strategy, supposing the big war to be in Europe and the contingency in Asia, and in 1971 the 7th Division was withdrawn from South Korea, leaving a single American division in garrison there. The virtual evacuation of Asia was made easier by the good relations which were established with China.

The doctrines of 'one-and-a-half wars' and allied self-help received a severe battering in the course of 1979. The regime in Iran, which had been a showpiece of its kind, succumbed to a fundamentalist Islamic revolution in January. September saw the outbreak of the Gulf War between Iran and Iraq, which further emphasised the instability of the Middle East, and finally in December the Soviets began their large-scale military intervention in Afghanistan.

The Americans now believed that they could detect an 'arc of crisis' which stretched across south-west Asia and threatened access to the oil of the Gulf of Persia. In his State of the Union Message on

20 January 1980 President Carter declared that 'any attempt by any outside force to gain control of the Persian Gulf region will be regarded as an assault on the vital interests of the United States of America, and such an assault will be repelled by any means necessary, including military force'.

The 'Carter Doctrine' was given practical effect with the setting up of a Rapid Deployment Joint Task Force, although no actual increase was made in the size of the mobile reserves (see p. 122).

The Reagan Administration entered office in 1981, and rejected the old 'fractioned' strategies as too mechanistic. Targets were set for genuinely increased force levels, including a 600-ship navy, and air- and seaborne mobility were improved.

We gain some inkling of the Reagan strategic priorities from an internal *Defense Guideline Paper*, which was circulated by Secretary of Defense Caspar Weinberger in the winter of 1983–4:

> The highest military priority is the defense of North America – including Hawaii, Alaska, Caribbean sea lines of communication and the Panama Canal; followed by NATO areas and lines of communication leading thereto. The next priority is ensuring access to oil in south-west Asia for our allies and ourselves, followed by the defense of American Pacific allies and lines of communication necessary therefor in the Indian and Pacific Oceans, and then defense of other friendly nations in Latin America and Africa. American actions in other parts of the world will protect essential American interests, exploit Soviet vulnerability and divert Soviet attention and forces from Europe and south-west Asia.

It is natural for Western Europeans to imagine that the defence of the European continent must have the chief claim on the attention of the Americans. Such is not necessarily the case, and although this book is about NATO we must pause briefly to consider some of America's interests in the non-European world.

The western outlook – the Pacific and the Indian Ocean

'THE OCEAN OF THE TWENTY-FIRST CENTURY'

There are many reasons why the Americans are looking westwards across the Pacific. The United States is concerned about the growth of Soviet naval and air power in the Pacific, and the dangers to sources of oil in the Persian Gulf. Between 1979 and 1983 North

America reduced its imports of Gulf oil from 13 per cent to a negligible 3 per cent, but oil from the Gulf matters more to Western Europe, and still more to Japan, and for this reason it also matters indirectly to the United States.

In part the renewed American interest in the Pacific is a projection of the westward movement of industries and perceptions within the United States (see p. 113). America by the 1980s was certainly very receptive to a notion that was first mooted in 1967, that of the existence of a Pacific Basin or Pacific Community. These are terms applied to the twenty or so states of the Old and New Worlds which border the Pacific. Japan is an industrial superpower and America's main trading partner in Asia, but the growth of economies like those of Singapore, Taiwan and South Korea has been still more phenomenal. In the early 1970s the American trade with the Pacific nations began to surpass that with the European Economic Community, and between 1979 and 1984 it went up by another 75 per cent. In 1983 most flights by the world's wide-bodied jets were still routed across the Atlantic, but in 1984 four out of seven took place over the Pacific.

Some of the new-found Pacific unities do not stand up to examination. There are huge divergences in culture and prosperity among the component nations. The distances must also not be underestimated. When the world is depicted on the pages of an atlas we almost invariably find that the Pacific has been cut in two. Globes of the world (now usually consigned to the schoolroom cupboard) give a much better idea of the immensity of that vast ocean. We are accustomed to talking about Old and New Worlds, and the northern or southern hemispheres, but it is just as realistic to proclaim a Pacific or watery hemisphere, and a matching land hemisphere which comprises the greater part of the continents.

However, ideas are facts in their own right, or at least they represent realities which have to be reckoned with, and if the Americans are persuaded that they have a Pacific destiny, then this is a conviction that demands respect from the Europeans.

AMERICAN FORCES AND BASES

The Americans have two fleets in the Pacific.

The Third Fleet is responsible for defending the more immediate approaches to the Americas, and it is firmly and widely anchored on national territory at Pearl Harbor (the headquarters) in the Hawaiian Islands, at San Francisco, Long Beach, San Diego and Whidbey Island in mainland United States, and at Adak in the Aleutians. In

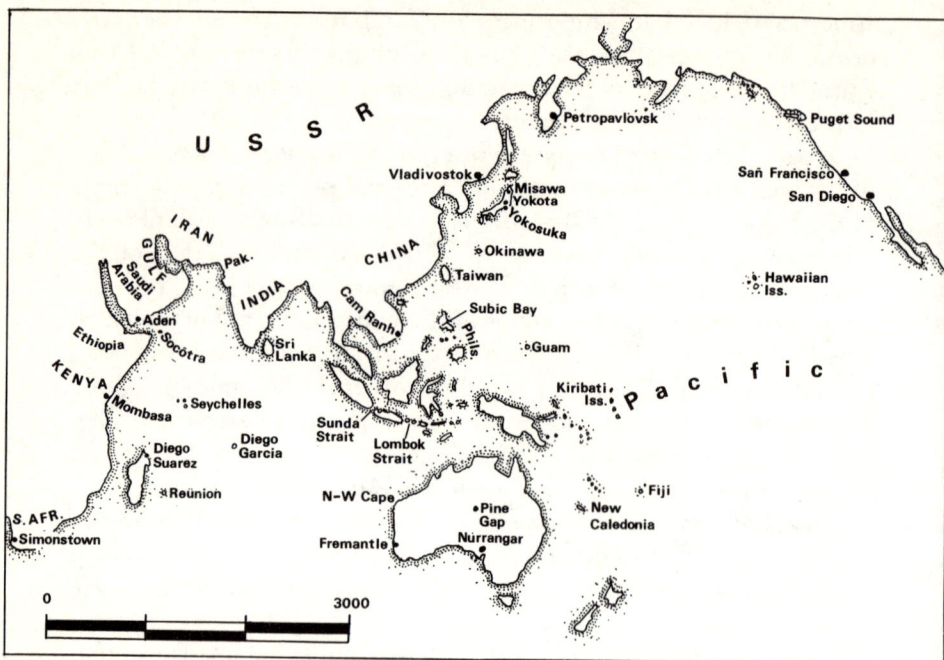

MAP 6   The Pacific and the Indian Ocean

the acutely sensitive north Pacific the Americans have an air base at
Shemya Island, well out along the Aleutians and only 400 kilometres
from Soviet territory.

The Third Fleet is large, and its extensive support facilities, and
especially those at San Diego, help to maintain the American
presence all the way across the Pacific Ocean. One of the high
priorities of this fleet is to track the Soviet Delta III nuclear missile
submarines, lurking off the continental United States, and to this
end it calls on its force of P-3 Orion maritime surveillance aircraft,
operating from Moffett Field just south of San Francisco. The Third
Fleet also helps to safeguard the exit of the American strategic
submarines, which use the deep-water channel into the Pacific from
their home in Puget Sound in Washington State.

The patrol areas of the Seventh Fleet lie further out in the Pacific
and in the waters of south-eastern and southern Asia, and it has a
special wartime interest in sealing the Japanese straits against the
Soviet Pacific Fleet. The Seventh Fleet has a rearward base on the
American island of Midway, but most of its establishments are
located on foreign territory. The headquarters are to be found in the

old base of the Japanese Imperial Navy at Yokosuka, and the main support facilities are at Subic Bay in the Philippines – where they are at the mercy of political developments in those troubled islands.

The 2nd Division in South Korea is the one remaining formation of the US Army in Asia. The principal Asian base of the US Marine Corps is on the Japanese island of Okinawa, which is the home of the 3rd Marine Amphibious Force.

Land-based tactical coverage of the Pacific is controlled by the headquarters of Pacific Air Forces (PACAF) at Hickham Field on Hawaii, and the most significant components are the fighters of the 5th Air Force in Japan, operating from Yokota close under Fujiyama, and from Misawa near the strategic Tsugaru Strait. The US Air Force has its most important advance base in Asia at the huge establishment of Clark Field on Luzon in the Philippines, more than 7,000 kilometres to the west of Hawaii.

B-52 strategic bombers have long been stationed on the island of Guam. There are maritime air patrol bases at Misawa, Agana on Guam, Kadena on Okinawa and Cubi Point in the Philippines, and finally exotic spyplanes operate from Guam, Kadena, Atsugi in Japan, Osan in South Korea and Peshawar in Pakistan.

Australia is of interest to the Americans as a naval port of call, and still more on account of a number of communications and intelligence establishments. On North West Cape the Americans have a new and very large 2,000,000-watt extra-low-frequency radio transmitter, which controls submerged nuclear missile submarines in the Pacific and is the only facility of its kind outside the mainland of the United States (see p. 40). North West Cape also accommodates an American signals intelligence base, and a high-frequency radio communications station.

Two American installations in Australia receive intelligence material 'dumped' from satellites on Polar orbit over the Soviet Union. Bursts of recorded radio transmissions are processed at the Merino Station at Pine Gap, in the middle of the Outback near Alice Springs. The comparable Casino Station at Nurrungar, about 960 kilometres to the south, takes the high-definition television pictures. Satellite intelligence of this kind has become all the more important to the Americans after they lost their ground stations in Iran in 1979.

The traditional naval and air bases do not give an adequate military coverage of the north-west Indian Ocean or the Gulf region, which lie beyond the logistical reach of the western United States, and at daunting distances from the Atlantic coast. With aerial refuelling, a C-5 Galaxy transport aircraft takes about fifteen hours to reach the Gulf from the eastern United States. The comparable sea voyage amounts to some 13,000 kilometres by way of the Suez Canal, and 21,600 around the Cape – or in the region of five or six weeks' steaming for a cargo ship.

In order to gain an 'in-theatre' base the Americans have therefore leased the British island of Diego Garcia, which stands in the centre of the Indian Ocean. Large-scale work on the installations began in 1971. The Americans now have the facility of a long runway capable of operating B-52 bombers and large transport aircraft. A submarine tender is anchored in the central lagoon, together with a small fleet of ships of the Military Sealift Command, which are packed with a great variety of weapons and military stores, representing the equivalent of many thousands of sorties by transport aircraft.

In the area of north-east Africa and the Gulf the Americans do not have heavy permanent installations like the Soviet submarine pens at Aden. Instead they make agreements with individual countries, providing for access to airports and airfields in time of need. Deals of this kind have probably been struck with Kenya, Somalia, Oman, Saudi Arabia, Sudan and Egypt.

In 1977 the Americans began to explore how they might move as many as 200,000 men from the central continental reserve to the Indian Ocean and the Persian Gulf in case of emergency. The structure of an appropriate Rapid Deployment Joint Task Force (RDJTF) was set up in March 1980. However, the intended region of operations fell uneasily between the areas of responsibility of two existing major American commands, namely the European (EUCOM) and the Pacific (PACOM). On 1 January 1983 the RDJTF disappeared, and a new Central Command (CENTCOM) sprang into being to control all American operations in a zone of nineteen countries, extending across north-east Africa, the Arabian peninsula and south-west Asia. The peacetime headquarters was established at MacDill Air Force Base in Florida, a very long way indeed from the Gulf.

This impressive array of titles conceals the fact that the Americans do not possess any intervention forces permanently assigned to the Indian Ocean and the Gulf. They have instead a command structure, a set of contingency plans, a series of basing agreements and some logistical preparations. In the context of a global war, as opposed to a local crisis, it is likely that most of the earmarked forces will be sent to Europe instead.

AMERICAN ASSOCIATES AND ALLIES

The West has a very complicated network of treaty obligations in Asia and the Pacific. The details have no place here. It is enough to mention that many of the arrangements are loose (and becoming looser still), and that America will always have to take the lead in upholding 'free world' interests in this region. Some of America's clients give particular cause for concern:

- *New Zealand* A Labour government assumed office in 1984, and refused permission for visits by nuclear-armed American warships. The US State Department declared that the denial of access was 'a matter of grave concern which goes to the core of our mutual obligations as allies'.
- *Australia* Here the socialists came to power in 1983. The Prime Minister, Bob Hawke, held Australian ports open to American visits, but in January 1985 he withdrew the offer of Australian facilities for American MX missile tests in the South Pacific.
- *Japan* The Japanese are industrial giants, but the coyly named 'Self-Defence Forces' are inhibited by politics and the terms of the constitution from making a proper contribution to regional security.
- *Thailand* Threatened by Communist Vietnam's domination of Indo China.
- *The Philippines* This country is the least stable of America's Asian allies. In April 1979 a report by the US Senate Foreign Relations Committee explored possible alternative sites for the American facilities at present located in these islands, where the present basing agreement expires in 1991.
- *Pakistan* Open to invasion from India and Soviet-garrisoned Afghanistan.

Amid all these uncertainties, the working relationship with the People's Republic of China remains an immense counterbalancing force to Soviet influence in Asia.

The southern outlook

AMERICAN INTERESTS

To many Europeans the Americans appear to become unduly excited by seemingly minor developments in the Caribbean and Latin America. What do they have at stake in this part of the world?

In the first place the Americans have become accustomed to treating the rest of the New World as a back garden. They served notice to the powers of the Old World to stand off when they proclaimed the Monroe Doctrine in 1823. The Spaniards were evicted from Cuba in 1898. Central America came under the virtual hegemony of the Americans in the 1940s and 1950s, and the Organization of American States has provided a traditionally favourable voting bloc in the United Nations. The intrusion of Marxist ideology in this region is therefore seen as an intolerable affront.

The Americans have very active economic interests in the Caribbean and Central and South America. About 20 per cent of the world deposits of bauxite are located in Jamaica, Surinam and Guyana. Oil and natural gas are found in several countries of Latin America, and the large reserves in Mexico and Venezuela are of potentially vital importance to the Americans in the long term. Coffee, sugar, special timbers and others of the less essential commodities also flow to the United States from Latin America. The return on American investments in these regions helps to compensate for the visible trade deficit of the United States, and has undergone a very dramatic rise in the late 1970s and in the 1980s, amounting to more than $15 billion in 1979, nearly $20 billion in 1980, and almost $27 billion in 1981, by which time the returns outstripped those from Europe, and represented the largest receipts from any single area of the world. Here it should be noted that American trade with the Pacific Basin is heavily in deficit.

Economic and military geography makes the Gulf and Caribbean sea lanes of high strategic concern. A long lease has given the Americans possession of the Canal Zone and the supremely important Panama Canal. This great waterway is eighty kilometres long, and truly lives up to President Theodore Roosevelt's intention that it should serve as the 'path between the oceans'. In 1983 the canal was traversed by 11,505 ships carrying 146,000 tons of cargo, and about three-quarters of this freight was destined for American ports. The canal is just as useful for strategic purposes, for it can take all the American warships except the supercarriers, which have to make the long passage around South America.

The United States imports between 40 and 45 per cent of her consumption of oil, but she is surprisingly ill-equipped to receive it. For a start there are few deep-draught channels by which large ships may sail direct to American ports or offloading terminals. Moreover, the refineries are concentrated along the eastern and Gulf shores of the United States, leaving the Pacific coast comparatively bare. Oil from Pacific sources (like Alaska or Ecuador) must therefore be shipped through the Panama Canal, or pumped through the Pacific–Atlantic pipeline to tankers waiting in the Caribbean. Similarly the oil from Venezuela and Africa reaches the American mainland in smallish tankers, having been forwarded as crude which has been offloaded from supertankers in Caribbean ports, or in the form of petroleum products which have already been processed at refineries in the West Indies. All of this makes for heavy traffic across the Caribbean.

In the event of a European war the Gulf will receive cargoes from the military depots in the Mississippi Basin, and serve as an assembly area for ships preparing to make the voyage across the central Atlantic (see p. 137). On the way out of the Gulf the shipping must pass to one side or another of the island of Cuba, whether through the Florida Strait, or the southerly route by way of the Yucatan Channel between Cuba and Mexico.

MILITARY BASES

Marxist military establishments on Cuba or anywhere else in Latin America can count their survival in a matter of hours if a major war ever breaks out between the United States and the Soviet Union. Meanwhile they afford the Soviets a platform for military surveillance, and regional pot-stirring of a kind which is very offensive to the Americans.

Fidel Castro's victory in the Cuban revolution in 1958 gave the Soviets their first chance to establish a geopolitical bridgehead in the Western hemisphere. At Cienfuegos the Soviet attack submarines have a port of call within easy reach of vital shipping lanes, and Cuban airfields support Soviet reconnaissance flights far up the eastern coast of the United States. There is, however, a most important prohibition on the use of Cuba as a base for nuclear warfare against the Americans. The Soviets were forced to concede as much at the end of the Cuban missile crisis in October 1962, and it appears that in the autumn of 1970 a secret American–Soviet agreement specifically extended the ban to nuclear missile submarines.

In the Caribbean generally a strategic vacuum was opened up when a number of microstates gained their independence from the colonial powers. On Grenada, the southernmost of the Windward Islands, a left-wing government imported 'security equipment' from the Soviet bloc and began to construct a runway which might or might not have been intended purely as a tourist facility. It was noted that Admiral Gorshkov was among the tourists to visit the island in 1980. After an extreme leftist internal coup the forces of America and a number of Caribbean states invaded Grenada on 25 October 1983, and put an end to any further 'progressive' developments.

On the north-eastern mainland of South America the state of Guyana, a former British colony, is regarded as a strategic extension of the Caribbean. In the middle 1970s Guyana gave the Soviets and Cubans a staging post for their flights to the scene of the civil war in Angola. Neighbouring Surinam is said in the 1980s to be likewise inclining to the left, which creates the possibility of the Soviets acquiring the use of a still wider stepping stone on the way to the South Atlantic.

Central America is the irregular and winding bridge between the northern and southern sub-continents of the New World. Nicaragua, with more than 148,000 square kilometres of surface, is the largest of the Central American states, and the Americans were deeply disturbed by the motivation behind the Nicaraguan 'Sandinista' revolution which ousted the Somoza family from power in 1979. The Cubans and Sandinistas have been accused of fomenting revolution in nearby El Salvador, and in 1984 the Nicaraguans completed one of those airfields which ring such loud alarm bells in American ears. The site is at Puenta Huete, near the shores of Lake Managua. The runway measures 3,200 metres, making it the longest in Central America, and it is constructed of concrete one metre thick, enabling it to serve the heaviest civilian and military aircraft. For the Soviets to station aircraft at Puenta Huete would be a momentous step, since they would have the means of extending reconnaissance flights all the way up the Pacific coast of the United States as far as the heavy concentration of naval establishments in Puget Sound.

In compensation the American military presence in the region is much longer established than that of the Marxists. In addition to their installations on the Gulf shore of the mainland United States, the Americans actually have an important military base at Guantánamo on the south-east coast of Cuba. This place was originally leased as a coaling station in 1903, shortly after the end of Spanish rule. There are further American bases (San Juan and Roosevelt Roads) on the island of Puerto Rico, which is a self-governing American territory at the eastern end of the Greater Antilles.

The Panama Canal Zone is the home of the US Southern Command, which was established in 1963, and now co-ordinates all the military activity of the United States in Central and South America.

The Southern Air Division is the air component, and operates from Howard Air Force Base. The sovereignty of the Canal Zone is due to revert to the Republic of Panama in 1999, but the United States is certain to retain the right of military intervention for a long time after that date.

At the time of writing the Americans are engaged in indirect but intensive military activity against Nicaragua. Anti-Sandinista 'contras' operate with American encouragement from the territory of Honduras and Costa Rica, and the new American airfields and bases in Honduras might lay the foundation for an enduring military presence in Central America after the Canal Zone lease expires.

Canada, the northern outlook

Area:	9,215,430 square kilometres
Population:	25,150,000
Land forces:	3 brigade groups, 1 special service force of 4,000 troops

AMERICAN INTERESTS

To the north the mainland of the United States shares a border of nearly 6,000 kilometres with Canada, a country which is still in many ways one of the least-known members of NATO and the Western world.

For the Americans, Canada is a northward geopolitical extension of their homeland. They have important economic concerns in the affairs of their neighbour. Canadian nickel (the largest reserves in the world), bauxite, copper, uranium and Arctic oil would be a notable addition to the resources of a 'Fortress America'. Also an independent and obstructive Quebec would offend American commercial interests, for this province lies athwart the navigational system of the Great Lakes and the St Lawrence, which convey bulk commodities to and from the American Midwest.

More important still, Canada is enmeshed in the American system of early warning against strategic nuclear attack. 'We are . . . the prisoners of our geography. Canada's territory provides for the United States the strategically essential "depth" granted to the USSR by its own Arctic. If we barred Americans from access to Canadian airspace for the early detection of hostile Soviet intentions, we would leave Washington with little choice but to invade our territory' (Newman, 1983, 16).

CANADIAN PROBLEMS AND CANADIAN NATIONAL SOVEREIGNTY

Canada is a country in which the geopolitical *bizarreries* of Russia and Australia are writ large. The population is very small in comparison with the great extent of the national territory. Most Canadians live in a very lengthy and shallow band of country just north of the border with the United States. In contrast Canada's Arctic North stretches for 3,500,000 square kilometres and is a wilderness surpassing Russia's Siberia, being unexploited – nay almost totally unvisited. In 1943 the crew of a German U-boat landed on the north shore of Labrador and set up a weather station. This was a not inconspicuous object, but it remained undetected on the open tundra until 1981, when one of the Germans wrote to the Canadians to ask what had happened to it.

The Canadians are divided among themselves. Only about 40 per cent of the population is of British descent, and much of the rest consists of unassimilated ethnic groups. The French make up the most significant element, with some 30 per cent of the whole. Their language is a Long John Silver kind of French which metropolitan Frenchmen compare to the way some of the very aged people used to speak in the north-western parts of old France.

These divergences are compounded by the very uneven way in which the natural and industrial resources are distributed. Quebec holds about one-quarter of Canada's industry and population, and feelings about Quebec's identity are at least as much provincial as cultural in inspiration. *Québécois* separatism built up a high head of steam in the later 1970s, but the pressure was reduced when an economic decline set in and English-speaking businessmen removed their money and their persons. However, the Canadian Federation still holds together rather badly. The poor and remote Maritime Provinces in the far east are separated by Quebec from the rest of anglophone Canada. The British Canadians are themselves at odds, since the four western provinces, where there is wealth in oil and wheat, resent the fact that political and commercial domination is still exercised by the eastern cities of Ottawa and Toronto.

The language heard in Canada about the United States sometimes echoes the kind of thing that Finnish or Norwegian politicians say about the Soviets:

Canada has to walk a fine line in its policies on North American air defence, balancing its own national requirements with the need to respond to the Soviet threat and the imperatives of its relationship with its neighbour. As Professor [David] Cox remarked, one requirement of an effective pursuit of national sovereignty is that Canada should not act 'in such a manner as to invite . . . an unsympathetic policy on the part of the United States'. (Special Committee of the Senate, 1985, 35)

Canadian sovereignty has been further eroded by a number of economic and technical developments. The coal-fired power stations of the American Midwest spread their pollution across the territory of Canada. American imports have helped to ruin the once-flourishing agriculture of the Niagara peninsula, a salient of Canadian territory which enjoys a relatively benign climate. Furthermore, computerised communications have persuaded many American companies to close down branch offices in Canada and run their Canadian subsidiaries directly from headquarters in the United States, with consequent injury to the pay and promotion of Canadian employees.

Defence is a precious ingredient of Canada's remaining sovereignty – defence not against an American invasion, which could not be resisted, but military capacity as a means of asserting national independence and interests in the presence of a mighty friend with whom Canada has so much in common.

Canadian military leaders were admitted to the secrets of the Air Defence Master Plan (1982), in which the Americans set out their designs for updating the strategic nuclear defences of North America (see p. 21). A Special Committee of the Canadian Senate investigated the matter in some detail, and reported in January 1985 that in most respects the needs of the Americans and Canadians could be treated as one. The Canadian population (heavily concentrated along the southern borders, as we have seen) would suffer equally from nuclear fallout spreading from the United States, and 'drop shorts' by Soviet bombs or missiles. It was, however, important that specific national interests should be borne in mind. For technical reasons (see p. 21) the coverage of the long-range American OTH-B radars could not be extended to the north. The new Seek Igloo radar system in Alaska would help to protect Canada's north-western flank, but there was still a very dangerous gap in the radar surveillance of Labrador. The Canadians hoped that the Americans would bear this deficiency in mind when they set up their North Warning System, which is intended to replace the DEW Line along the shores of the Arctic Ocean. The Pinetree Line, a purely Canadian responsibility, is to be phased out of service, leaving a void in the coverage of internal Canadian airspace which, so the Committee recommended, could be covered most effectively by AWACS aircraft.

Canada was a founding member of NATO, and the Canadians have long-standing commitments to the alliance in Europe quite separate from those of the United States: 'Western Europe is important to Canada for economic, political, cultural and security reasons. A continued strong and democratic Europe, free of Soviet control, remote or on site, gives Canada a viable and highly preferable alternative to "Fortress America" ' (Ørvik, 1984, 29).

In the middle 1980s the Canadians have about fifty aircraft in West Germany, together with a small mechanised brigade group which is based at Lahr. A battalion and two squadrons of aircraft are available for the NATO ACE Mobile Force (see p. 230), and an additional brigade, called the Canadian Air-Sea Transportable (CAST) Brigade Group, is specifically earmarked to reinforce the Norwegian army. There is an interesting Transatlantic traffic in the opposite direction, for Canada has put huge training areas at the disposal of the alliance, and British and West German armoured units travel regularly to perfect their skills on the Canadian prairies.

The Canadian ground forces are equipped with Leopard I tanks, and CF-18 Hornet aircraft are coming into service with the air element. Orders have been placed for a new model of patrol frigate, the first of which is due to enter service in 1989.

However, the Canadian forces are but a shadow of their former selves. They were severely pruned by Prime Minister Pierre Trudeau from 1968 onwards, and the present commitment to NATO, though reduced from earlier times, is still probably more than they can reasonably spare. The Canadian North is guarded by just 451 troops, and the air and naval cover is virtually non-existent, which permits the Americans and the Soviets to violate Canadian sovereignty in Arctic regions as a matter of routine.

The eastern outlook

AMERICAN INTERESTS IN EUROPE

The United States is linked to Western Europe by ties of heritage and common values. American business interests in Europe are considerable, and receipts from investments, albeit overtaken by those from Latin America, amounted in 1981 to the respectable total of more than $26^1/$_2$ billion. Moreover, the free use of the whole extent of the Atlantic helps to give the Americans access to world markets and raw materials.

Strategically, an independent Western Europe holds the Soviets away from warm water ports, and ties down some half a million Soviet troops, 10,000 tanks, 2,000 combat aircraft, 190 attack submarines and 370 major surface vessels which might otherwise be free for deployment elsewhere. Under Soviet domination Western Europe would most probably swing the global balance of force against the United States, and turn Euro-Asia into a formidably self-sufficient entity in which European technology could be used to open up the resources of Siberia.

American intercontinental and tactical nuclear systems are linked with the defence of Western Europe, and if we count the military families as well as the 350,000 service personnel, some half a million American citizens have been planted by the American authorities in Western Europe, and they represent so many hostages to European fortune. A passage in the *Defense Guidance* paper (see p. 118) states categorically that 'the security of Europe is vital to the security of the United States. This linkage is manifest in the long-term deployment of major American forces in and around western Europe, the maintenance of a major American reinforcing capacity, and the leading American role in NATO'.

Through sympathy, calculation of advantage, treaty obligations and physical presence, the defence of Western Europe has therefore become to a great degree synonymous with that of the United States. The two are not identical, however, and the distinction between them is underlined by differing perceptions of economic interest and the nature of the global Communist threat, and by what the Americans see as the unwillingness of some of NATO's European partners to share the costs and immediate dangers of alliance membership.

On their side European statesmen wonder whether the United States would in the last resort expose itself to the danger of nuclear attack for the sake of preserving Europe. For the Americans to sanction nuclear release in such a context would be an 'immensely grave' decision, in the understated words of the British Defence White Paper of 1980. The American commitment to Europe is strong, but in the nature of things it cannot be overriding and absolute.

THE TRANSATLANTIC BRIDGE

Two grand strategic movements will take place within the Western world in a period of high international tension or actual hostilities. One of them, on a relatively small scale, involves sending British reserves to the continent, and deploying the alliance's ACE Mobile

Force to the NATO flanks, and especially Scandinavia. The other transfer is a very considerable affair, the conveyance of men, machines and supplies from the continental reserve in the United States across the Atlantic to Europe. 'The key fact of the military balance in Europe is that one superpower lives there and the other does not' (Millar, 1981, 58). The problems have been aggravated by the principle of 'dual basing', adopted in 1967, whereby three of the American divisions were withdrawn to depots in the United States, leaving only their forward elements in a ghost-like III Corps with their countrymen and allies in Germany.

It is impossible for a layman to find out what reinforcements will cross the Atlantic in a particular span of time, and where exactly they will be deployed in Germany, but we will probably not be too far astray if we imagine an initial reinforcement of 1,500 combat aircraft and six divisions or divisional equivalents. The first three divisions (making up the III Corps) and one of the others might arrive in as little as ten days.

Expert authorities cannot agree about the character of the great Transatlantic passage. According to one school of thought, wars have a habit of lasting much longer than is generally believed at the outset, and NATO must accordingly prepare for a huge and long-drawn-out operation. These views are associated largely but not exclusively with the naval interest in NATO's forces (Whiteley, 1979, 23–6; Kidd, 1980, 196; Leach, 1982, 12). The land lubbers, on the other hand, point out that West Germany is the decisive theatre of war, where issues are likely to be settled in the first days or even hours of a conflict, and where the opportunities for warning and reinforcement will be minimal. What matters is the opposition that will be offered by the NATO forces already in place in Western Europe (Canby, 'Military Policy', 1978, 40–1; Dunn, 1979, 40; Krehbiel, 1980, 24–5; Spiers, 1982, 23).

Assuming for the sake of argument that the Transatlantic movement will be a major one, the alliance might seek to transport more than one million American personnel, twelve million tons of weapons, equipment, ammunition and stores, and seventeen million tons of petrol, oil and lubricants. Such estimates vary greatly, and they do not include the requirements of Europe's population and industries.

The overall scheme for the American reinforcement of Europe is NATO's Rapid Reinforcement Plan, which was approved on 7 July 1982. Inside Europe the movement of American and British reinforcements and supplies will be managed by a Joint Movements

Coordination Centre (JMCC), to be activated in time of crisis.

It is likely that about 830,000 tons of cargo and three or more of the American divisions will make a speedy and relatively safe passage by air. For this purpose the US Military Airlift Command has at its disposal its 'organic' fleet of about 570 transport aircraft. No less importantly, the Americans will call on the very considerable resources of the Civil Reserve Air Fleet (CRAF, set up in 1952), which will utilise aircraft of the civilian airlines.

We are left with the more than 90 per cent of the freight which will have to cross the Atlantic by sea, together with some at least of the follow-on troops. The US Military Sealift Command has a fleet of about sixty-five chartered or wholly owned tankers and cargo vessels, including a number of recently purchased fast container ships. Hundreds, possibly thousands, of further ships will have to be hired or commandeered from the merchant navies of the NATO countries, in which case the run-down state of Western merchant fleets and shipbuilding will prove something of an embarrassment.

The Transatlantic passage is just one component of the larger operation that will move troops and materiel from depots in the United States to where they are needed in Central Europe. American road and rail movement on both sides of the Atlantic is supervised by the US Military Traffic Management Command, which has its European headquarters in Rotterdam. There are a great number of appropriate 'host nation' agreements with the European civilian and military authorities. One of the most important of these documents is the US and West German deal of 22 April 1982, by which the Germans promised to make available civilian workers and more than 90,000 reservists to help to move and protect American supplies in the Federal Republic.

In 1968, as a consequence of the practice of 'dual-basing', the Americans held the first of their annual REFORGER exercises, rehearsing the Reinforcement of their Forces in Germany from the reserves in the United States. Since then REFORGER has grown in realism and scope. In 1976, for example, it was for the first time linked with NATO's Autumn Forge series of exercises, and activities were widened to include the forwarding of heavy equipment overland from the ports in Europe.

From 1977 stores of heavy equipment have been built up in West Germany and the Benelux countries for the use of specific reinforcing divisions, which will spare some of the labour of moving supplies across the Atlantic in terms of emergency. REFORGER units are now delivered directly to the gates of these depots, which bear the appallingly clumsy name of Prepositioning of Materiel Configured to Unit Sets (POMCUS). The last of the six divisional sized depots was completed in 1986.

The corresponding reinforcement exercise of the US Air Force is called Crested Cap (see p. 272). The British hold irregular exercises of their own, in which they practise the transportation of home-based regular units and the Territorial Army to West Germany, and joint operations there with the British Army of the Rhine (Crusader 1980, and the still bigger Lionheart 1984).

REFORGER, POMCUS and the other devices must be regarded as palliatives at best. The fact remains that Soviet forces are closer to depots and forward positions in West Germany than are many of the NATO troops who are supposed to make use of them. This is the ultimate product of the insular geopolitical character of the United States.

The Transatlantic movement will certainly be challenged by the Soviets. The most serious threats are posed by attack submarines and long-range maritime aircraft, reinforced by extensive mine-laying in the shallow waters off Western Europe. The role of the Soviet surface ships is less clear. If the Soviets fail to bring off a successful 'surge deployment' (see p. 77) the main NATO effort will probably go into blocking the Soviet egress from their bases. There is likely to be much activity in the areas of the Turkish Straits and the Baltic Approaches, but NATO will strive above all to deny the Northern Fleet an entry into the open Atlantic. This is the origin of the term 'the GIUK Gap', standing for the waters between Greenland, Iceland and the United Kingdom. Satellites, maritime reconnaissance aircraft and lines of SOSUS hydrophones (see p. 40) will help to identify surge deployments and attempted penetrations.

The main power of NATO resides in the Striking Fleet Atlantic, whose core will be the available carrier groups of the American Second Fleet. The British Royal Navy contributes about 30 per cent of NATO's naval forces in the eastern Atlantic, and among a variety of roles the most important will probably be to provide anti-submarine support to the American carrier groups, cover the approaches to Scandinavia, and lend depth to the contest for the GIUK Gap. For many years NATO strategists envisaged a layered defence, forming an outer screen of submarines, a main defence zone of submarines and aircraft, and a deep deployment of submarines, surface ships and aircraft between the GIUK Gap and the Atlantic shipping lanes.

A radical reappraisal became public knowledge in April 1985, when the American admiral Wesley McDonald, the Supreme Allied Commander Atlantic, announced that the Soviets had developed a long-range fighter which would operate from the Kola peninsula to escort Backfire bombers on shipping strikes, and protect the Soviet equivalent of AWACS. McDonald declared:

> I just cannot build a barrier at the Greenland–Iceland–United Kingdom Gap and not go into the Norwegian Sea.
>
> Such a policy allows the Soviets too much freedom in the Norwegian Sea and probably forecloses the fact that Norway is going to come under great pressure and may collapse under the pressure. Therefore you lose the flanks and you may lose the battle for the Atlantic.

The Americans were now prepared to operate their carrier groups ahead of the GIUK Gap.

We must pause for a moment to consider the elements of the much-debated Gap, taking them in order from the west.

We first encounter the 'back door' between Canada and Greenland, which might tempt Soviet submarines to steal under the Arctic ice and attempt to make the passage by way of Baffin Bay and the Davis Strait. On Greenland itself the Americans have had military establishments since the Second World War, and the fixed radar stations there are as vital for the strategic defence of North America as they are for safeguarding the Transatlantic passage. The BMEWS strategic early warning station at Thule is situated far up the west coast. A chain of four more conventional radars is strung along the ice cap, and is serviced from the American air base at Søndrestrøm-fjord.

Constitutionally Greenland is a self-governing part of Denmark. The small population (sadly ravaged by alcohol and the pox) voted to leave the European Economic Community in 1982. The formal parting of the ways took place on 1 February 1985, and at one stroke the EEC lost 60 per cent of its land area, though it was difficult to detect much concern written on the visages of the citizens of London, Paris or Bonn.

The Denmark Strait between Greenland and Iceland is narrow by oceanic standards, measuring only about 300 kilometres across, and the surface passage is restricted still further by the winter pack ice.

Iceland became a founding member of NATO in 1949, on the understanding that nobody expected this little country to raise any forces of its own. The Icelanders are an inward-looking people,

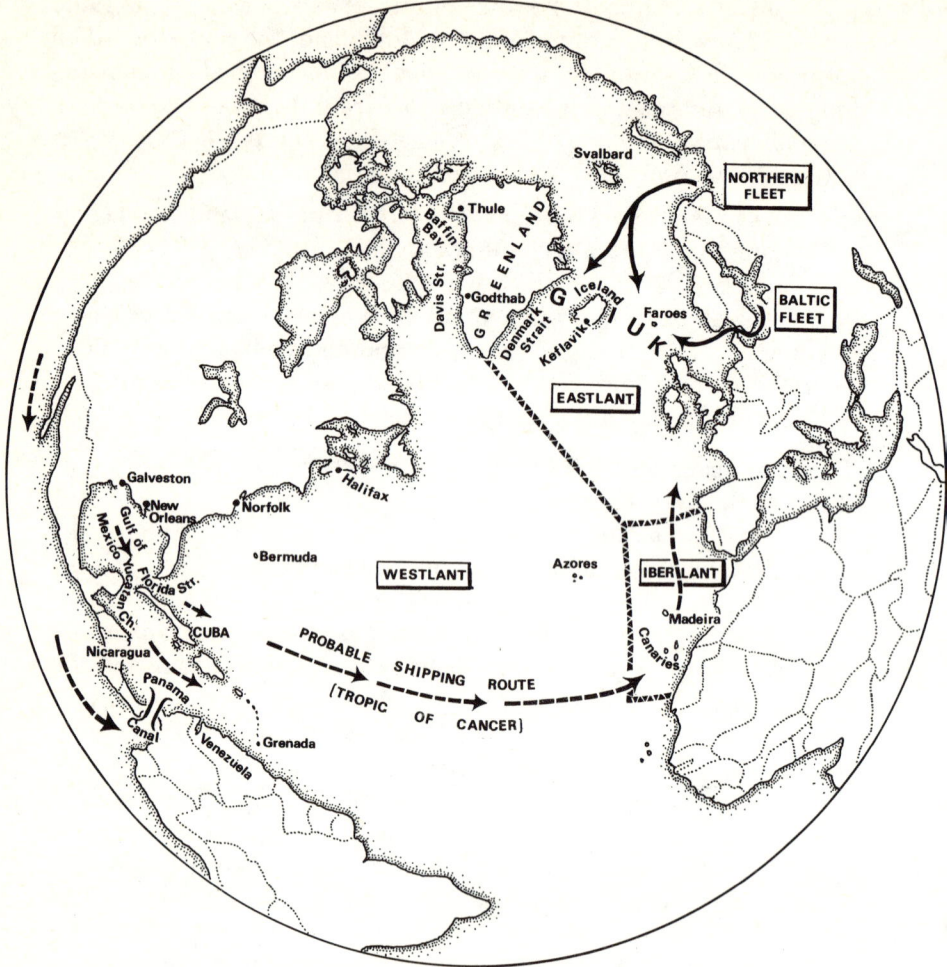

MAP 7   The Atlantic Bridge

interested above all in preserving their unique Viking culture and the fishing industry which is its economic base. In 1951, however, a bi-lateral treaty put the World War II airfield at Keflavík once more at the disposal of the United States, and in the 1980s the Icelanders became so concerned about the growing Soviet activity in their waters that they permitted the Americans to carry out improvements at this vital base. Keflavík field is now equipped with hardened aircraft shelters, improved fuel handling facilities, and a new military air terminal which enhances the value of Iceland as a staging post. F-4 Phantom combat aircraft have been replaced by F-15 Eagles, and the upgraded AWACS aircraft have sharpened NATO's surveillance of the centre of the GIUK Gap, assisted by new radars installed along the northern coast.

Eight hundred kilometres of the north-east Atlantic extend between Iceland and Scotland, and the distance to Europe widens to about 1,100 kilometres across the Norwegian Sea. The Faroe Islands (a Danish territory) are sited almost equidistant between Iceland, Scotland and Norway, and although they are weakly guarded they support some useful radar and radio stations. Northern Norway is effectively the right-hand flanking bastion of the GIUK Gap, which gives NATO's tenure of this region such a high strategic importance (see p. 232).

NATO's shipping lanes will cross the central Atlantic a good way south of the main convoy routes of the Second World War, so as to keep the freighters as far as possible from marauding Soviet maritime aircraft, which will approach from the north-east. The ships are expected to form up in the Gulf of Mexico and other southern waters, and cross the Atlantic at about the level of the Tropic of Cancer; the route then lies northwards up the coasts of north-west Africa and south-west Europe. Mid-ocean air cover will probably be extended from the Azores (see p. 197), and from the British western Atlantic island of Bermuda, where the Americans hold Kindley Field naval air station under a lease dating from 1941.

CHAPTER 6

NATO and Its Boundaries

EVOLUTION

On 4 April 1949, in an event of profound geopolitical significance, the United States, Canada and Iceland joined nine states of the Western European rimlands in a treaty of mutual defence. This league has proved to be extremely durable, and its thirty-fifth anniversary was celebrated formally in 1984.

The origins of the North Atlantic Treaty Organisation lay in the tensions in Europe in the years after the Second World War. Historians still argue about who was to blame for the ensuing 'Cold War', but it was in this period that a number of Western European governments perceived that a crude threat was shaping against their independence. Greece and Turkey were coming under heavy Soviet pressure, a Marxist internal coup took place in Czechoslovakia, and the Soviets imposed a land blockade on West Berlin.

The North Atlantic Treaty was signed by Belgium, Canada, Denmark, France, Iceland, Italy, Luxembourg, the Netherlands, Norway, Portugal, the United Kingdom and the United States. As such documents go, the treaty was very much to the point in its main provisions:

> Article 5
> The parties agree that an armed attack against one or more of them in Europe or North Africa shall be considered an attack against them all . . .

> Article 6
> For the purposes of Article 5 an armed atack upon one or more of the Parties is deemed to include an armed attack on the territory of any of the parties in Europe or North America, or the Algerian dependencies of France, on the occupation forces of any one party in France, on the islands under the jurisdiction of any party in the North Atlantic area north of the Tropic of Cancer or on the vessels or aircraft in this area of any of the parties

NATO has adapted to many changes over the long term. The first

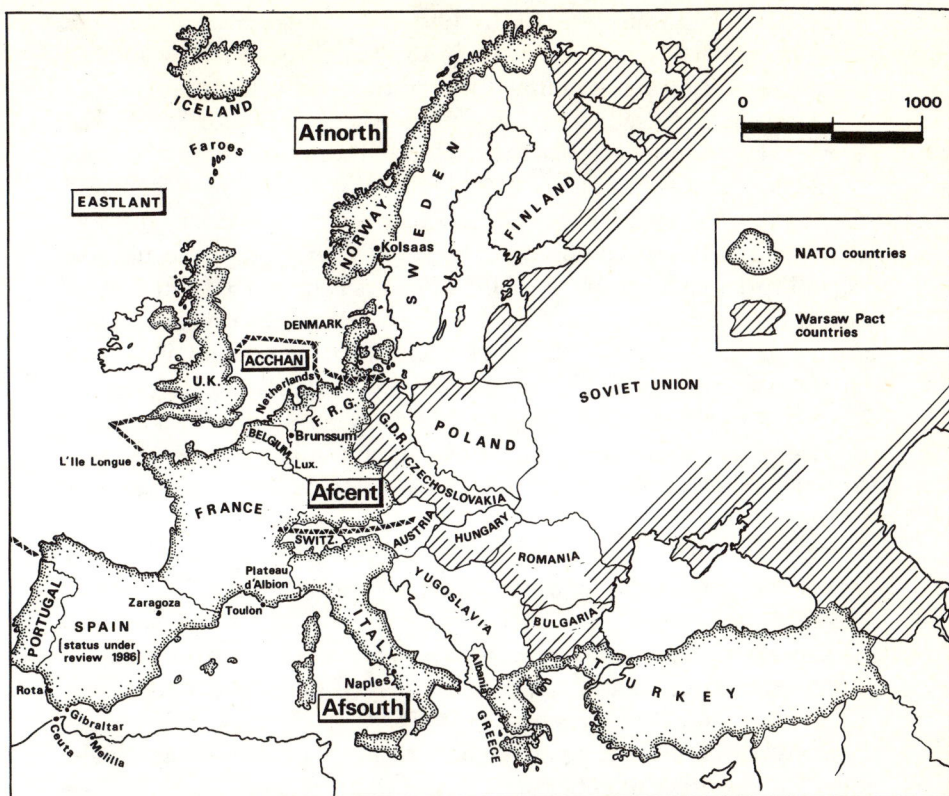

MAP 8   European NATO – Countries and Commands

surprise arrived very soon, in October 1949, when the Americans discovered that the Soviets had exploded their first atomic bomb. The United States had only just given a virtually unconditional guarantee to Europe, and now this pledge might expose the Americans to nuclear attack on their homeland. They nevertheless stood by their word.

In the early 1950s there followed a period of political, military and economic expansion. In 1951 and 1952, when international tensions were heightened by the Korean War, the former Allied Zones of Occupation in West Germany were converted into a military command structure. On 2 April 1951 General Dwight D. Eisenhower accordingly entered into office as the first Supreme Allied Commander Europe. Greece and semi-Asiatic Turkey were admitted to NATO on 18 February 1952. West Germany joined the alliance on 5 May 1955, and in 1958 the Treaty of Rome established the European

Economic Community (EEC). The EEC was not a branch of
NATO, but it indirectly served NATO ends by working for the
economic and ultimate political integration of Europe.

The French caused something of a sensation when, on 29 March
1966, they announced that they were withdrawing from the integrated command structure of NATO (but not the alliance itself), and
that all NATO establishments must leave French territory in short
order. There followed some complicated reshufflings and uproot-
ings. Supreme Headquarters Allied Powers Europe (SHAPE) abandoned Rocquencourt near Paris for a new home near Brussels, while
the headquarters of Allied Forces Central Europe betook itself to a
still-smoking coalmine at Brunssum in the Netherlands. The Americans had to reroute their logistical lines of communication around
France, which was inconvenient and operationally dangerous, and
American naval units were transferred from Mediterranean France
to Italy.

Over the 1970s and early 1980s the French gradually worked
themselves back into the inner military counsels of NATO, but at
this time the alliance experienced a wilting at the edges. Belgium, the
Netherlands, Denmark and Norway were all subject to degrees of
semi-neutralism, and the Greeks banished themselves from the
integrated command structure in 1974. Greece rejoined six years
later, though it became a partner only in a very qualified way. Spain
joined as a political member on 30 May 1982, but shortly afterwards a
new Socialist government made the continuing membership depend
on the result of a referendum, which was fixed for February 1986
(see p. 192).

STRUCTURE

Decision-making

The political leadership of NATO is formed of a Council of Ministers, with one representative from each member nation. The Council
is supported by frequent meetings of the NATO national ambassadors, and the important element of continuity is provided by the
permanent international staff of the Secretary General.

In time of crisis the Council of Ministers is supposed to determine
the levels of military response, ranging from Stage 1 (Military
Vigilance), to Stage 4 (General Alert) when hostilities begin. It is
difficult to imagine, however, that the ministers will find themselves

of one mind or that they will be able to determine quickly enough what ought to be done. In practice the running will probably be made by the American political and military command, and the other nations will follow the lead with greater or lesser enthusiasm.

MAJOR MILITARY COMMANDS

At the top of NATO's formal military structure stands the Military Committee, which advises the military and naval major commanders, and works with a number of specialised planning committees and groups. We now pass to the major commands themselves, of which there are three.

SACEUR

The land and air forces of the alliance in Europe stand under the Supreme Allied Commander Europe. He rules his kingdom from Mons, which is a good fifty kilometres south of Brussels, and he is therefore inconveniently separated from SHAPE, which is the administrative headquarters. SACEUR has always been an American general, which allows him to take a wide viewpoint on European affairs, and facilitates the vital process of nuclear decision-making.

SACEUR directs a number of subordinate commands. His strategic equivalent of a pocket pistol is the Allied Commander Europe's Mobile Force (ACE Mobile Force, or AMF) which was set up in 1960 as a 'small but highly mobile force, multi-national in composition, that is capable of quickly reinforcing any threatened point on the flanks of Europe'. It is generally assumed that the more important flank will be the northern one in Scandinavia, which is why it appears strange that the headquarters of the land element is located at Seckenheim near Heidelberg, well inland in West Germany.

SACEUR also exercises direct authority over the United Kingdom Air Forces (headquarters High Wycombe). This command has become of increasing importance to the alliance as a whole, for it helps to assure the air reinforcement of Europe.

SACEUR has three regional subordinate commands, corresponding to likely theatres of operation.

AFNORTH

The responsibilities of Allied Forces Northern Europe embrace Norway, Denmark and Schleswig-Holstein. The AFNORTH headquarters are at Kolsaas near Oslo in Norway, and a British general is invariably appointed as commander – a practice which helps to reconcile the Norwegians and Danes to their former German enemies, and which strengthens the British commitment to the reinforcement of Scandinavia.

AFCENT

Allied Forces Central Europe is a command of comparatively narrow geographical extent, but of crucial importance to the alliance. It takes in Benelux, and West Germany south from Hamburg to the borders with Switzerland and Austria. The commander, a German general, has his headquarters at Brunssum, in the southern Netherlands, and he directs a unified air command (Allied Air Forces Central Europe, headquarters Ramstein, West Germany), as well as the two component army groups of the land forces – Northern Army Group (NORTHAG, headquarters Mönchengladbach, West Germany) and the Central Army Group (CENTAG, headquarters Heidelberg, West Germany).

AFSOUTH

From his headquarters at Naples an American admiral is supposed to manage the sprawling and loose subordinate command of Allied Forces South, comprising Italy, Greece, Turkey and the Mediterranean waters. The AFSOUTH members of NATO are set apart by geography, history and culture, and two of them (Greece and Turkey) are on the worst possible terms short of war (see p. 154). It is fortunate that the American admiral has direct personal command of the US Sixth Fleet, which is by far the most mobile and effective force that the West possesses in the Mediterranean.

Such is the empire of SACEUR. The other two major commands are both naval, and they are of startlingly uneven size.

ACCHAN

Allied Command Channel manages to pack no less than five subordinate commands into its tiny but important area of responsibility in the Channel and the southern part of the North Sea. The commander (CINCHAN) is a British admiral who works from Northwood near London, and also directs the Eastern Atlantic (EASTLANT) major subordinate command under the authority of ACLANT.

ACLANT

The responsibilities of Allied Command Atlantic extend from the North Pole to the Tropic of Cancer, and from the eastern shores of the United States and Canada to the western coastlines of Europe and North Africa. The Supreme Allied Commander Atlantic (SAC-LANT) is an American admiral based at Norfolk, Virginia. He directs three geographical commands – the huge WESTLANT, EASTLANT (see above), and IBERLANT (Iberian and Atlantic, which was increased in size and upgraded in status in 1982).

NATO AS A GEOPOLITICAL ENTITY
THE TRANSATLANTIC DIVIDE

It is easy to create impressive effects by heaping numbers together. The NATO member states have a combined population of around 595,000,000 or 632,000,000 if we include Spain, which makes up about 15 per cent of the world total, and their combined gross national product is very approximately three times that of the members of the Warsaw Pact.

Inside NATO, however, geography has a very divisive effect. The Atlantic gives the West a certain passive strength (see p. 75), but this sundering ocean is otherwise a source of grave military weakness and potential conflicts of interest. Some European countries are increasingly inclined to think in continental rather than Transatlantic dimensions, and one of the reasons is obviously that they live so close to the Soviet Union. The French angered the United States when they invited President Brezhnev to a private mini-summit in May 1980, and the Americans were further affronted by the eagerness of continental Europeans to plug themselves into the Siberian natural gas pipeline. Conversely the Americans put their forces on unilateral nuclear alert during the Arab–Israeli War of 1973, and ten years later they invaded the island of Grenada without any reference to the head of state, the Queen of Great Britain.

The Americans are at a loss to know what to make of that unique continental phenomenon, the Eurocommunists, who proclaim with greater or lesser conviction that they are committed to Marxist ideals without being slavish adherents of the Moscow line. Dr Henry Kissinger commented: 'a Communist is a Communist whatever you put before or after his name, and the only safe procedure is to regard him as a potential opponent'.

However, the United States does not extend an enforced ideological empire to Western Europe, and on the whole the American military presence in NATO bulks much less large than that of the Soviet Union in the Warsaw Pact (see p. 95), even if there are some startling disproportions in a number of the categories of military effort. The United States furnishes NATO in Europe with between 20 and 25 per cent of its air forces, and supplies the West with about 97 per cent of its strategic nuclear deterrent. On the other hand the US Army's contribution to Europe is outclassed by that of the West Germans, who provide about half of the land forces on the Central Front and most of the available tanks. The Americans bear 60 per cent of the costs in the alliance, a burden which is about four times heavier per head of population than in Europe, but the 'parasites' can counter with the argument that the United States sells between three and a half and nine times more military equipment to the Europeans than it buys from them. The Europeans have never accomplished anything comparable with the celebrated 'deal of the century', when the Americans succeeded in selling F-16 combat aircraft over a period of time to five of the smaller members of continental NATO.

In defence of his European allies the SACEUR General Bernard Rogers declared in September 1984:

> If we go to war tomorrow, 90 per cent of the land forces and three-quarters of the air and navy will be West European. After thirty days of mobilisation, even under the most optimum conditions in the United States, still 75 per cent of the land forces and 50 per cent of the air and 30 per cent of the navy will be West European . . . many people do not realise the massive amount of hidden costs that West European nations pay . . . I also know that Western European nations provide many military facilities for which they get no return whatsoever.

EUROPE AS A SUPERPOWER

How realistic is it to talk about a 'Western European superpower'? Including France, but excluding Spain and Turkey, the little countries of European NATO teem with 284,000,000 people, which is 45,000,000 more than the United States and 8,000,000 more than the Soviet Union. The gross national product of Western Europe as a whole has now probably fallen behind that of the United States, but it is comfortably ahead of the Soviet Union.

Western European nations share basic political ideals, and their cultural heritage and standards are still unsurpassed. A specifically Western European outlook on world affairs is evident from time to time, as we have seen, and in 1982 the nations of the European Economic Community achieved a unity of a kind against Argentina, even if Ireland and Italy quickly broke ranks. Outside NATO additional platforms for European debate exist in the EEC, and in the less formal clubs of the Western European Union (established 1954) and the Eurogroup. The Western European Union was originally set up to monitor the rearmament of West Germany, and co-ordinate policies after the collapse of a project for a unified European Defence Community. In October 1984 a 'Declaration of Rome' gave the semi-moribund WEU a new role as an identifiably European voice in military debates. The membership of WEU happens to be a useful one, embracing France, but excluding neutral Ireland, faint-hearted Denmark and unreliable Greece.

By exercising a certain amount of imagination, learned men have detected certain historical and geographical continuities which are said to underly the whole. Thus the Napoleonic period is sometimes acclaimed as a unifying experience, for the mass conscript armies helped to overcome regionalism in the individual countries, and the French conquests began to spread the Napoleonic legal code in Europe. It has also been pointed out that the EEC originated in the lands of what is called 'Industrialised Lotharingia' or the 'Heavy Industrial Triangle', at the meeting of Wallonia, Lorraine, the Saar and the Ruhr – a region which corresponds roughly with part of the heritage of Charlemagne's great-grandson Lothair, way back in 843.

More tangibly, the developed core areas of Europe follow a pronounced north-west to south-east axis. This line originates in Midland Britain, jumps the sea to the Low Countries, and proceeds by way of the Rhine and the Rhône to the Alps. After another leap we are in northern Italy, with its urban traditions and heavily concentrated industries. (It is unfortunate that the axis in question is an eminently 'chewable' object, for much of it lies within close striking range of the frontiers of the Warsaw Pact.)

In almost every other respect Western Europe fails the tests that we normally apply to a superpower. It is politically divided, and the sovereignties of its component states, although eroded by the EEC, remain substantially intact. The two major institutions, NATO and the EEC, are by no means identical. Semi-Asiatic Turkey belongs to NATO but not yet to the EEC, and Ireland belongs to the EEC but not NATO. Again Britain and France from time to time respond to the urge of their 'out of area' interests, which may or may not be of advantage to the alliance.

The Soviet Union would never tolerate in the armed forces of the Warsaw Pact the wild divergences that are to be found in NATO. The project to form truly integrated forces in the European Defence Community collapsed in 1954, and the present alliance lacks real uniformity in military doctrine and command. Logistical support remains a matter of national responsibility, and our generals and admirals, sitting at Mons, Norfolk and the like, do not have any allied forces under control until the member nations release them to the hierarchy when war is about to break out. Strictly speaking, peace-time 'NATO forces' do not exist. The West Germans keep most of their powerful Territorial forces under purely national command. No less strikingly, the French have their troops garrisoned in West Germany under the terms of a bi-lateral agreement between Paris and Bonn, which owes nothing to NATO.

Furthermore, as a voluntary alliance of sovereign and capitalist nations, NATO does not have the will or the power to enforce the high degree of standardisation and interoperability which obtains in the military equipment of the Warsaw Pact. 'Defence' (i.e. military) contracts in the West have very high profit margins, and economies of scale are usually rejected in favour of the commercial gain which comes from selling expensive equipment to domestic and overseas clients. This is one of the reasons why NATO actually spends more on defence than the Warsaw Pact, and yet receives less hardware in return.

The forms of government of individual NATO nations are of diverse types, ranging from extreme multi-party democracies to military juntas which have ruled in Greece and Turkey. European industries are competitors rather than allies, and it is usually more tempting for a businessman to sell a commodity to America or Japan, where there is immediate access to a mass market, than to try to put together an elaborate deal with his counterparts in Europe. Mean-while Europe as a whole falls behind in high technology. A single US company, IBM, accounts for about half of all computer sales in the world. In the fundamentally important technology of semiconduc-tors, not a single British company was numbered in the world's top twenty-five in 1983, and only three were European.

Quite apart from its institutional weaknesses, European NATO does not have the proper size and shape for a superpower. Its lands (excluding Spain and Turkey) amount to 1,890,000 square kilometres, which is the equivalent of one-fifth of the area of the United States or one-twelfth of the Soviet Union. Much of the Western European space comprises islands and peninsulas, and the core area (West Germany and the Low Countries) lacks depth. The concentration of population is still impressive, as we have noted, but in both relative and absolute terms the European peoples will become of less significance in the world as a whole, and those of the EEC will decline to an estimated 3 per cent of the world total by the year 2025.

The members of the EEC and the military alliance have no common language or dominant racial group. They are divided by bodies of water (the Channel, North Sea, Baltic and Mediterranean), and by groups of neutral countries (Switzerland and Austria; Yugoslavia and Albania). They do not own the physical resources of the United States, let alone the near self-sufficiency of the Russians. The land of the Europeans has been transformed from a centre of world power to a collision zone of two alien geopolitical systems. The Europeans have lost their empires, and they have also lost control over many issues on which their survival depends.

BEYOND THE TROPIC OF CANCER

NATO was born in a certain geopolitical environment, not long after the Second World War, and since then the alliance has become vulnerable to developments in regions which stand well outside the original treaty limits. NATO's boundaries were extended to the east by special protocol, when Greece and Turkey were admitted to the league, but the southern border still runs along the Tropic of Cancer. This line was determined at the insistence of the Americans, who did not wish to become involved in military operations to protect the colonial empires of their European partners.

The Tropic of Cancer line takes in the tip of Florida but it does not cover those areas of the Caribbean and Central America which have since become of lively concern to the United States. On a wider scale the boundary falls very far short of those sources of raw materials which the Western world needs in order to survive.

In 1973 the producers of Middle Eastern oil brought on a world economic crisis by holding their consumers to ransom. Since then the West has learned to make more economical use of oil, and the countries of European NATO have diversified their sources of supply to the extent that by 1983 their dependence on oil from the Persian Gulf had been cut to about 29 per cent. However, some 60 per cent of global oil reserves are thought to lie in the Middle East, and Gulf oil is still the cheapest of all to extract and probably the easiest to distribute worldwide. A barrel can be filled with Saudi Arabian oil for a matter of cents, but the same quantity of North Sea oil takes about twelve dollars to bring to the surface.

It is doubtful whether the Soviet Union would take the risk of moving against the sources of Middle Eastern oil now that the Americans have staked out this area as being of 'vital interest' to the United States (see p. 118). The more immediate threat to Gulf oil comes from regional instability, whether resulting from internal revolutions or war between local powers.

The economic interests of NATO members are also closely engaged in Africa. Zaire, for example, is the world's main producer of cobalt. The Republic of South Africa is rich in gold and diamonds, and owns reserves amounting to an estimated two-thirds of the world deposits of chrome and vanadium, one-third of the manganese and four-fifths of the platinum. It is scarcely surprising that South Africa has become a very active trading partner of the Western world, or that Britain's investment there is the equivalent of 8 per cent of all its investments abroad.

South Africa is also important to the West because it lies on the heavy-draught shipping route from the Gulf and the Indian Ocean to Europe and the United States. In the event of general hostilities with the Soviet Union the British and American navies might well avail themselves of the deep water port at Walvis Bay (an enclave on the coast of Namibia), and the historic naval base of Simonstown, which lies on the Atlantic coast of South Africa in False Bay behind Table Mountain. The British and Americans hold stocks of naval fuel at Simonstown, and they helped to set up the South African naval intelligence station in the mountains nearby at Silvermine, where a computerised monitoring system extends a very wide surveillance across the Indian Ocean and the South Atlantic.

A number of NATO nations have already accumulated stockpiles of basic raw materials as a provision of a passive kind against the possibility of lines of supply being cut. The Americans began to lay down their strategic reserves in 1947, and nowadays the stores are measured in years of consumption and range across ninety-three commodities, from copper to pepper. For the same reason the Americans prefer to keep much of their reserves of oil untapped, and satisfy immediate demand with the help of imports.

In Western Europe the impetus was provided by the 1973–4 Middle Eastern oil embargo and the resulting recommendations of the International Energy Agency and the EEC. France, Italy, the Netherlands and West Germany have prudently laid up stocks of oil under a variety of arrangements. The Dutch, who are at the centre of the international oil market, can easily tap the considerable quantities of oil which are awaiting shipment at their ports.

Since 1952 NATO has operated a Petroleum Planning Committee, whose War Oil Organisation has the task of co-ordinating national supplies in the event of hostilities, but the question is often raised as to whether the West should take more active measures to secure its interests overseas. The Americans have already made elaborate contingency plans for long-range expeditions (see p. 122), and in May 1980 NATO agreed to allow the United States the freedom to use some of its 'European' reinforcements for possible operations in the Gulf. This was the first time that NATO had formally identified a security interest outside its treaty limits. In May 1984 NATO's North Atlantic Council went on to declare that 'the allies recognise that events outside the Treaty area may affect their common interests as members of the alliance. They will engage in timely consultation on such events, if it is established that their common interests are involved.'

On balance, however, NATO would probably derive little advantage from writing the Gulf or any other distant region into its treaties. Formal obligations can achieve little that cannot be accomplished by statements of intent, informal arrangements among existing allies or friendly regional states, or swift unilateral military intervention by the Americans. On the other hand an attempt to intervene through NATO forces *per se* might well bring on a general confrontation with the Warsaw Pact, hasten the polarisation of the 'Third World', and impose needless strains on the unity of the alliance.

One authority has suggested that European NATO could most readily help the United States by sending more warships to the Indian Oceans, where the Americans are thinly spread (Coker, 1984, 105). If, for whatever reason, it becomes important to set up a more elaborate joint Western task force, the process of decision-making might be fairly straightforward. The only conceivable partners of the Americans in such a major enterprise are Britain and France, and both powers own effective out-of-area intervention forces, as well as a comprehensive network of worldwide outstations and diplomatic agreements. The French in particular retain a very active interest in the succession states of their colonial empire, and they do not hesitate to stage military interventions in their African 'Near South' (see p. 199).

Taken on a superpower scale, the British and French mobile forces, like their overseas bases, clients and dependants, do not appear to amount to very much, but they may provide a physical and legal launching platform for wider Western military initiatives. They certainly offer an alternative to the momentous step of extending NATO's treaty obligations over the surface of the globe.

CHAPTER 7

The Southern Flank

THE MEDITERRANEAN AND THE RIVAL FLEETS

THE MEDITERRANEAN AS A HIGHWAY

The Mediterranean, together with its adjacent lands and sub-seas, makes up one of the most elaborate geopolitical systems in the world. These waters extend for well over 3,000 kilometres from the Strait of Gibraltar, past the cradles of the Carthaginian, Roman, Grecian, Minoan and Egyptian civilisations to the shores of Palestine, and the north-eastern extension through the Turkish Straits takes us across the Black Sea to the shores of ancient Tartary. The combined population of the modern Mediterranean countries has reached about 330,000,000, and the coastal nations have the most diverse standards and styles of life.

The hydrography is very complicated. The Mediterranean is divided into eastern and western basins by the Sicilian Channel (see p. 42). The eastern basin is much the larger of the two, and on its northern side it merges with the Adriatic and Aegean sub-seas. The choke points usually coincide with shallow water (which favours the employment of mines), and lurking submarines are able to take advantage of the mixing of temperatures and salinities to evade detection by hydrophones. Large surface ships are also at risk in the Mediterranean because they lack sea room and are vulnerable to land-based aircraft. Sea power has a revenge of sorts in the strategic dimension, for the Mediterranean provides a platform from which carrier aircraft and sea-launched missiles may strike at important targets in southern Europe, the Balkans, the south-western Soviet Union and the Middle East.

In peacetime the Mediterranean is a very busy sea, and at any given time it is being traversed by about 1,500 large cargo ships and 5,000 coasters. Some 60 per cent of Soviet seaborne trade passes through these waters, for a number of Russia's oldest-established industrial centres are located in the basin of the Black Sea. The Mediterranean is still more important for the economic life of southern and central Europe. In particular the Mediterranean is still the main short-haul route for Gulf oil, which is pumped to terminals on the eastern shores (like the Iraqi terminal at Kirkuk in Turkey), or carried through the Suez Canal, which has been widened to accept tankers up to a displacement of 150,000 tons. About 40 per cent of the oil consumption of France and West Germany passes through the Mediterranean, and Italy and Austria receive almost all of their imported oil by this path.

THE SOVIET MEDITERRANEAN SQUADRON

Active Soviet interest in the Mediterranean grew markedly in the 1960s, when this sea was opened to American nuclear forces. The Soviets noted potentially dangerous developments like the increasing range of American carrier aircraft, the successful testing of the Polaris A-2 missile in 1962, and the American–Spanish agreement of 26 September 1963, which gave the Americans the use of the Atlantic port of Rota, near Cadiz, as a base for a Mediterranean force of nuclear missile submarines.

The Soviet Mediterranean squadron (SOVMEDRON) first became a permanent presence in the Mediterranean in 1964, and three years later access to Egyptian ports helped the Soviets to complete the first stage in their deployment. Technically the Mediterranean flotilla forms one of the squadrons of the Black Sea Red Banner Fleet, from which it receives its major surface combatants; operationally, however, it is necessary for the Soviets to maintain the SOVMEDRON as an independent presence because the communication through the Turkish Straits could so easily be cut by NATO forces. Similarly, it is to avoid the complications involved in passing these straits that the Soviet submarines in the Mediterranean are provided by the Northern Fleet.

In 1972 the Soviets lost the use of their facilities in Egypt, but they are still sure of a friendly reception in Libyan and Syrian ports, and the Yugoslavs have been persuaded to service Soviet submarines (see p. 177). In international waters the Soviets continue to avail themselves of anchorages off the Spanish isle of Alboran and the Greek island of Kíthira – the one lying conveniently close to the Strait of Gibraltar, and the other in the channel between Crete and the Greek mainland. Soviet land-based aircraft are capable of ranging over the whole of the Mediterranean, which helps to compensate for the SOVMEDRON's weakness in 'organic' air cover.

With the militarisation of the Indian Ocean and the increasing range of submarine-borne missiles the Mediterranean has lost its former high importance on the intercontinental scale, and in the 1980s the SOVMEDRON has become more of a regional force. From the evidence of exercises, and deployments like the one which the Soviets staged during the 1973 Yom Kippur War, it is likely that the tasks of the squadron will be to attack the American Sixth Fleet, prevent the detachment of NATO forces from the Mediterranean to northern Europe, command choke points on NATO lines of communication, and assure the Soviets' own links with their friends in the Middle East and the Mediterranean.

THE UNITED STATES SIXTH FLEET

The American Sixth Fleet is based at Naples, Sigonella and La Maddalena in Italy, and at Rota in Spain. The headquarters is at Gaeta near Naples.

This force provides the unity and strength which are otherwise lacking in Mediterranean NATO. Its carrier aircraft are capable of carrying conventional or nuclear armament into the south-western Soviet Union. On the defensive they will protect sea lines of communication, lend support to any land battles which develop in Turkey, Greece or north-eastern Italy, and in general help to preserve SACEUR's freedom of options. 'It is often overlooked in Central Europe that whether we control, prevail and win in the Mediterranean will have a serious impact north of the Alps as well as on the Mediterranean countries' (Crowe, 1983, 11).

The Sixth Fleet nevertheless labours under serious operational disadvantages. Ideally a carrier-based force like this ought to roam the open seas, whereas in the Mediterranean the Americans are compelled to share the narrow waters with the SOVMEDRON and its very dangerous submarines. In the early 1970s the Sixth Fleet benefited from the redeployment of American forces after the Vietnam War, but in the winter of 1980–1 one of the carriers was dispatched to the Indian Ocean, leaving the forces in the Mediterranean with a single carrier group. The British had long since withdrawn their permanent naval presence from the Mediterranean, and it was fortunate for NATO that the weakening of the Anglo-Saxons was compensated by those supreme realists, the French, who in 1975 began to divert some of their naval forces from the Atlantic. In the 1980s the French fleet in the Mediterranean is a powerful and balanced force of attack submarines, light aircraft carriers and other major surface combatants.

NATO'S GEOGRAPHICAL AND POLITICAL PROBLEMS

NATO's members in the Mediterranean (excluding Spain) make up about 40 per cent of the land area and population of the European component of the alliance, which looks impressive as long as we forget how scattered and badly articulated the Mediterranean partners are. Italy is separated from Allied Forces Central Europe by the barrier of neutral Switzerland and Austria, and from Greece by Yugoslavia, Albania and the Ionian Sea. Greece and Turkey are joined only by a short land border in Thrace, and inside those two countries the road and rail networks are poor, and the logistical base as a whole is feebly developed. Effectively communication on NATO's southern flank is carried out by sea and air, which is one of the reasons why the commander of Allied Forces Southern Europe is an American naval person, who in addition has direct personal control of the Sixth Fleet. In contrast the 'Southern Tier' of the Warsaw Pact enjoys the advantages of a central position with regard to Mediterranean NATO, giving Soviet strategists the ability to marshal up to about fifteen divisions against eastern Turkey, thirty-four against Turkish Thrace and northern Greece, or ten against north-eastern Italy.

Politics have intervened to complicate matters still further. In no other part of the world is United States diplomacy so strongly influenced by considerations of domestic American politics, for many members of Congress are beholden to special interest groups who urge the cases of the Israelis and the Greeks. The Turks, who are really more important to the West, have few people to plead for them.

The inevitable ambiguities of American policy have sharpened the resentments between the Greeks and Turks, whose quarrel is by far the most destructive of the internal feuds of NATO. The history of Greek and Turkish relations is a sorry tale of massacre and atrocity, stretching back over the centuries. The Catholics and Protestants of Northern Ireland are forgetful and forgiving in comparison. When Turkey and Greece temporarily laid their quarrel aside and joined NATO in 1952, it was because both of these countries had experienced intolerable pressure from the Communist world. From 1946 to 1949 the Greek authorities were engaged in combat against a Communist insurrection which received support from Yugoslavia, Bulgaria and Albania. Just as Stalin demanded the return of the Soviet Union's three lost provinces in Armenia from the Turks, so Yugoslavia claimed Grecian Macedonia and the Bulgarians desired to open a corridor to the Aegean at Thessaloníki (Salonika).

At present there are two bones of contention between Greece and Turkey. One of them is the island of Cyprus. This former British possession was given its independence in 1960, on condition that union with Greece (*Enosis*) was forbidden, and that power was shared between the Greek Cypriots and the minority Turkish community. The British safeguarded their security interests by retaining the base areas of Akrotiri and Dhekelia in full sovereignty, and their electronic 'eyes' help NATO to maintain a surveillance over the Middle East and Soviet movements in the Black Sea.

Internal order broke down in Cyprus, and in July 1974 the Greek military junta instigated a coup which threatened to open the way to *Enosis*. The Turkish government responded by a full military invasion on the 20th of the same month, the result of which was to divide Cyprus in two parts, converting the northern third into a Turkish Cypriot state, and leaving the Greek Cypriots with the less favoured remainder of the island. Mediterranean NATO was threatened with dissolution. The American Congress forthwith imposed an embargo on the shipment of arms to Turkey, and Greece left the integrated command structure of the alliance. The Americans would dearly like to see a solution to the Cyprus problem, not least because they wish to regain the use of the large airfield at Lefkoniko, which now lies in the Turkish sector.

The second quarrel is a territorial one, concerning the Aegean. This near-landlocked sea forms the passageway between the Dardanelles and the open waters of the Mediterranean, and it is littered with about 2,500 islands. The great majority of these islands are Greek and some of them lie within sight of the Turkish coast – circumstances which make it difficult for the Turks to accept the normal provisions of the international law of the sea. A national zone of twelve nautical miles, drawn around the Greek islands, would leave the Turks with 10 per cent of the Aegean, and have the effect of blockading Turkey's Aegean coastline and denying the Turks any means of exploiting the reserves of oil and gas that lie under the sea. The Turks therefore claim that the central line between the two mainlands ought to determine the frontier for mineral exploitation and air and sea passage.

If the Greeks have the economic advantage of being the sitting tenants on the offshore islands, they pay the penalty of being exposed there to immediate attack. They would have little time to rush reinforcements from the Greek mainland, and so in 1974 they defied the provisions of the treaties of Lausanne and Montreux and began to fortify the islands lying nearest to the Turkish coast – Lésvos, Khíos, Samos and Ikaría. Likewise the forces on the mainland were redeployed in Thrace, under the command of a IV Corps headquarters at Xánthi. In 1975 the Turks responded by creating a Fourth Army, responsible for the security of the Aegean coastline. Thus the militarisation of the Aegean has proceeded apace.

Eventually the Americans tried to build some bridges, which was a very delicate process. The two nominal allies were not only outraged at any concessions which the United States made to the other, but they were eager to demonstrate their independence by opening relations with the Soviet Union.

The Turkish arms embargo was lifted in August 1978, and the Turks permitted the Americans to reactivate their bases and stations in Turkey under new terms. However, the high-altitude sky planes were not moved back to Turkey from their new home at Akrotiri on Cyprus, and in June 1979 the Turks notified the Americans that these aircraft could overfly Turkish territory only if the Soviets did not object – which was tantamount to a refusal.

NATO's disunity in the eastern Mediterranean has prevented the West from giving in full measure the many kinds of help which Turkey needs. This country faces problems of inflation, balance of payments deficits and a fast-rising birth rate which has more than doubled the population since 1950. The American arms embargo of 1974–8 postponed the urgently needed updating of the Turkish forces. The small and efficient navy and air force have since received some good new equipment, but it is much more difficult to modernise the Turkish army, a large, tough but rather primitive body of 450,000 men, which has important subsidiary roles as an employer and as a steward of political traditions.

In Greece the military junta fell from power after the Cypriot debacle. The new prime minister, Constantine Karamanlis, was a man of the centre-right, but he believed that the time had come to pursue a policy of greater even-handedness between East and West. In 1976 the Americans had to close down three of their bases in Greece altogether, and they were made to renegotiate their tenure of the remaining four.

Patient diplomacy persuaded Greece to rejoin the NATO command structure in 1980. In the next year, however, Karamanlis was voted out of power by his rival Andreas Papandreou, and the Americans were almost back to where they had begun. In 1982 the lease of the bases was confirmed, after a fresh bout of negotiations, but in most other respects the Greek membership of the alliance was no more than nominal. In 1983 Greece disrupted NATO's eastern Mediterranean autumn exercise (*Display Determination*) by denying the allies access to Greek territorial waters at the last moment, and while the hastily revised manoeuvres were still in progress a Soviet flotilla was admitted on a courtesy visit to Piraiévs, the port of Athens.

January 1985 brought the announcement of a 'new defence dogma', based on the supposition that 'the only visible military threat to Greece comes from the east' – in other words from Turkey, and not from Bulgaria to the north. In fact the declaration only confirmed the deployments which had existed since 1974, and in the last resort Greece is probably not prepared to make a break with the Western alliance, which is after all a source of modern weapons, and the best guarantee of a restraining hand on Turkey. However, the lease of the American bases in Greece comes up for renewal in 1988, and it would not be at all surprising if the Americans finally decided that they must uproot their establishments from the soil of this troublesome host.

TURKEY

Area:	779,452 square kilometres
Population:	49,500,000
Army:	17 divisions, 23 separate brigades

THE TURKISH BARRIER

Turkey occupies a crucial position at the meeting of Europe and the Middle East. Its importance as such was recognised by European statesmen as early as the 1720s and 1730s, when they began to worry about the southward expansion of the Russian empire.

The truncated remnant of Turkey in Europe still stands between the Soviet allies in south-eastern Europe and the Turkish Straits (see p. 163). In the 1780s the Russian drive through the Balkans was powered by Potemkin's vision of a new Byzantium, raised on the ruins of the Ottoman empire. Nowadays it is in the Soviet interest to secure the Bosphorus and the Dardanelles and guarantee the passage of merchantmen and warships from the Black Sea to the Mediterranean.

To the east of the Straits the mountainous block of Anatolia represents NATO's only bridgehead in Asia, and the alliance's

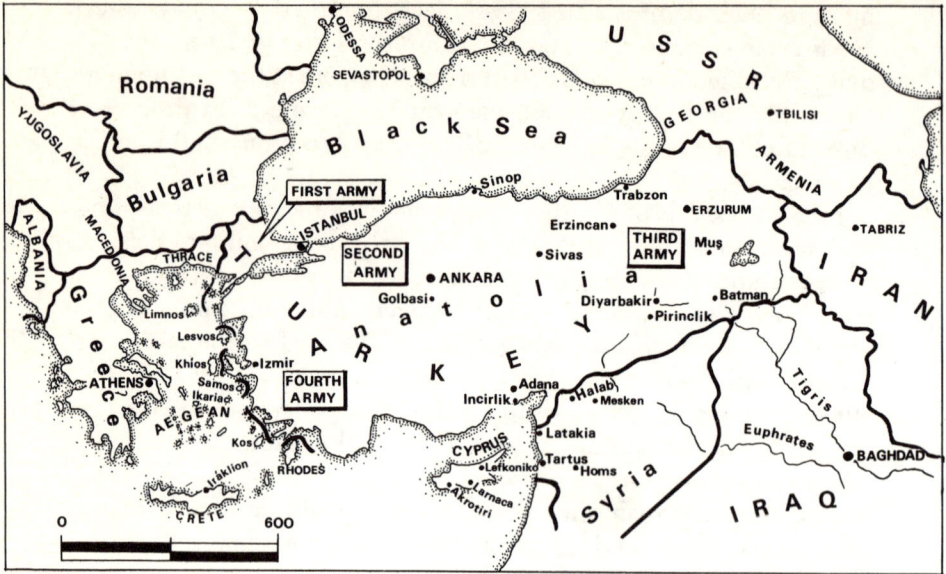

MAP 9   Turkey

second land border with the Soviet Union (the other is in northern
Norway). The geopolitical importance of the Anatolian salient has
increased over the years. When Turkey joined NATO in 1952 the
Mediterranean was a Western lake. Algeria was still counted as part
of metropolitan France. There were American bases in Libya,
British forces in Malta and the Canal Zone as well as in Cyprus, and
indirect Western influence extended through the Middle East. Gradually all of this fell away, which has left Turkey as an isolated
bastion, barring the overland route between the Soviet Union and
Syria, and standing on the flank of any Soviet advance against the
oilfields of the Gulf.

The Americans were evicted from their electronic intelligence-
gathering bases in Iran after the fundamentalist Islamic revolution of
1979, and this high-technological *hegira* underlined the need for the
Americans to repair their relations with Turkey and expand the
infrastructure of their air power and intelligence-gathering in Turkey.

The most considerable NATO air base in the region is the field in
southern Anatolia at Incirlik, on the far north-eastern corner of the
Mediterranean. A squadron of American fighters is based there
permanently, and Incirlik is a very useful standby base for intervention in the Middle East. The NATO air potential in eastern Anatolia
was greatly strengthened as the result of an American–Turkish

agreement in December 1981. The airfields at Erzurum and Batman have been modernised, and the chain is completed by a new base at Muş. All of these fields are capable of handling bombers and heavy cargo aircraft. Anatolian anti-aircraft radar stations were improved at about the same time, and twenty new defence communications centres have helped to integrate the Turkish systems into those of the rest of NATO.

Anatolia has an intercontinental as well as a regional importance, for it offers a 1,500-kilometre-long base for electronic surveillance of the Soviet Union. From here the West may track the movements of the Black Sea Fleet, intercept radio transmissions between Soviet aircraft and their bases, and 'see' into Soviet Central Asia – monitoring the underground nuclear tests at Semipalatinsk, the activity at the anti-satellite base at Tyuratam, and following rocket launches from Kapustin Yar and the Baikonur Cosmodrome at Leninsk in Kazakhstan (see p. 86). Likewise the south-eastern extremity of NATO's chain of anti-aircraft radars (NADGE) is represented by the golfball-like structures sitting on top of Mount Ararat.

Since 1979 the Americans have improved their surveillance, while giving the Turks greater control over what is going on at the appropriate bases. Among the most important of these establishments are the station at Golbasi (for monitoring underground nuclear tests), the long-range radar and communications centre at Pirinclik near Diyarbakir, and the station at Sinop on the Black Sea, which watches Soviet missile tests and naval movements.

Anatolia

One of the forgotten interrelationships in modern strategic geography is that a NATO member, Turkey, shares a border with a Soviet client in the Middle East. This is the heavily armed state of Syria, which fields eight modern divisions and about 500 combat aircraft. The shipments of Soviet arms arrive at Latakia and Tartus, and the second of these ports also provides an anchorage and shore facilities for Soviet warships and submarines. It is difficult to imagine a 'scenario' in which the Syrians will be fighting Turkey without having to cope with the Israelis as well, but the long-range Soviet SAM-5s at Mesken and other sites in northern Syria must present a danger to the airfields in Anatolia.

The immediate threat of attack on Antolia comes from the Soviets. For such an enterprise they could deploy about fifteen divisions from the Transcaucasus and Turkestan Military Districts, and it should

be noted that the Transcaucasus MD has a unique Mountain Warfare Directorate, which trains troops for operations in the kind of
terrain that will be encountered in Turkey. The defending forces,
the Turkish Third Army and Third Air Force, are at a disadvantage
of about three to one, and little reinforcement could be expected over
the long overland routes.

The border of eastern Anatolia, or Turkish Armenia, is the
ultimate product of generations of Russian campaigning in the
mountainous terrain between the Black Sea and the Caspian. The
first push dates from 1722, and was directed not against the Turks,
but around the eastern flank of the Caucasus against the Persian
fortresses on the Caspian. Persia was finally eliminated from the
scene in 1828, by which time the Russians had established themselves along the main chain of the Caucasus in the face of bitter
opposition from the local peoples. The Russians now controlled the
historic Cilician Gate (the Daryal Pass), from where their 'Georgian
Military Road' led down to Tiflis (Tbilisi) in Transcaucasia.
Another important strategic route, the Imeretian Military Road,
struck south-west towards the Black Sea, though the road and rail
communications along the coast were not opened up until the
twentieth century.

Beyond the valleys of Transcaucasia looms the tangled massif of
Turkish Armenia. The rim of the plateau is cut by the valleys of the
Çoruh, Kura and Aras, which have provided the main avenues of
penetration. The interior is generally barren, and comprises mountains, saddles, steep river valleys, volcanic lakes and extensive high
plains or plateaux. The going is undeniably difficult, whether for
historic or modern armies, but the record of campaigns in Armenia
shows that it is frequently possible for an attacking force to discover
hill tracks or neglected valleys which lead around the flanks of locally
strong defensive positions. The chief obstacle to progress has always
been the winter, which descends with literally killing cold, and
blankets much of the level ground with snow for about half the year.
The passes may be blocked by sudden and heavy blizzards as late as
April, and the thaw frequently ruins the side roads of 'stabilised
gravel'.

The present frontier is 610 kilometres long, and was delineated by
the Treaty of Lausanne in 1923, when the Turks regained the three
Armenian provinces of Artvin, Ardahan and Kars, which they had
lost to the Russians as a result of the disastrous war of 1877–8.

The recovery of Artvin advanced the border a useful distance
down the valley of the Çoruh, and gave additional defence to the

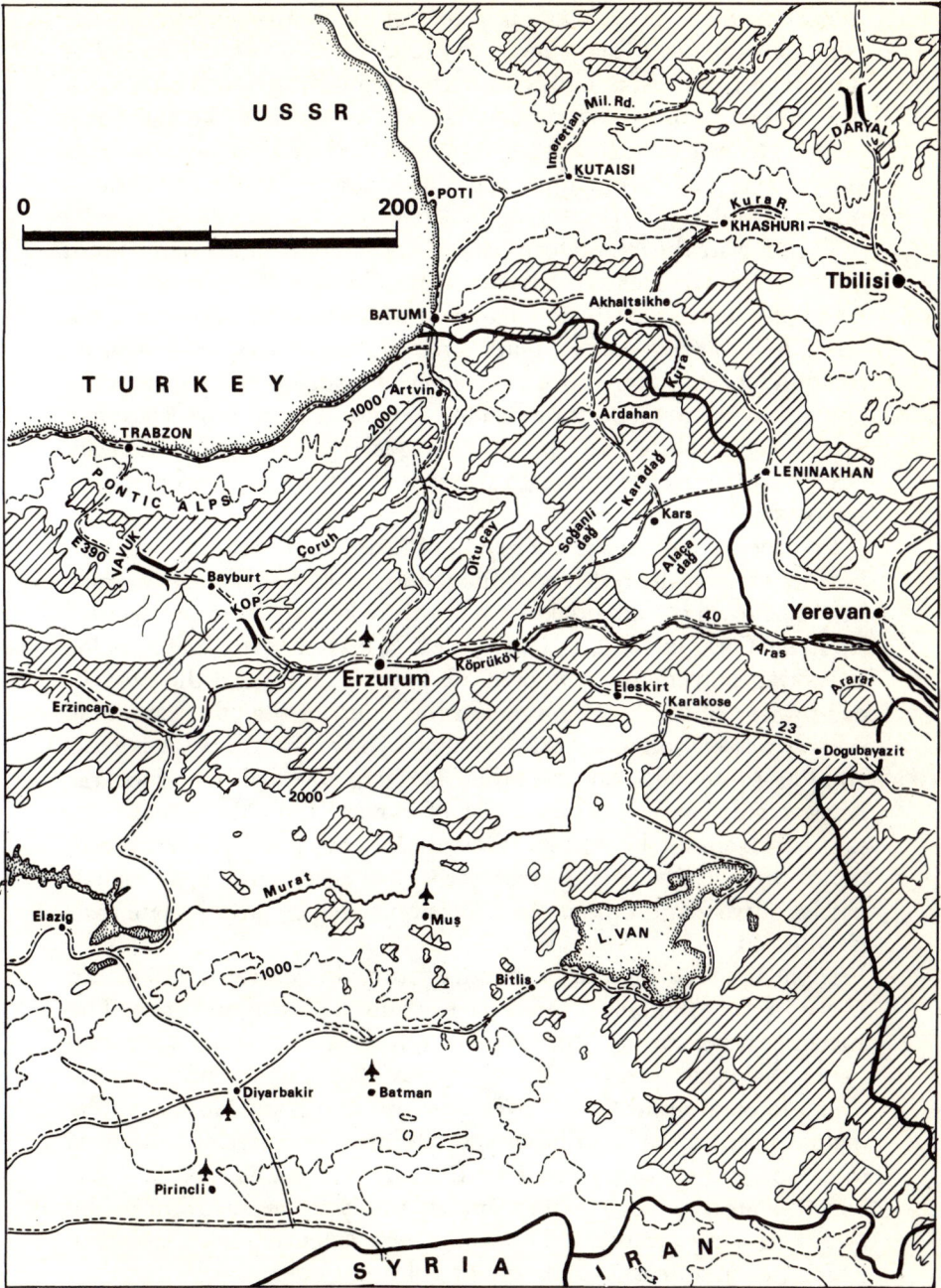

MAP 10   Eastern Anatolia

important road (E 390) which leads from Erzurum over the Pontic Alps to Trabzon (Trebizond), the main port of eastern Anatolia. The Black Sea coast is a difficult route for purely overland attack, for it is intersected by the numerous valleys which make the short descent from the Pontic Alps. The task becomes easier when it is supported by naval and amphibious action, as in General Lyakhov's push to Trabzon in the spring of 1916.

In past wars the inland fortress of Kars was the bastion of northern Anatolia against Russian advance from Georgia. Kars is sited in a basin of generally open downland, at an altitude of between 1,830 and 2,440 metres, and its chief strength has always resided in its outer defences – the forts on the steep Karadağ heights just to the north, the rearward positions on the Soganli dağ, and the Alaça dağ massif to the south. Kars was lost in 1828, 1855 and 1877, but only after it had absorbed the main Russian effort in those campaigning seasons.

For operations against the region of Kars the Soviets enjoy a wide base just inside the borders of the Georgian and Armenian Republics. The town of Akhaltsikhe, the historic key to Georgia, was won from the Turks in 1828, and now gives the Soviets an opportunity for a flanking movement around to the north of Kars and the Soganli dağ by way of the Kura gorge and the valley of the Oltu çay. This avenue was exploited by the Russians in 1877 and 1914. A corresponding route to the south of the Alaça dag is available up the Aras River from Yerevan, the capital of Soviet Armenia, which was captured from the Persians by General Paskevich in 1827. Formerly the narrowest part of the Aras gorge was accessible only to small parties of troops, but now the river is bordered by an adequate road (Route 40).

In the latter part of the twentieth century the central and southern sectors of the Anatolian border have acquired new significance. The ancient caravan route, running by way of Erzurum to Tabriz in Persia, has become a very busy highway (E 23) which provides the overland communication between Europe and Iran. Moreover, the main concentration of air bases and intelligence-gathering stations is to be found in southern and south-eastern Anatolia (see p. 159), which lends a strategic significance not only to the E 23 but to the routes running around Lake Van, a very extensive body of water which lies in an eerie landscape of volcanic peaks.

From 1828 these central and southern routes were repeatedly explored by Russian armies. Their first objective was usually the Turkish outpost of Doğubayazit (Bayazit), which is situated in the choke point between the towering massifs of Ararat and the Alaça dağ. Beyond Doğubayazit there is a choice of routes down the Murat to Muş (where there is one of the new airfields), or up the fertile valley of Eleskirt in the direction of Erzurum. In the First World War the main blocking position on the way to Erzurum was at Köprüköy, where the E23 crosses the Aras River and joins the road from Kars.

About ninety kilometres to the rear the historic fortress of Erzurum figures almost as largely in the history of the wars as Kars itself. Erzurum was extensively refortified by British and German engineers after 1878, but it fell to the Russians on 15 February 1916, after General Yudenich had seized the commanding Kargapazar dağ to the north-east and penetrated the lines of forts. The modern NATO airfield lies nine kilometres to the west of the town, and the Erzurum region must still be considered important for the defence of eastern Anatolia.

Behind Erzurum the highway divides in two. The E 390 (see p. 162) branches off north-west to the Black Sea at Trabzon, and is most easily blocked at the Kop Pass (where a Turkish division checked the Russians in 1916) and again at the Vavuk Pass in the Pontic Alps. Further south the E 23 continues its westward path through the road junctions at Erzincan and Sivas, which have long been considered the keys to central Anatolia.

The Straits and Turkey in Europe

In western Turkey the great prize for the Warsaw Pact is the three-hundred-kilometre passage of the Turkish Straits between the Black Sea and the Aegean. This avenue has three components. At the north-eastern end the entrance from the Black Sea is formed by the Bosporus, which is thirty kilometres long but only about two kilometres wide. This is the historic connection between Europe and Asia (traversed every year by millions of migrating birds), and the two continents have recently been joined by a bridge which connects the city of Istanbul with its eastern suburb Üsküdar (Scutari). The Black Sea shore on the neighbouring European coast is flat and sandy; the corresponding Asiatic shore is crowned by steep basalt cliffs, and is more obviously defensible.

Between the two straits proper the passage widens into the inland Sea of Marmara, which measures two hundred kilometres by seventy kilometres. At the south-west corner the waters are funnelled into the Dardanelles, which are about five kilometres wide, and lead for seventy winding kilometres to the Aegean.

The rights of navigation through the Turkish Straits are governed by the Montreux Convention of 1936, which was signed by the Black Sea coastal states and most of the major powers. The foreign Black Sea countries are allowed to book a passage for their warships, as long as they observe a limit on the tonnage which is en route at any given time; there is a prohibition on the passage of aircraft carriers, and the 'Black Sea' submarines must transit on the surface. The limits on non-Black Sea naval powers are more restrictive still. American and British surface warships make occasional and cautious forays through the Straits into the Black Sea, but they are forbidden to carry offensive missiles. Western submarines are denied the passage altogether.

In practice, the Turks make up their own minds as to how they will interpret the Montreux Convention, and they have not hesitated to avail themselves of this splendid opportunity to press home a political point. On 18 July 1976, when relations between Turkey and the United States were at a low ebb, the Turks allowed the new 40,000-ton carrier *Kiev* to sail through the Straits to the Mediterranean, accepting the Soviet declaration that the vessel in question was a 'specialised anti-submarine warfare cruiser'. The same issue will arise again in the middle 1990s, when the Soviets have completed the heavy carrier which is under construction at Nikolayev (see p. 37). It is inconceivable that this large vessel should be intended just for cruises inside the Black Sea.

According to Yugoslav commentators, who have followed Soviet exercises attentively, any Warsaw Pact attempt to open the Straits by force is likely to form part of a larger scheme, designed to open the way to the Middle East and ultimately the Indian Ocean. We gain some inkling of the scale of such an enterprise from the exercise Soyuz 84 (12–20 March 1984), which was commanded by Marshal Viktor Kulikov, and involved a number of divisions from the Odessa Military District and further Bulgarian and Hungarian divisions. Romanian forces did not take part physically, but were represented on maps. From evidence such as this, NATO might expect a direct air and amphibious assault on the shores adjoining the Bosporus. The main attack is likely to come overland from Bulgaria, and to involve Bulgarians and Soviets thrusting down the Maritsa River to the Aegean, dividing the Turkish and Greek forces in Thrace, and preparing or supporting a direct advance down the roads converging on Istanbul. About thirty-four divisions might be employed in such an offensive, and the Turks and Greeks could oppose them with only some twenty-five, consisting mainly of unmechanised infantry.

The Turkish Straits have been heavily fortified and garrisoned for centuries, and the defence now rests upon the Second Army, which is based on the Asiatic side, and the strong First Army, which is responsible for the security of the whole of Turkey in Europe. NATO's grand strategic interest will be in blocking the Turkish Straits to the Soviet Black Sea Fleet, and if the alliance is allowed to act in time it will be able to exploit geography to full advantage. The Bosporus and the Dardanelles are eminently suitable for mining, and much of the hydrography of the Straits favours the operation of small submarines, as was proved by the British underwater offensive in the Sea of Marmara in 1915. The Dardanelles are in fact an anti-submariner's nightmare, for a strong outflowing current of fresh water overlies a layer of salt water and the passage of sound is badly distorted as a result.

Turkey in Europe is the stub end of a mighty Ottoman empire which once reached almost to the gates of Vienna. The outer defence lines along the lower Danube and the Balkan Mountains (Stara Planina) were signed away in 1878, and the borders with modern Greece and Bulgaria run across the base of the narrowing isthmus which leads to Istanbul, between 140 and 230 kilometres away.

The terrain of Turkey in Europe is much less heavily accented than that of Anatolia. Edirne (Adrianople), the ancient gathering place of the armies of the Sultans, owed its strategic importance to its position on the Justinian Way (E 5N) at the confluence of the broad valleys of the Ardhas (Arda), Maritsa and Tunca. It fell to the Russians without opposition in 1829 and 1878, and in the latter year the Treaty of Berlin left it stranded on the new frontier. Construction of a thirty-five-kilometre-long circuit of forts was begun after this unfortunate settlement, and an outer zone of works in earth, concrete and steel was added from 1908. Edirne was now tactically strong, but it was, however, powerless to stop an invasion of Turkey in Europe on a wide frontage, and in the grand Bulgarian offensive of 1912 the Bulgarian Third Army was able to break across the border to the east and make directly for Kirklareli (Kirk Kilisse), where the Bulgars took up the secondary road (Route 20) which provides the northerly route down the isthmus.

Behind Kirklareli and Edirne the only obstacles are presented by the low wooded Yildiz daǧlari (the Istranja Balkan), and the valleys of the streams which flow through rolling downland on their way to the little river Ergene. Behind one of these rivulets, the Karacaaǧaç, the Turks checked the Bulgarian advance for five days (28 October–5 November) in 1912, in an action which became known as the battle of Lüleburgaz.

As the isthmus narrows towards the east, the last historic defensive position short of Istanbul is that of Çatalca, which extended from Karaburun on the Black Sea to Büyükçekmece on the Sea of Marmara. The line ran for a total of about forty kilometres, but it was effectively reduced to a more defensible twenty-four by lakes and arms of the sea. A first, incomplete position was evacuated by agreement with the Russians at the close of the war of 1877–8. Afterwards the Belgian engineer Brialmont helped the Turks to build a much more powerful line, which turned back the final offensive of the Bulgarians between 17 and 19 November 1912. The defensibility of the Çatalca position and indeed of the isthmus as a whole was also influenced by the command of the inshore waters on either side, and in 1912 this advantage clearly lay with the Turks.

GREECE

Area: 24,761 square kilometres
Population: 10,300,000
Army: 14 divisions, 7 separate brigades

GREEK DILEMMAS

Greece is a smallish country in land area and population, and yet she holds more than 2 per cent of her citizens under arms, which is a higher proportion than in any nation of the Warsaw Pact or the rest of NATO. This is the product of some unusually powerful forces of a political and geographical kind.

The Greeks are in the strange position of maintaining military readiness against both the Warsaw Pact and the Turks, their nominal allies in NATO. We have touched already on the troubled story of Greece as a member of the Western alliance. For NATO, Greece gives a measure of solidity to the defence of the eastern Mediterranean, lending indirect support to Turkey (however strongly the Greeks may deny this vocation), and in wartime presenting the Soviets with the problem of how to make the passage of the 600 kilometres of intricate and hostile Aegean waters between the Dardanelles and the open Mediterranean. In this context the defensive task of the Greek navy and air force is just the same as that of the Republic of Venice in the sixteenth and seventeenth centuries, when the strategy was to bottle up the Ottomans by a forward blockade of the Turkish Straits, while upholding a defence in depth down to Crete, the cork in the neck of the Aegean.

After Greece joined NATO the Americans operated seven bases on the national territory, and Piraévs became a frequent port of call for the Sixth Fleet. No less usefully, the Greeks accepted five NADGE early warning stations, which completed the line of NATO anti-air defences in the north-eastern Mediterranean.

In the 1970s the old quarrel with Turkey became of much greater immediacy than the wider confrontation between NATO and the Warsaw Pact, which in any case seemed to be losing its sharpness in this period of detente. In 1976 the Americans were forced to close down three of their installations (see p. 156), and they held on to the remaining four under restrictive conditions. Two of these establishments are on the Greek mainland – the air supply and standby base at Hellenikon Airport near Athens, and the very important naval communications centre at Nea Makri near Marathon. The other sites are on Crete, namely the air supply and communications base at Iráklion, and the Sixth Fleet's support base at Suda Bay.

Greece's relations with her northern neighbours are also somewhat intricate, since there is ample potential in this region for classic irredentist war in the old Balkan style. Here the Greeks appear to be treading lightly, if only to have their hands free to confront the Turks. In February 1984 Andreas Papandreou sought to put an end to an old quarrel with Albania, by renouncing all claims on 'Northern Epirus', a region of southern Albania where there is a large population of ethnic Greeks. Conversations with Yugoslavia began after Marshal Tito broke with the Soviet bloc in 1948, and the relationship was put on a formal footing by the Balkan Pact of 1953 and a further agreement in 1954, which not only relieved the Greeks of their immediate anxieties about the Yugoslav frontier but had the effect of holding the Albanians in awe. The Greek government sedulously avoids any provocation to its Bulgarian 'friends', though it is unlikely that the Marxist regime in Sofia will ever forget the national Bulgarian mission to reopen a corridor to the Aegean. The last frontier in the north, that with Turkey in Thrace, is one of the most tense and heavily guarded in Europe.

Greece, with its diverse and contradictory interests, is a country that has a desperate need for good internal communications. Unfortunately, geography is no help at all.

Away from Athens and Thessaloníki (Salonika), the population is dispersed over a multitude of islands comprising 17 per cent of the land area, and along the fringes of a mainland where 80 per cent of the ground is occupied by mountains. The two principal routes of overland communication are the E 19 and E 92 motorways, which run down the west and east coasts of the mainland, respectively. Otherwise the articulation depends on the free use of the Aegean. Some of the biggest industrial centres have developed along the coast, and the sea upholds the communication with the island groups which sprawl for 300 kilometres as far as the coast of Turkey and the open waters of the Mediterranean. It is not surprising that powerful air and naval forces are considered vital for national survival. The Greek army (like the Turkish one) is an old-fashioned body, and it probably cannot move very far or fast from wherever it happens to be garrisoned in peacetime.

THE STRATEGIC GEOGRAPHY OF THE LAND FRONTIERS

The northern Greek borderlands have been the scene of intense fighting in the first half of the twentieth century, notably in the Balkan Wars of 1912–13, the campaigns of 1916–18 in the First World War, the 'Italian' war of 1940, and the German *Blitzkrieg* in April 1941. The terrain, generally mountainous or otherwise inhospitable, has certainly produced long struggles for dominating features of the ground, but it has also yielded with startling suddenness to mobile forces which displayed the kind of 'savage vigour' demanded by the allied commander Franchet d'Esperey ('Desperate Frankie') in 1918. On 6 April 1941 the German mechanised columns skipped across the Rhodope Mountains into Thrace and Macedonia by tracks that are scarcely visible on large-scale maps. No less significant in its way was the feat of the French general Jouinot-Gambetta, who in September 1918 turned the Bulgarian positions in the Vardar valley by taking his cavalry brigade over the wooded heights of Karadžica.

Present-day Greece is militarily overextended, and the army is still more scattered than it was in 1941. Given the numerical preponderance of Bulgarian and other Warsaw Pact forces in a future conflict, it is unlikely that the geographical obstacles in northern Greece will exercise anything more than a temporary canalising effect.

The north Aegean coast

The least tenable ground on the frontier is patently the long-drawn-out strip of eastern Macedonia and Greek Thrace, which extends between the Aegean and the Bulgarian border. This corridor has an average width of only about forty kilometres, which gives it a passive strength against the Turks (who must approach end-on from the east), but its vulnerability must exercise an almost irresistible temptation for Bulgarian and Soviet forces, who can so easily thrust south to the sea. If the Greeks and Turks are fighting side by side, which will probably be the case in the event of a war between NATO and the Warsaw Pact, the obvious avenue is the plain of the Maritsa, for an advance in this direction will divide the allies (see p. 164). The frontier along the Rhodope Mountains further west appears to be easier to defend, but in April 1941 two German divisions crossed in a couple of days and reached the coastal plains at Alexandroúpolis, Komotiní and Xánthi. The modern Bulgarians have an added incentive to try their luck in this part of the world, for between 1913 and 1918 their hold on Alexandroúpolis (Dedéagach) and the adjacent coast gave them a national outlet to the Aegean.

In 1941 the Greek commander-in-chief General Papagos sought to check the further German progress by holding the prepared Metaxas Line, which stretched for more than 160 kilometres from the Kerkíni (Beles) Mountains and down the Néstos river to the sea. This position was tactically strong in places, but between 6 and 8 April it was unseated by the German XVIII Mountain Corps, which attacked frontally across the Rhodopes against Sérrai, and turned the left flank and rear by the avenues of the Struma and Vardar.

The Struma valley

In 1941 the Greeks would have done better to put more effort into holding their rearward defences, which ran along the Struma River to the rear of the Metaxas position. The Struma (Strimón) is doubly important. Along its northern reaches it is a corridor of military operations leading straight from the region of the Bulgarian capital, Sofia. However, downstream from the Rupel border pass it changes direction to the south-east, and along this stretch it serves as an outer defence for the major port of Thessaloníki. The high ground behind was the scene of the Greek and Serbian victory over the Bulgars at Kilkís in 1913, and between 1916 and 1918 the plain of the river itself formed one of the many static fronts of the First World War. At that period the Struma levels were a malarial swamp in summertime, and brimming with water during the autumn rains and the spring thaw. The broad central lake has since been drained, but the multiple channels and embankments offer some potential for halting an armoured advance.

The Vardar valley

Further to the west the Vardar (Axiós) is another river of more than passing interest. On the international scale it represents the main path of road and rail communication between the Danube basin and the Aegean. Inside Greece it is the key of Thessaloníki and the neighbouring coastal plain, which is one of the most intensively developed areas in the country. Here too the front was nearly static between 1916 and 1918. The heights to the south-west of the border lake of Dojran were contested in many battles, which did not deter a German panzer division from effecting a breakthrough in this sector in two days in 1941.

The Flórina Gap

Ninety kilometres west of the Vardar River the Flórina Gap provides a northern entry into the heart of mainland Greece, and a roundabout route to the plain of Thessaloníki. Once again we find little correspondence between the experience of the two world wars. In the Great War the campaigns of 1916–18 were dominated by the terrain and the climate. The valley floor, especially where it broadens to the north in the direction of Bitola (Monastir), became a near-impassable quagmire every October. There was bad going of a different kind on the two mountain flanks, and particularly to the east, where the notorious peak of the Kajmakcalan ('Butter Churn', 1,996 m) formed the corner bastion of the Vóras (Moglenitsa) Mountains.

The German XL Motorised Corps cruised through the gap in 1941, and encountered effective opposition only at the southern exit at the snowbound Vévi Pass, where a force of British and Australians stood their ground for four days until ordered to retreat. The present road (the E 20) is a considerable improvement on its predecessor. Beyond Vévi the way was clear for the Germans to exploit through Kozáni, and send columns south towards Thermopylae, and over the tangled Pindus Mountains and on by way of Ioánnina.

The western coastlands

The final stretch of the frontier, namely the border with Albania from the Pindus to the Ionian Sea, is dominated by parallel ridges and river valleys which follow a pronounced north-west to south-east direction. The military movements followed the same axes, in the victorious campaign of the Greeks against the Italians in 1940, and at that time only the narrow coastal lowlands were suitable for the operation of armour. This region appears to be tucked safely out of the way of any likely Warsaw Pact offensive, but it is notable that the excellent new coastal route (the E 19) bends inland by way of Ioánnina, which, as we have seen, is by no means immune from attack from the east.

Rearward positions

The campaign of 1941 draws our attention to the high ground where Greek and NATO forces might seek to halt an offensive short of the important fighter base at Lárisa and the good tank country of the plain of Thessaly. Early in April that year the British expeditionary force took over the defence of the Aliákmon Line, which was effectively the edge of the western Macedonian plateau facing east over the Vardar plain. The total length was about 110 kilometres. The left or northern flank was anchored on the Vevi Pass, the Kajmakcalan and the northern end of Lake Vegorítis. The right rested on Mount Olympus and the anti-tank ditch which the Australians dug in front. The Aliákmon Line was not equipped with forts and properly prepared positions like those of the Metaxas Line, but it commanded wide observation over the Vardar plain, and the frontal access by way of the passes at Edhessa and Véroia was (and is) steep and tactically difficult. The rearward defences ran from Klisoúra to the neighbourhood of Sérvia, where the ford on the swift-flowing Aliákmon proved to be impassable to German armoured vehicles. Since that time the opening of the E 92 motorway has increased the danger of an outflanking move along the narrow Aegean coastal plain and up the Piniós river behind Mount Olympus.

In 1941 the British evacuated the Aliákmon Line in some haste, following the collapse of Yugoslavia and the Metaxas positions, and after crossing the plain of Thessaly they sought to check the Germans in the last high ground of the mainland short of the isthmus of Corinth and the peninsula of the Pelepponese. The Germans were held for just a day in a second battle of Thermopylae. The ground of this historic blocking position had changed greatly since Leonidas and his Spartans stood their ground here in 480 BC. The seaward flank on the north used to be wide enough for a single chariot, but by 1941 the retreat of the water had created a five-kilometre wide marshy plain at Molós, which is now traversed by the E 92. The

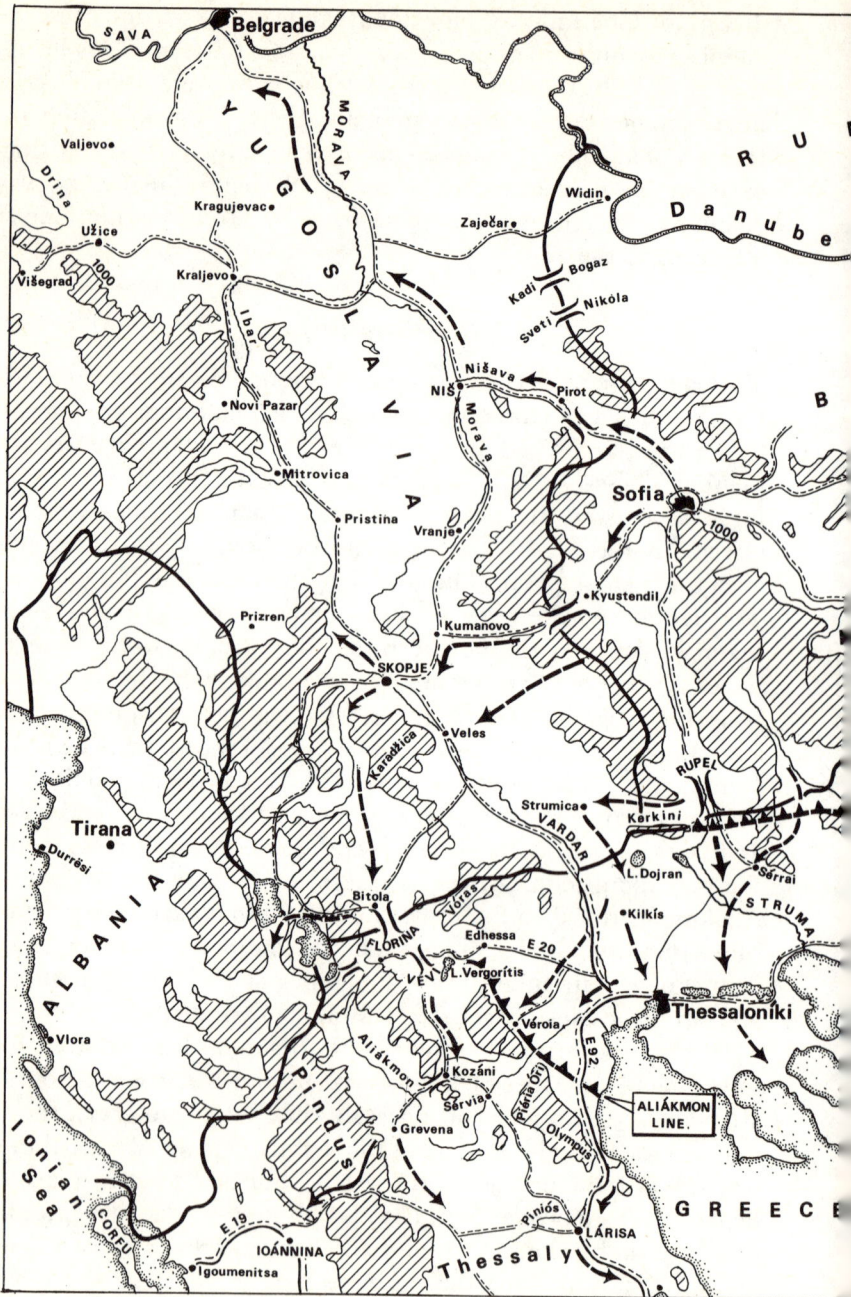

MAP 11   Macedonia and Thrace

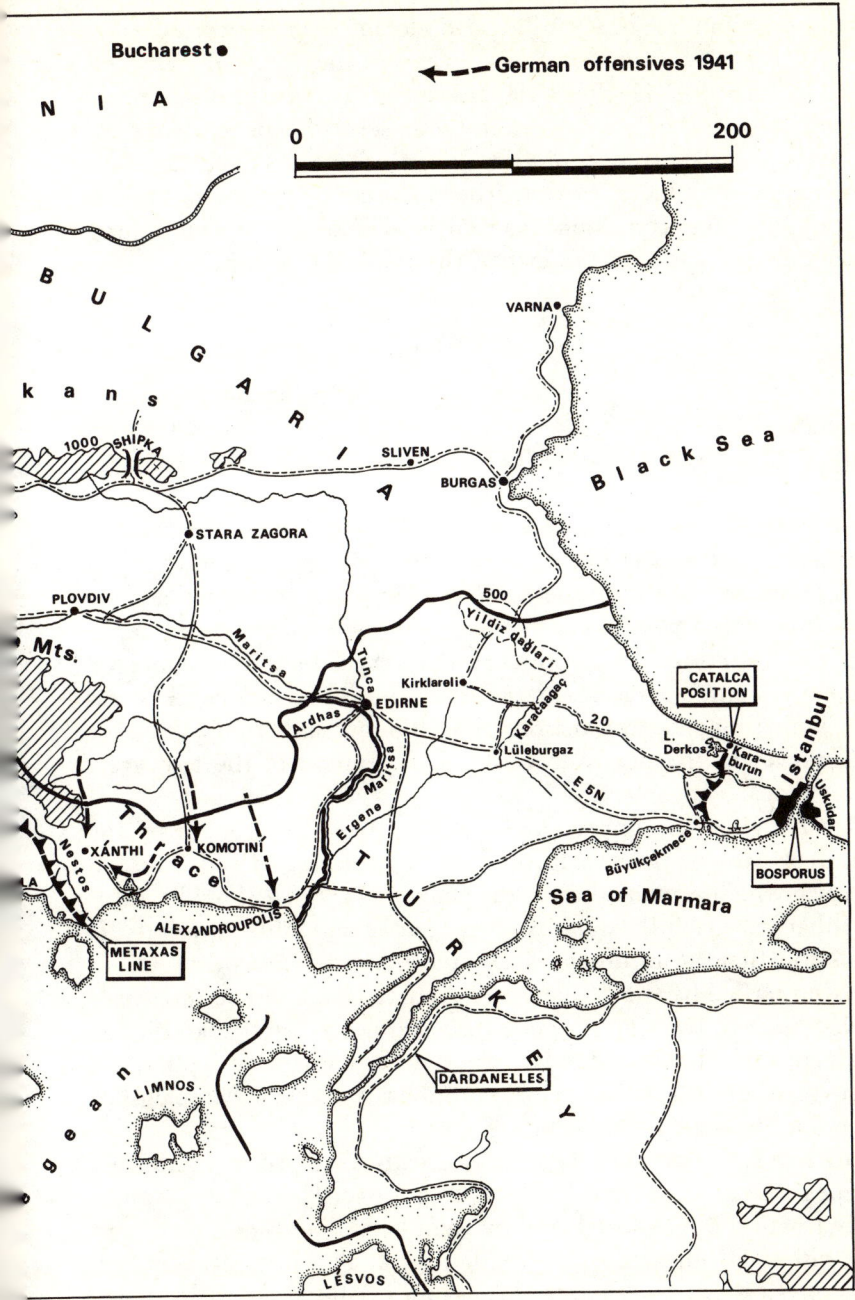

Bucharest●

←--- German offensives 1941

0 200

N I A

B U L G A R I A

k a n s

VARNA●

Black Sea

1000 SHIPKA

SLIVEN●

BURGAS●

●STARA ZAGORA

PLOVDIV●

500

Yildiz dağlari

Maritsa

Tunca

Mts.

Kirklareli●

EDIRNE●

CATALCA POSITION

Istanbul

Ardhas

20

Lüleburgaz●

Karaagaç

L. Derkos●

Kara-burun

Üsküdar

Maritsa

E 5 N

XÁNTHI●

Nestos

T h r a c e

KOMOTINI●

Ergene

T U R K E Y

Büyükçekmece●

BOSPORUS

Sea of Marmara

ALEXANDROUPOLIS●

METAXAS LINE

LIMNOS

DARDANELLES

g e a n

LÉSVOS

inland mountain route at Brállos had already been converted into a highway by 1941, and it is now designated the Route E 90.

On 26 April 1941 the Germans made a parachute assault at Corinth (Kórinthos), in an attempt to seize the bridge over the spectacular rocky trench of the Corinth Canal. The bridge was blown up in their faces. Soviet airborne forces might try to improve on the German performance, as well as to seize the important ferry passage near Pátrai, by the exit of the Gulf of Corinth.

ALBANIA

Area:	28,748 square kilometres
Population:	3,000,000
Army:	6 brigades

This strange little country forms, with Yugoslavia, the pair of neutral Marxist states which interrupt the geographical continuity of NATO in the Mediterranean. Together they make up a zone measuring about 900 kilometres long, and 300 kilometres in depth from the Adriatic coast. In both countries the Communists emerged as the dominant anti-German guerrilla groups in the Second World War, which gave the Marxist regimes a military and popular base for their power in the post-war world, independent of the two great power blocs.

Albania gives the impression of having been left behind by the march of history. It was formed out of a rump of old Turkish territory which remained after the Balkan Wars of 1912–13, and it has inherited a rich Balkan mix of irredentist and ethnic quarrels. It is possible that the argument with Greece over the Northern Epirus has been settled by the démarche of Andreas Papandreou in February 1984 (see p. 167), but Yugoslavia continues to fear that ambitions of a 'Greater Albania' extend to the southern Yugoslav republic of Kosovo, where the ethnic Albanian majority wages a campaign of intimidation against the Serbs.

Moreover, Albania has been ideologically alienated from Marxist regimes abroad. The hard-line president Enver Hoxha contrived to fall out with the Soviets when they went 'soft' after Stalin died, and then with the Chinese after the death of Mao. This fortress mentality finds physical expression in the thousands of military emplacements which line Albania's coastline and inland frontiers.

Albania is by no means devoid of international significance, in spite of its tiny area and inward-looking regime.

First of all by the middle 1980s there were distinct signs that in the declining years of Hoxha a younger leadership had become interested in breaking out of Albania's self-imposed isolation. The years 1983 and 1984 witnessed the construction of the first rail links with Yugoslavia, the inauguration of a ferry service from Trieste in Italy, and agreements with Turkey, Greece, Italy, Austria and Switzerland which opened Albania to foreign road haulage. In January 1985 Albania and Greece ceremonially removed the barriers at the main border crossing at Kakavia.

The venerable Hoxha died on 11 April 1985, and the incoming regime rejected the official Soviet message of condolence. At the time of writing there is no clear indication whether the Albanian government will develop its recent outgoing policies or return to its old self-imposed purdah.

The Albanian economy is still the poorest in Europe, thanks to Marxist mismanagement, but the low ground is very fertile, and there is real or potential self-sufficiency in energy (oil and hydroelectric power). The national territory contains vast reserves of iron ore, and the deposits of chrome are significant even on the global scale (see p. 5).

Strategists also know that Albania occupies an important position at the entrance to the Adriatic, which measures only about eighty kilometres across. The ancient Romans, who were master geopoliticians, made Durrachium (Durrës, Durazzo) the point of departure for the Via Egnatia leading to Constantinople. Nearby the southern prong of the last great Ottoman offensive was halted by the Venetians in 1717, when they successfully defended Corfu against a Turkish siege. In the First World War the geography of the narrows inspired the British, French and Italians to establish their 'Otranto Barrage' (1916–18), with the intention of halting the passage of Austrian and German U-boats. The Western allies had the facility of the harbours of Brindisi and Otranto on the Italian shore, and the deep water port at Vlora (Valone) on the Albanian side. The Barrage (which was not very effective) consisted of nets suspended from fishing boats, and a very extensive patrol zone that was covered by submarines, destroyers and smaller craft.

The middle of the strait is much deeper than most of the Adriatic, but vessels creeping inshore are vulnerable to mines of all sorts. In the First World War a dense minefield off Otranto was an important ingredient of the Barrage. On the opposite shore the British destroyers *Saumarez* and *Volage* were badly damaged by Albanian mines on 23 October 1946, while asserting the right of passage through the Corfu Channel.

These waters have lost none of their significance over the years. Enver Hoxha was determined that the Soviets would never regain the use of Vlora, and he recalled in his memoirs how he overheard the Soviet Minister of Defence, Marshal Malinovsky, remark to Khrushchev that Albania would make 'an ideal base for our submarines' (Artisien, 1985, 107).

YUGOSLAVIA

Area:	225,804 square kilometres
Population:	23,308,000
Army:	12 divisions, 21 separate brigades; Territorial Defence Force of between one and three million

Yugoslavia is a very sensitive area in the confrontation between NATO and the Warsaw Pact. There are three main reasons:

- It is a dangerously imprecise grey zone, which falls into the accepted spheres of influence of neither of the alliances.
- The likelihood of foreigners intervening has been increased by major internal problems.
- Yugoslavia is one of the classic 'pivotal areas', offering corridors of advance into north-east Italy and northern Greece.

YUGOSLAVIA AS A NEUTRAL

The Yugoslav leader Marshal Tito broke with the Soviet bloc on 28 June 1948. He was a formidable and ruthless dictator in his own right, but he was determined to develop his own revisionist form of Marxism, and he feared for the independence of Yugoslavia after the Soviet-inspired putsch in Czechoslovakia in February.

Yugoslavia has sedulously kept up its position as the acknowledged leader of the 'non-aligned' block, and cautious relations are maintained with both the rival alliances. During the Yom Kippur War in October 1973 the Yugoslavs allowed their airspace to become an important Soviet air supply corridor to Egypt and Syria, and the Yugoslav port of Rijeka continues to serve as a channel for the transfer of Soviet military equipment to clients in the Middle East. In 1974 a change in Yugoslav law permitted any five ships of a 'non-aggressive' power to use docking and repair facilities in national ports for up to six months. These provisions were clearly intended for the benefit of the Soviets, who ever since have availed themselves of the opportunity to have submarines serviced in Yugoslav ports, and naval crews landed there for rest and recreation.

On the other side a treaty in 1975 resolved a very long quarrel with Italy over the sovereignty of Trieste. The Italians were confirmed in possession of the city ('Zone A'), and the sovereignty of Yugoslavia was acknowledged over the territory to the south ('Zone B'). In 1981 Yugoslavia obtained favourable commercial terms from the EEC, and Yugoslavia continues to trade actively with countries on both sides of the Iron Curtain.

Yugoslav neutrality is also upheld by a high state of military preparedness. After the Soviet invasion of Czechoslovakia in 1968 the Yugoslav armed forces were restructured according to a strategy called Total National Defence. The job of the regular troops of the Yugoslav People's Army is to fight a delaying action in the northern plains, and make it possible for the government to mobilise the regular reserves and the hordes of the Territorial Defence Forces, who will wage a guerrilla war in the style of Tito's partisans in the Second World War.

Yugoslav commentators provide us with some of our most realistic assessments of Soviet intentions and capacities in southern Europe, and there is no doubt that most of Yugoslavia's military activity is orientated against invasion by the Warsaw Pact.

INTERNAL PROBLEMS

Yugoslavia held together better than many people had expected after Marshal Tito died on 4 May 1980, but the difficulties that faced the new collective leadership were as intractable as ever. Like other countries of south-eastern Europe, Yugoslavia has been cursed by high unemployment, rising inflation, and a daunting foreign debt. However, in Yugoslavia the dangers to national cohesion are exceptionally acute, and any foreign invaders will certainly try to turn the divisions to their own advantage, as the Germans did in 1941.

'Scientific atheism' makes little headway against the great numbers of believers, which detracts from the credibility of the national Communist party, the League of Communists. In turn the religious people are split among themselves. There are about 3,000,000 unregenerate Muslims, who have a full complement of genuine whirling dervishes. The Christianity of the 7,000,000 Catholics dates back to the eighth century, when the peoples of Croatia and

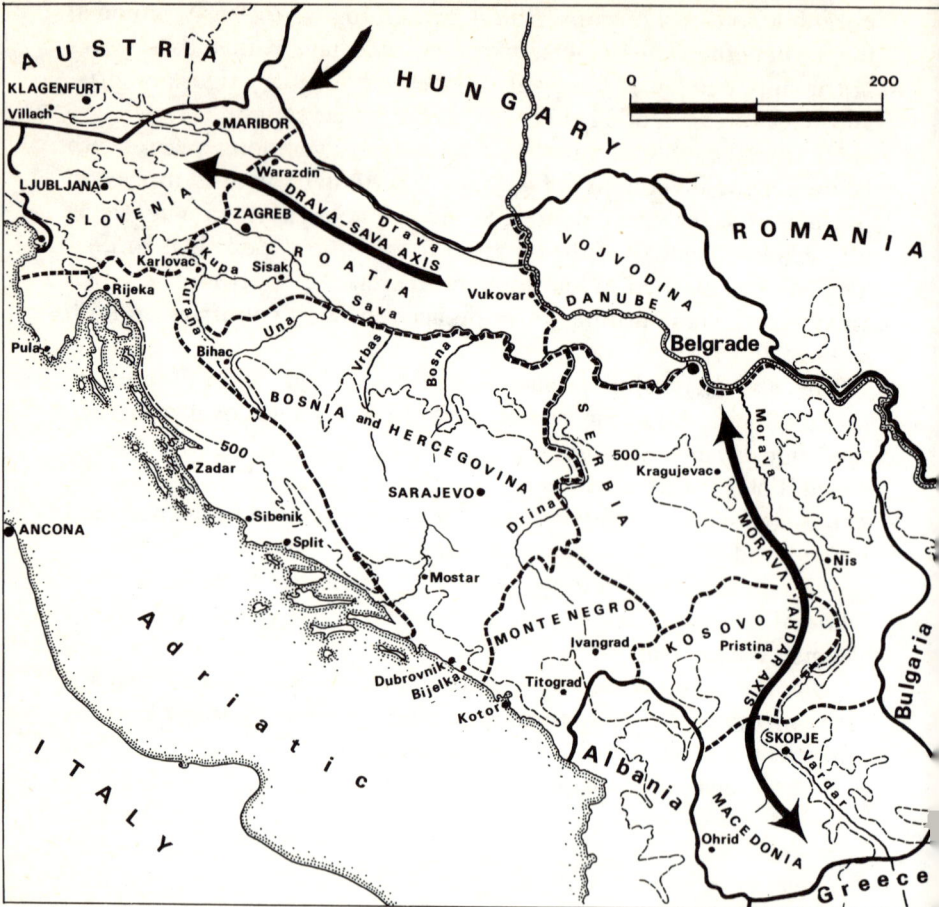

MAP 12   Yugoslavia

Slovenia were Christianised from Western Europe, and the religious allegiance of the Croats was confirmed by the experience of later times, when they were preserved from Ottoman rule by the Austrians and Venetians. In Serbia, on the other hand, Christianity arrived from Byzantium in the ninth century, along with the Cyrillic alphabet, and the Serbs continued to look east after the Great Schism.

The enduring strength of religion has reinforced the ethnic quarrels which sow division between and inside the six constituent republics of Yugoslavia.

The republic of *Serbia* represents in every dimension the core area of the state, and plays a role very similar to that of the Russian

Republic in the Soviet Union. It spreads down the eastern side of Yugoslavia, embracing the federal capital, Belgrade, and taking in more than one-third of the national population and surface. The centre forms the Serbian Republic proper (*c.* 5,500,000), where ethnic Serbs make up 90 per cent of the population. Moreover, the influence of the Serbs is felt throughout the Yugoslav state, for they dominate the political leadership and represent two-thirds of the officer corps of the regular army.

At both its northern and southern extremities the Serbian Republic embraces an internal 'autonomous province'. Serbians form a minority in the very mixed population (2,000,000) of the autonomous province of *Vojvodina*, extending across the sandy plains north of the Danube. At the other end of Serbia the autonomous province of *Kosovo* (*c.* 2,000,000) is a region of very different character, a poor and hilly place where the Serbs are heavily outnumbered by hostile Albanians.

Both the Albanians and the Yugoslavs have deep emotions invested in the issue of Kosovo. Hoxha's widow reaffirmed her dedication to the Albanians of Kosovo on her husband's coffin. The Serbian Yugoslavs, on the other hand, remember Kosovo as the core of the old Serbian kingdom, which was overthrown by the Turks as a result of the battle on the Kosovo Polje in 1389. To lose Kosovo yet again would represent a betrayal of the Serbian national mission.

The remaining five constituent republics may be divided into two main groups – northern provinces which own the main areas of industrial and agricultural production, and which are generally Western in tradition and outlook, and southern provinces of a decidedly Balkan aspect.

In the north the republics of Slovenia and Croatia were conjured out of old lands of the Habsburg empire at the end of the First World War. *Slovenia* is jammed against the Austrian and Hungarian borders. Ethnic Slovenes make up more than nine out of ten of the population of about 2,000,000, and they spill across the border with Austria, where some tension has arisen with their Germanic fellow-citizens. *Croatia* has a population of about 4,500,000, four out of five of them being of Croatian national stock. Croats are Catholics, like the Slovenes, and they resent the political domination of the Serbs and the subsidies that must be given to the southern republics. The Croats have important expatriate communities in the United States and Australia, which reinforces their sense of nationhood, and between 1941 and 1944 they formed an independent state under German protection.

In the large central republic of *Bosnia and Hercegovina* (*c.* 4,000,000) the Serbs and the Muslim nationals form the largest ethnic groups and they stand in rough equilibrium. Bosnia and Hercegovina shares the tourist trade with Croatia, and although it is not particularly prosperous it has some importance as a centre of arms production. The southern neighbour, *Montenegro*, is the smallest and most backward of the republics, and has a mixed population. In the far south the remote republic of *Macedonia* has foreign territory on three sides, and the Macedonians, who form the dominant racial group, have many blood brothers in Greece and Bulgaria.

YUGOSLAVIA AS A THEATRE OF OPERATIONS

The broad strategic shape of Yugoslavia may be compared with a triangle: ◁ . The slanting base on the left hand corresponds with the south-western highland zone, which is relevant primarily as a national redoubt in which a prolonged partisan war may be waged against the Soviets. The other two sides are of concern to NATO as well. Along the top or northern side the river lines of the Danube, the Sava and the Drava represent avenues leading towards Italy and neutral Austria. On the right the corridor of the Morava and the Vardar gives the Warsaw Pact an entry to Greece on a vulnerable inland flank.

The south-western highland zone

This region extends inland from the Adriatic for between 50 and 180 kilometres, and was the scene of Tito's campaign of guerrilla resistance against the Axis in the Second World War. For three years Bosnia and eastern Croatia were the principal stamping ground of the partisans, and then in the summer of 1944 the activity was extended into Serbia. Present-day Yugoslav strategy is therefore based on an intimate knowledge of the ground.

The Yugoslav army has eight tank brigades, and the three principal concentrations are clearly designed to defend the northern and eastern fringes of the highland zone. The northernmost grouping is at Sisak in Croatia, situated at the junction of the rivers Kupa and Sava. Sisak lies on or near the principal avenues into the highlands of Bosnia, and about one hour's drive by tank from the city of Zagreb (Agram), which has a major airport, and is politically significant as the capital of Croatia.

Another important concentration is at Kragujevac, which stands at the north-eastern edge of the highland zone close to the apex of our triangle. This was one of the most important arsenals of the old Serbian monarchy, and it served as the rallying-point for the success-ful mobilisation of August 1914. The three Austrian attacks in that year were checked in the high ground to the west, and in 1915 Kragujevac formed part of the last coherent line of defence before the Serbs were broken by the pressure of the Germans and Bulgarians.

Skopje in Macedonia is the last of the concentrations, and will be considered shortly in relation to the Morava–Vardar corridor.

The important exercise *Sloboda 71* (2–7 October 1971) was at once an affirmation of national independence and an indication as to how the Yugoslavs probably intend to conduct their defence. The scene was Croatia, where hostile 'Blue' armies struck south by way of Karlovac and Sisak. The Yugoslavs had an outpost line along the Sava, but they put up their main defence in the higher ground between the Kupa and Una rivers, where the 'Blue' advance was canalised into the Korana valley and turned back just short of Bihac. In a real war the same funnelling effect might be reproduced equally well in the valleys of rivers such as the Vrbas, Bosna or Drina.

The northern avenues

If *Sloboda 71* is to be taken as a model of Yugoslav strategy, there will be little to prevent the Soviets and Hungarians from exploiting the axes of the northern rivers for an offensive westwards into Italy. The history of twentieth-century wars suggests that Belgrade is unten-able, and that the lower Danube is too far advanced into the plain to serve as a serious line of defence. It is significant that the Soviet offensive in this region in October 1944 took the form of parallel advances by their Forty-Sixth and Fifty-Seventh Armies across the plains on either side of this great river. Upstream from Vukovar the Danube bends north, and so ceases to be of any use at all for stopping a move from the direction of Hungary. Worse still, for the purposes of NATO, the two main right-bank tributaries (the Drava and the Sava) offer natural avenues of advance into the 210-kilometre-deep corridor of Slovenia and southern Austria which is all that separates Hungary from northern Italy.

The Morava–Vardar corridor

The right-hand side of our triangle represents the valleys of the Morava and Vardar rivers, which form a path 500 kilometres long from the Danube below Belgrade to the Aegean at Thessaloníki. It is vulnerable almost all the way to offensives from the Bulgarian border, which runs at an average of about 80 kilometres to the east, and many of the same entries were exploited by the Bulgarians in 1915, the Germans in 1941 and the Soviets in 1944.

Along the northern sector the immediate objective has usually been the town of Niš on the Morava, and some of the most interesting passages thither have proved to be those at Zaječar (obstinately disputed in 1915), the Kadi Bogaz and Sveti Nikola passes, and the valley of the Nišava, where Pirot was another fortress which was defended gallantly by the Serbs in 1915.

In the south the corridor has been reached by invaders at Vranje, Skopje, Veles and Dojran.

Serbia, Kosovo and Yugoslav Macedonia become very difficult to defend once the enemy has reached the Morava–Vardar valley. After Bulgaria deserted to the Soviets on 9 September 1944 the Germans were forced to open a new rearward communication north-west from Skopje through Pristina, Mitrovica, Krajlevo, Užice and Višegrad. This road in turn became unusable once the Soviets reached the Ibar valley, and the Germans had to resort to the tracks leading through Novi Pazar.

The breaching of the great corridor is still more dangerous for the Greeks, for it opens approaches like those through Flórina, by which the enemy may turn the defences of Macedonia and Thrace from the flank and rear, as the Germans demonstrated so dramatically in April 1941 (see p. 170).

ITALY

Area:	301,245 square kilometres
Population:	57,150,000
Army:	4 divisions, 12 separate brigades, 2 amphibious battalions

UNITIES AND DIVISIONS

By 1871 the ruling family of the north-east Italian kingdom of Piedmont-Sardinia finally succeeded in creating a united Italy out of a congeries of separate states. This movement had wide if not universal popular support, and modern Italy still hangs together much better than Yugoslavia, despite some indications to the contrary. Certainly more than forty successive governments have entered office in Italy since the end of the Second World War, but many politicians serve in one administration after another, and the meetings of the Supreme Defence Council lend continuity to the management of military affairs.

Italian political traditions have proved robust enough to admit a powerful Italian Communist Party (which embraced Eurocommunism in an 'historic compromise' in 1975), and the Italian public has learnt to live with a weight of bureaucracy and a daily experience of strike action that would have wrecked almost any other society in Europe. When, in 1981, the Italian Parliament voted to accept cruise missiles at the Comiso base in Sicily, it was after an impressively well-informed and responsible debate in the public media.

When all of this has been said, the remaining divisions in Italy are of considerable indirect interest to NATO. More than a century after the political unification, the geography of this very long-drawn-out country helps to preserve something of the old regionalism. At the top the autonomous province of Alto Adige (South Tyrol) has a large Germanic population, and lies as far north as Burgundy in France. At the other end Sicily is an island of distinctively southern character; it is situated on a level with Tunisia and Algeria, and its landscapes have doubled for those of the American badlands in the 'spaghetti Westerns'. The physical divide is by no means to be underestimated, as was evident in 1980 when the Italian army faced considerable problems in sending units south to help in earthquake relief. The divorce also extends to mentalities and institutions, for the tradition of the army is still mostly in the keeping of the northerners, and more specifically the Piedmontese. The regiments of *Alpini* are by definition northern units, while the regiments of *Bersaglieri* and armoured cavalry claim descent from the old army of Piedmont-Sardinia.

Here it is perhaps worth mentioning that 'Italian military pride' is not a contradiction in terms. Even under fascist leadership in the first years of the Second World War the Italian performance was not so much bad as very patchy. A number of specialist forces gave a good account of themselves, the armoured formations fought with technical skill, and in few other theatres of war did the British have such heavy fighting as at Keren in Ethiopia in February and March 1941.

THE MEDITERRANEAN VOCATION

The celebrated lack of accord between the Italian army and navy is partly the outcome of the geopolitical forces which have pulled Italy in opposite directions, towards the heart of Europe and towards the Mediterranean.

Italy's value to NATO is associated largely, though not exclusively, with the situation of the peninsula jutting slantwise into the centre of the Mediterranean. For the Americans Italy is at once a potential station on the way to the Middle East and the Gulf, and a platform for projecting power over the Mediterranean and the adjoining states. The Sixth Fleet is based largely on Italian ports (see p. 153). Likewise the United States Air Force makes frequent use of the standby field at Aviano in north-east Italy, and trains aircrews in bombing and aerial combat at Decimomannu in Sardinia.

In the 1970s the Mediterranean became of declining importance in the global confrontation between America and the Soviet Union. Over the same period, however, the immediate threat to Italian interests increased. The Middle East was in turmoil, and Libya emerged as an unpredictable and aggressive power which had the capacity to challenge the passage of the central Mediterranean and the right of Italy to exploit the seabed. The Italians were only too well aware that all of their oil and 90 per cent of all imported raw materials came to them across the sea, and Italy reawakened to her Mediterranean destiny.

In 1980 a potentially dangerous dispute broke out with Libya, which warned off an Italian oil exploration rig which was working for Malta in a contested sea area. The very last British forces had left Malta in 1979, abandoning the finest natural habour in the Mediterranean, and there was a strategic vacuum waiting to be filled. In 1981 the Italians signed a bi-lateral treaty with Malta, guaranteeing its independence (effectively against Libya). However, the independent-minded Maltese government proceeded to re-establish its connections with Libya, and in 1984 the two countries signed a renewable treaty of friendship whereby the Libyans agreed to supply arms and training to the Maltese forces. The territorial dispute was referred to the International Court of Justice in The Hague. None of this was of any comfort to the Italians.

In 1981, by when such things had become all the rage in international military circles, the Italian Ministry of Defence proposed the setting up of a joint-service Rapid Intervention Force. This scheme ran into the usual difficulties of inter-service rivalries and lack of money, and the defence of national interests in the Mediterranean still rests in the first line upon the Italian navy.

The retreat of the British from the Mediterranean from 1975, together with the reduction of the presence of the Sixth Fleet, have left the resources of the Italians badly overstretched. The Italian navy has had to wage a very long fight for 'organic' air cover, and now the queen of its anti-submarine fleet is the single light carrier *Giuseppe Garibaldi*. The complement of mine countermeasures craft is also probably inadequate. The Italians have a responsibility for keeping open the strait between Sicily and Tunisia, and an important national interest in preserving swept channels through the Adriatic, where most of the waters are only between twenty-five and forty metres deep. The Italians have only a few naval ports on the Adriatic (Venice, Ancona, Brindisi), and the experience of the First World War suggests that their shores are vulnerable to warships dashing from behind the shelter of the islands which line the Yugoslav coast.

THE GUARD OF THE INLAND BORDERS

Since the Second World War the Italian army and air force have devoted their main attention to defending what is by any standard the Italian core area, namely the lowlands on either side of the river Po. The northern plain covers only 15 per cent of the land area of Italy, but it embraces by far the heaviest concentrations of population and industry. Milan is effectively the business capital of Italy, just as Turin is the heavy industrial powerhouse.

In strategic terms northern Italy belongs to Central Europe, not to the world of the Mediterranean. For centuries the two basic options in the wars between France and Austria were campaigns on one or other side of the Alps, in the valleys of the Danube or the Po, and the Austrians rightly regarded the defence of the Italian plain as the outer bastion of Vienna. Nowadays the threat to the security of northern Italy comes from the east, in the shape of a push by Soviet and Hungarian forces by way of the south-east corner of Austria and the Yugoslav provinces of Croatia and Slovenia (see p. 181). This is a reality which has scarcely penetrated the literature of modern strategic studies. Venice is geographically closer to Hungary than to Rome, and the north Italian core area lies within reach of new tactical and medium-range nuclear missiles which the Soviets deployed in Czechoslovakia in the summer of 1984.

All three of the fully constituted corps of the Italian army are stationed in the north. In the rear the III Corps (HQ Milan) functions as a reserve in depth, having an armoured division at Novara west of Milan, an infantry division at Turin, and another infantry division forward on the fringe of the Alps at Bergamo. The IV Corps (HQ Bolzano) sees to the defence of the high mountains, and its five component brigades of *Alpini* are garrisoned on the flanks

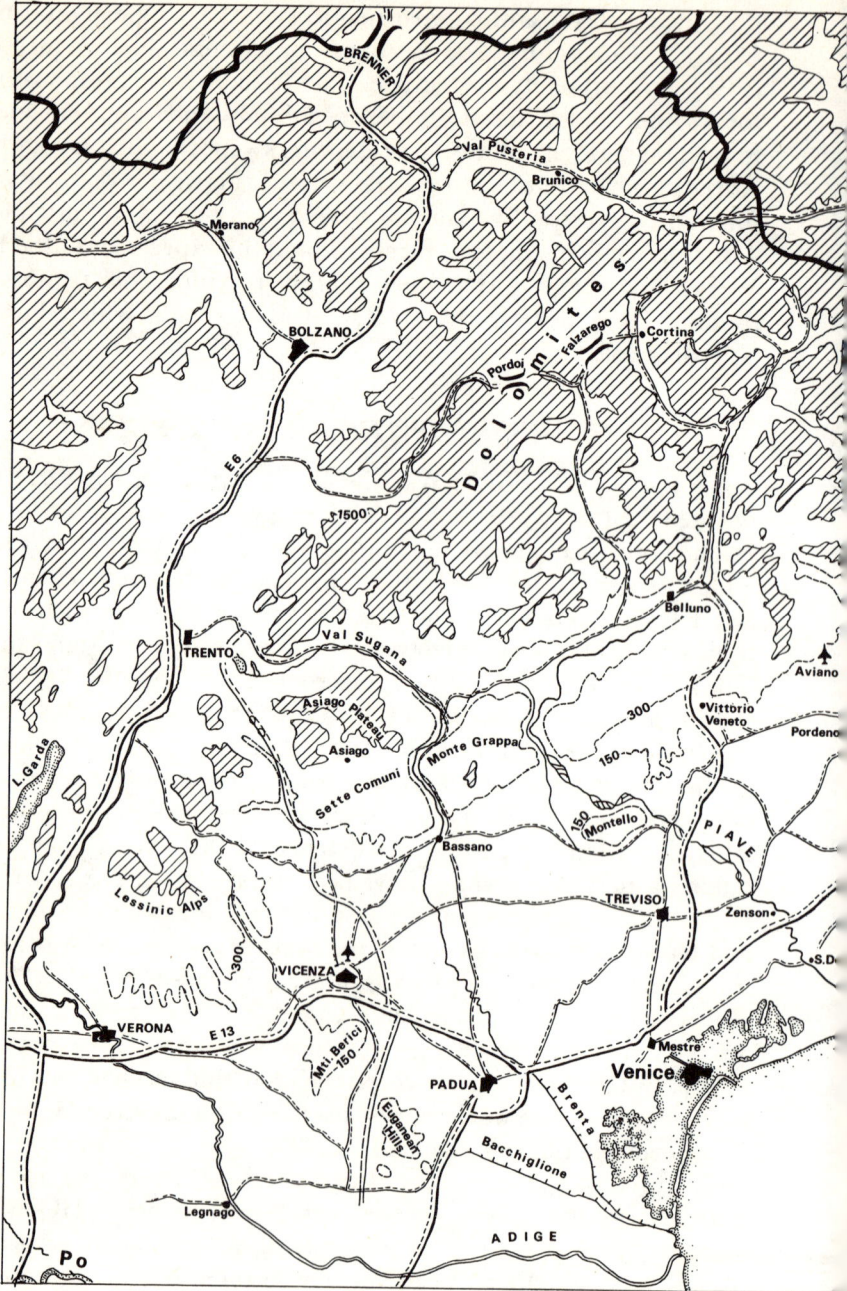

MAP 13   North-East Italy

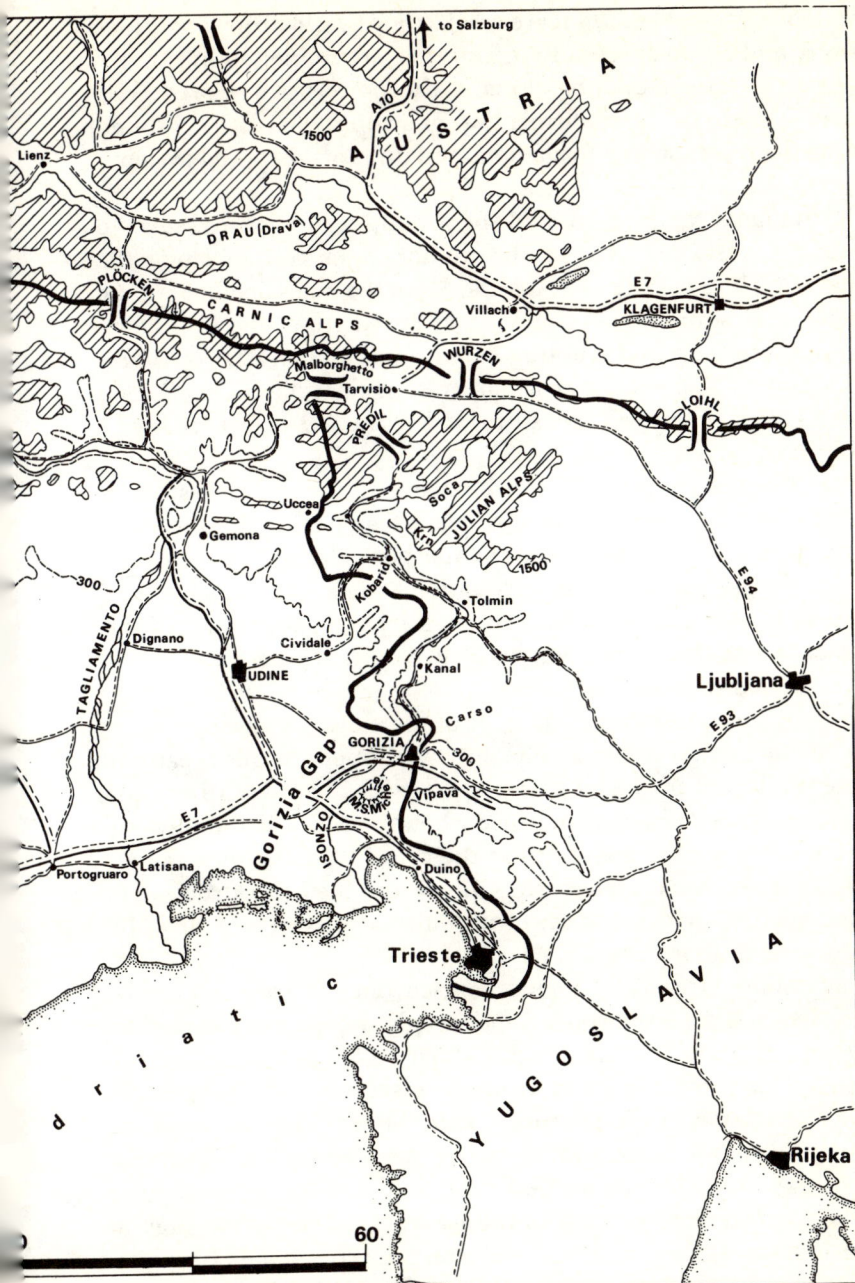

to Salzburg

A U S T R I A

A10

1500

Lienz

D R A U (Drava)

PLÖCKEN

C A R N I C   A L P S

Villach

E 7

KLAGENFURT

Malborghetto

WURZEN

Tarvisio

PREDIL

LOIBL

Uccea

Soča

J U L I A N   A L P S

Gemona

1500

Kobarid

Tolmin

E 94

300

Dignano

Cividale

Kanal

TAGLIAMENTO

UDINE

Carso

Ljubljana

GORIZIA

300

E 93

Gorizia Gap

Vipava

ISONZO

E 7

Portogruaro

Latisana

Duino

Trieste

A   d   r   i   a   t   i   c

Y U G O S L A V I A

Rijeka

60

of the Dolomites. The *Alpini* are crack troops with strong traditions of family and regional recruiting, and they are trained to live, move and fight in the mountains. Finally the powerful V Corps (HQ Vittorio Veneto) is responsible for guarding the flatter ground towards the coast, and its formations and units are disposed in depth along the approaches to Venice.

The Italian strategy is to hold the ground well forward, so as to exploit the obstacle value of the mountainous terrain along the borders with Yugoslavia and Austria. Here the main defence will be offered by armoured units, moving at speed from one hull-down position to another, and erupting in periodic counter-attacks. *Alpini* and helicopter-borne infantry will operate against the enemy flanks, and the valley floors will be saturated by fire and obstructed with demolitions.

If the Italians are pushed into the plains to the south-west, they will disperse into company-sized all-arms teams, which will seek to arrange tank killing-zones in the chequerboard landscape of towns, farm buildings, vegetation and irrigation canals.

Topographical studies, commissioned by the government, indicate that the medium tank will be Italy's most effective weapon in these two main types of terrain.

We shall now pause briefly at some of the more interesting sectors of the north-eastern frontier. The only war fought in this theatre in the twentieth century was the contest of 1915–18 between Italy and the Austro-Hungarian empire, since when the political and physical geography has greatly altered, and the art of war has undergone a transformation. Nevertheless, the climate and the basic structure of the land are unchanged, and they will continue to exercise a powerful influence on military operations.

Heavy snow is inimical to mechanised operations of all kinds, especially when it lies on wooded and steeply sloping ground, and on the north-east Italian theatre heights above 1,000 metres are likely to remain under snow from October to the second half of April. In many years the low ground becomes waterlogged in the season of the autumn and winter rains, and the course of the rivers is so short that even in high summer a spell of heavy rain in the mountains will cause rapid and unpredictable rises in the water level. Mists are slow to disperse in the mountain valleys and along the rivers, which favours the use of chemical weapons, and facilitated surprise on many occasions in the First World War.

The Gorizia Gap

The coastal plain at the northern corner of the Adriatic extends for just over twenty kilometres from the mountains near Gorizia to the Gulf of Trieste near Duino. It was known to the Ancients as the Barbarian Gate, and it represents in every way the most vulnerable sector of Italy's frontiers, being accessible from Yugoslavia by way of Ljubljana (Laibach) and Rijeka (Fiume), and offering the only terrain for mass armoured operations in the border regions.

At the present time the Gorizia Gap is traversed by a motorway and a network of highways, which puts a high value on the defensive potential of the remaining features of the ground. The one continuous frontal obstacle is the lower Isonzo River, which here runs through Italian territory. In front of the Isonzo stands an isolated kidney-shaped hill (Monte San Michele), and on the northern edge of the plain the town of Gorizia (Görz) is embraced by tongues of high ground reaching down from the limestone plateau of Carso (Karst). This upland lies within Yugoslav territory, and was notorious in the First World War as a bleak and waterless place, baking under the summer sun, or swept by the icy *Bora* mountain wind.

The upper Isonzo and the Julian and Carnic Alps

Upstream from Gorizia the Italian border retreats to about five kilometres to the west of the Isonzo, and follows a twisting ridge which leads north under the shadow of the Carnic Alps. The continuity is broken by a number of entries, like the one to the west of Kobarid (Caporetto, Karfreit), where Army Group Stein effected its devastating penetration of the rear of the Italian positions on 24 October 1917. North of Tolmin (Tolmino, Tolmein) the Julian Alps give most of the advantage of the high ground to forces on the eastern side of the Isonzo, and the towering peak of the Krn (2,245 metres) dominates the upper reaches of the Isonzo valley. The Austrians held this bank of the river in the First World War, and withstood no less than eleven Italian offensives along their Isonzo positions between 1915 and 1917.

Near the headwaters of the Isonzo the borders of Italy, Yugoslavia and Austria meet in an interesting cluster of passes. The Predil Pass gives an entry on the Italo-Yugoslav frontier. The no less historic Malborghetto passage covers the back entry to Gemona, and leads to Tarvisio, from where roads branch to Yugoslavia and across the great wall of the Carnic Alps (Karawanken) to Austria.

It is clear that the frontier line does not run very favourably from the Italian point of view. However, the Italian strategic position would be improved immeasurably by pre-emptive advances across the borders. The Soviets' approach through Croatia and Slovenia would be severely embarrassed if they found that the nodal road junction of Ljubljana was occupied by NATO forces or otherwise unusuable. An even shorter move north across the Carnic Alps into Austria might just as effectively block the Soviet advance up the valley of the Drau (Drava) by way of Klagenfurt and Villach.

Rearward positions

The multiple channels of the Tagliamento represent the first line of defences behind the Gorizia Gap, and this historic role has been reinforced by the modern Italian army, which has installed tank turrets at a number of important points. The main defect of the Tagliamento position is its excessive length, which reaches 120 kilometres or more, owing to the necessity to cover the upper valley in the mountains as well as the coastal plain.

In November 1917, after the rout at Caporetto, the Italians were able to regroup their army along the line of the Piave, which they held until they launched their great offensive on 26 October 1918. The left flank of the Piave position is buttressed by the high Dolomites, which are accessible only by difficult passes, and enemies who try to sneak down the valley of the upper Piave by way of Belluno are stopped short by the massif of Monte Grappa.

In the plain the course of the Piave amounts to less than eighty kilometres. The left or northern flank rests on Monte Grappa and the free-standing Montello hill, while the right is supported by the lagoon of Venice. The river itself is a considerable barrier, coursing rapidly through a number of beds and being passable only by boats. Treviso provides an excellent centre of communications from the rear, but it is unfortunate that a programme of road improvement has presented the Italians with the need to guard two autostradas across the Piave as well as three major highways.

At the beginning of the twentieth century the old Austrian frontier bulged south to within less than forty kilometres of the north Italian plain near Verona, and South Tyrol formed a heavily fortified outer bastion of the Habsburg Empire. The result was very heavy fighting in the First World War in the Lessinic Alps and on the plateaux of Asiago and the Sette Comuni.

Italy gained the South Tyrol (Alto Adige) in 1919, and the

modern Italian frontier runs about 130 kilometres to the north of the old demarcation, all the way up to the Brenner Pass. The Italians now have a high degree of security on this flank, unless the Soviets make a dash down the Val Pusteria, or something goes very badly wrong for NATO in southern Germany.

The tenable positions on the north-east Italian plain have therefore acquired much greater depth than in the First World War. Before Soviet forces can reach the Italian heartland they must advance through the successive lines of the Brenta River, the Monti Berici and the Euganean Hills, the Adige, and finally the Po and its left-bank tributaries.

SPAIN

Area:	504,750 square kilometres
Population:	39,500,000
Army:	3 divisions, 3 separate brigades

SPAIN AND THE ALLIANCE

The French historian Michelet declared that Africa began at the Pyrenees, and it is undeniable that Spain has always been recognised as something which stands apart from the other countries of Europe. Spain's integration into the geopolitical system of the West has therefore been an unpredictable and uneven process, and at the time of writing (1985) it is impossible to tell whether Spain will continue as a NATO ally or revert to neutrality.

In 1953 a series of three basing agreements with the United States aligned Spain for the first time with the West. A bi-lateral treaty with France in 1970 linked the two national air defence systems, and in 1976 a very comprehensive Treaty of Friendship and Co-operation with the Americans gave formal recognition to the 'contribution of Spain to the security of the West'. For a time political developments inside Spain were equally encouraging. General Franco died in 1975, which made the possibility of Spain joining NATO more acceptable to the European members, and constitutional government was restored three years later. Finally Spain was admitted as a political member of NATO in 1982.

In October 1982, very shortly after Spain joined NATO, the Socialist leader Felipe Gonzalez was voted into power with an overwhelming popular mandate, and once more everything was thrown into doubt. Gonzalez had already pledged himself to submit the continuing membership to a referendum (to take place in March 1986, before the publication of this book), and meanwhile the question of integrating Spain into NATO's military command was left in abeyance.

Spain would be a very awkward object to fit into the alliance as a military member. Its arrival would upset established interests among the existing members, demand a fundamental reshaping of the antiquated Spanish army, and compel NATO strategists to find something useful for the Spanish to do.

A Portuguese vice-admiral is in charge of the upgraded IBER-LANT command (see p. 197), and the Portuguese are determined to defend this privilege against any Spanish take-over. Similarly, any Spanish administrative empire-building will cause difficulties with the French in the Bay of Biscay, and with the British over Gibraltar.

One of NATO's most important interests in the matter is to make sure that a close surveillance is kept on the busy nineteen-kilometre-wide Strait of Gibraltar, which is the outlet of the Soviet Black Sea Fleet. Shipping movements are monitored from the underground British command centre in the rock of Gibraltar, and the appropriate intelligence is forwarded to NATO headquarters in Naples, Lisbon, Brussels and London.

Spain, as a fully-fledged member of NATO, would have to accelerate the modernisation of her armed forces. The difficulties here have much in common with those encountered by other Mediterranean countries. On 5 January 1984 King Juan Carlos appointed Admiral A.A. Lucini as Spain's first proper Chief of Defence Staff. The choice of a sailor was interesting, for it signified a break with the inward-looking ethos of the Spanish army, whose leadership was traditionally devoted to upholding the ideal of a unitary and very conservative Spain (It is not without relevance that the single armoured division, the *Brunete*, is stationed in the heart of Spain just outside Madrid – in other words conveniently on hand for political intervention in the capital.) In 1980 the updating of the army had begun in accordance with a DEMA, or Plan for Territorial Demarcation, but the progress was inevitably delayed by the existence of the large and elderly officer corps. The Spanish army had in fact been heavily over-officered ever since the close of the Peninsular War in 1813, and it still had more generals than the rest of European NATO put together.

The Spanish air force and navy are by far the most outgoing of the armed services. Modernising the air force has required little more than some very expensive purchases of aircraft. The navy, however, is confronted with the block obsolescence of its warships, which is much more difficult to remedy.

THE MILITARY ROLES OF SPAIN

Africa and the western Mediterranean

One of the inherited geopolitical tasks of the Spanish armed forces is to safeguard the glacis towards North Africa. The Spanish cannot ignore the unbridled ambitions of the Libyan leadership, the rise of Moroccan and Algerian air power, and the acquisition by Algeria of a powerful short-range fleet.

The Spaniards have abandoned the colonial outpost of the Spanish Sahara, but they still own the Canary Islands off the African shore, and they hang on to their two ancient enclaves on the Mediterranean coast of Morocco at Ceuta and Melilla (something that is forgotten when there is Spanish outrage at the British presence in Gibraltar).

The French present themselves as the most obvious partner for Spain in southern waters. French interest in the Mediterranean was rekindled in 1975 (see p. 153), and together the French and Spanish navies might help to rescue Italy from its partial isolation and safeguard the interests of NATO on the southern flank.

The American bases

By the middle 1980s Spain had already served for three decades as a base for American power in southern Europe, and the relevant agreements were last renewed in July 1982. Spain is the home of the American 16th Air Force, which has a fighter wing and a supply base at Torrejón field near Madrid, and runs an important air-to-air missile training base at Zaragoza in the north-east of the country. Since 1956 the port of Rota near Cadiz has given the Sixth Fleet its most accessible harbour on the European side of the Atlantic. The facilities here are geographically more secure than those at Naples, and yet the nearby Strait of Gibraltar is deep enough to permit the passage of submerged American nuclear-powered submarines into the Mediterranean.

Spain as a bridge to the Old World

In support of NATO activity in the eastern Atlantic the most

valuable contribution the Spanish could make would not be by their
venerable navy, but from opening up territorial waters and airspace
and further facilities on land, especially in the Canary Islands. The
Canary group not only lies right next to the established shipping
lanes off West Africa, but offers a landfall for the sea and air passage
of the central Atlantic from North America and the Caribbean – a
route that promises to be of very great strategic importance in
wartime (p. 137).

A number of Spanish strategists have been emboldened to propose
that Spain might provide a way station for the movement of American forces to the Gulf (Sanchez-Gijon, 1981, 49). The Americans
will probably be unwilling to rely too much on this facility. In
October 1973 Spain along with other Western European countries
denied the United States permission to use the American air bases on
their territory to ferry munitions to the hard-pressed Israelis. Possibly this experience encouraged the Americans to embark on building up their 'in theatre' logistical support in the Indian Ocean (see
p. 122).

Spain and the land war in Europe

It requires some effort to imagine how Spain might help to defend
Europe against overland attack. Possibly a battalion might be
attached to the ACE Mobile Force, or elements of the Spanish Rapid
Intervention Forces might arrive somewhere on the Central Front.
There is a precedent of sorts in the Second World War, when the
Spanish Blue Division served alongside the Germans near Lenin-
grad.

Both Spanish and Portuguese strategists have proposed that the
Iberian peninsula should act as a rearward support for NATO,
supplying the depth which is so deficient on the Central Front,
furnishing secure lines of communication, receiving damaged aircraft, and – if the worse comes to the worst – offering the Pyrenees as
a highly defensible line behind which the West might recruit its
forces for a counter-attack (Gomes Tardoso, 1980, 86; Sanchez-
Gijon, 1981, 46; Suarez de la Hidalga, 1982, 82).

Conceivably the Iberian writers are inspired by the example of the
celebrated Lines of Torres Vedras, which were built by Wellington
during his strategic defensive north of Lisbon in 1810–11. In more
modern times the closest parallel is that of the *réduit breton*, which
was mooted in the exciting month of May 1940 as a 'vast entrenched
camp into which shattered French forces might withdraw to reorga-

nise. Within this defence zone, the French Government would continue to function, pending the arrival of British reinforcements and, possibly, of American aid. The zone would then become a springboard for offensive operations'.

Churchill gave this scheme his serious consideration, but he finally rejected it on the advice of General Sir Alan Brooke. A comparable 'Iberian redoubt' would almost certainly be unacceptable to NATO today. Things would indeed be at a sorry pass if Western forces were ever driven to hiding behind the Pyrenees. Meanwhile talk of this kind in NATO official circles would smack of defeatism and betray a lack of confidence in the sacrosanct principle of forward defence in Germany.

CHAPTER 8

Western Partners and Peripheries

PORTUGAL

Area:	92,072 square kilometres
Population:	10,280,000
Army:	1 brigade, 15 regiments, 3 separate battalions

Portugal enjoys the status of a founding member of NATO, and its citizens are folk of a decidedly Atlantic outlook. It would therefore be something of an outrage to consider the Portuguese as components of a Southern Flank alongside the Turks, Greeks, Italians and Spaniards. All the same, Portuguese thinking shares many of the geopolitical perceptions of Spain when these two countries reflect on their relationships with the world.

For many years the Portuguese, like the Spanish, lived under the authoritarian rule of an austere and conservative leader, in this case Prime Minister Dr Antonio D'Oliveira Salazar (1932–70).

After Salazar died Portugal underwent a period of political turmoil (1974–6), during which the membership of NATO virtually lapsed and Portugal abandoned her colonies in Africa, where the campaigns against guerrillas in Angola, Mozambique and Portuguese Guinea had absorbed almost the whole of the Portuguese military effort since the early 1960s. Relatively stable constitutional government emerged in 1976, and slowly the Portuguese began to feel their way back into NATO. A NATO-assigned army brigade was set up in 1978, and in 1980 the Portuguese began to participate in nuclear planning and once more joined NATO exercises.

For the moment it seems that the contribution of Portugal to the alliance will be characteristic of those members like Iceland or Denmark, who are more important for being where they are than for what they do.

Modern Portuguese strategists like to identify the military vocation of their country with the concept of 'Atlanticity', which is based on commanding a 'Portuguese Strategic Triangle' which stretches from the archipelagoes of Madeira and the Azores to the mainland. Through this vast area run sea lines of communication from the Gulf and South Africa to the Western world, and from North America to the Mediterranean. Altogether two-thirds of Western Europe's imports of oil and raw materials must make the passage of these waters. The Triangle acquires additional importance during hostilities as an alternative to the north Atlantic sea lanes (see pp. 137, 194), and in time of peace the facilities on the Azores and Madeira help NATO to monitor the movements of Soviet shipping.

The history of the military establishments on the Azores dates back to 1943, when Churchill prevailed on Salazar to grant base facilities to the Allies. The Azores were used so extensively that they became known as the 'Grand Central Station of the Atlantic', and after the war the British base on Terceira Island passed into the hands of the Americans. Lajes Field on Terceira is still important to the Americans as an aerial refuelling stop, but their continuing right of access depends on delicate negotiations with the Portuguese.

The second leg of the triangle is the archipelago of Madeira, where the military facilities are on Porto Santo Island. On the Portuguese mainland, the third leg of the triangle, NATO maritime reconnaissance planes are able to refuel at Ovar, in the south of the country, and the port of Lisbon holds stores of petrol, oil and ammunition which have been deposited for the use of the warships of the 'declared nations' Britain and the United States.

Portugal's 'Atlanticity' has been institutionalised in the command structure of NATO. The Portuguese mainland actually falls under the overall authority of the Supreme Allied Commander Atlantic, and in 1967 Portugal and the waters to the south and west were constituted as IBERLANT, one of SACLANT's subordinate commands. In 1982 there was talk of a Spanish takeover, but at the time of writing IBERLANT remains under Portuguese control.

FRANCE, THE UNKNOWN PARTNER

Area:	543,965 square kilometres
Population:	55,170,000
Army:	About 15 divisions

GEOPOLITICAL CHARACTER

France is a country of generally advantageous shape, size and situation. The national territory makes up an irregular quadrilateral measuring 650 by 650 kilometres, and amounts to almost the size of Britain, West Germany and Benelux combined. By European standards the population is small, in relation to the area, and in the nineteenth and early twentieth centuries demographically minded French strategists were worried by the knowledge that the population of united Germany was so much greater. Since the Second World War these fears have been set at rest by the cordial relations obtaining between the French and West German governments, and also (though nobody will admit it) by the division of Germany.

The French body politic was one of the earliest centralised states of Europe, and (outside Corsica) local separatism is enfeebled by metropolitan culture, a very tight bureaucracy and the inroads of high technology. If France is poorly endowed with mineral wealth, this is a problem she shares with many countries of the West, and one which has been ameliorated by nuclear and hydroelectric power.

The strategic role of France is historically active and prominent. In the wars of Louis XIV and Napoleon the French were able to exploit interior lines in order to concentrate their forces in whatever direction was most advantageous – whether in the Low Countries, Germany, northern Italy or Spain. The French also have an outlook on the Channel, the open Atlantic and the Mediterranean, and France is inevitably a sea power as well as a land power, though striking the right balance between the two vocations has often proved very difficult.

FRANCE AND NATO

France is still a member of NATO. The confusion on this point derives from the dramatic events of 1966, when President de Gaulle withdrew France from the integrated command structure of the alliance, and required all foreign powers to vacate their bases on national territory (see p. 140). However, France remains a fully paid-up political member, and she is fully committed to the central Article 5 of the treaty of alliance (the one about an attack on any partner being considered an attack on all).

Over the years the French have preserved a remarkable internal consensus about the necessity of armed strength, and indeed in defence matters the left-wing politicians have proved to be some of the most hard-headed of the lot, which contrasts notably with the situation in Britain. It is now largely irrelevant whether France decides to rejoin the overt NATO structure of command or not.

France and her allies keep up contacts at every other official level, and French military men participate very actively in NATO exercises and joint planning.

FRENCH MILITARY ROLES

Intervention overseas

On the global scale there is no necessary coincidence of interests between France and other individual nations of the capitalist world. In the distant Pacific the Australians and New Zealanders are incensed by the nuclear tests conducted by the French at Muroroa Atoll. France in the early 1980s was not afraid to trumpet the success of the French-made Exocet missiles in the Falklands War, which offended the sensibilities of the British, and French weapons continued to pour into Iraq, regardless of the reservations expressed by the Americans. The French in their turn resented the growing influence of the United States in former French colonies. At the same time the very high level of French interest in regions of Africa and Asia helps to reduce the risk of NATO having to assume formal 'out of area' responsibilities, and complements the new American effort in the Indian Ocean.

In Africa the French have not hesitated to stage military interventions in Zaire and Chad. There are small French units deployed in Senegal, the Ivory Coast and Gabon (usefully arranged along the coast of West Africa), in their power centre the Central African Republic, and in Djibouti at the mouth of the Red Sea. The French-owned and French-garrisoned territories overseas include the islands of Martinique in the Caribbean, Réunion in the Indian Ocean, and Tahiti and New Caledonia in the Pacific.

In addition to the troops already stationed overseas, the French are in the process of building up a *Force d'Action Rapide* (FAR), which has a planned establishment of 47,000 personnel. The FAR is intended for speedy intervention in the many areas of French strategic concern beyond Europe, as well as on the Central Front or the NATO flanks.

Nuclear forces

For a comparatively small power, France has an unusually comprehensive arsenal of nuclear weapons. These too lend indirect support to the alliance. French governments have never accepted the official

NATO doctrine of Flexible Response (see p. 259). Rather they have made it clear that a threat to French 'vital interests' will be answered very smartly by a warning shot by tactical nuclear weapons, and that if these fail to produce the desired effect the use of strategic weapons will unfailingly follow. The 'vital interest' was once assumed to be the security of the Rhine, but by the 1980s it seemed to have marched a good way further east.

The tactical nuclear weapons in question are airborne bombs, and ground-launched missiles. The Hades, the newest of the army's missiles, is credited with a range of at least 320 kilometres, which will permit it to be fired from the west side of the Rhine and still hit targets beyond the Inner German Border.

The French strategic nuclear triad consists of:

– Short-range (100-kilometre) missiles launched by aircraft.
– Land-based S-3 missiles, whose range of 3,500 kilometres takes in almost the whole of European Russia. They are installed in two batteries of nine silos each in the lonely region of the Plateau d'Albion, which lies between Avignon, Sault and Apt in south-eastern France.
– A flotilla of nuclear missile submarines, based on L'Île Longue outside Brest.

An all-out nuclear exchange would certainly involve the destruction of France. However, the government hopes that the Soviets are persuaded that France would not go under before it had succeeded in 'tearing a limb off the Soviet Union'. Meanwhile the French independent nuclear deterrent sows a seed of doubt in the minds of Soviet planners. It might not be impossible for the Soviets to form a reasoned judgment about the nuclear responses of the Americans or the British, but it would be a foolhardy Russian who gambled on what the French might do if they were pushed too far.

Strategic depth in Europe

NATO's Central Front in Europe is notoriously thin, and the availability of French territory in time of emergency gives the alliance a much more useful kind of depth than the commodity offered by the Iberian strategists. There can be little doubt that detailed contingency plans have been made to permit NATO allies to store fuel in hardened bunkers in France, and to enjoy access to French airfields and ports. The Americans in particular will benefit from a new covered communication running perpendicularly to the

Central Front, as a supplement to the dreadfully exposed right-angled supply line which enters by way of the North Sea ports. French assistance must also benefit NATO's lateral cohesion in Europe. French national territory extends across the rear of Belgium, Luxembourg and West Germany, and also gives the alliance its only means of overland communication with Italy, which is otherwise cut off by neutral Switzerland and Austria.

The French conventional forces, somewhat neglected by de Gaulle and his immediate successors, began to acquire new strength from about the middle 1970s. In this process the Gaullist freedom of action has not been cast aside; instead it has been sublimated in order to make the French armed services available to NATO as an uncommitted reserve.

The complement of the air force will be stabilised at about 450 modern aircraft. The navy is a balanced force of attack submarines, surface combat vessels, and floating and land-based maritime aviation. The naval bases are at Cherbourg, Brest and Lorient on the north and west coasts, and at Toulon on the Mediterranean. Formerly the main force was held in north-western waters, but in 1975 the French strengthened their fleet in the Mediterranean to make up for the impending departure of the British. 'This demonstrated with customary French neatness a realistic appreciation of the realities of life [and] the danger of a power vacuum in this – to France – vital sea' (Hill-Norton, 1978, 75).

The remodelling of the French army dates from 1976, and it now includes the fast-moving FAR (see p. 199), and the First Army, which has been redesigned to support NATO on the Central Front. This work is still far from complete, since the French are lavishly equipped with medium and light tanks and armoured cars, but are lacking in heavy modern main battle tanks.

It perhaps comes as something of a surprise to discover that the French have a powerful force in Germany. From July 1963 the French garrisons in West Germany (a relic of the old Zone of Occupation), were withdrawn from forward positions in Bavaria, leaving a void on CENTAG's southern flank which has still not been completely filled (see p. 302). However, the French retained the legal right to keep troops on German soil through a bi-lateral Status of Forces agreement with West Germany (see p. 146), and in the 1980s the powerful French II Corps in south-west Germany has come to figure in NATO calculations as a mobile reserve on the Central Front. Its headquarters are at Baden-Baden, and it is equipped with more than 500 tanks, which are organised in three small armoured divisions.

Between 1984 the French III Corps was redeployed from the neighbourhood of Paris to that of Lille near the Belgian border, from where it will be in a position to cover the northern flank of the national territory against a Warsaw Pact breakthrough on the northern plain. The I Corps, the last component of the First Army, remains in position in eastern France.

These deployments help to confirm the impression that the French are to be considered NATO's effective second line in Europe.

WEST GERMANY (FEDERAL REPUBLIC OF GERMANY)

Area: 248,687 square kilometres
Population: 61,400,000 (incl. W.Berlin)
Army: 12 divisions, 12 Territorial Army brigades

West Germany is of supreme importance to NATO. This country is located along the dividing line between the two main geopolitical systems of the world, and is an immediate target of potential Warsaw Pact attack. West Germany is also the most wealthy state of Europe, and provides the Western alliance with by far its most powerful ground forces on the continent. Oddly enough, it is difficult to uncover any specifically West German geopolitics, so strongly are they influenced by the history of the first half of the twentieth century, and so closely are they entangled with the alliance strategies which will come under review in a later chapter.

WEST GERMANY AND ITS ALLIES

The Federal Republic emerged as a sovereign state between 1949 and 1952. The new nation joined NATO on 5 May 1955, and its rearmament began in November the same year.

Formal restrictions on West German armed strength are enshrined in documents like the Brussels Treaty of 1948, the Paris Agreement of October 1954, and the Fundamental Law of the West German constitution. The final limitations on the acquisition of long-range conventional armament were lifted in 1984, but West Germany is still forbidden to manufacture nuclear, chemical or biological weapons. The Germans have no general staff, and they must make no preparations for offensive action, nor seek to alter their boundaries by force. The ceiling of the Field Army is fixed at twelve divisions, and the 'layer cake deployment' (see p. 270) of the NATO corps on the Central Front makes it impossible for the Germans to concentrate their army in a single mass.

West Germany has lived since its inception as a model ally and a model Western European democratic state. Its armed forces were not created on its own initiative, but summoned forth by NATO allies in order to hold the line on the Central Front. For all this, the admiration and respect which West Germany commands in international circles are flavoured with a tincture of disquiet. This unease, which is unfounded, unfair and harmful to the Western alliance, is not easy to trace to its source. It cannot arise from fear of German revanchism or military force. Probably it has more to do with the belief that a reunited Germany would be a superpower in European terms, and more than the international system could handle. 'Both halves of Germany separately have established themselves as major economic powers. In comparison with their united strength, the rest of Europe would be dwarfed almost as completely as it is today by the United States' (Howard, 1984, 188).

We are left with a fundamental contradiction between one of the declared wishes of the NATO alliance, which is a reunited Germany, and the reservations (however unjustified) of individual members. In 1984 no less a personage than the Italian Foreign Minister Giulio Andreotti blurted out that 'Pan-Germanism must be overcome. There are two German states, and they must remain two.'

THE ARMED FORCES

History and geography have combined to focus the West German military effort to a remarkable degree. The Soviet Union, the United States and leading third-rank powers like Britain and France all have to make provision against a variety of contingencies, but West Germany's 'out of area' activity is confined to isolated forays by the navy into distant waters, and rendering military and economic aid to deserving countries. Virtually all of West German military resources may therefore be concentrated on training and equipping the services for operations in Central Europe and inshore waters.

The small but efficient West German navy is a predominantly professional force, and it is particularly well armed with small coastal submarines. The naval bases are at Flensburg-Murwick, Olpenitz, Eckernförde and Kiel on the Baltic, and at Wilhelmshaven on the North Sea. The necessary air cover is extended from the land bases of the naval air arm. The air force proper has about 500 combat planes.

The West German ground forces are lavishly and expensively armed, and their complement of 4,250 main battle tanks is the largest of any NATO contingent in Europe, not excluding the Americans. The establishment of the Field Army is held at the legal limit of twelve divisions, but a clause of the Paris Agreement has allowed the Germans to build up a powerful Territorial Army, which is assuming a direct combat role in addition to its main responsibilities for rear area security. The Territorial Army remains largely under German national control, independent of NATO, and (unlike the British Territorials) it is made up of professional soldiers and conscripts, just like the Field Army.

The training of the West German army is as impressive as its equipment. However, the long-term effectiveness of the German forces is threatened by the rapid decline in the birthrate which set in from the middle 1960s and leaves the average West German woman with an average of 1.4 children. West Germany still has the largest population in European NATO, but the reserve of manpower of military age is drying up fast. In 1984 the annual requirement of 250 conscripts was drawn without difficulty from the pool of about 310,000 young men, but by 1992 the number available will have shrunk to 160,000, which will add to the difficulty of defending the Central Front by conventional means.

STRATEGIC ISSUES

Forward Defence

The interests of West Germany have had a very strong influence on the doctrine of Forward Defence (see p. 260), which NATO embraced in 1967 as one of the foundations of its strategy for the Central Front. Forward Defence was made physically possible by the fact that West German forces were now at hand to thicken up the order of battle. More importantly, it paid regard to the West German desire to hold the scene of conflict as far distant as possible from the core areas of the national territory. The tenets of Forward Defence have remained holy ever since. In 1982 the West German Defence Minister Manfred Wörner reaffirmed to some of his senior officers: 'The principle of Forward Defence is the heart of our strategy and is vitally important to our state and the people who live in it. Alternative concepts which abolish the principle of Forward Defence and substitute a war of attrition waged in our territory are unacceptable.'

Nuclear weapons and the American commitment

Less welcome to German strategists was another shift in NATO thinking in the 1960s, this time away from the doctrine of Massive Retaliation, whereby the United States threatened to meet Eastern aggression at any level by the use of its strategic nuclear forces. Massive Retaliation was a crude all-or-nothing strategy, which ceased to make sense when the Soviets acquired the means to retaliate massively in their turn. It had nevertheless been a source of comfort to the West Germans, for it had amounted to an unreserved American commitment to the defence of German territory.

The new policy was that of Flexible Response (see p. 259), which by admitting the possibility of a conventional phase of combat, or indeed of an all-conventional war, no longer put the American heartland immediately at risk if the Soviets ever crossed the Inner German Border. Many Germans believe that the American pledge to the security of their country has been weakened accordingly. It was the Socialist cabinet of Helmut Schmidt which in December 1979 acceded to the 'dual-track' agreement with its allies (see p. 23), and invited the Americans to station cruise missiles and Pershing IIs on German territory. The German hope was to advance America's nuclear frontier once more to the IGB, but the motivation behind the deal has been represented differently by the movement for unilateral nuclear disarmament, which claims that the Americans were only too delighted to exploit this opportunity to use West Germany as a launching-pad for possible nuclear war against the Soviet Union.

The Benelux countries

LUXEMBOURG

Area:	2,586 square kilometres
Population:	367,000
Army:	1 battalion, 1 company

BELGIUM

Area:	30,519 square kilometres
Population:	9,900,000
Army:	2 division equivalents

THE NETHERLANDS

Area:	33,938 square kilometres
Population:	14,500,000
Army:	3 division equivalents

The Grand Duchy of Luxembourg is a little country shaped like a pear, and measures about seventy kilometres from north to south and forty from east to west. This territory holds a NATO air base, and saw the passage of significant German forces during the offensives of May 1940 and December 1944.

The Luxembourg army consists of a single though rather good airmobile battalion, which is committed to the ACE Mobile Force. For legal reasons all the NATO joint AWACS aircraft are given Luxembourg registration, which endows the Grand Duchy with an air armada of seemingly miraculous size. The reigning Grand Duke is an ex-officer of the British Guards.

Belgium and the still more densely crowded Netherlands share an almost identical strategic environment. Their territory is of great importance to NATO in time of emergency, for ports like Zeebrugge, Antwerp and Rotterdam will receive reinforcements and supplies from Britain and the United States, and the men and material will be forwarded overland to the Central Front. Belgium in addition houses the peacetime political and military headquarters of NATO, and much of the alliance's war effort will be directed from command centres on Belgian and Dutch territory.

The two air forces have been equipped with modern aircraft, and the navies own a useful complement of mine countermeasures vessels. The latter are needed to help to clear the approaches to the North Sea ports, where the narrow shipping lanes, the shifting sands, the muddy and shallow waters, and the density of traffic all favour Soviet minelaying. Moreover, the Royal Dutch Marines are considered to be a very effective component of the NATO mobile reserves, and train regularly with their British counterparts.

In other dimensions the Belgian and Dutch effort has been less than wholehearted. In the early 1980s the Belgians left an important gap in NATO's anti-aircraft coverage when they disbanded four of their eight squadrons of Nike-Hercules missiles before they had made any provision to acquire modern Patriots in their place. The Belgians at least stood by their commitment to station forty-eight cruise missiles at Florennes, twenty kilometres west of Dinant in Namur province. In June 1984, however, the Dutch Parliament reneged on a resolution of 1982, and deferred the deployment of their quota of forty-eight missiles at Woensdrecht, in the south-west of the country, until the Dutch could be certain that the Soviets were continuing to build up their force of SS-20s. On 1 November 1985 a centre-right coalition cabinet finally took the plunge and decided in favour of accepting the missiles. As some kind of compensation, the government went on to announce that it must now drop two of its remaining NATO nuclear roles, those relating to nuclear depth charges and airborne nuclear bombs.

Most embarrassing of all for NATO, in operational terms, has been the failure of the Belgians and Dutch to live up to their promise to keep adequate forces on the Central Front. On paper the two countries each appear to have a full army corps deployed behind important sectors of the Inner German border (see p. 289), but in fact the bulk of the forces are held back in the homelands.

GREAT BRITAIN

Area:	244,754 square kilometres
Population:	56,020,000
Army:	4 full divisions, 2 brigades in N. Ireland, home-based defence and rapid intervention forces

THE CONTRACTION OF BRITAIN'S IMPERIAL AND MILITARY ROLE

No other nation in European NATO is forced to make so many geopolitical choices as Britain, poised as she is between the strategic systems of the continental mainland and the world oceans. This multiplicity of options worked mostly to Britain's advantage as long as seaborne mobility had clear advantages over land transport, when Britain had no industrial competitors on the continent, and regional powers had yet to arise in Asia.

The foundations of empire were undercut as long ago as the 1850s, when continental Europe began to embrace the Industrial Revolution, and by 1910 British industrial production had sunk below that of Germany, and amounted to less than half that of the United States. As the twentieth century wore on, many of Britain's former opportunities were clearly established as embarrassments. Again and again Britain was compelled to conform with external forces, such as those represented by the crisis of the pound sterling in 1967, or by the humiliations heaped on the British by Japanese arms in 1941–2, or by nominal American allies at the time of the Suez expedition in October–November 1956.

British India was dissolved in 1947, which detracted from the relevance of many of the bases and possessions which Britain still retained in the Indian Ocean and south-east Asia, and Prime Minister Macmillan's celebrated 'wind of change' speech in February 1960 was followed by the end of British rule in Africa as state after state gained independence in rapid succession. The overseas military presence 'East of Suez' lingered for a short time longer, but the Defence White Papers of July 1967 and February 1968 precipitated the withdrawal of forces from Malaysia, Singapore and the Persian Gulf. Henceforward Britain's military effort was to be 'concentrated in Europe and the North Atlantic area'. More startling, perhaps, was the Defence White Paper of 1975, which not only terminated the Simonstown naval base agreement with South Africa, but ended the permanent British naval presence in the Mediterranean.

By the 1980s about 90 per cent of British military resources were committed directly or indirectly to NATO. However, Britain remains a world presence long after ceasing to be a world empire. Britain is a signatory of the South-East Asia Collective Defence Treaty, and the Five Power Defence Agreement with Australia, New Zealand, Malaysia and Singapore. The British have security responsibilities concerning Bermuda and a number of the Caribbean islands, Belize, St Helena and its dependencies, the British Antarctic Territory, the Chagos Archipelago, Pitcairn Island, and the foreign states of South Korea, Sri Lanka (Ceylon), Kenya, Oman, Qatar, Bahrain and the United Arab Emirates. The Americans, the former anti-imperialists, are now only too glad to avail themselves of British hospitality for United States military bases in locations like Bermuda, Ascension Island (one of the dependencies of St Helena in the South Atlantic) and Diego Garcia in the Chagos Archipelago.

In virtue of 'residual commitments' Britain still has forces stationed in Gibraltar, the sovereign base areas of Cyprus, Belize, Brunei, Hong Kong, and in the Falklands where the British re-established themselves by going to war with Argentina. 'The Falklands campaign of April–June 1982 was not military intervention, but rather the liberation and reoccupation of sovereign territory . . . to suggest that the Falklands experience supports arguments for an expanded surface fleet and a return to a major power-projection role beyond the North Atlantic is seriously to misunderstand some of the strategic lessons of the conflict and to underestimate the political and economic costs' (Wyllie, 1984, 96, 102). These penalties have been considerable, for precious assets of the Royal Navy were diverted to the South Atlantic, and the post-war garrison of the islands amounted to about 4,000 troops, who likewise could ill be spared from Europe.

Britain as a leader of the Commonwealth has influence and contacts in the 'Third World' independent of any system of military alliances. The English and foreign language broadcasts of the BBC command wide respect, in spite of enforced economies, and a British academic or vocational training is still part of the basic equipment of many professional men and women in African, Asian and West Indian countries, which engenders a goodwill that cannot be measured in purely monetary terms.

In historical perspective the essentials of British geopolitics have changed remarkably little over the centuries. The worldwide post-imperial interests are by no means to be underestimated, as we have noted. Moreover, some fundamental strategic arguments, which long preceded the British Empire, have been sharpened by new technologies and new systems of alliance.

THE DEFENCE OF THE HOME BASE

Air defence

Britain's primordial duty of self-defence no longer serves exclusively national interests, but concerns the ability of the Americans to support European NATO as a whole in time of emergency. In 1975 the task of securing the aerial approaches to Europe was entrusted to a new major subordinate command, that of the United Kingdom Air Defence Region (UKADR), whose area of responsibility extends from the Channel to the Faroes, and from the North Sea to well out into the Atlantic.

'The all-round threat to the United Kingdom is founded on the concept that more protracted conventional operations are now possible than seemed likely a few years ago, and the certainty in these circumstances of the United Kingdom being used not only as a staging post for reinforcements coming from the United States by sea and air but also as a main base for many of the US reinforcement aircraft' (Cairns, 1980, 20–1).

As a matter of routine Soviet long-range Tu-95 aircraft fly close to the fringes of British airspace, whether on intelligence-gathering missions or in transit to distant Cuba. It is now said that the threat has been greatly augmented by the new Backfire and Fencer aircraft, which have the theoretical ability to subject Britain to attack from every point of the compass. Here is a danger not only to the American staging bases, but to fields like the ones that were used extensively by the British during the reinforcement phase of Exercise Lionheart in September 1984, namely the RAF's two transport fields at Lyneham and Brize Norton, and the civilian airports at Heathrow (London), Gatwick, Luton, Manchester, Newcastle, Glasgow and Belfast.

In the 1980s Britain's chain of NADGE sites has been improved, and new radar stations have extended the early warning system to the north and west of the British Isles. The most important radar sites appear to be at Saxa Vord on the isle of Uist in the Shetlands, Benbecula in the Hebrides, Bishopscourt in Northern Ireland, and Hartland Point and Portreath in Cornwall. Stations extend down the east coast of Britain at Buchan (north of Aberdeen), Boulmer in Northumberland and Neatishead in Norfolk, and there is a further station inland in the Chilterns at High Wycombe.

Contracts were placed for Nimrod AWACS aircraft to replace the aged Shackletons as aerial radar pickets, though deliveries were delayed on account of some difficulty with the computers. The ground-based anti-aircraft missile defence was considerably thick-ened up at the same period. Short-range Rapier missiles defend the American air bases and the British fields at Leuchars and Los-siemouth, while the modernised long-range Bloodhounds are de-ployed in a line at Bawdsey, North Coates, Wyton, Barkston Heath, West Raynham and Wattisham.

The air defence squadrons of the RAF are on constant alert to challenge any intrusions into airspace. The fighters are based at Wattisham in Suffolk, Coningsby and Binbrook in Lincolnshire, and the vital and busy field at Leuchars in north-east Scotland. Among the other British airfields, Marham and Honington are important as long-range conventional strike bases, while Culdrose, Yeovilton and Portland accommodate elements of the Fleet Air Arm when they are not on board ship.

Naval defence

During a large reinforcement operation of European NATO, the harbours on the British west coast will receive considerable quanti-ties of American supplies and forces, while those on the east and south-east coast, and especially Felixstowe, Harwich, Dover and Folkestone, will be busy forwarding British and American troops and equipment to the continent.

Next to providing Britain with her independent nuclear deterrent, the main job of the Royal Navy is to safeguard the movement of this shipping, and the British presently make up about 70 per cent of NATO naval forces on the maritime approaches to north-west Europe. NATO's effort in the region is managed by the British, and since 1966 the posts of commanding officer in the Channel and the Eastern Atlantic (see p. 142) have always been combined in the person of a British admiral, who has his peacetime headquarters at Northwood near London.

In the North Sea (see p. 206) the Royal Navy's base is at Rosyth, which is within a couple of days' steaming time of the North Cape of Norway. On the far side of the North Sea the corresponding bases of the NATO allies are at Bergen (Norway), Wilhelmshaven (West Germany), Den Helder and Flushing (the Netherlands) and Kallo, Ostend and Zeebrugge (Belgium).

The area of the Channel major command is very small by NATO standards, but it covers the southern part of the North Sea as well as the Channel proper, and it will be the scene of the most intense activity in wartime. Traffic passing up and down the main shipping lanes will intersect with that of the cross-Channel ferries. The Channel lends itself only too well to mining, like the North Sea. The deepest water is the long trench north of the Channel Islands, where the seabed descends to just over one hundred metres; elsewhere it is uncommon to find depths greater than seventy metres, and many of the waters are less than forty metres deep. Ground mines may therefore be employed over most of the Channel. The task of identifying and destroying these objects is complicated by the murky waters, the strong and frequent tides, and the wrecks which litter the seabed – conditions which also favour the operations of submarines, which would otherwise be at a disadvantage in such narrow and shallow waters.

Liverpool and the ports of the Firth of Clyde and the Bristol Channel will be significant as eastern abutments of the American Transatlantic bridge. These western waters have also acquired great importance in the intercontinental nuclear dimension, for the Firth of Clyde accommodates both the forward base of the American Poseidon nuclear missile submarines at Holy Loch, and the home of the four British Polaris submarines at Faslane.

The Firth of Clyde is a narrow dog-leg channel, and beyond the exit the submarines must still make the passage around Ireland – either turning right (north) between Scotland and Northern Ireland, or left by way of the North Channel, the Irish Sea and St George's Channel. There is in consequence a great deal of naval interest in the western channels. Joint NATO mine countermeasures exercises are frequently held there, and every now and then a peaceful trawler catches a very large mechanical fish and receives an unsolicited tow.

The necessary low-frequency signals (see p. 40) for the British submarines at sea are projected from powerful transmitters at Rugby in the Midlands, Criggion in Shropshire and Anthorn on the Solway Firth. Rosyth, on the east coast of Scotland, is an important base for destroyers, and has been chosen as the refitting (as opposed to operational) base for the British nuclear missile submarines into the next century.

Land defence

Some authorities do not entirely discount a direct attack on the British mainland. Large-scale amphibious or airborne assaults would be very dangerous and technically difficult for the Soviets. More feasible is a campaign of sabotage and assassination waged by Soviet special forces (*Spetsnaz*), who could be infiltrated into Britain by covert means. In the early 1980s the British government set up a small and experimental Home Service Force, to act as an auxiliary to the thinly spread regular and Territorial forces who would remain in Britain in wartime. This measure did not satisfy the demand of a number of recently retired senior officers, who believed that nothing short of a full citizen militia would be of any use.

IRELAND, NORTH AND SOUTH

Northern Ireland is a constitutional part of the United Kingdom, but since 1969 it has been safeguarded as such only with the help of a powerful contingent of the British Regular Army. From a peak of 21,000 troops in the early 1970s the military presence fell to under 10,000 in the middle 1980s, which still represents a very considerable diversion of force from NATO, amounting to the equivalent of almost one-fifth of the British garrison in Germany. Furthermore, as a bone of contention with the Irish Republic, the unresolved issue of Northern Ireland indirectly damages the Western alliance by obstructing any move to link the South with NATO.

Early in 1949, when NATO was in the process of conception, the Irish president De Valera rejected an informal approach from the Americans to join the league. However, Irish neutrality is not the product of centuries-old tradition, as in Switzerland, or imposed from without by treaty, as is the case in Austria and Finland, and the debate came to life again in the early 1980s, when several retired Irish army officers (as vocal as their counterparts in Britain) spoke out in favour of joining the alliance.

The effective but very small Irish armed forces could not be expected to make a direct contribution to NATO, except in token form. The real usefulness of Ireland as an ally or associate would come from its position, which extends Europe more than 300 kilometres into the North Atlantic.

In the First World War the whole of Ireland was still part of the United Kingdom, and without the use of Irish ports it is doubtful whether Britain could have survived the crisis of the U-boat campaign in 1917. Four years later Ireland was partitioned, but the British retained properties and rights at the bases of Berehaven, Queenstown (Cobh) and Lough Swilly. During the negotiations the Republican spokesman Michael Collins had given the assurance 'Of course you must have the ports, they are necessary for your life.' Afterwards the Irish facilities were signed away by Neville Chamberlain (one of the lesser-known of that man's masterstrokes), and in the Second World War Winston Churchill contemplated extreme political and military measures to regain the use of them. Churchill finally decided to repose his trust in the naval and air bases in Northern Ireland. 'Without them, Hitler would have won the second Battle of the Atlantic, and Britain, in Churchill's words, would have been confronted with "slavery or death" ' (Biggs-Davison, 1981, 44).

Ireland has acquired still greater potential importance towards the end of the twentieth century, for it offers NATO greater operational depth and the means of strengthening the 'Atlanticity' of the alliance. Access to Irish territory and airspace would certainly make it easier and safer for the Americans to reinforce continental NATO in an emergency. There can be little doubt that the alliance would be only too happy to avail itself of any invitation to overfly the Republic, set its planes down at Shannon and other airports, establish mobile 'gap filler' radars around the Irish coastline, and make use of the sheltered base of the south-west coast and the ports of the south and south-east.

It is possibly significant that a very large contingent of eighty Irish officers visited NATO's military headquarters in 1983, and that with the help of the EEC the Irish have been building microwave communications stations at Middletown (Co. Cork), Sligo and on Malin Head.

'THE BRITISH WAY IN WARFARE'

Over the centuries a number of strategic writers and military men have examined the geographical position of Britain, and persuaded themselves that it is costly and unnecessary to consign large British forces to wars on the continent. The Royal Navy, on the other hand, not only gives the British the mastery of the defensive moat of the Channel, but provides them with the means of injecting amphibious and light expeditionary forces into locations of strategic interest on the periphery of the European continent. Thus, while the continentals are massacring one another in their hundreds of thousands, the British are at liberty to engage in an elegant and effective form of warfare, uniquely suited to their geopolitical circumstances. The glimmerings of the notion are already present in the writings of Jonathan Swift, who opposed the commitment of the British army to the War of the Spanish Succession at the beginning of the eighteenth century. The ideas were developed by Julian Corbett, who by no means underestimated the importance of land warfare *per se* (*Some Principles of Maritime Strategy*, London, 1911), and in a more extreme form by Captain B.H. Liddell Hart (*The British Way in Warfare*, London, 1932).

With the arrival of the 1980s Britain still possessed the means of strategic projection in her reduced but still respectable navy, and the 'out of area' reserve provided by the 5th Airborne Brigade and the units of the Parachute Regiment, the SAS and the Royal Marines.

It now seemed to some British commentators that the best service that Britain could render to herself and the alliance would be to concentrate her limited finances on building up light intervention forces and her naval strength. Meanwhile 'it should . . . be the purpose of any sensible national strategy to ensure that "the main body of the enemy" is fought by somebody else' (Cable, 1983, 38; also Hill-Norton, 1978, 154; Longworth, 1983, *passim*). Inspired by the more extreme naval lobby a leading article in *The Times* (18 June 1984) went so far as to claim that the 'devotion to forward strategy and the so-called conventional options, which involve a large permanent garrison in the Rhine Army, is not dissimilar from the army's loyalty to the horse between the two World Wars'.

THE CONTINENTAL STRATEGY

Another tradition in British thought has argued with no less cogency that Britain is not just an island, but an island lying off a continent where the big and decisive battles have always been fought. Only by making a direct contribution to the struggle could Britain exercise a political and military influence on the outcome. Such was the conviction of the 'warmongering' Duke of Marlborough early in the eighteenth century, and of the Secretary of State for War Lord Haldane who refashioned the British army for continental intervention two hundred years later. Half way between these two periods the Duke of Wellington defended the costly military effort in the Iberian Peninsula, which was the only locality at that time where it was possible to engage large forces of the French. The Iron Duke argued that in the last resort it was better to fight the French on the continent than leave them free to attack Britain. 'Then indeed would commence an expensive contest; then would His Majesty's subjects discover what are the miseries of war, of which, by the blessing of God, they have hitherto had no knowledge; and the cultivation, and the beauty and the progress of the country and the virtue and happiness of its inhabitants would be destroyed' (to Lord Liverpool, 23 March 1811).

The original British commitment to the defence of West Germany dates from the London and Paris Agreements of October 1954, whereby the British undertook to maintain four army divisions and a tactical air force on the European continent until 1998, or such time as it proved necessary to withdraw this contingent on grounds of 'an acute overseas emergency' or 'too great a strain on the external finances of the United Kingdom'.

In its unreinforced state the British Army of the Rhine consists of about 56,800 troops (the 3,000 British troops in West Berlin are not counted as part of its establishment). The costs of BAOR are undoubtedly high. Britain took on her obligations in Germany when the West Germans were still recovering from the war and BAOR amounted to only about 14 per cent of the British Army. Now in the 1980s West Germany is an economic giant. The British commitment to Germany was slightly reduced in the later 1950s, but the overall size of the British Army has contracted much further still, so that BAOR now accounts for about one-third of the whole, or proportionately more than twice as much as in 1954. To the numbers of the troops we must add the 10,000 personnel of the RAF in Germany, and a train of some 80,000 wives and children together with all the supporting apparatus of housing, schools, hospitals and 25,000 locally employed Germans. The system of 'offset payments', by which the Germans shared some of the burden, was reduced over the years and finally expired in 1980, and much of the cost to Britain must be met in one of the hardest of the hard currencies. The return on all of this investment seems to be poor, since BAOR is outnumbered six to one by its West German allies, and outmatched in combat troops, armour and artillery by the Soviet Third Shock Army across the border.

In other dimensions the costs of withdrawing the garrison from Germany, in whole or in part, might prove to be higher still. There is a risk attached to arranging to have the main body of the enemy fought by 'somebody else'. In the Second World War the somebody else proved to be the Americans (who were no friends at that time of the British Empire), and the Soviets who proceeded to advance their strategic borders into the heart of Europe. Without forces on the spot in Germany, the British could well be reduced to being spectators of a war that was decided before reinforcements could arrive on the theatre, let alone before the activity of navies had time to take affect. In peacetime the presence of BAOR and its families is taken by continental allies as an important pledge of support, and it encourages the Americans to maintain their forces in West Germany. If the British pulled out, then the pressure within the United States to retrieve the American garrison would become very strong, and threaten to precipitate the dreaded 'decoupling' of America from Europe.

Even these arguments might be of little avail in the face of financial necessity. Britain's North Sea oil wealth has bought an economic stay of execution, but Britain's manufacturing base, like her merchant shipping, appears to be in irreversible decline, and the price of military equipment continues to rise at a rate well above that of inflation. The defence cuts in the 1960s and 1970s bit ever more painfully and closer to home, and if something more has to be sacrificed in the later 1980s and the 1990s it will inevitably be at the expense of a national interest that has hitherto been considered vital.

NUCLEAR FORCES

Britain's independent nuclear deterrent is invested in her flotilla of nuclear missile submarines, and the cost of keeping this force up to date has contributed to the difficulties in military finance. In 1980 the government decided to make provision against the approaching obsolescence of the Polaris/Chevaline force, and on 15 July of that year the Trident Accords arranged for the acquisition of Trident I (C-4) missiles with American help. This updating proved more expensive than was at first envisaged. In 1981 the Reagan Administration pressed ahead with the development of the more elaborate Trident II (D-5) missile, and the British fell into line for the sake of 'commonality'. Moreover, in the following years the dollar (in which many of the costs were to be paid) gained very heavily in strength against the pound sterling, which threw out the original calculations.

Quite separately from the British national nuclear forces and the American nuclear missile submarine base at Holy Loch, American weapons in Britain provide much of the nuclear umbrella which the United States extends over Europe. About 160 of the swing-wing F-111 low-level bombers are stationed at Lakenheath in Suffolk and Upper Heyford in Oxfordshire, from where they are capable of striking at targets as far distant as European Russia. Britain has also taken on board a generous share of the American cruise missiles. Ninety-six missiles are based at Greenham Common in Berkshire, and 1988 sees a further sixty-four being deposited at Molesworth in Cambridgeshire.

A nuclear war involving Britain is likely to prove a highly destructive affair in every respect. The accuracy of the British submarine-borne deterrent is inherently limited, which prevents the British from exercising much discrimination in their targets. Nor would an enemy be able to show much restraint, for Britain is a little island in which large civilian communities lie close alongside prime military objectives.

'THE UNSINKABLE AIRCRAFT CARRIER'

In the Second World War British national territory served as America's most important stepping stone to Europe, and at the time of writing Britain is still the principal component of the Atlanticity of NATO, functioning even now as a physical and psychological bridge between the Americans and the continent.

The watery barrier of the North Sea and the Channel lends the American bases in Britain more security than is available to their establishments in Central Europe, and the British have proved to be remarkably accommodating and undemanding hosts. Internal political stability has also helped to recommend Britain to the Americans. In 1984, however, a long tradition of consensus was broken when the opposition Labour Party declared that if it was ever returned to power it would not only abolish the British nuclear deterrent, but require the Americans to remove their nuclear weapons from British soil and retain their conventional forces only under restrictive conditions.

Britain is an outpost and an essential link in the American systems of intelligence, communications and navigation. One of the stations of the BMEWs line is located on Fylingdales Moor (see p. 20), and Pitreavie in Scotland and Brawdy near Pembroke serve as eastern terminals of the chains of SOSUS underwater listening devices which monitor the movement of Soviet submarines through the GIUK Gap (see pp. 41, 135). American signals intelligence (SIGINT) and satellite-tracking agencies also have facilities on British soil, and high-altitude spy planes operate from the field at Alconbury in Suffolk.

More than one-fifth of the strength of the United States Air Force overseas is already stationed in Britain under the command of the Third Air Force (HQ Mildenhall), and many more aircraft will be flown to Co-located Operating Bases in Britain and on the continent in time of tension. Britain became all the more important for the rearward support of the Central Front after the Americans were evicted from France in 1966–7. The US Army owns very large stocks of pre-positioned equipment at Burtonwood in Cheshire, and it has a big store of ammunition tucked away on the Welsh borders at Caerwent, close to the major M4 motorway. About one hundred of the specialised A-10 ground attack aircraft from the dual base of Bentwaters and Woodbridge in Suffolk, providing a useful reserve of tactical firepower for the Central Front. Further inland the busy transportation field at Mildenhall receives the giant C-141 Starlifters and C-5 Galaxies on their way from the United States to the continent in the annual REFORGER exercises.

CHAPTER 9

The Northern Flank

SCANDINAVIA AND NATO

The Scandinavian world is a kind of northern European Mediterranean. In both of these regions the distances are huge, and the overland communications are poor and fragmented. They each have an inland sea at their heart, and the NATO partners are separated by bodies of water, by neutral states, and by the limitations which they choose to observe on their participation in the alliance. The main difference between the two theatres is that the Scandinavian one is the more important. Scandinavia faces the Soviet heartlands along a broad frontage; it closes up the flank of the Central Front, and it gives NATO the potential of blockading two of the four fleets of the Soviet Union.

Among the Scandinavian countries, Denmark and Norway are members of NATO. In the allied chain of command they fall within the area of responsibility of Allied Forces North (AFNORTH), which also embraces the northernmost part of the Federal Republic of Germany. The geographical extent of this command is impressive. Denmark and Norway by themselves cover 366,975 square kilometres. AFNORTH's north–south axis is some 2,300 kilometres long. Kirkenes in Finnmark lies about 260 kilometres to the north of the Arctic Circle (and further east than Istanbul). Hamburg at AFNORTH's southern end is on the same latitude as Manchester in England. The distances from east to west are very much less, and at one point Norway measures only seven kilometres across – from the head of Otofjord to the Swedish frontier.

AFNORTH's empire touches the territory of the Warsaw Pact at the two extremities, along the Inner German Border near Hamburg, and on the Norwegian–Soviet frontier near Kirkenes. This is one of the reasons why the outcome of the contest for power in Scandinavia has a bearing on the course of potential combat on the Central Front, the long-term tenability of Europe in the face of Soviet attack, and probably also the balance of nuclear advantage between the superpowers.

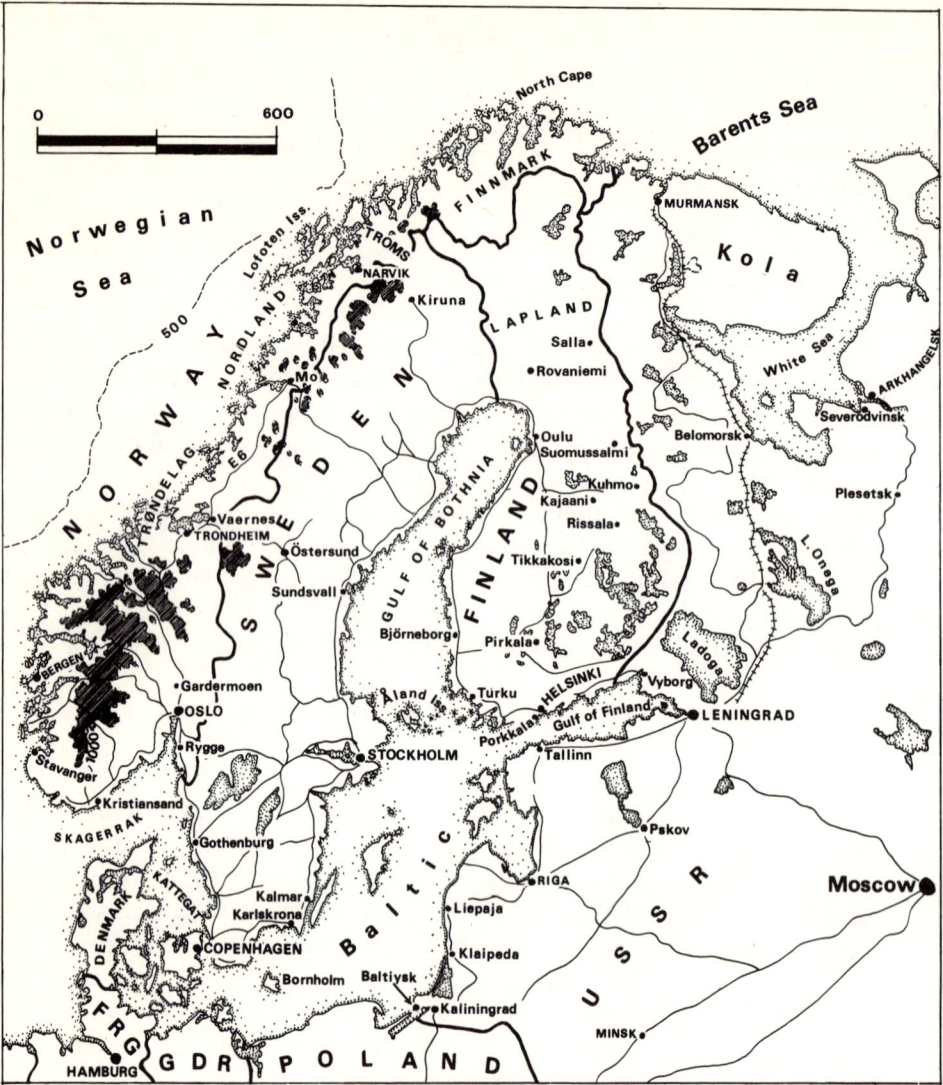

MAP 14   The Scandinavian Countries

DENMARK

Area: 43,080 square kilometres (excluding the
                                    Faroes and Greenland)
Population: 5,150,000
Army: 10 battalions

DENMARK AND NATO

The Danes were a European force in the early Middle Ages, and they remained a significant regional power until the early eighteenth century. Thereafter Denmark underwent brutal treatment from a variety of foreign countries. The British bombarded Copenhagen in 1801 and 1807. A number of German states assailed the land borders in 1848–50, and then in 1863–4 a second attack compelled Denmark to cede the rich southern provinces of Schleswig and Holstein. Finally in April 1940 the Germans overran Denmark in a single day.

Denmark is universally admitted to be one of the weaker links in NATO. Denmark was a founding member of the league, but the Danes were unable to overcome their disappointment at the collapse of the project for a Nordic military alliance, which had been proposed by Sweden in 1948. 'As the one Scandinavian country geographically linked with the European continent, Denmark is, for psychological reasons, anxious to stress her Nordic identity lest she should be written off as belonging in all respects to the continent' (Hagerup, 1975, 25). The NATO connection was seen as something of a second best, and in 1953 the Danes announced that the Western allies were thenceforward forbidden to station forces on Danish soil, or to store nuclear weapons there.

The Danish army amounts to only two divisional equivalents, and it suffers from the cuts in the length of conscript service that were made in 1973 and 1975. The navy has a useful force of coastal submarines, but it is still somewhat weak in anti-submarine warfare and mine countermeasures. The Danish air force has been updated with F-16 fighters, and its principal bases are at Skrydstrup near the West German border, Karup and Ålborg in central and northern Jutland, and Vaerløse near Copenhagen. In general the Danish forces have been starved by the politicians. Rear-Admiral Jorgen Bork, the commander-in-chief of operational command, complained that these people take 'a miserly and emotional view of defence matters, and they hardly ever look at them in their proper perspective – as a means of defending the country'.

Danish membership of NATO is nevertheless of great value to the alliance, for the national territory forms the left flank of the Central Front on the mainland of Europe, and helps to keep two of the Soviet fleets bottled up in their northern fastnesses – namely the Baltic Fleet, and the very important Northern Fleet. The Danes have been rewarded with a prominent place in the AFNORTH hierarchy. A Danish admiral has always been in charge of the unified Danish–

RANDERS

KARUP

Århus

JUTLAND

HORSENS

VEJLE

Fredericia

Esbjerg

KOLDING

Middelfart

Little Belt

Odense

NYBORG

FYN

Gt. Belt

Sejerø Bay

Kalundborg

Sj

Slagelse

Slagels

KORSØR

SKRYDSTRUP

A10

Denmark

Sonderborg

LANGELAND

Nakskov

Lo

Westerland

F. R. G.

LECK

FLENSBURG

Fortress

Rødbyhavr

SYLT

Olpenitz

SCHLESWIG

Schlei

Treene

HUSUM

Eckernförde

FEHMARN

RENDSBURG

Kiel

HEIDE

Kiel Can.

Elder

NEUMÜNSTER

Lübeck

Brunsbüttel

ITZEHOE

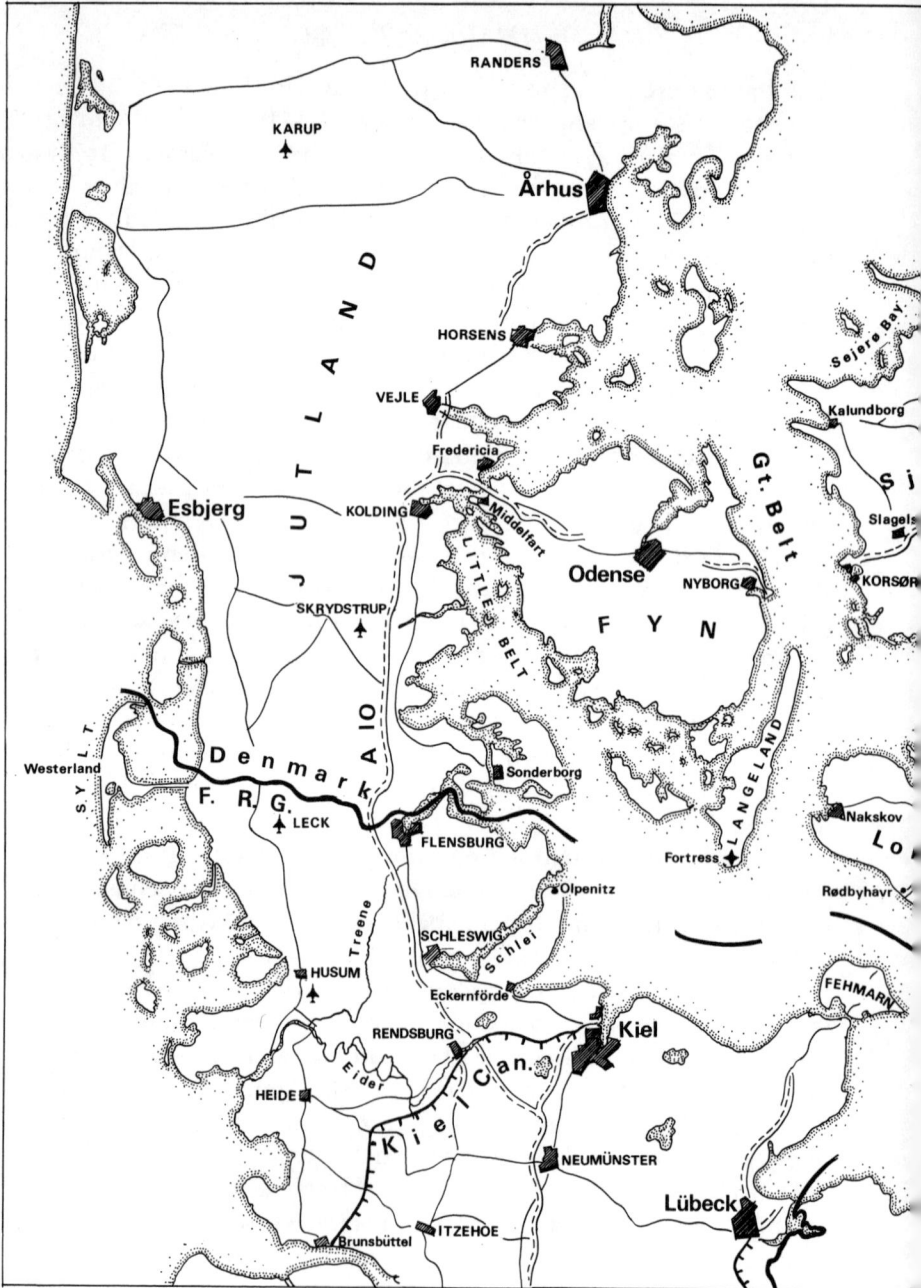

MAP 15   The Baltic Approaches

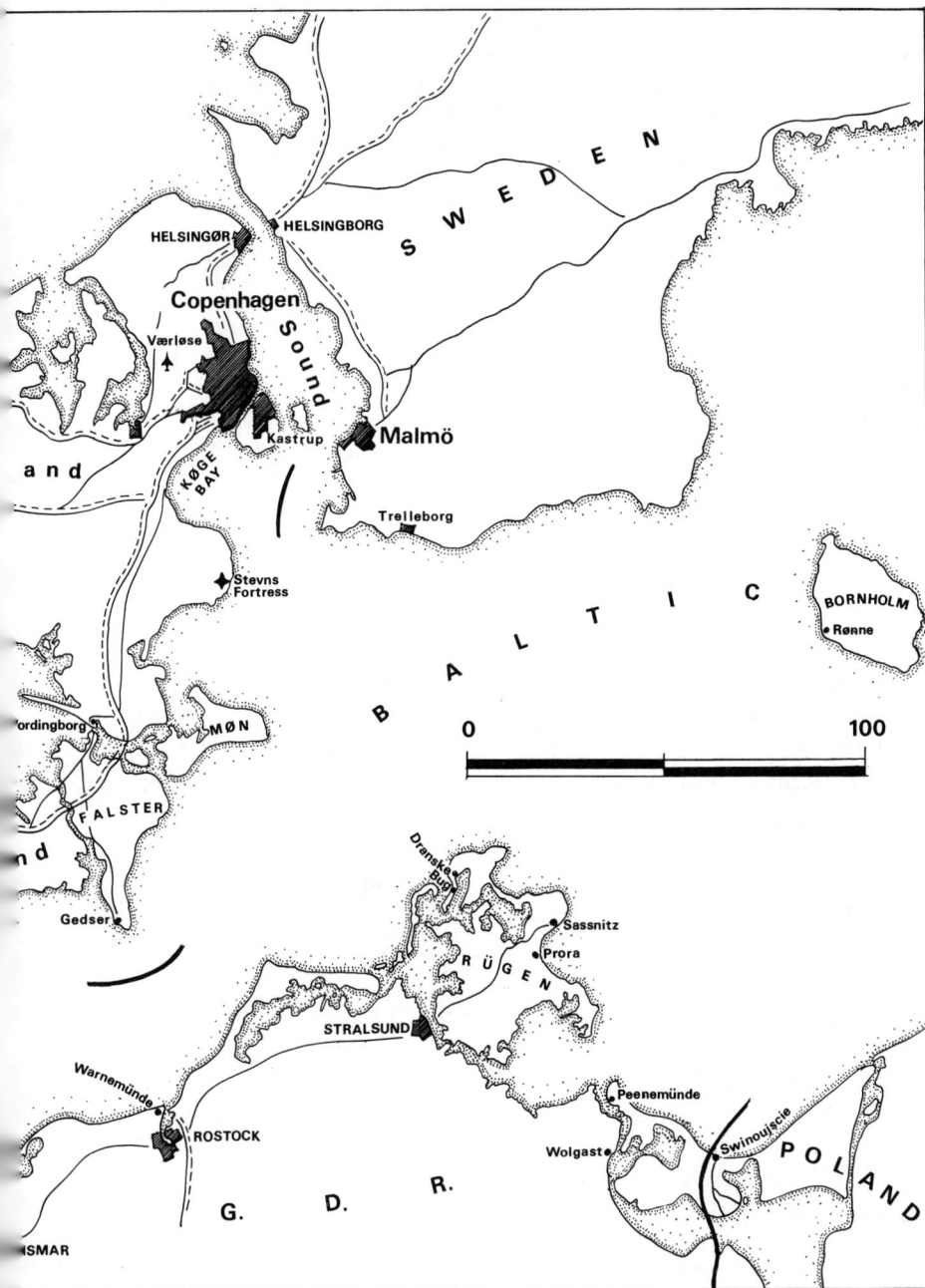

SWEDEN

HELSINGØR HELSINGBORG

Copenhagen

Værløse

Sound

Kastrup Malmö

KØGE BAY

Trelleborg

Stevns Fortress

B A L T I C

BORNHOLM
Rønne

and

ordingborg MØN

0 100

FALSTER

nd

Gedser

Dranske Bug

Sassnitz

R Ü G E N Prora

STRALSUND

Warnemünde

Peenemünde

ROSTOCK

Wolgast Swinoujscie

P O L A N D

G. D. R.

ISMAR

German Baltic Approaches (BALTAP) subordinate command, whose area of responsibility covers the southern half of the Skagerrak, the Kattegat, the Danish Straits, the western Baltic and Schleswig-Holstein – in other words taking in a slice of north Germany. This is a compensation of sorts for the humiliations inflicted on Denmark in 1864.

THE IMPORTANCE OF DANISH TERRITORY

The GIUK Gap

One of the most vital objectives of NATO strategy is to prevent the forces of the Soviet Northern Fleet from reaching the North Atlantic. By leave of Denmark, the Danish possessions of Greenland and the Faroes form integral components of the potential naval and air barrier which extends from the New World to Scotland and Norway (see pp. 135–7).

The northern flank of the Central Front

Denmark occupies now, as she did at the time of her greatness, a crucial position at the junction of Scandinavia and Central Europe, where the base of the Jutland peninsula merges into the north German plain. This ground will be reviewed in due course, as part of the geography of the Central Front, and we shall pause only to note that a Warsaw Pact breakthrough on this flank would threaten the rear of the eastward-facing lines of battle along the Inner German Border.

The standing forces in this region comprise the three Danish mechanised brigades in Jutland, and two thinly stretched West German formations – the 6th Mechanised Infantry Division, and the mechanised 51st Territorial Home Defence Brigade (based at Eutin, and under NATO command).

In 1982 the autumn exercise Northern Wedding indicated the scale of the operations required to bring in help from outside. The Dutch 1st Amphibious Combat Group and the American 4th Marine Amphibious Brigade carried out a landing near Esbjerg in Jutland, and joined the Danes and the West Germans in securing the vital ports and canals in Schleswig-Holstein. A continuation exercise involved landings on Danish islands in the Baltic, and the expulsion of 'enemy' forces from Lolland.

Warning time is at a premium for NATO in the Baltic

Approaches, where every hour is vital for dispersing forces or getting them under cover from air attack, pouring mines into the Danish Straits (below), preparing the coastal defence of the Danish islands, summoning up reservists and home defence forces, and calling on assistance from the Standing Naval Force Atlantic, the ACE Mobile Force and the British 1st Infantry Brigade.

The Baltic and the Danish Straits

No less importantly for NATO, Danish national territory commands the straits where the Baltic blends with the waters of the North Sea. What happens in the Baltic concerns the whole of the Baltic world, and is therefore of great interest to the rival alliance systems.

THE BALTIC SEA

The Baltic follows a general south-west to north-east axis. The most significant stretch of open water runs from the area of Bornholm for about 800 kilometres to south-west Finland, where the sea divides into two branches – the Gulf of Bothnia reaching 700 kilometres to the north, and the Gulf of Finland which extends for 500 kilometres to its head near Leningrad. The average width of the Baltic is only about 200 kilometres, and the total area of 420,000 square kilometres is very much smaller than that of the Mediterranean.

The Swedish and Finnish coasts are for the most part heavily indented and bestrewn with stony islands. From the air the inland lakes are frequently indistinguishable from arms of the sea, which helps to create the impression of a generalised amphibious environment made up of rocks, conifers and sheets of water. In contrast the eastern and southern shores are characterised by dunes, sandspits, lagoons and estuaries.

The difficulties of navigating the Baltic are considerable, even in peacetime. The Baltic is nearly tideless, but large ships are in danger of running aground on reefs and shallows, for the average depth is only between 100 and 200 metres, and strong north-easterly winds have the effect of whipping up choppy seas, which are unpleasant or hazardous for the navigation of small craft. The winter pack ice imprisons the gulfs of Bothnia, Finland and Riga and the bay of Kaliningrad, and reaches well down the Swedish coast from Stockholm. Ice-free harbours like Karlskrona are a precious asset, though drift ice presents a potential danger even in the open waters, and in the very hard winter of 1984–5 the sea was frozen all the way from East Germany to Sweden.

The naval mine is a child of the Baltic. It was employed by the Prussians to bar Kiel harbour against the Danes during the Schleswig-Holstein crisis of 1848–51, and mines were sown in profusion by the Russians in the Crimean War. Baltic conditions also lend themselves to the employment of coastal submarines. The salinity is low, but like the temperatures it shows enough variations to distort the passage of sound. The difficulties of locating under-water objects are magnified in the Swedish archipelago, where the bottom is littered with rocky outcrops and debris.

SOVIET INTERESTS

Whereas NATO is accustomed to talking about a Northern *Flank*, the Soviets give this region a central place in their order of priorities.

In the event of war the Soviet operations here might be conducted by a single headquarters, controlling a Theatre of Military Operations that reaches from Murmansk north of the Arctic Circle down to the East German coast. Alternatively the Western Theatre of Military Operations could be expanded north to embrace Denmark and southern Norway and Sweden, taking under control a 'coastal axis' of advance along the Baltic, which would combine the drive along the north German plain with short-range amphibious hooks. Such an arrangement would have the great advantage of striking at the junction of the AFNORTH and AFCENT commands, and also bring some important political targets under co-ordinated attack, namely Copenhagen and Hamburg.

We must not forget that the Warsaw Pact has some dangerous weaknesses of its own on the Baltic flank. It is not impossible that NATO could launch some kind of amphibious operation against the Polish coast. More realistically, the Baltic offers an avenue by which NATO aircraft could outflank the great concentration of radars and SAMs in the buffer zone in Eastern Europe, and then strike south against the rearward lines of communications of the Soviet forces in Central Europe, and south-west against the Soviet Union's Baltic shores and hinterland, which contain Leningrad, the second city of Russia, and important concentrations of military bases and industries. One of the reasons why the Soviet Union went to war with Finland in 1939 was to improve the security of Leningrad. Stalin flatly informed the Finns: 'We cannot do anything about geography, nor can you. Since Leningrad cannot be transported away, the frontier must be moved further off.'

The Soviet force in the Baltic is built around the Red Banner Baltic Fleet. Its principal bases are on Kronstadt Island near

Leningrad, Paldiski near Tallinn in Estonia, Riga and Liepaja in Latvia, Klaipeda in Lithuania, and the headquarters at Baltiysk near Kaliningrad in an annexed corner of old East Prussia.

Some characteristics are very pronounced. One is that the Baltic Fleet is based closer than any other to the Soviet heartland, and that it consequently contains about 60 per cent of the entire dockyard facilities of the Soviet Union. The yards at Leningrad and Kaliningrad have become by far the most important of the Soviet establishments for building and repairing surface warships, and the lavish basing facilities in the Baltic support many of the tenders and auxiliaries which in their turn maintain the Soviet flotillas on the high seas.

In a war of any length the Soviets would therefore find it extremely useful to have a secure passage of the Danish Straits, permitting ships of the Baltic Fleet to reach the North Sea, and allowing battered and depleted units of the Northern Fleet to gain access to the Baltic. Domination of the area of the Baltic outlets would in addition allow the Soviets to plant effective air defence systems well to the west along a much narrower frontage than on their Baltic coasts, and gain the use of airfields in north Germany, Jutland and southern Sweden and Norway, from where they could carry the air war more easily to Britain, and turn the line of NATO forces and missile belts on the Central Front. Behind the shelter of these lodgments the Soviets could keep up a secure communication to their forces in East Germany. Until 1982 the reinforcement of the GSFG depended on movement through Polish territory and airspace (see p. 110). Since then the Baltic Fleet's complement of hovercraft and landing vessels has been increased, and the Soviets have built extra airstrips for heavy transport aircraft along their coast, all of which indicates that the support for the military presence in East Germany is being extensively rerouted over the Baltic.

Another distinguishing feature of the Baltic Fleet is that it is very strong in the short-range power required to seize the Baltic Straits and objectives on the nearby coasts. The capacity of the Northern Fleet, on the other hand, lies more in the long-range strategic dimension. For operations in the Baltic the Soviets may call not only on the resources of the Red Banner Fleet and its Naval Infantry, but on the 76th Airborne Division of the Leningrad Military District, the Polish 6th Airborne Division, and the amphibious flotillas of Poland and East Germany. In naval force alone the Warsaw Pact has a superiority over the Danes and West Germans of about five to one. Moreover, a number of Warsaw Pact airfields are only a few minutes' flying time from targets in the Danish Straits.

Amphibious landings on the southern shores of the Baltic have figured prominently in major Warsaw Pact exercises like *Waffenbruderschaft-80, Soyuz-81, Zapad-81* and *Soyuz-83*, and the techniques that were rehearsed here could be applied equally well to coasts further west. The Warsaw Pact's naval surveillance of the Danish Straits began in 1956, and Soviet, East German and Polish naval forces regularly circumnavigate the major island of Sjaelland.

THE DANISH STRAITS

The navigation around or through the Danish islands and capes constitutes a funnel 750 kilometres long between Bornholm Island in the Baltic and the open waters of the North Sea.

As the Baltic narrows to the west between the coasts of Sweden and Germany, the shipping must pass to one side or another of the Danish island of Bornholm, a rocky plateau measuring twenty by thirty kilometres, and which is stranded in the Baltic about 120 kilometres to the east of the nearest national territory. This location puts it north of the border between East Germany and Poland, and very nearly on a level with the Soviet headquarters base at Baltiysk some 350 kilometres to the east. Bornholm gives NATO a window into the heart of the territory of the Warsaw Pact, and it is scarcely surprising that this island has become a base for NADGE and other far-seeing installations.

The garrison is made up of one Danish battalion. Bornholm is obviously untenable against any kind of serious attack, but its defence might act as a trigger, forcing Danish politicians willy-nilly to commit their country to a common struggle against the Warsaw Pact. The Danish standing *General Operational Instructions* declare:

> In the event of an attack being launched against Danish territory or Danish military units outside Danish territory, the forces being attacked will, without delay, engage the enemy without awaiting or trying to obtain orders, even if the declaration of the state of war is unknown to the commanders concerned.

At its far western end the Baltic terminates at the Jutland peninsula, which is impenetrable to shipping except at the base, where the Kiel Canal has been carved through German territory. All the other traffic must pass through the Danish Straits, which see more than 60,000 sailings a year. It is now possible to appreciate something of the maritime character of the Danish environment, where the coastline of Jutland and the islands amounts to no less than 5,314 kilometres in length.

The Little Belt (Lille Baelt) between Jutland and the island of Fyn (Fünen) is forty-eight kilometres long but only about half a kilometre wide at its narrowest point, and it is too shallow for large ships. A road bridge now vaults across the channel, greatly facilitating Danish internal communications.

Next in line comes the Great Belt (Store Baelt), which is eighteen kilometres wide at its narrowest point and forms the most important avenue for international shipping. The main crossing is by way of the ferry between Nyborg on Fyn and Korsør on Sjaelland.

Sjaelland (Zealand) is the main island of Denmark, and contains the city of Copenhagen and more than half of the national population. Two of the Danish mechanised brigades are garrisoned here, which testifies to the importance the Danes attach to this home island. The most interesting of the political landing beaches for the Warsaw Pact is the broad sweep of Køge Bay, just south of Copenhagen. However, the embankment of the coastal railway has some defensive potential, and there is a multitude of possible firing positions in the 'Atlantic Wall' of housing development.

At the far end of Sjaelland the channel of the Sound (Öresund) is four kilometres wide at its narrowest point between Denmark and Sweden. These historic waters are churned up by intense ferry and cargo traffic, though the bottom is too shallow for large ocean-going vessels.

Two artillery forts are still in commission on the islands, namely a work at the southern end of Langeland (defending the access to the two Belts), and the Stevns Fortress at the southern entrance to the Sound. More importantly, the mine defences of the Straits are held in a high state of readiness, and the Danes hope to take a heavy toll of approaching invasion forces by strikes from aircraft, submarines and fast attack craft, and mobile land-based missile launchers.

In the 'long war scenario' already discussed, the Warsaw Pact is likely to make the considerable effort that would be required to force and clear the Straits. In a short war, which is more likely, the Soviets would probably be content to leave Copenhagen and the Straits in the hands of NATO, and concentrate their efforts on the decisive push in north Germany and along the Baltic coast. In either event the seaborne attacking forces will have the advantage of operating on interior lines, whereas the NATO defenders must be scattered on a long arc across Schleswig-Holstein, Jutland and the Danish islands.

NORWAY

Area:	323,895 square kilometres (excluding Svalbard)
Population:	4,150,000
Army:	2 brigade groups

THE KOLA PENINSULA AND THE SOVIET INTEREST

At the risk of appearing eccentric we begin our review of Norway by reminding ourselves of what the Soviet Union has at stake in its adjacent border region in the Kola peninsula. Since 1940 the population of Kola has risen from about 360,000 to 1,000,000, and an American Secretary of the Navy has described it as 'the most desirable piece of real estate on the earth' (John Lehman, 1982). The reasons are not to be found in the beauty or amenities of the surroundings. Murmansk, the principal town, stands about 200 kilometres to the north of the Arctic Circle, and is shrouded in winter darkness for fifty days of the year.

Nuclear defence

Kola lies between the western Russian heartland and the Arctic, on the direct path of potential American missile and bomber attack. The peninsula bristles with the appropriate warning systems.

Nuclear attack

The Kola peninsula offers the Soviets a unique combination of advantages over their other base complexes. Murmansk and the other ports of the Kola Inlet are ice-free throughout the year, thanks to the warming influence of the Gulf Stream. Moreover, the Soviets enjoy from here a direct run to the high seas, if not immediately into the North Atlantic. For these reasons the Northern Fleet has become the largest and most modern of the Soviet armadas, and the strongest in nuclear missile submarines and attack submarines.

The Soviets have deployed the nuclear missile submarines from Kola in three main ways. The older Yankee-class submarines with their relatively short-range missiles (2,400–3,900 kilometres) must still make the voyage to their patrol areas in the North Atlantic. The longer-range missiles of the Delta classes permit these more modern submarines to stand back in the sea defence area of the Barents Sea,

N O R W A Y

Vadsø

VARANGER FJORD

B a r e n t s
S e a

0 100

RYBACHIY PEN.

KIRKENES

PECHENGA

Titovka

NIKEL

ZAPOLYARNYY

Luostari

Salmiyarvi

Kildin

FINLAND

Koshka-Yavr

Titovka R.

L. Inari

Litsa R.

Rosta

POLYARNYY

Stednaya Guba

SEVEROMORSK

Severomorsk

Kilp-Yavr

Pasvikelva

Nautsi

Murmansk

Murmansk N.-E.

Kola

Mal-Yavr

IVALO

Murmashi-S.

T U L O M A

Taybola-N.W.

Olenegorsk

OLENEGORSK

Lovozero

Monchegorsk

MONCHEGORSK

Kovdor

Kirovsk

Aatity

Umbozero

Kirovsk S.

Afrikanda

Umbozero-S.

Alakurtti

KANDALAKSHA

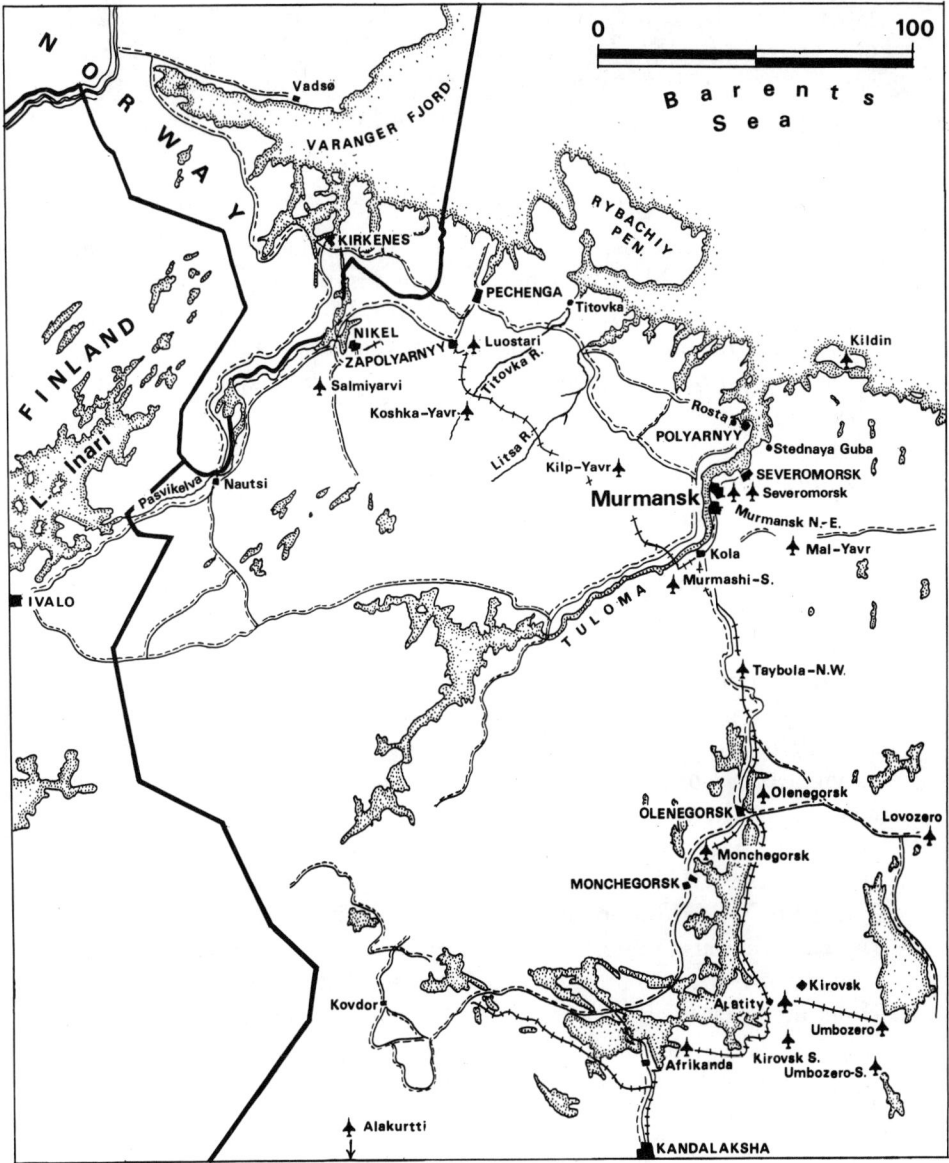

MAP 16   The Kola Bases

where they have the protection of surface ships and land-based aircraft (see p. 18). Lastly submarines from Kola are capable of making long voyages under the Arctic Ocean and launching their missiles through the permanent covering of pack ice.

Conventional maritime attack

The surface warships, attack submarines and naval aircraft of the Soviet Northern Fleet have been assigned important tasks in northern waters, whether to push through the GIUK Gap against the Transatlantic shipping lanes, or maintain a forward defence for the Kola installations and the Barents Sea defence area. In either event a strike into northern Norway will enable the Soviets to turn the flank of the GIUK Gap by denying or seizing the Norwegian air bases and the multitude of deep-water fjords. There are echoes here of the strategy once urged on Germany by Vice-Admiral Wegener, who pointed out that German control of Norway would break the grip of the British 'hunger blockade' in the North Sea, and turn Britain's strategic position from the north (*Die Seestrategie des Weltkrieges*, Berlin, 1929).

The implications for Nordic security were explored in 1978 by a Norwegian governmental Defence Review Commission. This body identified two possible 'scenarios' in which national territory might be violated. In one of them, Soviet forces launch a pre-emptive strike against northern Norway in a time of rising tension, seeking to spread the base area from Kola, and gain Norwegian facilities on the flank of the GIUK Gap. The second case is that of a general European War. The Soviets again attack Norway at the outset, but this time they also undertake hostilities in southern Norway as part of a larger operation to force an exit from the Baltic. The Commission concluded that in either eventuality the defence of northern Norway must be given the priority, and that most of the standing forces should be deployed there.

Physical aspects of the Kola bases

The Barents Sea is relatively shallow, and some of its deepest waters (100 metres or more) extend in a narrow trench close to the shore. Submarines are normally vulnerable in such an environment, but here the Soviet vessels operate under surface and air cover, and along the edges of the Gulf Stream the contrasts of salinity and temperature make underwater detection difficult. Once they have passed the north-western corner of Norway the submarines can slide down to the depths of the Greenland Sea, but southwards again the bottom rises to the potentially dangerous underwater ridge which follows the line of the GIUK Gap.

The submariners have a safer voyage if they first strike north in the deep waters beneath the frozen surface of the Arctic Ocean. In winter the pack ice reaches out to embrace the east coast of Greenland, the Svalbard archipelago, and all of the Russian coast except the ice-free zone around Murmansk. In summer the Gulf Stream is at last able to make a dramatic clearance to the north-west, releasing the Russian coast, and liberating Novaya Zemlya, Svalbard, Jan Mayen Island and all save the north-eastern corner of Greenland.

The major installations of the Northern Fleet are packed into a sixty-kilometre stretch of coast. Murmansk is situated about forty kilometres up the Kola Inlet, and it has very important construction and repair facilities on these sheltered waters. The fleet headquarters is located a little further down the same eastern shore of the inlet at Severomorsk. Considerable quantities of munitions are stored here, and the Northern Fleet lost much of its stock of missiles when the Severomorsk bunkers were devastated by a series of accidental explosions between 13 and 18 May 1984. The flotilla of nuclear missile submarines is based at Polyarnyy, on the western side of the Kola Inlet near the entrance to the Barents Sea. Nearby Rosta is the Northern Fleet's repair and maintenance base. These ports together constitute the largest naval base complex in the world.

The White Sea is tucked behind the Kola peninsula. It is frozen during the winter, but there is a naval base at Arkhangelsk (Archangel), and the great covered yards at Severodvinsk nearby are used to build super-large submarines, like the first of the Typhoon class.

The Kola peninsula accommodates more than 200 fixed-wing aircraft, and these numbers may be very rapidly augmented by long-range and high-performance aircraft like the Backfire and the new Blackjack. There are about forty airfields in all, and the major fields are probably those at Salmiyarvi, Luostari, Kilp-Yavr, Kildin, Severomorsk, Murmansk North-East, Mal-Yavr, Olenegorsk (the principal long-range base), Monchegorsk, Umbozero North, Afrikanda, Alakurttii and Loukhi West.

The communications between Kola and the interior are long and tenuous, and they were even more exposed before the Soviets compelled the Finns to cede the ground to the east of Salla and Kuusamo. The road and railway touch the White Sea at the port of

Kandalaksha, and again at the south-west corner of the sea at Belomorsk, where the lines to Leningrad and Arkhangelsk divide. Belomorsk is also the northern outlet of the Baltic–White Sea Canal, which has been widened to accommodate craft of up to 5,200 tons, giving smaller ships and submarines the means of making an inland passage between the Baltic and the northern seas.

Eastwards beyond the White Sea one of the bleakest sea lanes in the world (see p. 72) gives access to the Novaya Zemlya islands (with their nuclear missile testing grounds), and to Tiksi and the other lonely ports scattered along the northern coast of Russia. In the summer months the pack ice retreats just far enough to permit ships to steam all the way to the Bering Strait and the Pacific, but the waters are frozen right up to the coast for most of the year, and even the most powerful icebreakers are not always able to release shipping which does not make its escape in time.

Mineral resources and the Svalbard dispute

The mineral wealth of the Kola peninsula has added still more to the geopolitical importance of this region. Phosphates are mined at Apatity, iron ore at Olenegorsk and Yeno-Kovdor, and nickel, the most precious commodity of all, at Monchegorsk and at the town of Nikel. The facility of extracting nickel became one of the most important reasons why the Germans held their positions in the Kola peninsula until October 1944. When the Soviets went on to acquire Pechenga (Petsamo) from the Finns it was not just to give additional security to Murmansk, but to acquire the means of shipping minerals from the interior.

It is suspected that further very considerable wealth lies under the waters to the north. There is already profitable fishing in the Barents Sea, and the prospect of exploitable oil and natural gas in the sea bed. The floor of the Arctic Ocean beyond is a uniform body of sedimentary geology which promises to contain still greater reserves of oil and gas. Norway and the Soviet Union are in dispute about the rights of exploitation. Their quarrel owes nothing directly to the confrontation between the superpowers, but it is of some interest as being the only active territorial argument between members of European NATO and the Warsaw Pact.

The Soviets contend that the relevant dividing line ought to be drawn due north from the seaward end of the Soviet–Norwegian land border. The Norwegians, on the other hand, invoke the principle of the median line between the Svalbard archipelago (which belongs to Norway) and the Soviet Novaya Zemlya group. The overlap between the two lines amounts to about 180,000 square kilometres, though both the area and the shape have been difficult to establish.

The status of the Svalbard group itself was supposed to have been settled once and for all by the multi-national Svalbard Treaty in 1920. This agreement consigned Svalbard to Norway in what was called 'full and absolute sovereignty', though in fact military installations were forbidden there, and all of the signatory states were given access to the territory for purposes of economic activity. Even now Svalbard, and therefore 24 per cent of Norway's land surface, lies outside the NATO area of responsibility.

After some delay the Soviets too appended their signature. In 1944, however, they began to agitate for extra concessions. Not content with their coalmines on Svalbard, they mounted what was by the 1980s a *de facto* challenge to Norwegian sovereignty. They brought in wives and children to join the menfolk working there (effectively establishing a settlement), they sent warships on visits, they prepared harbours and airfields and set up a radar and helicopter station on Cape Heer.

THE DEFENCE OF NORWAY

NATO interests

The West's interest in Norway derives both from the obligation to uphold an ally and from the wider strategy of containing the Soviet fleets in their ports, of which the Kola complex is the most important. These remote lands and seemingly empty seas are figuratively pulsating with NATO activity. While CAPTOR mines and the SOSUS hydrophones wait patiently on the sea bed, Western maritime reconnaissance aircraft range the waters from Keflavík in Iceland, St Mawgan and Kinloss in Britain, Bergen, Bodø, Bardufoss and Banak in mainland Norway, and Andøya in the Lofoten Islands. Bodø is also important as a base from which Norwegian fighters intercept Soviet aircraft along the fringes of national airspace. There are further Norwegian airfields at Evenes and Kautokeino in the north, Vaernes near Trondheim, and Gardermoen and Rygge on either side of Oslo.

Norway also acts as host to some important electronic installations, including fourteen of NATO's NADGE radar stations, and the Loran-C navigational transmitter at Boe, which works with stations at Keflavík in Iceland, Ejde in the Faroes and Westerland on Sylt to provide super-accurate navigational fixes for nuclear missile submarines. All of these installations demand protection, over and above the necessity of denying the Soviets access to Norwegian fjords and airfields.

National policy and strategy

Norway is a very long-strung-out and thinly settled country, and it comes as no surprise that political resolve has shown some weakening in the presence of the Soviet Union. The Norwegians are aware that they are doubly offensive to the Soviets, both as members of NATO and as economic rivals in the northern seas, and their government is at pains to maintain a 'correct atmosphere' with their powerful neighbour. Little was done to implement the proposals of the Defence Review Commission (see p. 232), and the Norwegians continue to hold their allies at arm's length. Foreign NATO forces are certainly permitted to train and exercise in Norway, and in 1981 the Americans gained leave to establish POMCUS depots of equipment in Trøndelag. However, the allies are still forbidden to plant permanent garrisons on Norwegian territory, or to keep nuclear weapons there in peacetime. No joint exercises may take place near the sensitive border in Finnmark, lest any offence should be offered to the Soviets, and even the Trøndelag depots are situated embarrassingly far from the probable scenes of action.

In the event of a surprise attack by the Soviet Union, the Norwegians will for a time be thrown largely on their own resources. They have undeniable strengths. The F-16 fighters of the air force and the navy's coastal submarines and fast-attack craft are well suited to the geographical environment, and the tough and independent national character is manifest in the very enthusiastic Home Guards. Where the Norwegians are very weak is in ground forces capable of defending the borders with the Soviet Union, Finland and Sweden in the far north.

The resoundingly named South Varanger Garrison is just a border tripwire of sentries, and the only regular force within close reach is the Brigade Group North (about 4,000 troops), based at Bardufoss near Tromsø. Northern Norway in fact presents the problems of Norwegian defence in exaggerated form. The three counties (Finnmark, Troms, Nordland) make up 40 per cent of the national territory but have only 12 per cent of the population. The Home Guard is correspondingly weak, and the communications are poorly developed.

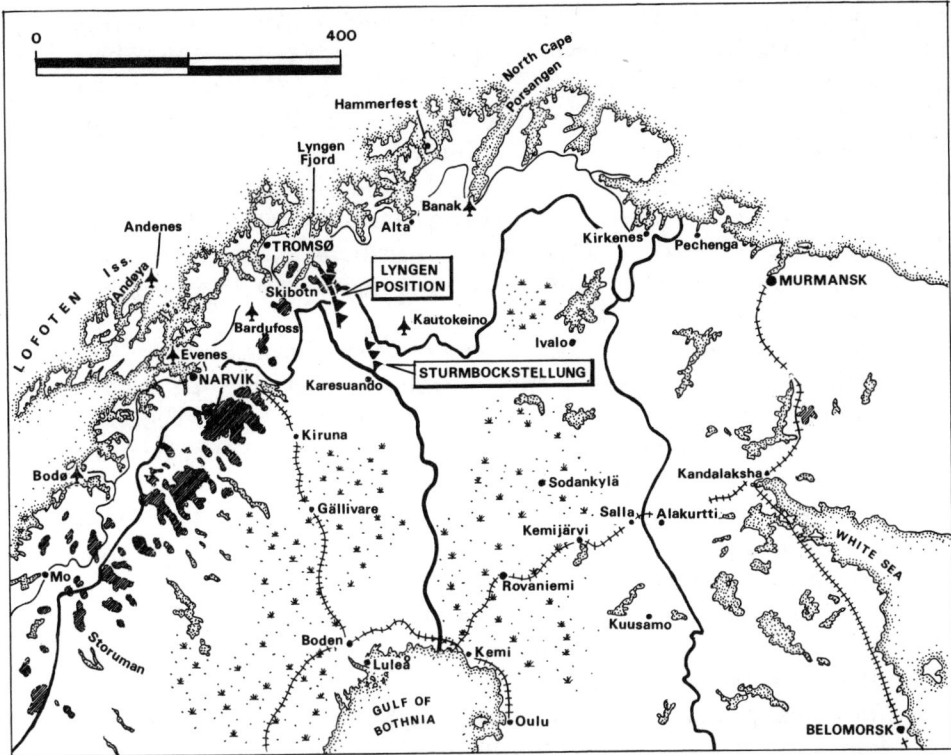

MAP 17   Northern Scandinavia

The general (COMNOM) in charge of Northern Command must therefore look for support to Southern Command, which holds the mass of the reservists and the only other regular standing force – a small all-arms group of one infantry battalion with supporting armour and artillery. Everything else must come from NATO allies.

The reinforcement of Norway

In 1960 NATO began to make provision to rush help to Norway in case of emergency. The relevant forces are among those assigned to SACEUR's ACE Mobile Force, and they are likely to include a US Marine Amphibious Force of 4,000 men, the Canadian air-sea transportable brigade (see p. 130), the joint Dutch and British amphibious force of about 3,000 marines, and a battalion each from Britain, Belgium, Luxembourg and the FRG. The air component is provided by the United States, Britain, Canada and the Netherlands. However, it must be noted that, with the possible exception of the Canadian contingent, these forces are not specifically earmarked for Norway, and their services might be urgently required elsewhere in Europe.

The passage of the ACE Mobile Force will be lengthy, lasting between ten and thirty days according to some estimates, and it is all too possible that some of the intended points of disembarkation will prove to be inoperable or already in Soviet hands, forcing the allies to divert the reinforcements south to destinations like Bergen or Stavanger just when the Norwegians were switching their national reserves to their Northern Command.

The movement of the ACE Mobile Force will probably take place in the context of a general reinforcement of northern Europe, such as was tried out in the concurrent Teamwork-84 and Avalanche Express exercises in the spring of 1984. Three hundred combat aircraft were involved, together with 150 warships and submarines. The needs of Norway might assume secondary importance if it appeared that the issue of the war was going to be decided on the Central Front in a matter of days.

All of this adds to the difficulty of working out whether NATO or the Soviet Union has the military advantage in the northern region. The Soviet resident forces too are surprisingly weak, in relation to the potentially great issues at stake. The Northern Fleet is geared to long-range strategic projection. Its naval aviation could very readily be used to attack Norwegian airfields, but the amphibious force is confined to a single brigade of naval infantry, and the two 'in-theatre' Army motor rifle divisions are scarcely more than might have been expected for safeguarding the Kola bases and their communications. It is by no means certain that the Leningrad Military District's resident airborne division (the 76th) could be spared for operations in the distant north.

For the Soviet Union, as well as NATO, large-scale operations in the north must wait until reinforcements arrive from outside the theatre. One calculation puts the attacking force at a minimum of seven divisions (Croker, 1984, 29), but the immediate threat to Norway probably comes from mobile and relatively small forces. The Germans demonstrated as much in April 1940, when they carried out their airborne or amphibious *coups de main* against Kristiansand, Oslo, Bergen, Trondheim and Narvik. Air superiority also counts for a great deal, for the narrow fjords and the sparse and cramped roads do not lend themselves to dispersing ships or troops. Conversely NATO's best defence is likely to be its vigilance. Full-scale surprise will be difficult for the Soviets to achieve, since the activity on the Kola peninsula is monitored by AWACS aircraft and the NADGE stations, and the hills on the Norwegian side of Pasvikelva River afford good optical vision into Soviet territory.

The geography of the land war

GENERAL PHYSICAL CONDITIONS

In no other potential theatre of war do weather and geography count for more than in Scandinavia. The climate is dominated by seasonal extremes. In late summer genuinely hot days may be encountered north of the Arctic Circle (see p. 50), but October is usually the last month in which it is possible to conduct conventional operations on a scale to compare with the Soviet Fourteenth Army's Pechenga – Kirkenes offensive in 1944 (7–29 October). For sheer cold the bitterest weather is encountered east of the Scandinavian watershed. The narrow Norwegian coastlands benefit from the Gulf Stream, and the fjords remain unfrozen in the depths of winter, but the collision of maritime and Arctic air masses triggers off heavy falls of dense and wet snow which is inimical to the movement of armoured vehicles.

For more than six weeks from late November the far north is afflicted with almost unrelieved darkness, which further discourages military enterprise, especially in the air, but the daylight returns with the approach of the late northern spring, and suitably trained and equipped troops enjoy a new 'window of opportunity' before the thaw of May and June makes overland movement virtually impossible over large regions of northern Scandinavia. In the Second World War all of the armies made extensive use of ski troops, and in the middle of April 1940, when the valleys around Oslo were still deep in snow, the German battlegroups progressed at an average rate of thirty-six kilometres per day, employing conventional forces along the roads, and ski troops for outflanking movements.

It is another matter to keep overland supply lines open during the winter, especially in northern Norway, where the difficulties of the climate are compounded by the fact that there is so little open ground between the mountains and the sea. Norway contains landscapes as diverse as the rocky and boggy tundras of Finnmark in the north and the green plains of Ostfold in the south-east, but the typical terrain is very much like the scenes which appear in the travel posters, with their pictures of mountains, fjords and rocky islands. From cape to cape the coastline measures 2,650 kilometres, but it amounts to

21,115 if you include all the inlets.

The German Reichstrasse 50 between Narvik and Kirkenes was frequently blocked by snow in spring and early summer until, through stupendous efforts, the section as far as Lakselv was 'winter-proofed' by snow fences and wooden tunnels. Only recently has a programme of road and bridge building completed the Norwegian E 6 north from Oslo to the county of Troms, eliminating a number of ferry crossings. However, this tenuous lifeline is liable to be closed by snow, and it still does not extend into the northern border country of Finnmark. At many points north of Trondheim the E 6 touches on fjords, or runs along their sides, and it is extremely vulnerable to attack from the sea. The few side roads are surfaced with uncompacted gravel, and they become unusable in the thaw.

Sea transport becomes all the more important on account of the inadequacy of the roads, and it is fortunate that the channels between the mainland and the islands enable shipping to make a sheltered passage along much of the coast. These avenues are called the 'Inner Leads', and they offer favourable conditions for the defending aircraft, submarines and fast attack craft. Mining is facilitated by the existence of choke points, but the great depths detract from the efficacy of mines of the bottom-mounted variety. Sonar conditions are generally poor.

Nowhere in the Soviet Union is there terrain which looks anything like the mountains and the fjords of Norway. The advantages of the knowledge of the theatre lie almost exclusively with the Norwegians and the allied troops who train there. A full-scale overland invasion will offer few attractions for the Soviets, except in the context of a long-drawn-out war.

THE NORTHERN COUNTIES

Collectively the three northern counties of Norway (Finnmark, Troms and Nordland) are known as the 'Fydde'. Whatever the scenario of war, the Soviet 45th Motor Rifle Division will be certain to seize the town of Kirkenes and overrun the NATO early warning systems in the corner of Finnmark closest to the Kola peninsula. The Norwegians have an inkling of what is in store for them from the events of June 1968, when the Soviets sent two divisions to this stretch of the border and the rumble of the tanks carried clearly to Kirkenes. This is the one area where the Soviets are at home on the ground, for the tundra zone extends across the border without a break, and they fought the Germans here in the Great Patriotic War. After a short offensive by the German Mountain Corps of General

Dietel, in the summer of 1941, the front bogged down only a short way inside the Kola peninsula along the line of the Litsa River. The Soviets proceeded to improve their road network and their cross-country mobility, and sweeping movements over the tundra (together with amphibious hooks) formed important surprise ingredients of their victorious Pechenga–Kirkenes operation in 1944.

The capture of the borderlands around Kirkenes is more relevant to the security of the Soviet bases in Kola than to NATO's defence of Norway. The true strategic frontier of Norway lies more than 400 kilometres (as the crow flies) to the West, in the very interesting area of Skibotn, where the head of the Lyngenfjord approaches the high ground at the junction of the borders of Norway, Sweden and Finland.

The value of the Skibotn blocking position was fully appreciated by the Germans, who fell back in this direction when they abandoned Pechenga and Finnmark towards the end of 1944. At that time the XVIII Mountain Corps occupied an outer position (the *Sturmbockstellung*) to the north-west of Karesuando. The *Sturmbockstellung* has lost its relevance, for in 1944 the Germans made the assumption (which NATO surely cannot) that the Soviets would not dare to launch an outflanking movement to the west through neutral Swedish territory. However, the main 'Lyngen Position' near Skibotn is as potentially useful as ever, for it helps to bar the way to the airfields and ports of Troms and Nordland.

If they kept inside Norwegian territory, the Soviets would have to approach Skibotn over the broad high plateau of central Finnmark (the 'Finnmarksvidda'). However, there must be a strong temptation for the Soviets to come at Troms and the Skibottsdal from the east by barging across Finnish and Swedish Lapland, where the forest tracks have been considerably extended and improved in recent years – they have firm surfaces of oil- or water-bound sand and gravel, and they are probably at least as good as most roads in Russia. The most likely spearhead is the 54th Motor Rifle Division, setting out from the area of Kandalaksha and Alakurtti, and taking the route by way of Rovaniemi and the road which follows the Finnish–Swedish border (the E 78). The Swedes have taken due notice to these developments, and in July 1985 they deepened the restricted and fortified 'security zone' which runs along the Finnish frontier.

An important southerly route across Lapland was developed with the purpose of opening up the reserves of high-grade iron ore at Gällivare and Kiruna in Sweden. In summertime the ore is transported down the railway to Luleå, at the head of the Gulf of Bothnia.

The gulf is icebound in winter, and at that season the ore must be carried over the mountains for transhipment from Norway. The track in this direction was completed in 1902, and the Norwegian terminus at Narvik became a boom town. This axis of communication has a double strategic importance, as an entry into northern Norway, and a channel by which Western forces might reach the heart of northern Scandinavia, as the British and French strategists appreciated in March 1940.

Here we must enter some qualifications. By striking across Finland or Sweden the Soviets would sacrifice all surprise for the attack on Norway, they would encounter resistance that will be at least locally effective, and the logistical problems must be formidable. The very shortest route to Skibotn, that by Rovaniemi, still comes to about 600 kilometres. The Soviet ground forces in the far northern theatre are small, and they are unlikely to be increased at the expense of the vital battle on the Central Front.

SOUTHERN NORWAY

The national capital at Oslo sits on the edge of the Ostfold plain. The AFNORTH headquarters at Kolsaas is just a few kilometres away, and the airfields at Oslo and Kristiansand must also be counted as tempting targets for Soviet airborne strikes or assault, not least because they help to command the Skagerrak. North from Oslo the valleys of the Glåma (Osterdal) and the Lågen (Gudbrandsdal) in April 1940 gave the Germans the means of executing a rapid advance to cut off the south-west bulge of Norway from the narrow coastal strip from the north. To the west a vast mountain plateau divides the Oslo core region from Stavanger and Bergen. These ports have long been of strategic interest because they provide the shortest and safest communication between Norway and the British Isles.

The Scandinavian neutrals

FINLAND

Area:	304,623 square kilometres
Population:	4,825,000
Army:	8 brigades

FINNISH–SOVIET RELATIONS

Finland was originally a component of the Swedish Baltic empire. In 1809 the territory of Finland became a grand duchy of Russia, but the Finns clung to their sense of national identity and in 1918 they finally gained their independence.

When Finland is nowadays mentioned in the literature of international affairs it is usually in the context of what is called 'finlandisation'. This term, which is deeply offensive to the Finns, describes the situation of a country which retains domestic self-rule while deferring to the Soviet Union in matters of foreign policy.

Finland was forced into finlandisation not through any weakening of national will and character, but through bloody and recent wars which reminded her that she is physically much closer to the Soviet Union than to the West. In the words of President J.K. Passikiui, 'the recognition of reality is the beginning of all wisdom'.

The courageous Finnish refusal of Stalin's territorial demands led to the Winter War of 1939–40. After heavy losses and humiliating defeats the Soviets finally succeeded in breaking through the celebrated Mannerheim Line, and in March 1940 the Finns had to buy peace at the price of ceding the Karelian isthmus and the shores of Lake Ladoga, the high ground towards Kuusamo and Salla, and the Finnish half of the Rybachiy peninsula in the Arctic.

In the War of Continuation, which broke out in 1941, Finland renewed the battle with the Soviets as a co-belligerent of the Germans, though not as a formal ally. Once again the Finns did well, but in 1944 they negotiated a change of sides with the Soviets, who by that time were clearly gaining the advantage over the Germans. According to the settlement in September the Soviets annexed the port of Pechenga (the Finnish Petsamo), which advanced the Soviet frontier up to that of Norway.

Altogether the losses in 1940 and 1944 amounted to 42,934 square kilometres, and in detail they were very painful indeed. With Pechenga went valuable reserves of nickel and Finland's last corridor to the Arctic. The ground that was forfeit in Karelia included Vyborg, the second city in Finland, along with important harbours, hydroelectric plants, and the papermills and sawmills of the Vuoksi River industrial complex.

In 1947 the multi-national Treaty of Paris imposed military restrictions on Finland, limiting the army to 34,400 troops, the navy to 4,500 men and 10,000 tons of shipping, and the air force to 3,000 personnel and sixty combat aircraft. Offensive weapons (bombers, submarines, missiles) were forbidden, though a useful modification in 1963 allowed Finland to acquire defensive missiles.

Finally in 1948 a bi-lateral Finnish–Soviet Treaty of Friendship, Co-operation and Mutual Assistance established the 'finlandised'

Finland. The most important military clause begins:

> In the eventuality of Finland, or the Soviet Union through
> Finnish territory, becoming the object of an armed attack by
> Germany or any state allied with the latter, Finland will, true to
> her obligations as an independent state, fight to repel the attack.
> Finland will in such cases use all her available forces to defend
> her territorial integrity by land, sea and air and will do so within
> the frontiers of Finland in accordance with the obligations
> defined in the present agreement and, if necessary, with the
> assistance of, or jointly with, the Soviet Union.

The original duration of the 1948 treaty was for ten years, but it was
given overlapping twenty-year extensions in 1955, 1970 and 1983.

Finland and the Soviet Union continue to pay one another a wary
respect. In 1955 the Soviets voluntarily relinquished their lease on
the naval base of Porkkala near Helsinki, and they did not object
when in 1953 the Finns made economic arrangements with the EEC
as well as with COMECON. Most of Finland's foreign trade is with
the capitalist world, but the connection with the Soviet Union has
given access to a vast market. Finnish consumer goods are highly
prized by Soviet customers, and Finnish construction teams have
used their mastery of Arctic technology to build factories and even
whole towns in Russia.

No doubt some of the Soviet complaisance is due to the deterrent
value of the Finnish armed forces, which are very formidable in their
environment. However, the Soviets are pleased at Finland's good
behaviour in international issues, and the Soviet strategic interest is
not so much to conquer Finland *per se*, but rather to eliminate
Finland as a springboard for Western attack and carve out security
zones in front of Leningrad and Murmansk. It is probably no
coincidence that the present border in Karelia corresponds closely to
the frontier established by Peter the Great in 1721.

FINNISH STRATEGY AND FRONTIERS

While the Finns are careful to observe all the treaty limitations, they
have built up a very large force of trained reservists, who can be
recalled to the colours at short notice. The field artillery is good, and
the coastal artillery (mostly installed in the southern archipelago) is
being re-equipped with 130 mm turrets. Helsinki and Turku are the
principal naval bases, and the fighter airfields are at Pirkala, Björne-
borg and Tikkakoski in the south-west, Rissa in the centre, and

Rovaniemi in Lapland.

Like the other Scandinavian countries, Finland is drawn out along a north–south axis, in this case measuring 1,160 kilometres in length. The land frontiers amount to 586 kilometres with Sweden, 716 with Norway and 1,219 with the Soviet Union.

The coastlines along the gulfs of Bothnia and Finland are ice-bound in winter. Lakes and rivers make up 25 per cent of the national territory, and the proportion of swamps in the north amounts to between 50 and 60 per cent. Most of the land surface is covered with forest, which reduces the average line of sight to below 100 metres. Altogether only about 10 per cent of Finnish territory is suitable for armoured operations.

Finnish Lapland is the most likely part of the country to be violated by foreigners, since it forms a corridor between the Kola peninsula and prime targets in northern Norway (see p. 241). The Finns have brigade-sized concentrations here at Kajaani, Oulu and their main garrison at Sodankylä.

The most sensitive region of Lapland is the zone of high ground (200 or more metres) which straddles the Finnish–Soviet border. To the east Kandalaksha and other points on the Kola-Leningrad communication were dangerously exposed during the Winter War, and in the settlement of 12 March 1940 one of the primary Soviet concerns was to win ground in the direction of Salla and Kuusamo. The danger to Finland's own wasp waist was increased accordingly, and a humiliating clause of the 1940 treaty forced the Finns to build a railway from the Gulf of Bothnia by way of Kemijärvi to Salla, while the Soviets completed the link to the Murmansk railway. Nowadays the Salla–Kemijärvi route comes into account as a potential avenue of Soviet advance across Finnish Lapland, along with the roads further south by way of Kuusamo, Suomussalmi and Kuhmo, all of which were bitterly contested in the Winter War or the War of Continuation.

In the interior of Finnish Lapland the town of Rovaniemi proved to be the most important of the road junctions, and especially during the German retreat in 1944. The ground in the neighbourhood is lower than along the frontier, but the swamps and the rivers slowing into the head of the Gulf of Bothnia offer very considerable obstacles to armoured operations.

War in southern Finland is less likely than in Lapland, but at the same time it would be much more dangerous for Finnish national life, for the south holds the main concentrations of agriculture, industry and population.

The southern sector of the border follows a line much less favourable than the frontier which existed in 1939. The old delineation ran across the Karelian isthmus, which not only gave the Finns 100 kilometres' greater depth of defence but enabled them to construct the short and strong Mannerheim Line, taking advantage of water obstacles. Even after the old political frontier had been pushed back, by the settlement of 1940, the Finns and Germans were able to fight the War of Continuation well ahead along the Karelian isthmus and the neck of land between the lakes of Ladoga and Onega.

All of this is now in the possession of the Soviets, who have gained a forward base for operations against Helsinki and the other cities of southern Finland. The main road is hemmed in between the woods and the sea, but it is capable of being cut by flanking movements along forest paths (as the Russian field-marshal Peter Lacy showed in 1743), or by light armour crossing the frozen gulf in the depths of winter.

The Åland Islands are strategically important Finnish territory at the meeting of the Gulf of Bothnia and the central Baltic. Their status is governed by a treaty between the Baltic countries in 1921, the Finno-Soviet treaties of 1940 and 1944, and the Paris Treaty of 1947. Finland is forbidden to fortify the islands or keep permanent garrisons there, although in the words of the 1921 treaty, 'in the eventuality of the Åland Islands, or through them the mainland of Finland, becoming the object of a sudden attack endangering the neutrality of the zone, Finland is to take necessary measures in the zone to stop or repel the aggression'. Soviet submarines utilise the channels between the islands and the Finnish mainland as a transit route for their submarines out of reach of Swedish surveillance.

SWEDEN

Area:	411,506 square kilometres
Population:	8,343,000
Army:	28 brigades

TRADITIONAL SWEDISH NON-ALIGNMENT

Early in the twentieth century the Swedes, having managed to keep out of wars for a hundred years, began to believe that they must have a national vocation of neutrality. In foreign affairs the Swedes observe an even-handedness in their dealings with the two power blocs. Most of the military establishments are orientated against the

Soviet Union, but measures are taken to counter 'secondary violation' by the West, such as any attempt to dispatch cruise missiles through Swedish airspace against the Kola peninsula.

Sweden has meanwhile sought to cocoon herself in arrangements for regional security. In 1948 Sweden put to her neighbours a proposal for a Scandinavian defence union. The Danish government was enthusiastic (see p. 221), but the Norwegians were aware that they belonged as much to the Atlantic as to Scandinavia, and they decided instead to throw in their lot with the emerging Western alliance.

In the course of time the concept of a 'Nordic balance' arose as a very acceptable alternative to a formal treaty. This notion received wide currency in Scandinavia, and it was particularly flattering to the Swedes, whose powerful armed neutrality was seen as extending a benign influence well beyond their borders. The Finns were reassured of their independence in the face of the Soviet Union, while the Norwegians and Danes could safely keep up their membership of NATO on minimal conditions. International tension was thereby reduced.

SWEDISH DILEMMAS

Sweden's non-alignment, or rather the suppositions on which it was founded, underwent serious erosion in the 1970s and early 1980s. Swedish manufactured products still enjoyed a high reputation, but the economy was badly hit by the world recession and the heavy burden of the cradle-to-grave welfare system. Simultaneously the proud tradition of self-sufficiency in arms production became difficult to sustain in this era of expensive high technology. Not only was the anti-submarine warfare capacity of the navy proving embarrassingly inadequate, but the army needed a new main battle tank, and the air force was committed to purchasing a costly modern fighter, the JAS-39 Grippen.

The nature of the threat to Swedish security underwent a number of changes, each conflicting with some of the assumptions of the national defence policy. By the middle 1970s it was clear that Scandinavia had become of increasing importance in the superpower confrontation. In 1978 an official Defence Committee drew attention to possible threats to Swedish Lapland and the broad and flat southern provinces, though at this period it was still possible to believe that Sweden herself was a target of altogether secondary importance:

Sweden assigns herself a low strategic value; control of her territory, or acces to Swedish resources are thought to become significant only as a preparation for or as a part of operations aiming at more far-reaching goals . . . only a marginal part of the military strength of a superpower could be used in an attack on Sweden. This doctrine is important in that it gives credibility to Swedish defence. (Andrén, 1976, 27–8)

The 1980s revealed how little Swedish non-alignment was respected by the Soviets, and how ill-prepared the Swedish forces were to ward off intrusion by even the 'marginal' forces of a superpower. Since at least the early 1960s Soviet submarines had been probing the coasts of Sweden and the other Scandinavian countries. These violations now assumed an altogether greater magnitude and impudence. On 27 October 1981 the Soviet Whisky-class submarine No. 137 ran very publicly onto the rocks outside the historic naval base at Karlskrona on the south-eastern coast of Sweden. The Soviets were unabashed, and in 1982 the number of detected intrusions reached about forty, with significant concentrations in the Stockholm archipelago and especially outside the sensitive Muskö naval base, where bottom-crawling tracked mini-submarines roamed with impunity. To the outside world it appeared as if the Swedes had acquired their equivalent of the Loch Ness monster.

It is not easy to understand the political motivation behind these blatant affronts to Swedish sovereignty, which run directly counter to the Soviet peace offensive in Scandinavia. The military implications were explored by a Swedish parliamentary Submarine Defence Committee, which made its report on 26 April 1983. The tenor was that the Soviets must be rehearsing and preparing for attacks on Swedish installations.

Sweden was now caught up directly in the wider superpower confrontation across the North Atlantic and the Central Front. It will take Soviet provocation on a still higher order to persuade the Swedes to make open arrangements with the Western alliance, but never before has Sweden been made so painfully aware of the costs of supporting a declared policy of 'non-alignment in peace leading to neutrality in war'.

CHAPTER 10

━━━

The Central Front – Doctrines and Deployments

THE IMPORTANCE OF THE CENTRAL FRONT

By the Central Front is usually understood the divide between the two great world geopolitical systems, in the region of the two Germanies and western Czechoslovakia. If we include the neighbouring Benelux countries and north-eastern France, then we are talking about the industrial heartland of Europe and some of its most important political centres.

Nowhere else is there such an accumulation of armed force, nowhere else are the limits of operational space and time so narrowly defined, and nowhere is political and military movement fraught with such heavy consequences. The likelihood of war or dangerous miscalculation is undeniably greater in the Balkans, the eastern Mediterranean or the Middle East, just as remote and thinly settled northern Norway lends itself better to Soviet risk-taking, but none of these theatres have the potential to affect the balance of power between the Eastern and Western blocs as immediately as in Central Europe.

FORCES

TABLE 10.1

Item	NATO	Warsaw Pact
Divisions or divisional equivalents	26	57
Tanks	8,050	16,620
Artillery pieces (excl. mortars)	4,400	10,270
Infantry fighting vehicles and carriers	24,600	26,900
Fixed wing combat aircraft	1,800	4,060

All of the above figures are subject to very wide variations, according to the sources consulted, and the degree of 'massaging' which the statistics have undergone.

The Warsaw Pact total comprises the nineteen Soviet divisions in East Germany, the five in Czechoslovakia, the two in Poland and the satellite divisions – six first-line East German, ten Czech and fifteen Polish. Out of these fifty-seven divisions forty-eight are at Category A readiness, which means that they are fully up to strength in equipment and have three-quarters or more of their manpower immediately at hand. All of the twenty-six Soviet divisions in East Germany, Czechoslovakia and Poland are at Category A status, together with all six of the East German divisions.

The reinforcement ratios strongly favour the Soviets. Not only are their reserves much deeper than those of the West, but they have less far to go and they do not need to pass oceans and seas.

Until the 1970s the technical superiority of the West compensated for the numerical advantages of the Warsaw Pact. This is something which NATO can no longer take for granted, for the Soviet forces have acquired new firepower and mobility, and made particularly impressive advances in anti-aircraft coverage, self-propelled artillery, helicopter gunships, and long-range offensive aircraft.

SOVIET OPERATIONAL DOCTRINE

The Soviet forces are equipped and trained to execute a wide variety of operations, from all-out nuclear, biological and chemical warfare down to short-range conventional incursions targeted at bargaining counters like Hamburg or the Hanover conurbation.

In recent years the more limited options have seemed to offer the greater attractions. If the Warsaw Pact attained a rapid victory inside NATO's forward defensive zone the West would be faced with a choice between reaching into its nuclear arsenal or listening to what the Soviets had to say. In such circumstances it might seem reasonable to many Western Europeans to consent to dissolve NATO and the EEC, and require the Americans to vacate Europe.

Whatever the ultimate goal might be, offensive action is seen by the Soviets as a key tenet of their doctrine. The Soviets uphold the offensive as the superior form of warfare in its own right, and they regard any defensive fighting as a local and temporary state of affairs, to be tolerated only as a preparation for a counter-attack. Moreover, the safest protection for the Soviet motherland is to make sure that any war is carried from east to west, and not from west to east as in 1812 or 1941.

The Soviets attach great importance to surprise as a means of attaining a decisive edge of advantage in their offensives. Surprise will be much enhanced by successful *maskirovka*, a term which extends to campaigns or political deception or softening-up, as well as concealing physical preparations and choosing unexpected places and time for the attack. Summer is the best season for rapid exploitations, but there is a better chance of taking NATO off its guard from October to March, during the murk of the long German winter. Higher than normal quantities of troops are available to the Warsaw Pact during exercises (like the one which preceded the invasion of Czechoslovakia in August 1968), or the twice-yearly seasons of troop rotations between Russia and the Group of Soviet Forces in Germany, in April–May and October–November.

Conversely the NATO formations are thinned by leave in July and August, and by the dislike of working on Sundays or over the Easter or Christmas period. Civilian traffic surges onto the West German roads on the occasion of public holidays, occasioning lengthy jams in many places.

Any Soviet attack will be inaugurated by a massive strike by aircraft and missiles. This blow, whether conventional, chemical or nuclear, is designed to neutralise or destroy NATO airfields, missiles and nuclear artillery.

Soviet military doctrine holds that everything that follows must support a 'high rate of operations'. The first attacks are likely to be on a very broad frontage. Once the Soviets have detected gaps or weak spots they will attempt to feed in highly mobile penetration forces, probably in the shape of reinforced divisions, which have the task of making for key geographical political and economic objectives in the deep rear. These so-called 'Operational Manoeuvre Groups' will be distinct from the less independent second echelon (wave) of the main forces.

Taken together, the initial strike and the fulminating attack are intended to destroy NATO's forward defences before they can be properly formed, and set the Warsaw Pact well on the way to victory before the West can gather its wits to sanction nuclear release.

Everything is geared to keeping up the same high rate of operations, even if outright victory eludes the Soviets in the 'initial period' of the war. The Soviets will not bother to repair or reinforce the burnt-out divisions at the spearpoint. Rather they will replace them by intact formations from the rear. 'Whereas the first echelon armies might lead off the attack from their barracks in East Germany, the second echelon armies would not be slow to come forward from

Poland and Western Russia. Their overall effect would be to land a remorseless succession of blows upon a few chosen points in the NATO line' (Dinter and Griffith, 1983, 37).

Most Soviet vehicles are theoretically capable of travelling up to 500 kilometres without refuelling, especially if they move along the roads, and the Soviet divisions have integral fleets of supply trucks which can sustain the combat units in ammunition and fuel for about five days of fighting. Resupply (for many years one of the weaker points in Soviet logistics) will be facilitated by fuel pipelines and stockpiles in 'hardened' bunkers, and by making extensive use of railways, heavy cargo aircraft, and new road transport vehicles like the seven-ton truck.

The Soviets have had many years in which to plan how to maintain their high rate of operations in the terrain of West Germany. The rivers and canals have summoned forth an array of tracked assault bridges, and truck-borne pontoons, bridging sections and ferries (see p. 52), and their 122 mm self-propelled gun and their infantry fighting vehicles are capable of swimming without adaptation. The relevant Soviet experience goes back to their Great Patriotic War, when some of their river-crossing operations were huge affairs. During the passage of the Dnieper in 1943 nineteen armies attacked simultaneously along a front of 750 kilometres, and built more than sixty crossings of that very considerable river.

Movement by road is very attractive to the Soviets, for this gives them the opportunity of going very fast while keeping the movement under control and conserving fuel, tracks and suspensions. Engineer route-clearing detachments are trained to make new paths where none existed before, adding to the potential for surprise, and NATO forces must also be on their guard against penetrations down the German forest tracks.

Airborne *Desants* offer the possibility of laying down a 'magic carpet' for the ground forces by seizing bridgeheads, road junctions, and other objectives along the axes of advance. It seems unlikely that the Soviets will employ their specialised Airborne Divisions in mass Arnhem-type drops or landings. However, the independent Air Assault Brigades might be committed in support of the Operational Manoeuvre Groups, and the conventional ground divisions have helicopter squadrons or detachments capable of depositing infantry on short-range objectives. Long-range sabotage, assassination and reconnaissance is the business of the companies and 'Diversionary Brigades' of the Soviet special forces (*Spetsnaz*).

By the later stages of the Great Patriotic War the Soviets had worked out elaborate routines for attacking towns. They first encircled the target city, then divided it into manageable segments by concentric thrusts, and finally eliminated the central core. The concentrations of force were gigantic, and the Soviets brought up no less than 41,600 guns and 2,100 rocket launchers for their grand assault on Berlin (16 April – 8 May 1945).

Berlin was a prize of supreme political importance, and cost the Soviets the lives of about 305,000 of their soldiers. Present-day Soviet military doctrine puts the emphasis on keeping up the momentum, and in a future war it is likely that the Soviets will try to avoid the city centres if they cannot seize them rapidly and economically by *coups de main*.

In the countryside the emphasis will be on brisk attacks on any defended villages that are found in the way of the advance. If at all possible, movements will be executed in columns and along the roads, which puts a premium on bouncing the enemy out of their positions with the least delay.

It is very difficult to form an overall impression of the possible shape of air action on the Central Front, for we are dealing with the most fluid and fast-moving of all kinds of war, and an environment which is disputed by rival forces operating to the very limits of the available technology. Put in the most rudimentary terms, the main advantages of the Warsaw Pact lie in the great number of its Main Operating Bases and alternative fields, and the superior numbers of its aircraft. A qualitative improvement was first evident in about 1971, and produced aircraft of an altogether higher order of range, payload and versatility than before. Where the Soviets fall short is in their overcentralised control, a lack of the most advanced technology and a curious deficiency in flying skills and time in the air.

In wartime the first task of the Soviet air forces will probably be to send their Flogger and Fitter fighter-bombers to punch holes through the 'Hawk Belt' (see p. 274) of NATO anti-aircraft missiles along the Elbe and the Weser. The medium bombers are then supposed to wing their way to deep targets while the Soviets fight to gain at least temporary and local superiority over the battlefield, and so create an environment in which they can strike at the NATO ground positions. The Soviet surface forces are largely responsible for seeing to their own immediate anti-aircraft defence, but the Soviets have an equivalent to the linear defences of NATO in their chain of long-range SAM-5 missiles, which was constructed between 1979 and 1983 and extends all the way from the Baltic to Hungary.

SOVIET AND SATELLITE DEPLOYMENTS

The Soviet forces in East Germany are deployed on straightforward operational principles. The terms 'Shock' or 'Guards' are honorifics dating from the Great Patriotic War, and they have no organisational significance. Three of the armies are positioned roughly in a line behind the border:

- Second Guards Tank Army, near the Baltic
- Third Shock Army, on the north German plain around Magdeburg opposite the main forces of NORTHAG
- Eighth Guards Army, in a pivotal position around Weimar near the 'wasp waist' of West Germany

Two further armies are in support:

- Twentieth Guards Army, to the west of Berlin
- First Guards Tank Army, around Dresden

Together these five armies comprise the Group of Soviet Forces in Germany. The six Category A divisions of the East German Army form an integral part of the Warsaw Pact's first line of order of battle.

For operational purposes the whole of the Central Front will probably be designated a unified Theatre of Military Operations (TVD). Inside this theatre the formations will be organised into Fronts (army groups). The arrangement is a matter of speculation, but three such Fronts might be formed, for example:

- a Northern Front (Second Guards Tank Army, Third Shock Army, Twentieth Guards Army)
- a Central Front (Eighth Guards Army, Twentieth Guards Army, First Guards Tank Army)
- a Southern Front (Soviet Central Group of Forces in Czechoslovakia, Czech Army, Soviet Southern Group of Forces in Hungary, Hungarian Army)

Here is probably the most convenient place to present the Warsaw Pact deployments on the Central Front in schematic form:

IN EAST GERMANY

1 Group of Soviet Forces in Germany (GSFG) (HQ Zossen-Wünsdorf)

SECOND GUARDS ARMY (HQ Fürstenberg)
16th Guards Tank Division (Neustrelitz)
21st Motor Rifle Division (Perleberg)
207th Motor Rifle Division (Stendal)
94th Guards Motor Rifle Division (Schwerin)

THIRD SHOCK ARMY (HQ Magdeburg)
10th Guards Tank Division (Altengrabow)
12th Guards Tank Division (Neuruppin)
47th Guards Tank Division (Hillersleben)
7th Guards Tank Division (Rosslau)

EIGHTH GUARDS ARMY (HQ Weimar-Nohra)
27th Guards Motor Rifle Division (Halle)
39th Guards Motor Rifle Division (Ohrdruf)
57th Guards Motor Rifle Division (Naumburg)
79th Tank Division (Jena)

TWENTIETH GUARDS ARMY (HQ Eberswalde)
6th Guards Motor Rifle Division (Bernau)
32nd Guards Tank Division (Jüterbog)
35th Motor Rifle Division (Dallgow)
25th Tank Division (Templin)

FIRST GUARDS TANK ARMY (HQ Dresden)
9th Guards Tank Division (Riesa)
11th Guards Tank Division (Dresden)
20th Guards Motor Rifle Division (Grimma)

2 East German Army
9th Tank Division (Eggesin)
8th Motor Rifle Division (Schwerin)
1st Motor Rifle Division (Potsdam)
4th Motor Rifle Division (Erfurt)
11th Motor Rifle Division (Halle)
7th Motor Rifle Division (Dresden)
Airborne Battalion (Prora)

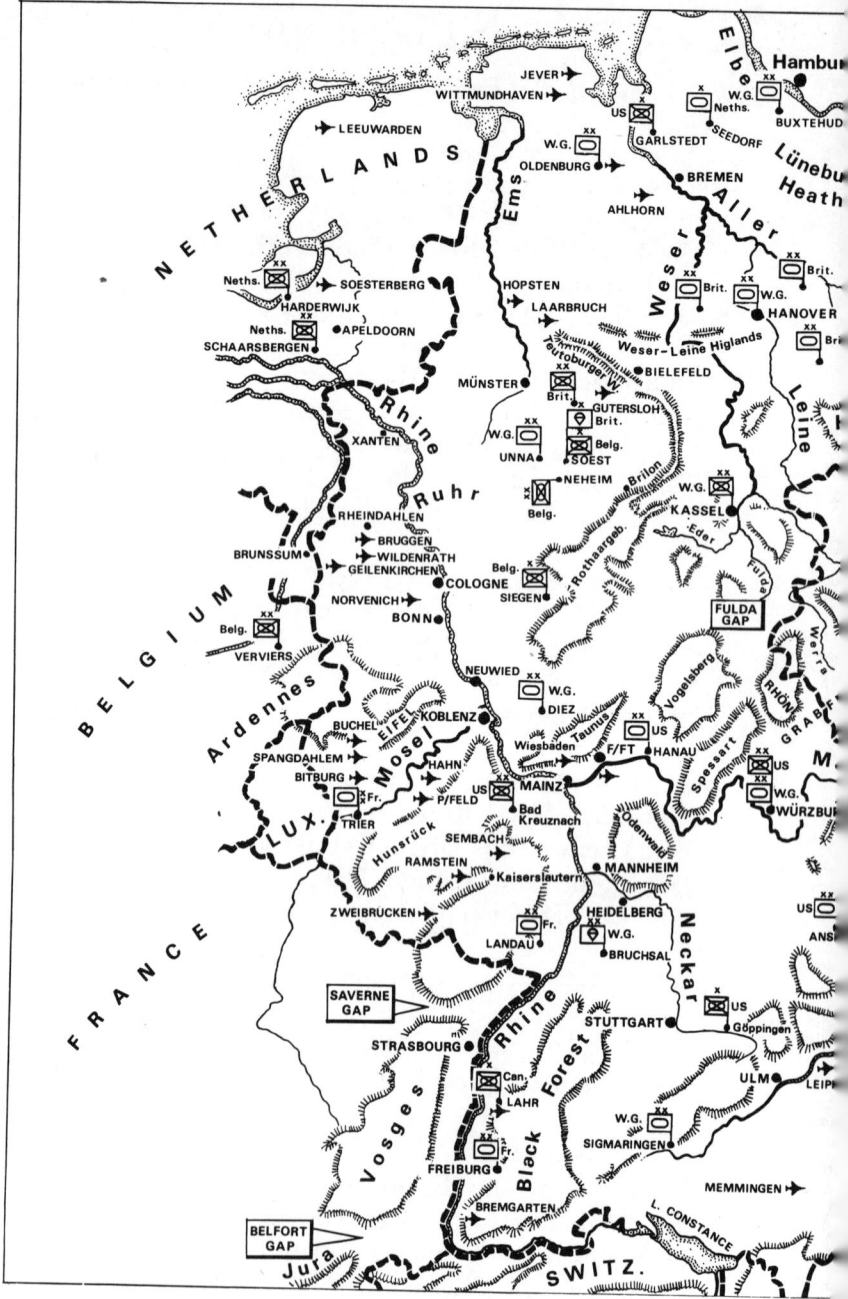

MAP 18   The Central Front

Map legend:

Symbol	Meaning
BRIGADE	BRIGADE
DIVISION	DIVISION
ARMOURED (TANK)	ARMOURED (TANK)
MECHANISED (MOTOR RIFLE)	MECHANISED (MOTOR RIFLE)
AIRMOBILE	AIRMOBILE
MOUNTAIN	MOUNTAIN
TERRITORIAL under NATO command	TERRITORIAL under NATO command

0   200

3 Soviet tactical air forces in East Germany (HQ Zossen-Wünsdorf)

Principal airfields in north: Finow, Damgarten, Wittstock, Neuruppin, Mirow, Templin. Stendal and Parchim (helicopter)
Principal airfields in south: Zerbst, Jüterbog, Köthen, Merseberg, Falkenberg, Altenburg, Finsterwalde, Brand, Grossenhain. Leipzig (helicopter)

4 East German air forces

Principal airfields in north: Trollenhagen, Peenemünde. Basepohl (helicopter)
Principal airfields in south: Cottbus, Dresden, Drewitz, Marxwalde

IN CZECHOSLOVAKIA

1 Soviet Central Group of Forces (HQ Milovice near Prague)
66th Motor Rifle Division (Zvolen)
55th Motor Rifle Division (Vysoké Mýto)
16th Motor Rifle Division (Mladá Boleslav)
10th Tank Division (Milovice)
31st Tank Division (Bruntál)

2 Czech Army

WESTERN MILITARY DISTRICT (HQ Tabor)
1st Tank Division (Slany)
4th Tank Division (Havličkuv Brod)
2nd Motor Rifle Division (Susice)
3rd Motor Rifle Division (Kromeřiž)
15th Motor Rifle Division (Cěské Budějovice)
18th Motor Rifle Division (Plzeň)
20th Motor Rifle Division (Karlovy Vary)
9th Tank Division (Tabor)

EASTERN MILITARY DISTRICT (HQ Trenčin)
13th Tank Division (Topol'čany)
14th Tank Division (Prešov)

3 Soviet air forces in Czechoslovakia

Headquarters and principal airfield: Milovice

4 Czech air forces

Principal airfields: Chotusice, Bechyne, Brno, Zatec

(NB The sources show very many contradictions. All of the above details are subject to correction and updating.)

NATO OPERATIONAL DOCTRINE

NATO does not possess an operational doctrine, or rather it has nothing to compare with the thoroughly thought-through corpus of teachings which the Soviets call the 'Soviet Military Art'. What the West offers instead is a handful of basic guiding principles, some military manuals, a number of programmes for re-equipping the alliance with new weapons and communications systems, and a great variety of theoretical *ballons d'essai* which are released into the air by military men, professional defence consultants, arms salesmen and university professors.

DOCUMENT MC 14/3 – FLEXIBLE RESPONSE

Among the basic principles of the West the most fundamental is that of Flexible Response (see p. 205), which was formally adopted by the NATO Defence Council on 14 December 1967. While NATO retained its full range of nuclear weapons, and the right of nuclear first use on the battlefield, it now set itself the task of building up forces that were capable of defeating aggression by conventional means before affairs deteriorated so badly that the alliance was forced to reach into its nuclear arsenal. Meanwhile the Soviets were to be kept in uncertainty as to the level at which NATO would pitch its military response.

Most NATO war plans enshrine Flexible Response in the notion of a 'conventional phase' of operations. However, the West has been very slow to provide the necessary physical means. The West Germans still hanker after the days of Massive Retaliation, which seemed a cast-iron guarantee of the American commitment to the defence of Europe (see p. 205). Moreover, tactical nuclear weapons are invitingly cheap, in comparison with their great destructive power, and Western Europe as a whole has preferred to keep its comfortable standard of living rather than pay the cost of large armies with their full complements of manpower, guns, spare parts, ammunition and all the other paraphernalia of conventional warfare.

FORWARD DEFENCE

This, the second strategic guideline, is a doctrine whose acceptance in NATO marched with the growing importance of West Germany in the alliance (see p. 204). In the 1950s the defence of continental Europe was still based on fallback positions behind the Rhine – 'we really were not particularly sensitive to what happened to people on the other side of the Rhine' (Carver, 1983, 7). By 1959 the main defensive zone crept forward to the lines of the Weser, the Fulda and the Lech, and then in the second half of 1963 NATO made up its mind to hold West Germany all the way up to the borders with East Germany and Czechoslovakia.

We have already noted how difficult it is for NATO to live up to its statements of principle. The West has been undeniably reluctant to work out what Forward Defence means in operational terms, and the British forces have probably been the least enthusiastic of all about the basic inspiration. Temperament, equipment, historical experience and local geography have all inclined the British to envisage an extended battle in depth, whereby a screening force action gives way to a succession of giant ambushes, and these in turn create favourable conditions for counterstrokes. No less characteristically the Germans prefer a highly aggressive kind of defence, which combines elements of positional warfare with powerful armoured thrusts which cut into the flanks of the enemy columns.

Since the middle 1970s NATO has sought to reconcile these differences in a common doctrine of Active Defence. Total uniformity has been neither attained nor desired, for the terrain is not identical all along the Central Front, but in the process every NATO contingent has had to sacrifice some of its sacred cows, with the British probably giving up most, and the Germans the least.

Forward Defence is open to some important objections. It appears to be the negation of hallowed military principles of manoeuvre and depth, making so little sense in defensive terms that the Soviets claim that it can only be intended to provide the springboard for an offensive. It compels reinforcements and supplies to make long journeys against the flood of refugees and under the threat of air and missile attack; the Rhine, once valued as a defensive barrier, now becomes a potentially serious obstacle to NATO communications.

Most seriously of all, the credibility of Forward Defence is being undermined in the 1980s by flexible Soviet operational principles (see p. 251), which might enable the forces of the Warsaw Pact to snatch a quick victory close inside the West German border, where they could seize the intended NATO deployment areas, breach the Improved Hawk missile zone, and overrun NATO's tactical nuclear artillery. The heavy concentration of tactical nuclear weapons (missiles and heavy artillery) in the forward defensive zone compels NATO to keep these weapons dispersed and on the move, to avoid presenting easy targets, and in the event of a surprise Soviet attack the NATO military and political command would be rapidly brought face to face with the dilemma of 'use 'em or lose 'em'.

Nobody has come up with a realistic alternative to Forward Defence, in spite of its manifest shortcomings. No other scheme can meet the desires and interests of the West Germans, who have about 25 per cent of their industries and 30 per cent of their population located within one hundred kilometres of the border. West German territory would be unfailingly devastated by any kind of war in depth. In any case nothing particularly brilliant in the way of manoeuvre could be expected of the NATO forces as they are at present constituted, for the variegated national corps structure is a 'mighty impediment to good command and control' (Mearsheimer, 1981–2, 114).

Physical geography also demands respect. The most defensible ground in West Germany happens to run within about thirty kilometres of the frontiers, and a prolonged slugging-match on this terrain would certainly run counter to Soviet operational and political purposes. Moreover, successive step-backs from the border will place NATO at progressively greater disadvantages. The sacrifice of one hundred kilometres entails the loss of communication with Denmark and the lower Danube valley. If NATO gives up another fifty kilometres the battle for Germany (and very much more) will probably be lost, for the ports, airfields and pre-positioned stores along the lower Weser are gone, and the enemy forces will be at Frankfurt and along the middle Rhine, sitting astride the communications between NATO's northern and southern army groups.

Manstein and other German commanders in the Second World War earned a reputation as masters of an offensive-defensive style of warfare – rolling with the punch and hitting back hard – which naturally suggests that such a way of fighting might offer an alternative to NATO's Forward Defence. However, this parallel is somewhat misleading, since much more space and time was available to

Manstein in the Ukraine in 1943 than will be at the disposal of NATO generals today. Also a close historical study has revealed that the Germans never voluntarily ceded ground in the Second World War, and that even somebody as lively as Rommel ended up by putting his trust in minefields and anti-tank weapons (Alford, 1977, *passim*).

Giving up ground on the Central Front would also be hazardous for political reasons. The fighting might come to a very sudden end if things were pushed to the verge of nuclear war, and in that case the new frontiers would probably congeal along the existing forward edge of the battle area, before the defenders had the opportunity to deliver their grand counterstroke.

Force multipliers

By the term 'force multiplier' is conveyed something which makes much out of little, the 'little' in this case being the NATO forces on the Central Front.

More than 5,000 tactical nuclear warheads still provide the West with its most formidable multiplier in the region, though these devices are regarded as weapons of last resort, to be employed only if the battle is being hopelessly lost on the conventional level.

More immediately palatable is the notion of engulfing the invader with swarms of gnat-like space-age *francs tireurs*, armed with anti-tank and anti-craft guided weapons (see p. 46). The effectiveness of these missiles is, however, open to question, at least in the lighter versions suitable for partisans, and in the circumstances of modern Central Europe it would be very difficult to reproduce the conditions which made guerrilla warfare so effective in recent history in south-east Asia and Africa, or in theatres like Yugoslavia or Russia in the Second World War. This is not to deny that continental NATO could make better use of its great potential in trained conscripts. These men, who are produced at a rate of half a million a year, are very suitable material for territorial forces who might hold cities, broken ground or other areas suitable for unmechanized infantry action, and so give greater freedom to the regular forces.

Three further multipliers are worthy of particular attention:

AIR FORCES

NATO's first operational warning of an impending attack could well come from intelligence satellites, or from its aircraft – high-flying spy planes, or AWACS orbiting from the Geilenkirchen field. Once the fighting starts, the inherent resilience, mobility and destructive power of aircraft will make them invaluable to the West on the Central Front, where the ground forces are faced with long and hazardous movements, and firepower must be brought to bear against sudden enemy breakthroughs. A number of aircraft will be told off for ground support of the latter kind, but the main effort will be directed against Warsaw Pact airfields and lines of communication.

TECHNOLOGY AND THE DEEP ATTACK

By the 1980s it became evident that the Americans, though still committed to deterrence and a reactive strategy on the Central Front, were determined that a first blow by the Warsaw Pact must be answered by extremely vigorous counter-offensive action.

The war-winning tactics and strategies have been explored in a number of official American documents – the USAF's *Air Force 2000: Air Power Entering the 21st* Century (1982), the current Army Field Manual *100–5 Operations* (1982), and the long paper *AirLand Battle 2000* (now renamed *Army 21*) produced by the Army's Training and Doctrine Command (1982) for operations at the corps level.

These documents do not add up to a coherent and received corpus of NATO doctrine. They are intended for use by the American forces, they differ greatly in scope, and they are not readily available for consultation in the alliance. *Air Force 2000* is a classified paper, which does not appear in normal military libraries. The Field Manual (much quoted at second or third hand) is not secret, but it has been read by no more than a tiny number of allied officers. The American general Bernard Rogers, who became SACEUR in 1979, nevertheless drew together a number of strands of thought in his theatre-level *Follow-on Force Attack Concept*, which was approved by NATO's planners on 9 November 1984.

Common to all true believers is the conviction that high technology makes a very attractive force multiplier, offering on the one hand an effective alternative to nuclear weapons, and on the other a substitute for 'old-fashioned' conventional forces, with their barracks, boots and bits of muddy equipment.

In broad terms the Americans intend not only to put more destructive weapons at the service of the forward defence, but to strike with missiles and aircraft against bridges, road junctions and other choke points well in the enemy rear, thereby causing huge traffic jams, creating fresh targets, and depriving the Warsaw Pact first echelon of support from the 'follow-on' forces. Targets will be 'acquired' by pilotless drones, airborne radars and the like, and new systems of communications will keep commanders constantly in touch with what is going on.

America's allies have not greeted the high technology concept with unreserved enthusiasm, and they fear that this novel style of warfare will enrich the American industrial corporations without adding much to the strength of continental NATO. Meanwhile the search for other force multipliers continues unabated.

FIXED DEFENCES AND FORTIFICATIONS

Sowing obstacles in the path of an invader has always been part of the currency of warfare, and modern NATO forces have the technical ability to plant nuclear mines, lay or project mine barriers with unprecedented speed, and reduce forests to tangled wreckage by nuclear or high-explosive tree-blowndown. West German bridges are built with demolition chambers as a matter of routine. Since the middle 1970s, however, there has been a remarkable revival of interest in engineered defences of a more systematic and comprehensive kind.

One of the sources of inspiration has been the closing-in and urbanisation of the West German landscape. Conurbations now reach out to one another along lengthy axes of development, and tree plantations cover increasing areas of the countryside, thereby hindering access and reducing the lines of sight (Bracken, 1977, 36–9; Burberry, 1978, 3). All of this has suggested possible military uses. 'If NATO were to exploit the conventional defence potential of cities, it would create, in effect, a super Maginot Line, echeloned in depth across Western Europe, which would constitute the largest man-made military fortification in history. As with all schemes of fortified defence, large mobile reserves would be essential, in addition to the use of the suburban and urban zones of Europe as a gigantic antitank barrier' (Bracken, 1977, 39).

Unfortunately, the German conurbations have developed in directions which are of little use for the forward defence (see p. 279). They may be compared in shape with a gallows or the Russian letter Г. The main axis parallels the Rhine, and therefore stands well back from the Iron Curtain, while the prolongation east towards Hanover runs perpendicularly to the border, and is consequently of little use as a frontal barrier. Moreover, the militarisation of civilian structures, whether tower blocks, suburban houses or villages, is something which demands a great deal in resources and time.

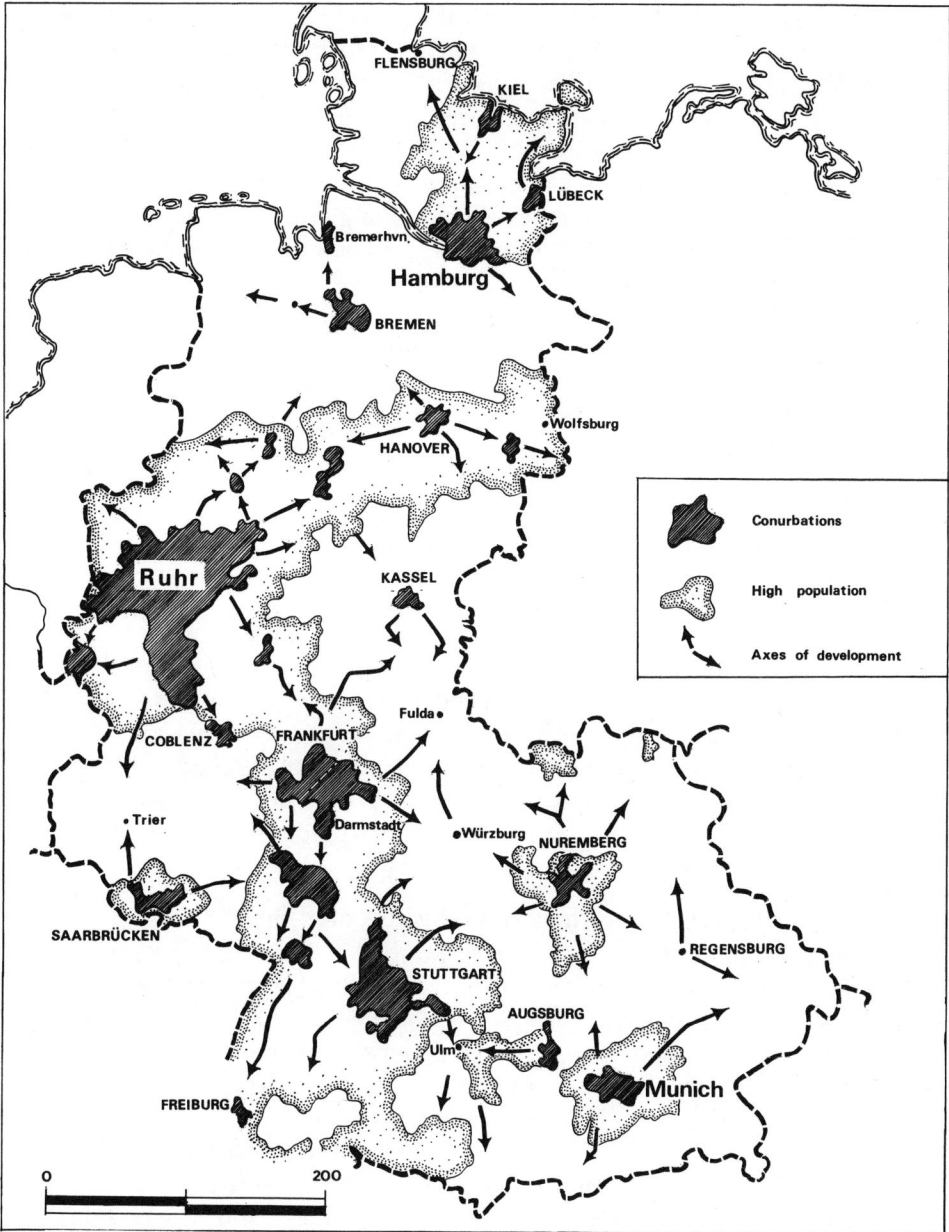

MAP 19   Urban Germany

In the same way no less than three feet of overhead cover is considered necessary to protect entrenched positions in the open field against modern artillery. Fields of fire must be surveyed and allocated, artillery 'Defensive Fires' arranged, and weapons and vehicles dug in and camouflaged. With adequate engineering support a brigade needs some eighteen hours to build its 'primary' fighting positions, with emplacements for anti-tank guided weapons. About seventy-two hours are required to build something more solid, with full 'secondary' defences.

It is the saving of time which, I venture to suggest, has always been a precious asset of permanent fortifications, and one which entitles it to earnest consideration as a modern force multiplier. The other properties of prepared defences – the economy of force, the high degree of protection, and so on (see p. 48) – have already undergone serious examination in recent years.

When Israeli veterans tour the Central Front they are surprised by the inactivity of the NATO engineers:

> Only conscientious preparation of the combat zone – that is, the creation of a well-planned and preconstructed system of obstacles, fortified emplacements and other defensive works capable of delaying or blunting a determined enemy attack – can provide the defender with the means to carry out his mission. To assume that a forward zone defence can be implemented by mobile forces alone, however well-trained and equipped, is, at best, wishful thinking, or, more accurately, total self-deception.
> (Anon., 'Strategic Concepts', 1984, 24)

Many expert writers have investigated how the Central Front might be prepared in suitable ways. If we heap their proposals together, we come up with a fortified zone about 800 kilometres long, anchored on the Baltic in the north and the Alps in the south. The infantry is sheltered in prepared positions, and command centres, observation posts and long-range anti-tank guided weapons are sited in concrete bunkers. Farm buildings might be adapted for these purposes, and obsolescent tanks could be dug in to serve as pill boxes. Anti-tank ditches can be pre-excavated or created instantaneously by exploding underground pipelines, and works and approaches may be covered by the normal minefields and barbed wire entanglements (Alford, 1977, 14; Tillson, 1981, *passim*; Freeman, 1981, *passim*; Simpkin, 1982, 15; Hackett, 1982, 131; Dinter and Griffith, 1983, 32; McKitrick, 1983, 198; Bailey, 1984, 887–92; Cross, 1985, 23).

What are the principal objections to this kind of defence? The first is that 'fortification' is still (*pace* Richard Simpkin) very far from being a 'printable word'. Any proposals for engineered defences will probably have a better chance of surviving the first knee-jerk rejection if they are presented as what they are – schemes for the physical preparation of the potential theatre of war.

Critics who look into the matter more deeply will point out that the location of emplacements and obstructions will be known to the enemy in advance. This is perfectly correct, but the same holds true for the natural obstacles by which NATO sets such store, and which have been recorded by the Soviets in the most meticulous detail. It is one thing to see a barrier or fortification on the map, but something quite different to locate it in the stressful conditions of the battlefield. Every kind of defended position has the effect of complicating the task of the attackers, who must either make arrangements to mask or by-pass it, or allocate forces, materiel and time for a direct assault.

The environmental protests will be loudly voiced, but the local populations generally have a greater understanding of military needs the closer you approach the Inner German Border, and in any case careful engineering will make the violence to the countryside more acceptable:

> The landscaping programme should enhance natural obstacles and reduce the need for artifical obstacles, such as minefields, that could be installed only after mobilisation. The programme would include forestation, walled terracing, construction of recreation and irrigation lakes and ditches, and hedgerow planting. (Tillson, 1981, 70)

The wider political objections are not so easily overcome. A strategic barrier zone could be construed as a Western equivalent of the Iron Curtain, perpetuating the division of the two Germanies, symbolically writing off the East Germans and the Czechs, and abandoning the Austrians to their fate. Here the experience of the 1930s offers a baleful precedent. Considerations of this kind deterred the French from extending the Maginot Line along the borders with neutral Belgium, and the Greeks from prolonging the Metaxas positions to bar the avenues from Yugoslavia.

NATO DEPLOYMENTS

GROUND FORCES

The arrangement of the NATO forces in West Germany owes almost everything to politics, economics, history and inertia, and very little to operational considerations. The pattern was set by the Zones of Occupation which were established in Germany in 1945, and these in turn were the outcome of the last campaigns of the war. The British were on the left and the Americans were on the right, just as they had come ashore in Normandy on 6 June 1944.

In the first years of peace the allied forces were fitted into whatever ex-Wehrmacht and Luftwaffe barracks best answered the purposes of occupation. The NATO army groups and command structure were established in the early 1950s, and occupation status was formally ended in May 1955. In theory the various allied corps now became standing expeditionary forces, but in fact the transition from the days of occupation was very incomplete. Thus the British retain an 'area of interest' from Lübeck to the neighbourhood of Göttingen, and their peacetime quarters are scattered across the old Zone of Occupation in thirteen main garrisons and many smaller posts from Mönchengladbach to the areas of Soltau, Celle and Wolfenbüttel. The area where the British are supposed to fight, near Hanover, is very much smaller, and is actually garrisoned by a division of the I West German Corps. Separate headquarters still run the British Army of the Rhine (BAOR), and the I British Corps, which is the same formation in its operational guise.

Arrangements like these are none the less odd for having been sanctified by time. It is as if France in the 1850s was still garrisoned by the victorious allies of 1815, and the British and Prussians preserved the alignment they had taken up at Waterloo.

Deployment on the east–west axis

Over the years the horizontal arrangement of the NATO troops has been stretched ever more thinly by forces pulling from opposite directions. On the one side the hypothetical fighting front has been drawn east according to the principle of Forward Defence, but meanwhile the military presence in West Germany has been thinned out by the departure of forces for their homelands. The 1960s witnessed the disappearance first of the French troops from Bavaria, and then of the dual-based American divisions. In the 1970s most of

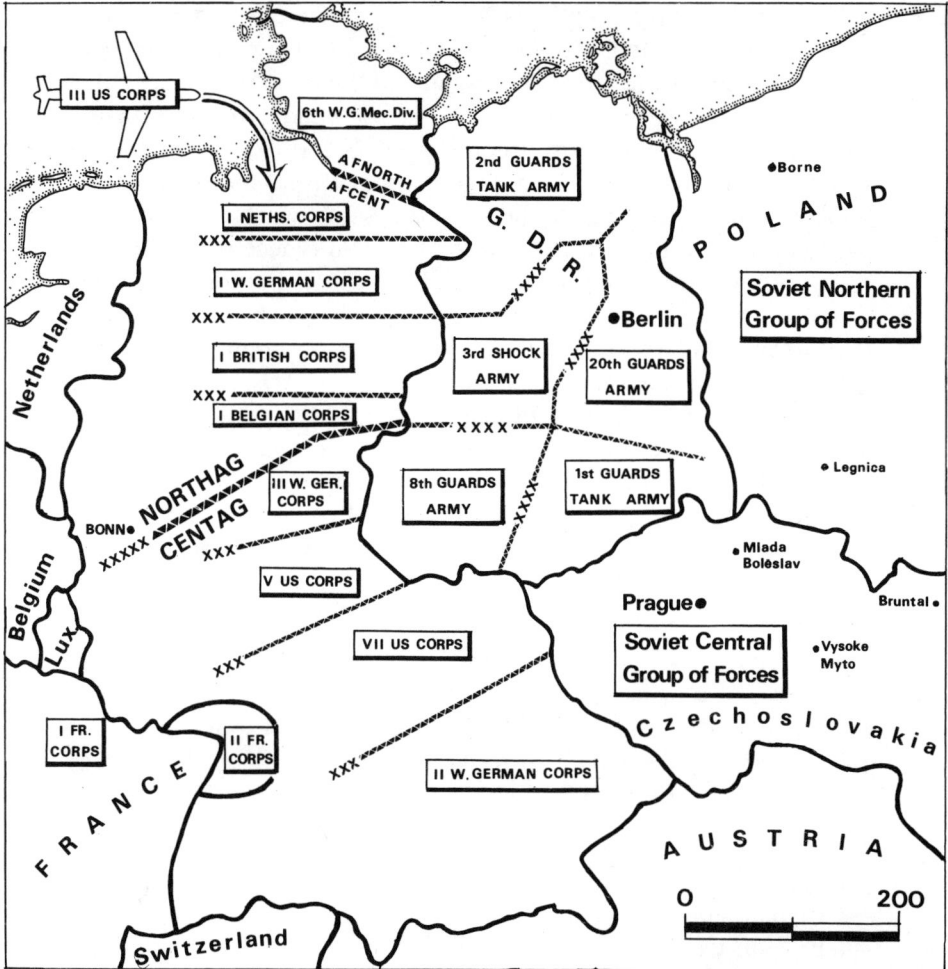

MAP 20   The Central Front – Major Formations

the Dutch and Belgians were whisked back over the borders, leaving little more than a nominal representation up front in Germany. The main force of the British still holds firm, in spite of the great financial cost, but one of the three brigades of the 3rd Armoured Division is based at Colchester, and the 2nd Infantry Division has only a small element stationed in Germany, waiting for its regular brigade and its two Territorial brigades to arrive from Britain in time of emergency.

The outcome is that significant elements of NATO's order of battle, especially in the north of the country, are faced with very long treks from home bases to their assigned stations in Germany.

Genuine military 'depth' is something different – a matter of having powerful and mobile formations available in your rear. NATO's second-line forces are few and all the more precious on that account. The nearest thing to a NATO *masse de manoeuvre*, capable of intervening in either the CENTAG or NORTHAG sectors, is the II French Corps on the upper Rhine and the Moselle. Smaller outfits that might help in the same work are the West German parachute division, and the Canadian mechanised brigade group. A second line in the north might be formed of the III French Corps operating from Lille, and the US III Corps REFORGER reinforcements – which are more likely to be committed in the NORTHAG sector than in the south.

The main concentrations of major headquarters, airfields, depots and other rearward establishments are held as far back as is physically possible in this rather narrow theatre. There are two significant groupings – one on the left centre between Brunssum and Cologne, and the other on the right centre between Trier and Heidelberg.

Deployment from north to south

The governing principle of NATO's vertical deployment is that of the 'layer cake', whereby operational areas of responsibility are assigned to eight corps of different nations, standing shoulder to shoulder along the border, namely:

- I Netherlands Corps
- I West German Corps
- I British Corps
- I Belgian Corps
- III West German Corps
- V US Corps
- VII US Corps
- II West German Corps

It will be noted that the two resident American corps are neighbours, but that the three West German formations are widely scattered. This is by deliberate design. There would have been some international unease if all the Germans had been grouped together (though nobody says so). More positively, the Germans desire to defend as many different sectors of the national territory as they can, and the allies see the need to share risk-taking to the full:

It is impossible . . . to overestimate the political value of such an arrangement, which ensures that an assault by the Warsaw Pact will not fall exclusively on German forces and the territory of the Federal Republic, but must also constitute an immediate attack upon the forces of several allies and therefore indirectly on their territories as well . . . This circumstance is a vital element of deterrence. (Hubatschek and Farwick, 1978, 45)

There are some penalties. The layer cake arrangement is a complicated one, and because the garrison areas do not necessarily coincide with the operational sectors there will have to be much criss-crossing of paths when the national contingents strive to reach the front line. The British difficulties have already been mentioned, but some of the other forces are also badly placed. The US 8th Mechanised Infantry Division is very awkwardly situated in the far rear at Bad Kreuznach on the west side of the Rhine, while the march of the US 3rd Mechanised Infantry Division from Würzburg lies through the garrison area of part of the West German 12th Armoured Division.

Worse still, the layer cake has made it difficult to even out the imbalances along the line of battle. Although it is a grave oversimplification to state outright that NATO's right is strong and the left is weak (see p. 302), the fact remains that the better going for tanks and the more important targets for the Warsaw Pact are to be found in the north, where the NATO contingents are ill-assorted and scattered.

It would be especially useful to achieve the right deployments in peacetime, because sideways movements along the line of battle (say by Americans into NORTHAG) are very difficult. Not only might the forces in the south be pinned down by enemy attacks, but the grain of the German country tells against south–north movement by a ratio of 4:1 in the hills, and 2:1 in the plains.

NATO first addressed itself to these problems in 1966, but little progress had been made by the time the retired German general Ulrich de Maizière delivered a comprehensive report to the Assembly of Western European Union in 1975 (Document No. 663, *Rational Deployment of Forces on the Central Front*). Maizière recommended that NORTHAG ought to be bolstered in case of emergency by sending the reinforcements from the United States to northern rather than to southern Germany – a principle which has been incorporated in the REFORGER exercises and NATO's war contingency plans. Maizière found that it would be much more difficult to rearrange the resident forces in Germany. A relatively simple move, like that of a mechanised infantry battalion to an existing base, was costed by Maizière at 1,700,000 Deutschmarks at the 1975 rate. The price was much greater when a new base had to be constructed, and amounted to 53,000,000 Deutschmarks for a mechanised infantry battalion – a bill which did not include the purchase of land, or the elaborate housing and other base facilities required by foreign regular units and their families, like those of the Americans or British.

The training areas in West Germany are very restricted and crowded, which puts further obstacles in the way of reshuffling the forces. As it is, British and West German tank crews must travel to battle ranges on the prairies of Alberta in Canada, and the British have found it expedient to build typical 'German' villages in training areas in the United Kingdom.

AIR FORCES AND ANTI-AIRCRAFT DEFENCE

The NATO air forces on the Central Front stand under the unified command of Allied Air Forces Central Europe (AAFCE), which was formed in the summer of 1974. The two major components are the Second Allied Tactical Air Force, which corresponds to the NORTHAG land command, and the Fourth Allied Tactical Air Force, which matches CENTAG.

Considered as a whole, the air bases in West Germany form a long and rather thin constellation of sites, located to the west of the buffer zone formed by the Improved Hawk Belt (see p. 274), whose inner edge runs along the approximate line of Schleswig-Holstein, Bremen, Frankfurt and Nuremberg. The number of fields is inadequate for the aircraft assigned to them, particularly for the reinforcements that are earmarked to fly from the United States, but NATO is better provided than the Warsaw Pact with Hardened Aircraft Shelters.

It is curious to reflect that many individual air bases now have a history stretching back to the limit of human memory. Thus the home of the West German 'Richthofen' fighter wing at Wittmundhafen is an old Zeppelin base. Many of the other fields in Germany show the influence of more recent history. This is clearly evident in the extraordinarily high concentration of American bases in the area of the Palatinate and Frankfurt, which is partly the product of the events of 1966, when the French evacuated their air bases in Germany and made way for the American squadrons which were being simultaneously evicted from France.

The backbone of AAFCE is the US 17th Air Force, which specialises in fighters. The headquarters is at Sembach, from where the Americans also command their mobile radars and their airborne and ground forward air controllers. Nearby Ramstein is the largest and busiest American air base in Europe, accommodating a tactical fighter wing, and the headquarters of AAFCE, the United States Air Force Europe and the European branch of the US Military Airlift Command. There are further American fighter wings at Bitburg and Hahn, and a mixed force of fighters and 'Wild Weasel' radar suppressive aircraft is based at Spangdahlem a short distance away.

The Royal Air Force has four Main Operating Bases in West Germany. Bruggen and Wildenrath lie close together between Cologne and the Dutch border. Laarbruch is located further north on the edge of the Reichswald near Hopsten. Finally the advanced base at Gütersloh, near Bielefeld, is the home of the Harriers and helicopters which provide close support to the ground forces.

The Main Operating Bases of the West German air force are found in three main groupings. The reconnaissance base at Pferdsfeld and the ground attack bases at Büchel and Norvenich are situated in the area of the central 'wasp waist'. There is a heavy concentration of bases in the north at Hopsten near the Dutch border, at Ahlhorn, Oldenburg, Wittmundhaven and Jever in the Ems country, and at Husum and Leck in Schleswig-Holstein. In southern Germany Bremgarten is tucked away near Basel on the Swiss border, but all the other fields are grouped in an arc to the west and north of Munich at Memmingen, Lechfeld, Leipheim, Fürstenfeldbruck and Neuburg.

The Canadians have their solitary European air base at Lahr in south-west Germany. The French air bases will probably be put at the disposal of NATO in case of emergency, giving a very needful depth to the air defence of the Central Front. No less valuable are the fields in Denmark (Skrydstrup, Karup and Ålborg), the Netherlands (Leeuwarden, Vokel, De Peel, Gilze-Rijn, Soesterberg and Twenthe), and in Belgium (Beauvechain, Kleine Brogel, Bierset, Florennes).

The air bases are among the principal customers of the networks of NATO underground fuel pipelines, which were begun in 1953, and now extend across Europe for more than 10,000 kilometres, of which 5,500 are to be found in Western Europe. The pipelines are designed to withstand nuclear and aerial attack, though a series of terrorist bombings on 11 December 1984 indicated that the pumping stations are vulnerable to sabotage.

NATO's heavy anti-air defence on the Central Front is arranged like a double Maginot Line. Mobile low-level radars are deployed immediately behind the borders with the Warsaw Pact, and are

backed up by a first defensive zone consisting of mobile Improved
Hawk surface-to-air missiles, which have a forty-kilometre horizontal range and can reach up to eighteen kilometres. The Improved
Hawk Belt offers an outer defence for the NATO airfields and rear
areas. About eighty kilometres to the rear of the Improved Hawk
Belt we encounter a barrier of high-altitude missiles. The original
Nike/Hercules missiles were installed in static positions, and this
system is now being replaced by mobile Patriots (horizontal range
sixty kilometres, maximum altitude twenty-four kilometres). All of
these missiles are of American manufacture, but they are purchased
by individual NATO countries, and operated by their contingents
inside their areas of responsibility.

NATO DEPLOYMENTS ON THE CENTRAL FRONT

This representation follows the same north–south sequence as the
one adopted for the forces of the Warsaw Pact.

West Germany to the north of the Elbe falls under the command of
AFNORTH in Oslo, which therefore controls the West German 6th
Mechanised Infantry Division (Neumünster) and the West German
51st Territorial Home Defence Brigade (Eutin).

The Central Front from the Elbe to the Alps forms the command
of Allied Forces Central Europe, and the dividing line between its
two component army groups (NORTHAG and CENTAG) runs
from near Bonn to near Göttingen. Unless indicated otherwise, the
divisional locations given are those of peacetime headquarters:

**Allied Forces Central Europe (AFCENT) (HQ Brunssum,
southern Netherlands)**

1 Northern Army Group (NORTHAG) (HQ Rheindahlen)

I NETHERLANDS CORPS (HQ Apeldoorn, Netherlands)
41st Reinforced Armoured Brigade (Seedorf)
1st Mechanised Infantry Division (Schaarsbergen,
Netherlands)
4th Mechanised Infantry Division (Harderwijk, Netherlands)

I WEST GERMAN CORPS (HQ Münster)
3rd Armoured Division (Buxtehude)
11th Armoured Division (Oldenburg)
1st Armoured Division (Hanover)

7th Armoured Division (Unna)

I BRITISH CORPS (HQ Bielefeld; BAOR administrative
headquarters at Rheindahlen)
1st Armoured Division (deployed posn N-E of Hanover)
4th Armoured Division (deployed posn S-E of Hanover)
3rd Armoured Division (deployed posn neighbourhood of
Hanover)
2nd Infantry Division (forward element only in West Germany)

I BELGIAN CORPS (HQ Cologne-Weiden)
16th Mechanised Infantry Division (Neheim)
1st Mechanised Infantry Division (Verviers, Belgium)

2 *Central Army Group (CENTAG) (HQ Mannheim-Seckenheim)*

III WEST GERMAN CORPS (HQ Coblenz)
2nd Mechanised Infantry Division (Kassel)
5th Armoured Division (Diez)
12th Armoured Division (Würzburg)

US SEVENTH ARMY (HQ Heidelberg), comprising:
US V Corps (HQ Frankfurt)
3rd Armoured Division (Hanau)
8th Mechanised Infantry Division (Bad Kreuznach)

US VII CORPS (HQ Stuttgart)
1st Armoured Division (Ansbach)
3rd Mechanised Infantry Division (Würzburg)

II WEST GERMAN CORPS (HQ Ulm)
9th Parachute Division (Bruchsal)
4th Mechanised Infantry Division (Regensburg)
10th Armoured Division (Sigmaringen)
8th Mountain Division (Garmisch-Partenkirchen)

CANADIAN LAND FORCES EUROPE (HQ Lahr)
4th Mechanised Brigade Group (Lahr)

3 *Other forces*
US III CORPS REFORGER reinforcement (HQ Fort Hood, Texas.
Home-based in US, with POMCVS and one brigade each

forward-based in West Germany).
1st Mechanised Infantry Division (Fort Riley, Kansas)
2nd Armoured Division (Fort Hood)
4th Mechanised Infantry Division (Fort Carson, Colorado)

West German Territorial Army
56th Home Defence Brigade (Neuburg)

Not under NATO command are 4 Home Defence Brigades, 6
equipment-holding Home Defence Brigades, 15 Home Defence
Regiments, 150 Home Defence Companies

French forces in Germany (not under NATO command)
II FRENCH CORPS (HQ Baden-Baden)
1st Armoured Division (Trier)
5th Armoured Division (Landau)
3rd Armoured Division (Freiburg)

CHAPTER 11

The Central Front – Ground

In the published literature the ground of the Central Front is discussed in language which suggests a ritual incantation, or a clearing of the throat. Again and again we hear about preordained axes of Warsaw Pact advance – the 'north German plain', 'the Fulda Gap', 'the Hof Corridor'. We are rarely told what they mean in geographical terms, or reminded of the fact that the Soviets have the forces to burst across the frontiers along a multitude of axes.

It would be agreeable to imagine that all professional military men are somewhat more alert to the nature of the ground. We must suppose that this is indeed the case among senior officers, but there can be no denying that many of their juniors are content to live in hoggish ignorance of their surroundings. Thus it was once shown that the lieutenants and younger captains of a highly regarded NATO battalion, which was stationed for many years in Westphalia, acquired an intimate acquaintance of the geography of gaming clubs in London's Mayfair, but were by no means so confident about the location of the Harz Mountains. All but one of the young gentlemen went along with the consensus that the Harz must be somewhere to the north of the garrison area. The solitary exception knew better, for he had once been on a skiing holiday to the mountains, and he had been much impressed by the sight of the frozen river Elbe stretching through the middle (i.e. the reservoirs on the Oker north of Altenau).

GENERAL CHARACTERISTICS

SIZE AND SHAPE

Excluding West Berlin the territory of West Germany amounts to 248,144 square kilometres, which makes the Federal Republic a medium-sized European state – half as big as France, but slightly larger than Britain. West Germany is more than 850 kilometres long from north to south, but only about one third of that distance broad, and there is a very pronounced 'wasp waist' measuring just 225 kilometres across.

The Federal Republic's western borders amount to 1,303 kilometres (450 with France; 129 with Luxembourg; 152 with Belgium; 572 with the Netherlands). To the north there is a North Sea coast of 415 kilometres (excluding islands), a 67-kilometre land border with Denmark, and a 313-kilometre Baltic coast (including Fehmarn but not the other islands).

In the east the 'Iron Curtain' stretches for 1,737 kilometres (Inner German Border, 1,381; border with Czechoslovakia, 356). The borders with the southern neutrals are 1,118 kilometres long, not including Lake Constance (namely 784 with Austria and 334 with Switzerland).

FEATURES OF THE GROUND

The main agricultural areas of West Germany are located in the northern plains, Lower Bavaria, and in Upper Bavaria north of a line between Munich and Altötting. The historic woodlands of Germany are not so much the dark coniferous forests of popular imagery, but spreads of beech and oak. Much of the coniferous cover is the result of comparatively recent planting, and as a general rule the conifers are to be found on the poorer soils and at the higher altitudes. Though suffering from pollution and drought, German woodlands are increasing at a rate of 0.8 per cent per year, and they now cover 29 per cent of the national territory as a whole, and naturally a much higher proportion of the hilly ground. This makes West Germany a heavily wooded country, and helps to bring the average line of sight to below 2,000 metres. Nobody who proposes to employ woods for military purposes can afford to ignore the place which this greenery occupies in the German imagination as a symbol of peace, freedom and unspoilt nature. Children, young couples, latter-day romantics and middle-aged walkers all regard the German woodlands as something more than a mass of growing timber.

The river systems of West Germany are dominated by the regimes of the Elbe, the Rhine and the Danube. The Rhine and the Danube rise in the high Alps, and the seasonal variation in their water levels is therefore determined by the melting of the upland snows; the waters are highest in early summer and lowest in the winter. The Weser and the Main are important tributaries which are born in the comparatively low Central Highlands; their waters usually reach their highest levels in March and their lowest in September.

Inland navigation still has a considerable place in the West German economy. In 1977 the total length of the navigable waterways was 4,297 kilometres, and in that year they carried nearly one-quarter by tonnage of the total West German freight traffic. The canals (1,192 kilometres, or 27.5 per cent of the whole) are much wider and much better maintained than their British counterparts, and they have great potential as military barriers.

Along a given axis of advance into West Germany a body of troops will encounter a minor water obstacle on an average every 5 to 10 kilometres, a medium water obstacle up to 100 metres wide every 30 to 60 kilometres, and something bigger like the Weser, the Inn, the Rhine or the Danube (100 to 300 metres wide) every 100 to 150 kilometres.

West Germany is an intensively developed country which the Americans compare in general terms with their own eastern coastal corridor. The Gross Domestic Product attained $652,567 billion in 1983, which makes West Germany an economic giant, and the population is settled at the high rate of 248 per square kilometre, or about twenty more than in Britain. There are a number of important military consequences.

Between 4.5 and 9 per cent of the national territory is covered by built-up areas, according to how closely that term is defined, and these urbanisations accommodate about 85 per cent of the population.

Probably the largest concentration of 'smokestack' industries and textile working is still to be found in the Ruhr. A belt of mixed industrial development extends up the zone of the western conurbations (see p. 264) to Stuttgart, and there are important outstations to the east at Hamburg, Hanover, Brunswick, Wolfsburg, Kassel, Nuremberg, Augsburg and Munich.

The main centre of high finance is located at Frankfurt, on the river Main. The federal capital at Bonn is a small place, and is invested with little of the symbolic importance of London, Paris or Berlin itself. Local allegiances are still strong. Bavaria covers 70,546 square kilometres or 28.4 per cent of the national territory, and it has emerged as by far the most important of the federal states (*Länder*). It is the home of many of the new 'sunrise' industries, and it has gained indirectly from the extinction of Prussia.

The density of the West German road network falls below that of Britain, Belgium or Denmark, and in spite of an intensive programme of construction the roads are inadequate for the vast volume of traffic that they must bear. The main trunk routes (*Bundesfernstrassen*) are still for the most part furnished with only two lanes, and the absence of hard verges adds to the difficulty of bypassing any obstructions. The old Hitlerian autobahns need extensive repair and widening, and many of their newer counterparts are even now being built with just four lanes.

Modern West German road building appears to have been determined almost wholly by economic considerations. The Ruhr, the middle Rhine and Stuttgart are comparatively well provided with new roads, but east of the Frankfurt conurbation the single crowded A7/E4 autobahn represents the main lateral north–south communication. In contrast some excellent new east–west autobahns and highways have been driven across the frontiers with an apparent disregard for strategic logic. We may cite the first-class A24/E15 to Hamburg, the improved A2/E8 to Hanover and the Ruhr, the A9/E6 through the Hof Corridor to Nuremberg, and the widened Route 20 from the Czech border to Cham. Some excellent new roads form bypasses around towns which used to be notorious bottlenecks. They make for faster motoring, but the obstacle value of the towns has been reduced accordingly.

Routes of all kinds are in danger of becoming choked with refugees in wartime. NATO contingency plans therefore provide for allocating permitted roads to civilians, and keeping the refugees away from the designated Main Supply Routes (MSR).

In 1981 the length of West German rail routes amounted to 28,393 kilometres, and the *Budesbahn* must be reckoned as an important ancillary means of moving material. Indeed, the Dutch depend on the German railways for getting their armour to their assigned place on the Central Front (see p. 56). About 40 per cent of the system is electrified, but diesel locomotives are capable of using the whole length if the electrical installations happen to be knocked out.

One of the vulnerabilities of the *Bundesbahn* is that it has few bridges across the rivers. There are only three railway bridges on the 180 kilometres of the Ems between Münster and Emden, and none at all on the 90-kilometre stretch of the Rhine between Cologne and Neuwied.

It is worth mentioning that the rail system of East Germany will play an important part in any concentration of forces by the Warsaw Pact. There are rail connections to the Baltic ports of Sassnitz and Warnemünde, in addition to the eleven railway crossings from Poland and the seven from Czechoslovakia.

CLIMATE

West Germany has a generally temperate climate, though the more extreme continental character becomes more pronounced towards the south-east. The prevailing winds blow from the west throughout the year, carrying moist air which produces above-average precipitation in the Central Highlands and the Alps. The falls of snow increase with altitude, and above 700 metres the ground lies under snow for long periods from November to April; in the northern plain the snow coverage is more sporadic, but the winters there are still pretty grim by the standards of Western Europe. The final thaw usually sets in at the turn of February and March, but it can be hastened by the arrival of a mass of warm air which will produce unexpected flooding along the river valleys. Cross-country movement becomes difficult in both the temporary thaws of early winter and the permanent unfreezing in the spring.

As a general rule fog is most frequently encountered on the northern plain in winter, and in the southern mountains in summer. Local concentrations result from the miasma exuding from river estuaries, marshes and industrialised basins. Frankfurt experiences an average of 60.7 foggy days a year, and Essen 62.5. The Ruhr (unlike British industrial centres) is heavily polluted by smoke, and the critical point in the formation of smog is reckoned to be 1.7 milligrammes of pollutant per cubic metre of air, beyond which industries and vehicles are ordered to halt.

Cloud cover presses below 2,000 feet (about 600 metres) for 16 per cent of the time in summer and 43 per cent in winter. In the depths of the latter season the sun sets at between three and half past three in the afternoon, and heaves itself reluctantly over the horizon (if the horizon can be seen) at about eight in the morning. Adding the hours of darkness to the bad weather during the day, about 80 per cent of the time in West Germany is unfavourable for visual flying, making advanced 'avionics' nearly essential for high-performance aircraft. The same murky conditions restrict observation and movement on the ground, but add to the opportunities for pulling off surprises.

INDIVIDUAL REGIONS

WEST BERLIN

This city is an enclave stranded inside East German territory, about 150 kilometres from the nearest crossing of the Inner German

Border at Helmstedt. West Berlin covers the respectable total of 480 square kilometres, and the considerable tracts of woodlands and lakes help to reduce some of the psychological pressure on the population of 1,040,000 souls.

The citizens withstood the blockade by the Soviets in 1948–9, and the building of the famous Wall in 1961, which interposed a physical barrier with East Berlin. The Wall proper runs along the dividing line between the two Berlins. It is 46 kilometres long and stands about 3.5 metres high. The remaining city boundary is shared with the territory of East Germany, and here the border is barred by 120 kilometres of walls or fencing.

The occupying allied powers of 1945 continue to exercise sovereignty over Berlin, and West German forces are still excluded from West Berlin (which does not deter East German troops from parading in the eastern part of the city). West Berlin is garrisoned by three allied powers – a brigade of Americans, a brigade and an armoured squadron of British, and an armoured regiment and an infantry regiment of French, or about 10,000 troops in all. Article 6 of the North Atlantic Treaty of 1949 links the defence of West Berlin directly with the important Article 5, the one about mutual assistance in the case of attack, and the presence of the Americans, British and French ensures that a violent change in the status of the city will not go unchallenged. Prolonged military resistance is impossible, for West Berlin is surrounded by about 95,000 Soviet and East German troops, but the commitment to West Berlin is a symbol of Western guarantees to West Germany as a whole.

THE 'IRON CURTAIN'

The frontier between West and East Germany measures 1,381 kilometres, or about 400 along a notional median line which ignores the intricate re-entrants and salients. The border has no inherent military significance, and it originates from a British diplomatic paper of 15 January 1944, which proposed that after Nazi Germany was finally conquered the delineation between the temporary Western and Soviet zones of occupation ought to correspond with the old boundaries of Mecklenburg, Saxony, Anhalt and Thuringia – states or provinces which existed in Germany before the Prussians formed the united Empire in 1871.

The British hoped that ancient regional spirits might once more spring to life:

Any such movements will . . . almost certainly be based on the
revival of old loyalties to States and Provinces with certain
natural internal boundaries dictated by geography, history and
economic considerations . . . An anti-Prussian bias may well be
developed in certain areas, and there are strong grounds for
weakening the present preponderance of Prussia.
(Quoted in Bailey, 1983, 20)

The proposed boundaries were adopted in the London Protocol of 14
September 1944, and in July 1945 the Americans nobly agreed to
evacuate the gains they had made to the east of this line in the final
days of the war.

The border is a 'softish' one in geographical terms, but political
divisions and man-made barriers have made it very hard indeed in
other respects. On 26 May 1952 the East Germans began to close off
the frontier with barricades and a barbed wire fence. Work on a new
double border fence began on 13 August 1961, simultaneously with
the foundation of the Berlin Wall. The Soviets and East Germans
considered that these structures were essential for safeguarding the
state consciousness of the German Democratic Republic, and halting the emigration that was bleeding its economy white. The first
concrete observation towers made their appearance in 1969. These
were the slender eleven-metre-high 'BT-11s', which proved to be
unstable in high winds. A more solid angular model was introduced
in 1976.

The Berlin Wall is now something of a tourist sight, but along
most of the Inner German Border the barrier stands back discreetly
several hundred metres from the political boundary, which is
marked only by demarcation posts and stones. The East Germans
exercise the right to patrol right up to the political limit, which
increases the danger of accidental or deliberately created border
incidents along this acutely sensitive frontier.

The barrier zone is about 500 metres deep, and it undergoes a
continual process of updating. Thus in 1984 the much-publicised
removal of the SM-70 anti-personnel mines (which was good for
public relations) coincided with the start of work on new defences
which will make the border more impassable than ever.

In its fully developed form the barrier zone will be about 500
metres deep will comprise the following elements, taken in sequence
from the east (the viewpoint of the refugee):

  – inner wall or fence, about 3 metres high
  – parallel metal fence with electronic alarms

- open zone with watch towers and observation bunkers
- patrol road
- anti-vehicle ditch and obstructions
- 10-metre-wide 'death strip', ploughed and raked to reveal the presence of intruders.
- outer wall or 3.2-metre-high fence of expanded metal mesh

The refugee must finally reckon with the possibility of being shot or intercepted anywhere on the open ground up to the political border. Soviet armoured formations will be able to crunch across the barrier zone without any difficulty.

A five-kilometre zone inside East Germany is forbidden to ordinary traffic, and closely patrolled by border guards and police. The authorised crossing points consist of nine roads, eight railway passages, two navigable waterways and three air transit corridors.

The Soviet troops are held well back from the Inner German Border, and all the duties of construction, maintenance, patrolling and surveillance are left to the 15,000 personnel of the East German border police.

In 1953 West Germany took on the prime responsibility for the western side of the Inner German Border, and patrols are maintained by the West German customs police and the 20,000 men of the well-equipped Federal Border Guard (*Bundesgrenzschutz*). Allied military personnel are normally excluded from the border, though they make tours of the line for the purposes of surveillance and familiarisation. The British patrols are accompanied by the surviving personnel of the vastly experienced British Frontier Service, which was raised in 1946 to control both the eastern and western borders of the old British Zone of Occupation. The founder of the British Frontier Service was a sea captain, and it makes an incongruous sight to see elderly gentlemen patrolling Central European woods in a uniform which clearly derives from that of the Royal Navy.

Without the supervision of the *Bundesgrenzschutz* individual West German soldiers must not come closer to the border than one kilometre, or formations closer than five kilometres.

The 356 kilometres of the border with Czechoslovakia follow the very old demarcation between the Electorate of Bavaria and the Bohemian lands of the Habsburg Empire. Here the barriers are lighter, less well maintained, and stand further back from the political border than they do along the Inner German Border.

SCHLESWIG-HOLSTEIN

Schleswig-Holstein forms the geographical base of the Jutland peninsula, and constitutes the northernmost part of the territory of the Federal Republic. This is one of those pivotal areas beloved, of geopoliticians, and it is just as important for securing the mouth of the Baltic as it is for guarding the northern flank of NATO's Central Front (see p. 224). NATO has allocated everything north of the Elbe to the BALTAP subordinate command of AFNORTH, in other words to the Scandinavian command structure, but it would be pushing pedantry too far to exclude Hamburg and Schleswig-Holstein from a review of West German geography.

This generally flat region shows an unexpectedly wide variety of landscapes. In the south the city of Hamburg on the Elbe is West Germany's largest port (population 1,700,000), and receives 35 per cent of the national imports. The river broadens out considerably here, but it still has 110 kilometres to go before it mingles its dark polluted waters with the open sea.

Along the western side of the peninsula the North Sea surges against the North Frisian coastline, which is made up of marshy flats and wind-blasted sandy islands – Sylt, Föhr and their smaller sisters. In contrast the Baltic coast is sheltered, and is formed of grassy headlands, sandy coves and deep inlets. Inland the ground rises to the badly misnamed Schleswig-Holstein Hill Region, which turns out to be a countryside of undulating agricultural land. Both the scenery and the local dialects carry reminders of the ancient Anglo-Saxon connections with England.

The prime responsibility for defending Schleswig-Holstein rests upon the West German 6th Mechanised Infantry Division, which is garrisoned at the important road junction of Neumünster. It has the support of a mechanised Territorial Home Defence Brigade which (unusually for such outfits) stands at the direction of NATO, and not the German national command.

In the event of hostilities the British are likely to rush the 1st Infantry Brigade (formerly 6th Field Force) to the BALTAP area, which would afford some relief to the Germans, and help is also supposed to be forthcoming from the Danish mechanised brigades in Jutland, and from the I Netherlands Corps, whose operational deployment area is immediately south of the Elbe.

One of NATO's problems in the BALTAP region is the shortage of sizeable ports on the western coasts of Denmark and Germany. Hamburg stands dangerously far inland and dangerously near the

Inner German Border. Bremerhaven and Wilhelmshaven are more secure, though reinforcements from Britain and other allies will have their most convenient entry by way of the Danish port of Esbjerg. It is unfortunate that the narrow and seemingly endless channel leads through a zone of sinister sandbanks, making the approaches to Esbjerg vulnerable to mining or obstruction.

Adequate warning time and resolute political decisions will greatly increase the chances of a successful defence, enabling the NATO forces to exploit the useful defensive potential of the Schleswig-Holstein theatre. The Soviet Second Guards Tank Army has its two forward divisions stationed at Schwerin and Perleberg, where they are undeniably well placed for a dash along the routes A1 and A24. However, the narrow frontage (sixty kilometres) between the Baltic and the Elbe will restrict the numbers which can be employed in the Warsaw Pact first echelon, and if the Soviets are compelled to make a deliberate assault they must force the passage of the Elbe-Lübeck Canal (25–32 metres wide, 2.5 metres deep), which runs just inside the border. Behind the canal the attackers will encounter the remnants of the wild Sachsenwald, and the zone of industrial development which is spreading between Hamburg and the port of Lübeck on the Baltic.

If Hamburg and Lübeck are given up for lost, a fighting retreat in the direction of Denmark will be favoured by the useful way the peninsula is obstructed by marshy ground, lakes and inlets, and by the thick hedgerows (*Knicks*) which are peculiar to this part of Germany. Terrain of this kind restricts the approaches to the Kiel Canal (*Nord-Ostsee-Kanal*). This waterway is a formidable obstacle on its own account. It is 104 metres wide and 11 metres deep, and extends for about eighty kilometres from the Elbe estuary at Brunsbüttel to Kiel Bay. In order to nullify this barrier, the amphibious forces of the Warsaw Pact might well seek to land on the bays of Kiel and Eckernförde and sweep inland along the two banks. The canal bridges and tunnels, and especially the central crossing at Rendsburg, are likewise tempting targets for airborne assault.

Behind the Kiel Canal the levels of the Eider and the Treene lead to the ancient strategic borderlands between Germans and Danes, where the peninsula narrows to about thirty kilometres between the North Sea at Husum and the long narrow Schlei inlet leading from the Baltic to Schleswig town. Here and there you can still see stretches of the early medieval Dannewerk embankment, which was built by the Danes to impede Germanic raiding parties. To the north the ground broadens into the Angeln peninsula, and then narrows to a last construction on German soil, running parallel with the Danish border as far as Flensburg Förde. The terrain here is relatively open and dry, and Flensburg town is now outflanked by a good bypass and by the important A10/E3 autobahn, which extends a long way up the peninsula.

We shall now enter the realm of Allied Forces Central Europe. The main component regions will be discussed in turn, from north to south, and each section is introduced by a few words on its general character and strategic importance.

NORTHERN ARMY GROUP AREA OF RESPONSIBILITY

'Whoever is master of north Germany is master of all Germany' (Blumentritt).

The North German Plain

   I Netherlands Corps
   I West German Corps
III US Corps (dual-based REFORGER reinforcement)

The plain of north Germany is part of the European lowlands which sweep without interruption from the Urals to northern France. In German territory the plain curls to the south-west around the corner of the Teutoburger Wald and merges with the Westphalian basin, while the southern border is sharply defined by the hammerhead of the Weser-Leine Heights and the Harz Mountains.

This region is interesting for a number of reasons. It is the flattest ground in Central Europe, and offers the Warsaw Pact a direct avenue to the ports of the Netherlands and Belgium, turning the northern flanks of the central German highlands and the Ruhr industrial region. It also has a grand strategic dimension. The area of the lower Weser holds the pre-positioned stores and other reception facilities for the US III Corps, which is the main Transatlantic reinforcement for the Central Front; the peacetime communications with the two American corps in southern Germany enter by the same channel, and have done so ever since the direct routes through France were cut in 1966.

Any Soviet attack across the plain will probably be shared between the Second Guards Tank Army, which will spare one or more of its divisions for the purpose, and the Third Shock Army, which has its headquarters at Magdeburg just forty kilometres from the Inner German Border.

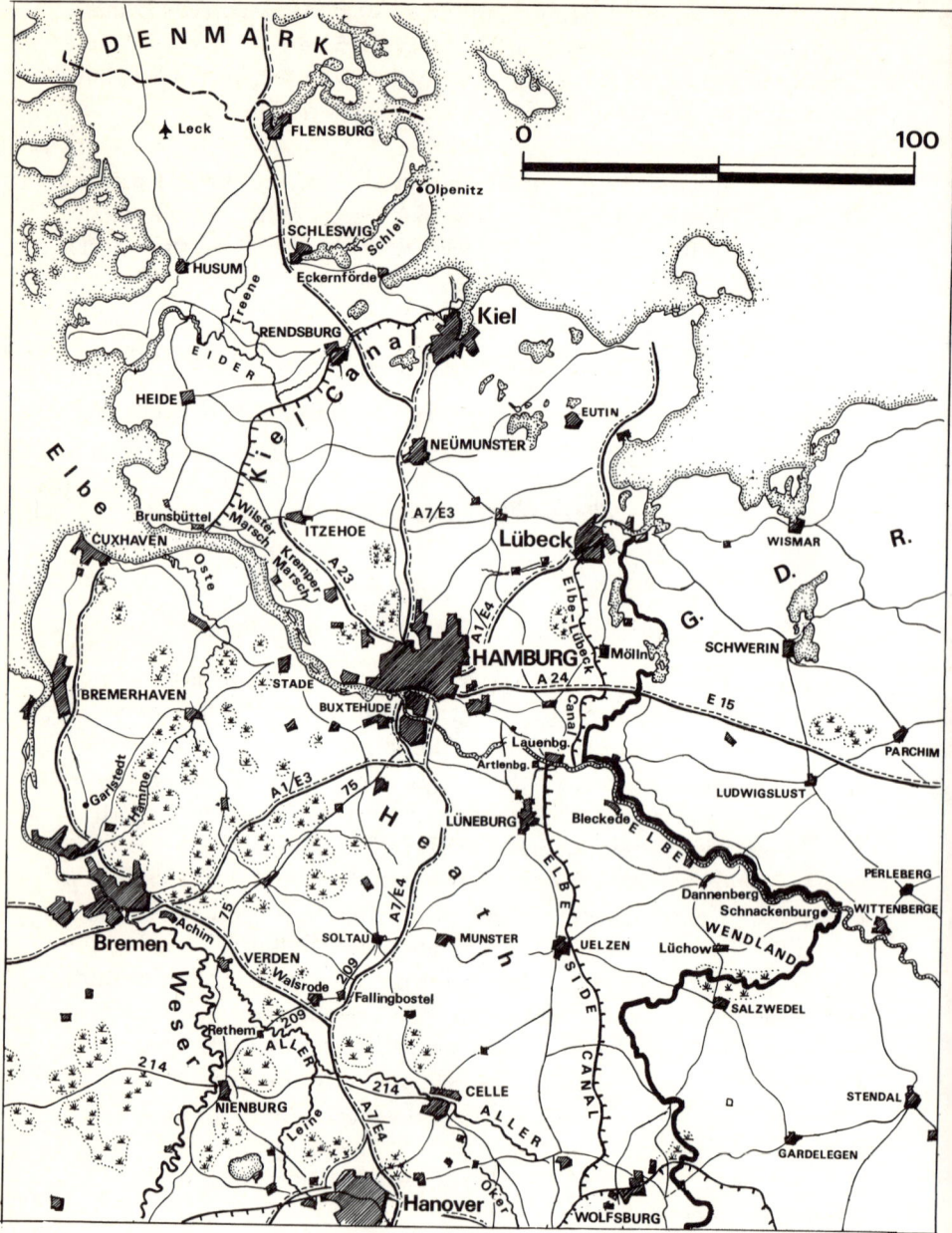

MAP 21   The Northern Plain

On the NATO side the I Netherlands Corps has the responsibility of holding the sector nearest the Elbe. In fact only a reinforced armoured brigade is forward-deployed in Germany, and the two mechanised infantry divisions are held back in the Netherlands. The immediate burden of defending Lower Saxony therefore falls on the I West German Corps. This formation is not only the largest corps in the West German army, but also the biggest and best-armed of the NATO national contingents in the NORTHAG area. It comprises four armoured divisions, which are deployed 'two up and two back'. In the first echelon the 3rd Armoured Division (HQ Buxtehude) is garrisoned on the south bank of the Elbe and secures the northern part of the corps sector; its mirror image in the south is the 1st Armoured Division (HQ Hanover), which will fight in a rough line with the I British Corps. To the rear the 11th Armoured Division (HQ Oldenburg) is located in peacetime behind the lower Weser, and will probably help to secure the avenue of American reinforcement. Finally the 7th Armoured Division (HQ Unna) is tucked away in deep reserve in front of the Ruhr. The Americans have a brigade in the region of the lower Weser, which serves as one of the advance elements of the dual-based US III Corps. The Americans hope that their reinforcements will arrive in West Germany before the Soviets do.

THE ELBE FRONTIER

The Inner German Border follows the Elbe for the eighty kilometres between Schnackenburg and Lauenburg, and makes up the most geographically distinct part of the whole frontier. For most of this stretch the river is bordered by unspoilt pastureland and woods, and the sight of the grazing cows and red-roofed farmbuildings on the East German bank helps to soften the impact made by the concrete watchtowers and the barrier fence. On the West German side the meadows are overlooked by a row of steep and heavily wooded hills, which help to seal off the base of the patently untenable Wendland salient on the east.

The river is about 330 metres wide. The average depth is 2 metres, but more in the shipping channel, and the current is swift enough to reduce the barge traffic passing upstream to a slow walking pace.

In 1945 this formidable barrier imposed a delay of ten days on the British advance north into Schleswig-Holstein after the Germans demolished the bridge at Lauenburg. The new German jet aircraft pounded the left bank wherever they could detect signs of preparations for a river crossing, but early on 29 April the VIII British Corps effected a passage at Artlenburg by amphibious carriers, and about twenty-four hours later a battalion of the US XVIII Airborne Corps established a bridgehead to the right near Bleckede. At both locations the German resistance was sporadic, and in fifteen hours the US Engineers completed a bridge capable of bearing heavy traffic.

THE ELBE AND WESER ESTUARIES

These are broad and marshy-banked bodies of water which represent a geographical extension of the Frisian wetlands south-east into Lower Saxony.

Cuxhaven at the mouth of the Elbe is a distant outstation of Hamburg, and it is a busy fishing and ferry port in its own right. Similarly there are two ports on the Weser. The historic commercial centre is the old city of Bremen, while the deep-water port is seventy kilometres downstream at Bremerhaven, where the first docks were opened in 1827. Bremerhaven and neighbouring depots like Garlstedt are important for the resupply and reinforcement of the American forces in Germany, though the communications with the south are not particularly good. The A1/E3 autobahn is a safe but roundabout route to the CENTAG sector, leading through the Rhine valley; the A7/E4 is much more direct but also much more vulnerable, since it passes within a perilous thirty kilometres of the Inner German Border in the region of the Harz Mountains.

THE GEEST

The western side of the Lower Saxon plain is the region of the infertile *Geest*, where tracts of sandy open ground are interspersed with scattered woodlands, and considerable peat deposits (*Moor*) such as those which extend north-west of Minden and north of Bremen, and are prolonged towards the Ems in the west. In April and early May 1945 this soggy countryside slowed down the advance of the Canadian and Polish forces, and even now the main communications are routed around the patches of soft going, though the general trend of the principal roads and the A1/E3 autobahn is from north-east to south-west – in other words an alignment which assists an offensive by the Warsaw Pact.

LÜNEBURG HEATH

The most celebrated topographical feature of Lower Saxony is Lüneburg Heath, which occupies most of the eastern half of the plain. It retains much of its classic landscapes even though it is being eroded around the fringes by agricultural reclamation, and industrial development is spreading rapidly eastwards from Lüneburg town. The heath is generally higher, drier and more heavily wooded than the *Geest* country to the west. There are small hollows, open grasslands ornamented by gnarled bushes of juniper, and very considerable forests of pine, spruce, beech and birch. Most of the main roads are separated by expanses of woodland, and over much of the region the scale of the landscape is small, and by no means unfavourable for defensive purposes. In the centre of the heath the ground in places like Soltau is very well known to the German and British forces, if only because they do so much of their training there.

In the campaign of 1945 Lüneburg Heath came into prominence when the allies discovered the concentration camp at Bergen-Belsen, and again when they encountered very fierce opposition from the scratch *Panzerdivision Clausewitz* in the neighbourhood of Uelzen. Uelzen retains its strategic importance today, for it receives three roads which converge from the east, and it stands close behind the very useful barrier of the Elbe Side Canal, which runs from the Elbe at Artlenburg south to the Mittelland Canal near Wolfsburg.

THE WESER–ALLER PLAIN (Weser–Aller Flachland)

To the south and south-west Lüneburg Heath gives way to the more open and more cultivated land along the Aller and the lower reaches of the Leine and the Weser. In the area of Walsrode and Verden in particular artistic-minded people will detect many resemblances to the Netherlands. Occasional windmills rise above the dykes and the grassy levels, and the typical old farmbuildings are built of dark brown brick, and are overhung with shady trees in best Old Dutch Master style.

The Weser–Aller plain is of interest to the Warsaw Pact, for it offers their forces an unurbanised corridor passing between the conurbations of Bremen to the north and Hanover to the south. The most naturally defensible features are the river lines and the areas of woods and damp pastureland.

The outermost barrier is formed by the Aller, which winds in a general west-north-west direction. This river receives the Oker stream above Celle, where it measures 30 metres wide and 1.8 deep. Half way to Verden the Leine (50 × 1.6 metres) swells the river to 65 × 2.1 metres, and just below Verden the Aller itself becomes a tributary of the north-flowing Weser. The Weser measures 110 × 2.8 metres at the confluence, and after a series of wiggles in the region of Achim it arrives at Bremen and broadens into its long estuarine reach.

The Weser is fed from the Central Highlands, and reaches its maximum volume in the spring thaw (see p. 278). Immediately above Bremen it has an average velocity of one metre per second, but in February the speed can reach two metres or more. The Aller and the Leine are also fairly fast-flowing waters, and after heavy rains all the three rivers are subject to sudden increases in volume.

Where are the best places for the Soviets to cross the river barriers? Out of many possible passages the most direct is along the axis of Route 209 by way of Fallingbostel, Rethem and Nienburg, almost equidistant between Bremen and Hanover. The XII British Corps advanced along this avenue in the opposite direction in 1945. On 11 April it met stiff resistance at Rethem from the German 2nd Naval Division, and the British were finally compelled to make a flanking move by an unguarded crossing eight kilometres further down the Aller.

At the present time the A7/E4 autobahn offers the opportunity for a rapid advance across the upper Aller and south in the direction of Hanover. An alternative is to cross the river barriers by their northern flank, making use of the nearly parallel Route 75 and the A1/E3 autobahn which lead to the lower Weser above Bremen, where there is firm ground in the region of Achim. This right-flanking move was recommended to posterity by the eighteenth-century engineer Jakob Mauvillon, who accompanied Duke Ferdinand of Brunswick in the Seven Years Wars: 'It is a general rule in warfare that when you have several rivers in front of you, the best thing is to pass the barrier below their confluence, so that you effectively cross them all in one go, instead of having to take them one after another' (*Geschichte Ferdinands Herzogs von Braunschweig-Lüneburg*, 2 vols, Leipzig 1794, I,271)

THE BÖRDE, THE WESER-LEINE HIGHLANDS AND THE HARZ
I British Corps
I Belgian Corps

This area takes in the southernmost edge of the north German plain, and the beginning of the Central Highlands – a complicated zone of hilly ground which extends as far south as the Danube valley. If it was necessary to determine the most vulnerable and important sector along the Central Front, this part of the world must have a first claim on our attention. The avenues of communication lead directly to the first-class objectives of the Ruhr and the ports of the Low Countries. The organic weaknesses of the NATO forces are more evident than anywhere else, for contingents of four separate nations are crammed into a frontage of 120 kilometres, if we include the formations immediately to the north and south, and the 'layer cake' deployment here becomes something of a puff pastry. The Soviets believe that alliances are inherently weak, and one of the dangers for NATO along this sector must be that what is 'everybody's business' might easily turn out to be 'nobody's business'.

The I British Corps looks after the northern part of the sector, along a frontage of about sixty kilometres from the neighbourhood of Wolfsburg to that of Goslar. According to newspaper reports the organisation and the planned operational deployment of the British have been altered as a result of Exercise *Crusader*, which was held in 1980. The I Corps now comprises three armoured divisions and one division of infantry. The armour will be deployed 'two up and one back', with the 1st Armoured Division acting somewhere to the north-east of Hanover, the 4th Armoured Division to the south-east of the city, and the 3rd Armoured Division held back in mobile reserve. A 6th Airmobile Brigade (drawn from the 4th Armoured Division) is garrisoned back at Soest, and forms a reserve of fast-moving anti-tank firepower.

The strengths and weaknesses of the British are well established. They are strong in 'small-unit cohesion' and they have been comprehensively rearmed and re-equipped, but the British are historically clumsy at combining little actions into bigger ones, and at the present time I Corps is heavily dependent on reinforcements from the homeland to fill it out to its wartime strength. The Belgians on the right flank are in a still worse case, which leaves the British vulnerable to the south.

For the Warsaw Pact, therefore, this region affords the chance of grabbing a quick victory, as well as an opportunity for long-range penetration. An advance of just eighty kilometres will breach the NATO forward defensive zone in this sector, and carry away the important economic and symbolic prizes of Wolfsburg, Brunswick and Hanover.

BRUNSWICK, HANOVER AND THE BÖRDE Lying immediately under the low wall of the Weser-Leine Highlands, the southern edge of the plain of Lower Saxony is a scene of intense economic activity. Three towns or small cities extend along the axis of the A2/E8 autobahn. Wolfsburg is a 'company town' *par excellence*, and the production lines of the Volkswagen plant extend to within a few kilometres of the Inner German Border. There is an important branch of the Volkswagen concern at Brunswick – a growing industrial town which lies

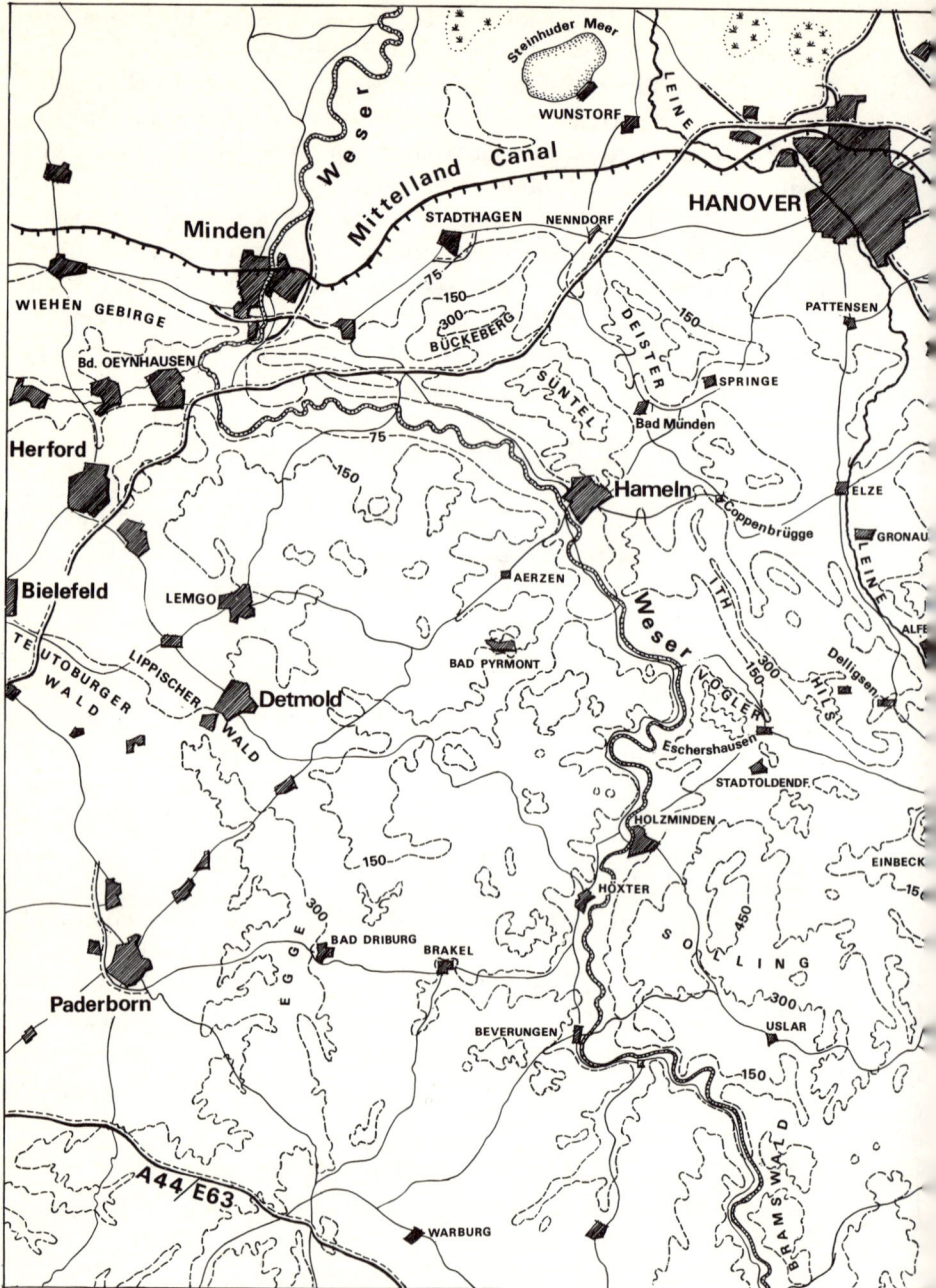

MAP 22   Hanover and the Harz

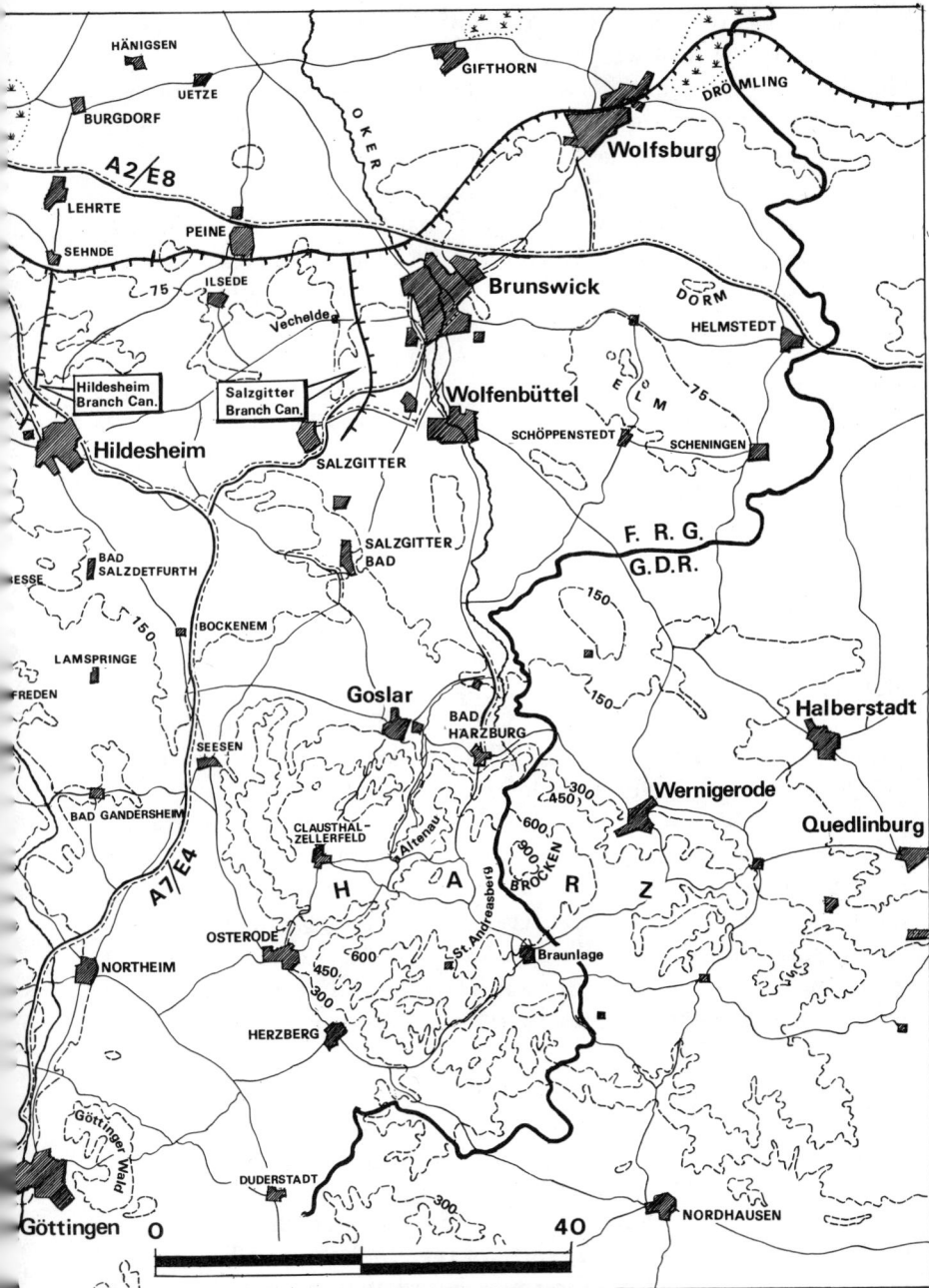

on the southern side of the autobahn. Fifty kilometres along the
autobahn to the west we arrive in Hanover (pop. 560,000), which is
another important manufacturing city, and comes into the public eye
through its springtime industrial fair (the largest of the kind in the
world) and the air displays at its busy modern airport.

Communications of all kinds are highly developed. The impressive and well-maintained Mittelland Canal (40–53 metres wide, 3–4
metres deep) is the most substantial artificial navigation in north
Germany, except for the Kiel Canal. It connects the Elbe with the
Rhine, running west roughly parallel with the A2/E8 autobahn,
which sustains most of the modern economic life of the region. The
feeder routes have increased the already considerable road density,
which is much greater than that on Lüneburg Heath.

Hanover is growing along the axis of the autobahn east towards
Brunswick and west in the direction of Minden and Osnabrück,
which gives a chance for the Soviets to execute a 'city-hugging'
strategy, hopping from the suburbs of one conurbation to the next,
until they reach the more continuous urbanisation of the Ruhr.
However, the towns are still embraced on most sides by intensively
worked agricultural land, for this is the *Börde*, a region of fertile
alluvial topsoil which stretches along the foot of the Weser-Leine
Highlands. The average width is about fifteen kilometres – narrowest at the western tip near Minden, and widest up the Leine
valley south of Hanover and along the Inner German Border.

The characteristic landscape is flat and open cultivated ground,
affording fields of fire of up to three or four kilometres, and
interspersed with large and isolated blocks of woodland. More than
most terrain in Germany the terrain favours long-range weapons,
and it is significant that on 9 April 1945 the sixty-seven anti-aircraft
guns emplaced around the Hermann Göring Works near Brunswick
were able to wreak some execution on the armour of the Ninth US
Army.

The *Börde* region lies along the most direct axis of advance
between Berlin, Magdeburg, Hanover and the Ruhr, and the Third
Soviet Shock Army might well strike against the junction of the I
West German Corps and the I British Corps. There appear to be few
opportunities for establishing a continuous line of defence immediately along the border. North of the autobahn the Soviets will
probably bypass the Drömling marsh and Wolfsburg. The Dorm
ridge immediately south of the autobahn near Helmstedt is very
narrow. The nearby Elm hill is much more substantial, and covered
with a forest of beech, but it is separated from the Dorm by open

agricultural land, and it is outflanked to the south by a salient of East German territory which reaches out to the neighbourhood of Schladen across a bare and sinister plain of fertile black earth.

The British will find more tenable ground further to the rear, possibly making use of features like the Brunswick–Wolfenbüttel conurbation, the Salzgitter and Hildesheim Branch Canals, and the isolated wooded ridges. (Here it must be stressed again that the author writes entirely from first principles, and has no knowledge whatsoever of NATO contingency plans.)

It is not easy to identify any comparable features north of the autobahn where the *Börde* region runs into Lüneburg Heath, roughly along the operational boundary between the British and German corps. To the west the Hanover autobahn dips into the Weser-Leine Highlands and so loses some of its potential as an avenue of advance. On the other hand a number of routes converge from the east into Celle, and from there Route 214 turns almost due west across the southern part of Lüneburg Heath, bypassing on the way all the areas of soft ground.

It is unfortunate for the British and West Germans that the principal canal of this region, the Mittelland Canal, runs on an east–west axis, and gives the Soviets the means of flank protection for a dash across the plain.

THE WESER-LEINE HIGHLANDS

The British area of responsibility covers two geographically very distinct areas. The northern flank runs along the southern edge of the Lower Saxon plain, as we have seen. The right flank corresponds with the Weser-Leine Highlands. This region is made up of a complex of fifteen ridges and ranges. They are nowhere particularly high, but they form a clear division between the north German plain and the Rhineland. Two further sub-divisions may be distinguished:

THE SALIENT OF THE WESERGEBIRGE, THE WIEHENGEBIRGE AND THE TEUTOBURGER WALD   The western part of the Highlands consists of two approximately parallel ridges which converge gradually on Osnabrück to the north-west, and enclose a region of considerable urban development around Herford.

The northern ridge (the Wiehengebirge and the Wesergebirge) looks bigger than it really is when you view it from the plain, and it is breached quite dramatically by the Weser as it cuts north at Porta Westfalica near Minden.

The rearward ridge begins with the Teutoburger Wald near

Osnabrück, and it gradually bends in a wide arc down to the south (the Lippischer Wald, the Eggebirge, the Briloner Plateau) gaining in breadth all the way until it merges with the Sauerland and the Rothaargebirge. The ridge is crossed every twenty kilometres or so by main roads or autobahns, but it forms one of the most impressively continuous features of the landscape of West Germany, and it must qualify as an outer barrier for the Ruhr.

The Teutoburger Wald has greater importance in European history, for somewhere in these woods the Germanic tribes annihilated the three legions of the Roman general Varus, nine years after the birth of Christ, putting an end to the Roman ambition to expand beyond the Rhine to the Elbe. In 1875 the Teutonic leader Arminius was commemorated by a huge statue near Detmold, familiar to generations of British soldiery as 'Herman the German'.

The ground between the Teutoburger Wald and the Ruhr is a plain with a dense road network, and lends itself to large-scale movements like the one by which the Ninth and First US Armies completed the encirclement of the Ruhr pocket on 1 April 1945.

THE WESER-LEINE HIGHLANDS EAST OF THE WESER   This is an agreeably undulating kind of country, which hints at the landscapes of central Germany. For once we shall begin our review from the east. As you approach from the foot of the Harz you first encounter a zone of open basins, where the neat little towns and red-roofed villages are scattered widely over the cultivated hills. The hollows in question are those of Bockenem, Bad Gandersheim and Einbeck.

To the rear we enter a much more thinly settled and strongly grained country, where the valleys of Sibesse, Alfeld, Eschershausen and Stadtoldendorf are narrowed to two kilometres or less by long ridges, which rise to three or four hundred metres in height and are densely clad in beech and spruce. Movement is therefore channelled along a south-east and north-west axis. The ground opens up along the Leine stream towards Hanover, but in the direction of Hameln it is crushed between new hills and the Weser, and here the most important defile is that of Coppenbrügge, a dozen kilometres short of Hameln.

The whole area between Bad Gandersheim and Hameln was the scene of much movement in the campaigns of the Seven Years War between the French and their British and German enemies. The battle of Hastenbeck (1757) was fought just to the south-east of Hameln, though most of the valleys were found to be too narrow to accommodate eighteenth-century armies in full panoply. The river

Leine did not figure largely in the events of April 1945, except as a phase line for the Ninth US Army, but it is an awkward little obstacle for armour, since the banks are steep in places, and they are liable to flooding after periods of heavy rain. At the present time locations like the 'Sibesse gap' are written as a matter of routine into the scenarios of many NATO exercises.

To the north the broad hill features of the Deister, the Süntel and the Bückeberg prolong the Highlands on either side of the A2/E8 autobahn. Westwards the approaches to the middle Weser find their way through or around the Solling and Vogler forests. The Weser along this stretch is a picturesque stream (60 × 2 metres), winding through meadows or steep-sided valleys. The river is fordable in summertime at Holzminden, and once an enemy has passed here, or crossed at somewhere like Beverungen, Höxter or Hameln, he has a widely radiating network of routes at his immediate disposal on the west bank. It is easy to imagine how these points could become the targets of Soviet airborne assaults, just as the line of the Weser might offer the British their last tenable position short of the western Highlands and the Teutoburger ridge.

In 1945 the Germans did not have the opportunity to organise a proper defence of the Weser, and on 5–7 April the Ninth and First US Armies were able to accomplish assault crossings near Hameln and upstream at Münden.

The British have good reason to be anxious about the security of the Weser-Leine Highlands, for the Soviets might very easily push through the Belgian area of responsibility to the south, and then break across the Weser on a broad frontage and push north-west to cut behind the British positions on the *Börde*. For this grand left hook the Soviets could employ a substantial part of their Eighth Guards Army, and call in support from the First Guards Tank Army, which forms the main uncommitted reserve of the Group of Soviet Forces in Germany. The Belgians have just two brigades on German soil (see p. 300), and only one of these is located in peacetime anywhere near the assigned national sector in the region of the Harz.

The Weser-Leine Highlands are therefore strategically open to the south-east. In compensation the ground is magnificently suited for the tactical defensive, for the pronounced funnelling effect of the terrain (see p. 260) will probably force the Soviet armoured columns to run the gauntlet of the narrow valleys.

THE HARZ MOUNTAINS

The so-called Belgian sector is about forty kilometres long and corresponds largely with the Harz Mountains, and in spite of the defensive advantages of much of the terrain it represents one of the most vulnerable components of the Central Front. The fundamental problem is that the Belgians are not available in sufficient force to withstand a surprise attack.

The I Belgian Corps comprises two mechanised infantry divisions, but only one of these, the 16th, is present in West Germany in strength, and even here it stands well back from the Harz in peacetime. It has the headquarters of its mechanised infantry brigade at Soest, and that of its armoured brigade at Siegen, and the Belgian barracks are scattered widely over both sides of the Rhine in the area of Cologne, Spich, Werl and Aachen. The headquarters of the other Belgian division, the 1st, is located across the border at Verviers in Belgium.

The Harz Mountains are a massif of heavily folded rock straddling the Inner German Border. On West German territory the peaks stand between 600 and 700 metres high and fall into gorge-like valleys, thus coming into the Soviet definition of 'low mountainous terrain'. The rocky slopes have a mantle of spruce, fringed with beech at the lower altitudes, and man-made lakes extend along the floors of three of the central valleys. The highest ground is east of the border. Here the dominating Brocken Hill (1,142 metres) was once the scene of witches' sabbaths and pagan survivals, and nowadays there is still something just as ominous about that domed summit, which is bald except for an array of Soviet radio masts and antennae.

It is difficult to determine how important the Harz Mountains ought to be considered in the context of modern warfare. In the first place they cast a long 'radar shadow', which gives Soviet aircraft the opportunity to sneak up on the Inner German Border at low altitude. Surprise for ground attack is assisted by the Harz microclimate. These heights are the north-western cornerstone of the great range of Central European hills and mountains which extend from here almost all the way to the Black Sea, and they intercept the humid winds from the Atlantic, causing heavy rains in summer, considerable snowfalls in winter and dense mists at any season of the year.

Actual progress on the surface will obviously be slowed down by the steep and heavily wooded terrain, and something of the defensive possibilities of the Harz was revealed by General Lucht's Eleventh Army, which held out there against the Americans in 1945. The

Germans had little artillery and only about twenty-five tanks and they rarely stood their ground against serious attack, but by utilising mines and barricades of felled trees they drew considerable forces from the Ninth and First US Armies. The fighting in the Harz began on 11 April. The radio station on the Brocken was taken by a formal assault seven days later, and mopping-up operations continued until the 23rd, when Lucht's mobile headquarters was run to ground near Blankenburg.

The very difficulties of attacking through the Harz might exercise a positive attraction for the Soviets, if they believed that surprise could thereby be enhanced. They know that the whole of the Harz on the West German side of the border is criss-crossed by forestry paths, and that no area of the mountains lies more than about four kilometres from the roads which radiate from the tourist resorts of Clausthal-Zellerfeld, Altenau, St Andreasberg and Braunlage.

It is therefore natural to draw comparisons between the Harz and the supposedly impassable Ardennes, where the Germans effected their *Blitzkrieg* breakthrough in May 1940, and where they attacked again in December 1944. Upon a closer examination, however, the parallels do not stand up particularly well. NATO is at least aware of the weakness of the Harz sector, whereas the Allies were oblivious of the dangers presented by the lightly-held Ardennes. Moreover, the West German share of the Harz is a stub-end measuring a maximum of twenty-five by thirty kilometres, which is much smaller than the Ardennes, and it is doubtful whether the Soviets would go out of their way to give themselves a bad time just for the sake of springing a local surprise in the Harz, when this tangled country may be so easily bypassed through the much flatter and easier ground on either side, namely through the Goslar Corridor to the north, and by way of the Göttingen Gap in the south.

THE CENTRAL ARMY GROUP AREA OF RESPONSIBILITY

The Göttingen Gap, the Fulda Gap, the Grabfeld

III West German Corps
V US Corps

It is often stated that NATO has a comparatively easy defensive task on the southern side of the Central Front, where the terrain favours the defensive more than in the north, and where the NATO forces are powerful and homogeneous contingents of Americans and West

Germans. We must enter some qualifications. The generally hilly and wooded country is opened by a number of deep corridors of much more accessible ground. Moreover, the Americans and Germans are forced to spread themselves very thinly in order to fill the void left by the departure of the French from the front line in the 1960s. Not only is the immediate frontier with the Warsaw Pact countries more than twice as long as that in NORTHAG (about 590 kilometres as the crow flies as opposed to 210), but the commander of CENTAG must make provision against a Warsaw Pact thrust across the Austrian border anywhere from the Böhmerwald to the neighbourhood of Salzburg, which effectively adds another 170 kilometres to the total.

The landscape changes perceptibly as we progress through Germany. On the eastern side of the Inner German Border the open plains of Magdeburg give way to the wooded heights of Thuringia. In West German territory the highlands widen to the south of a line drawn between Paderborn and Göttingen, offering NATO a great depth of defensive positions, and in place of the knife-edge ridges of the Weser-Leine Heights we have grand and broad features like the Vogelsberg or the Rhön. Long-range anti-tank weapons may be emplaced on the forward slopes, where the vegetation permits, and penny packets of armour are capable of commanding the flanking valleys.

This terrain may therefore be considered tactically strong, compared with much of the ground in NORTHAG, but it gives NATO a number of causes for concern on the strategic plane. It adjoins the boundary between AFCENT's two component army groups, and dividing lines of this kind are always a source of weakness. Furthermore, the bulge of East German territory gives the advantage of interior lines to the Warsaw Pact, and nobody in NATO can be sure whether the Eighth Soviet Guards Army will put in its main effort west towards the Rhine or south into Bavaria. The First Guards Army will in any event be fighting alongside or in close support.

The Soviets will have some splendid targets close at hand if they come surging across the borders at West Germany's 'wasp waist'. A push of 110 kilometres brings them to the city of Frankfurt and the autobahns which carry NATO's main communications between northern and southern Germany. By advancing 200 kilometres the Soviets can reach the federal political capital at Bonn, the nearest point on the French border, the huge US Army supply depot at Kaiserslautern and the very heavy concentration of air bases nearby.

THE GÖTTINGEN GAP

The literature on the Central Front is oddly selective, as we have had occasion to remark, and for every twenty times that the 'Fulda Gap' finds its way into the journals, there is perhaps one reference to the scarcely less dangerous avenue of penetration around Göttingen, at the boundary between the NORTHAG and the CENTAG areas of responsibility. The Göttingen Gap extends for about forty-five kilometres from the south-western slopes of the Harz at Osterode and Herzberg to the lower Werra near Witzenhausen. The Soviets can reach it very easily across the plain from Nordhausen in the east, or from the higher ground formed by the Ohmgebirge and the Eichsfeld, which run down to the border in the south-east. The terrain of the gap is undulating and only lightly wooded, and the ancient university town of Göttingen is embraced by open ground on all sides except to the east, where it is screened by the Göttinger Wald.

On the further side of the Göttingen Gap the invading forces appear to have two tempting avenues for exploitation. One lies north-west across the basins of Einbeck and Bad Gandersheim against the right flank of the I British Corps, and the other due west on a broad frontage across the upper Weser, and then either pushing directly for the Ruhr along the axis of the A44/E63 autobahn, or turning half right along the foot of the Teutoburger Wald against the deep rear of the British. A third exploitation, south-west towards Bonn, is by no means a physical impossibility, but this path carries the intruders into the difficult country of the Sauerland and the Rothaargebirge.

The CENTAG formation nearest the Göttingen Gap is the III West German Corps, which has its 2nd Mechanised Division garrisoned in peacetime up front at Kassel, the 5th Armoured division at Diez on the river Lahn, forty-five kilometres north of Frankfurt, and the 12th Armoured Division well to the south at Würzburg.

Immediately south of the Göttingen Gap stretches the zone of what for the sake of convenience we shall call the 'Werra Woods', where the ground close to the Inner German Border is much more tenable. The woods in question are those of the Reinhardswald, the Kaufunger Wald, the Meissner nature reserve and the Riedforst, which describe a semi-circle around the industrial town of Kassel. At many points the beechwoods reach down to the Werra River itself, which for thirty kilometres flows just within the West German side of the border. In military terms the Werra is a minor but useful forward

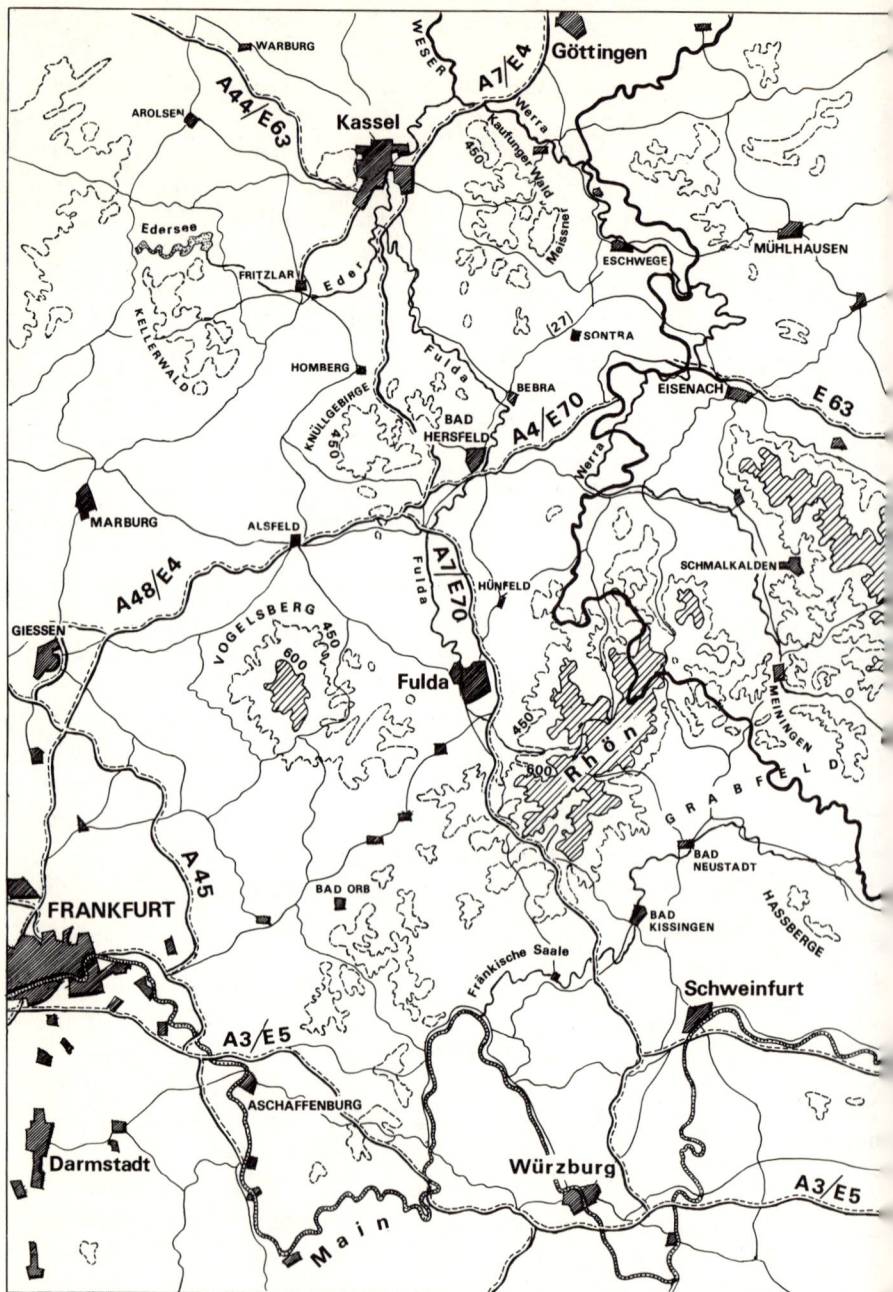

MAP 23   Fulda, Hof and Weiden

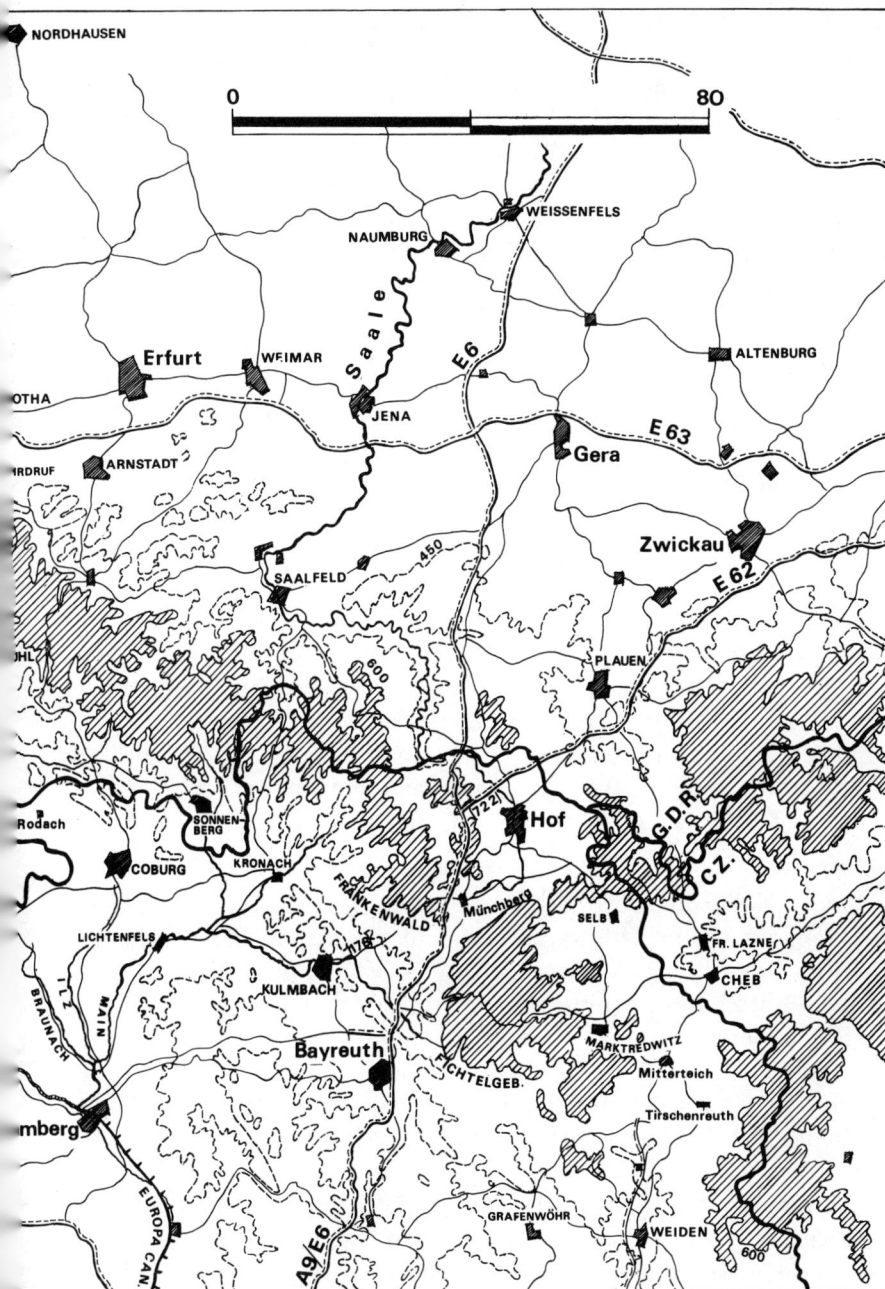

obstacle. The average width is about 35 metres, the depth 1.7 metres and the velocity 1.5 metres per second. The volume of the Werra is usually greatest in the early spring, but the river becomes fordable during the summertime.

Behind the Werra Woods the Kassel conurbation has an inherent defensive value, and it was the scene of four days of bloody fighting in early April 1945. The corridor of flat ground to the south, although penetrated by autobahns, might be inundated by breaching the Eder Dam (one of the targets of the British 'Dambusters' in 1943).

THE FULDA GAP

The Fulda Gap is the most celebrated of all the possible directions of Soviet advance into West Germany, but strangely enough some effort is needed to identify this passage on the ground, for no single feature has startling gap-like characteristics. Fulda town does not count, for it lies well to the south, while the Fulda river is an insignificant stream, about twenty metres wide and under two metres deep, which corresponds with the likely axis of a Warsaw Pact penetration for no more than a dozen kilometres. In effect the Gap turns out to be a zone of relatively accessible ground which reaches from the Inner German Border near Eisenach south-west to the neighbourhood of Frankfurt.

Close to the border the two principal frontier avenues converge on the basin of Bad Hersfeld, which is a busy and expanding town.

- Route 27 comes from the north-east over hilly ground. It meets the Fulda River at Bebra and runs alongside it to Bad Hersfeld; the beechwoods accompany the west bank for most of the way, but the right bank forms a flat and open plain which stretches a couple of kilometres to the east.
- The other approach is from the north-west along the East German autobahn E63, which stops at the Inner German Border, and is joined with the West German autobahn A4/E70 by means of a short stretch of hilly road. For strategic purposes the E63 and the E70 may be regarded as a single system, connecting the garrisons of the Eighth Soviet Guards Army with the Fulda Gap. Pivoting on Eisenach the Soviets may drive directly down the main axis, or advance on a broad front from the east across the valley of the upper Werra.

Behind Bad Hersfeld the road network branches out in a wide arc, and here the German and American forces will probably resort to a defence in depth, based on the principal hill features. The Knüll-gebirge (max. 636 metres) offer a forward flanking position to the north of the corridor. The sprawling Vogelsberg (max. 772) extends across the centre of the avenue, and to the south another volcanic massif, the considerable and heavily wooded Rhön (max. 950), forms the buttress on the right flank.

THE GRABFELD

We leave the Fulda Gap and follow the Inner German Border for a short distance where it inclines to the east. On its eastern side the Rhön looms impressively over the green, flat and fertile plain of the Grabfeld. Like the Göttingen Gap, this is one of those entries which figure very little in the published literature on the Central Front. The Grabfeld does not lead directly to important objectives like Frankfurt, but it could well be utilised by the Warsaw Pact to turn the defences of the Fulda Gap from the east. The approach from East Germany lies across flat ground, and a push south into Lower Franconia will carry the invaders through one of the most geographically open regions in the CENTAG area of responsibility. Once established along the valley of the Fränkische Saale, in the region of Bad Neustadt and Kissingen, the Soviets will be able to execute a right turn and advance over the many roads and tracks which lead north-west across the Rhön, hitting the NATO forces in the right flank just when they are battling to hold the Fulda Gap against the frontal assault. The Germans left the Rhön unguarded in 1945, and the Americans experienced little difficulty in passing over this apparently formidable natural feature.

Schweinfurt is an isolated industrial town on the upper Main. The wooded ridge of the Hassberge screens the direct approach from East Germany, though Schweinfurt might be difficult to protect against a side-swipe coming from the Fränkische Saale.

The Coburg Entry, the Hof Corridor, the Weiden Gap

This sector of the frontier follows the south side of the East German bulge and ends in the corner near Cheb, at the meeting of the borders of the two Germanies and Czechoslovakia. A possible objective of the Warsaw Pact might be to strike south and south-west in the direction of prizes like Regensburg, Nuremberg and Würzburg, engaging the American and West German forces so closely that they could not be deployed elsewhere. On the other hand the unique direction of the frontier in this region offers NATO an opportunity

for counter-attacks north into the East German bulge, following the
general plan of Napoleon's advance in the early stages of the Jena
campaign in 1806. A short-range NATO counterstroke might dis-
turb the Warsaw Pact offensive through the Fulda Gap; a large
counter-offensive directly across the Thüringer Wald could threaten
the rear areas and second echelon of any forces operating in the
region of Göttingen and the Harz.

THE 'COBURG ENTRY'

East of the Grabfeld and the Hassberge the first feature of interest is
what might be termed the 'Coburg Entry'. This is a three-sided
enclave of West German territory jutting about ten kilometres to the
north of the general line of the Inner German Border. The southern
or open side merges with the highly populated valley of the upper
Main, and the area as a whole is a busy and small-scale landscape
which is characterised by fields, scattered woods and numerous
villages. The principal towns are Coburg and Lichtenfels.

The Coburg Entry is probably indefensible against Soviet attack
across the border from the wooded hills of the Thüringer Wald, but
on the southern side the valleys of the Braunach, the Itz and the
upper Main will tend to jam the invaders together on the approaches
to Bamberg. Any further advance in the direction of Nuremberg will
be flanked by the heights of the Fränkische Alb to the east, which is
one of many examples of the depth of defence available to NATO
forces in southern Germany.

THE HOF CORRIDOR

The avenue in question figures almost prominently in strategic
literature as the Fulda Gap, and, unlike its rival in fame, it at least
forms a recognisable geographical entity.

The wild Frankenwald forms the left-hand side of the corridor.
The peaks of the Frankenwald nowhere rise above 800 metres, but
they seem to be much higher than they really are since the slopes are
very steep and are clad in a very dense mantle of spruce, which
renders cross-country movement virtually impossible for vehicles.
Along some stretches the major east–west route, the 173, is enclosed
by a narrow valley or gorge, and when you pass through in misty
weather it is easy to imagine that you have been transported to
somewhere as remote as the North American Rockies.

The Fichtelgebirge rises on the corresponding eastern or right-
hand side of the corridor. In contrast to the precipitous ridges of the

Frankenwald, this feature is a great swelling in the ground reaching in two locations to more than 1,000 metres. The slopes are a little more gentle than in the Frankenwald, and the forest cover is not quite so dense. However, the principal route, the 303, could be barred quickly and easily by felling the tall spruce which line the roadside, and over extensive areas the ground away from the paths and tracks is strewn with massive boulders. Some of the blocks stand naked and open. Others have a light covering of grass or moss, which gives the scenery the appearance of some old abandoned battlefield, like the woods around Verdun.

Between these two hill groups the Hof Corridor represents an irregular zone of relatively flat ground measuring very approximately six kilometres wide and forty kilometres long along the north–south axis. The entry from East Germany is swift and easy. The E6 is a continuous autobahn which passes the garrison locations of the Eighth Soviet Guards Army, then runs across the Inner German Border and down the Hof Corridor and continues in the direction of Nuremberg. This city is a nodal point of communications in northern Bavaria, and a place of some economic and historic importance for the Germans. Another autobahn, the E62, arrives at the head of the corridor from the north-west, and it might serve as a channel for the First Soviet Guards Tank Army in Saxony.

The floor of the Hof Corridor lies at more than 450 metres, which is higher than the Fulda Gap, but the local climate is not particularly wet or snowy, and the landscape is a gentle one, made up of open cultivated fields and frequent blocks of spruce woodland. The 3rd US Mechanised Infantry Division has the immediate responsibility for guarding the corridor, and the chequerboard character of the terrain suggests that the Americans might adopt a mobile defence based on anti-tank helicopters and fast-moving armour.

THE WEIDEN GAP

The Czech frontier begins at one of the corners of the Hof Corridor, and it immediately assumes its characteristic south-easterly trend. We very soon arrive at the historic trading and military route which runs up the valley of the Ohre to the frontier town of Cheb (Eger), and branches out on the German side of the border to Bamberg, Nuremberg and Regensburg. Out of the latter routes the one by way of Weiden to Regensburg has become the most important, thanks to the building of the A93 autobahn.

This Weiden Gap is yet another of those entries which have been forgotten in the debates about the security of the Central Front. The

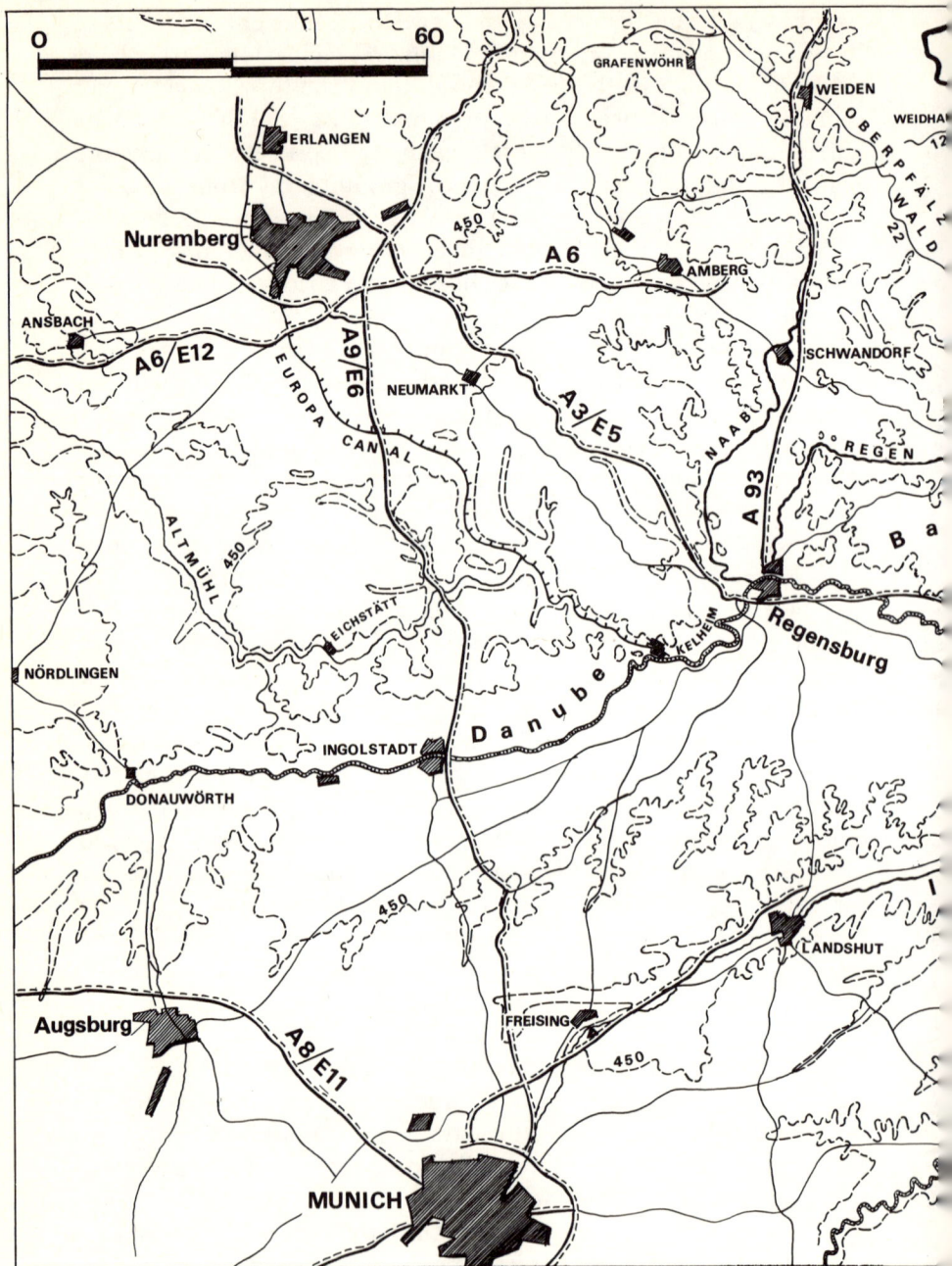

MAP 24   The Böhmerwald and the Danube

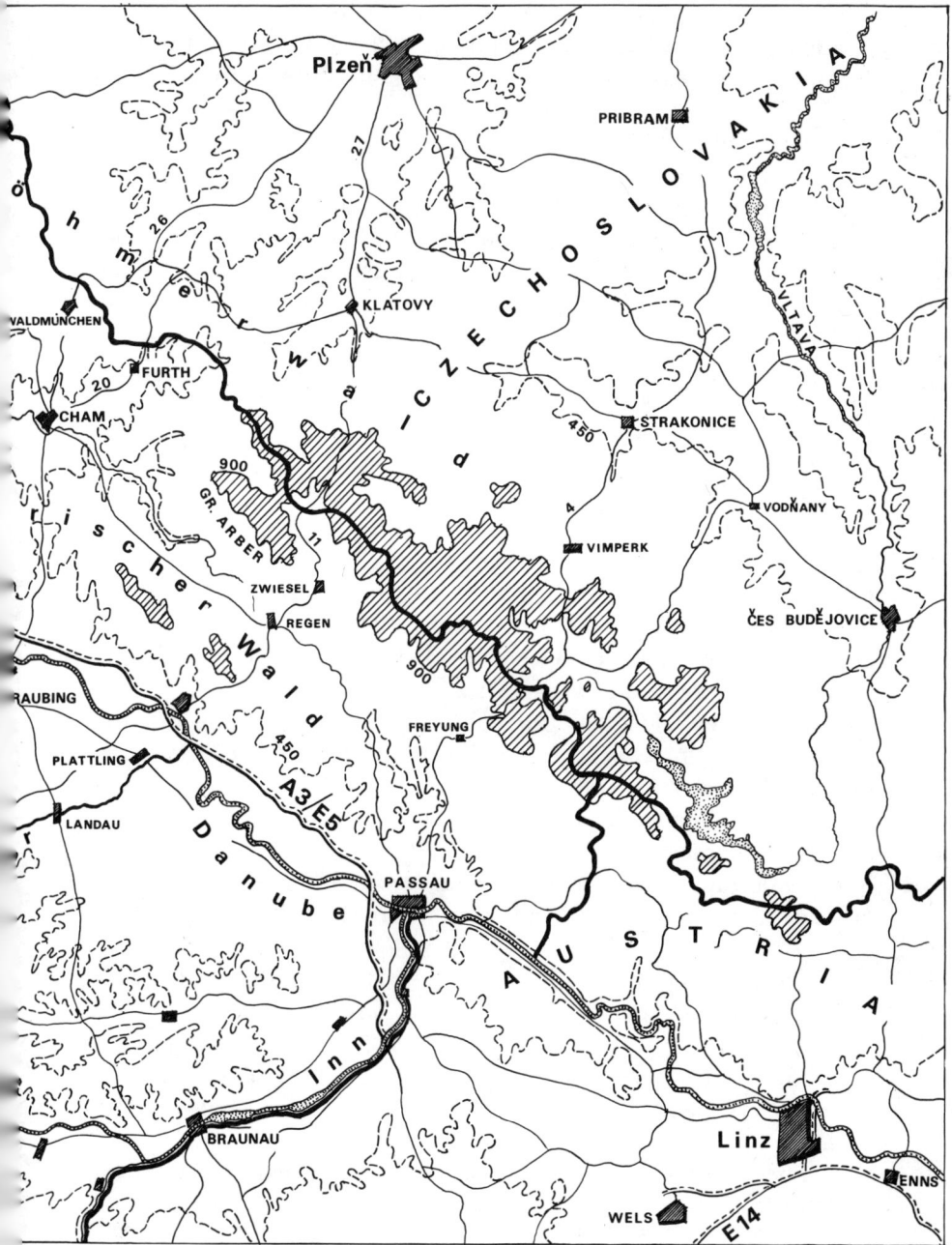

altitudes in this region are deceptive, as we have already noted in relation to the Hof Corridor, and the relative height of the local features deserves as much attention as their absolute height above sea level. The tract of high-lying ground to the north and east of Weiden looks fairly formidable on a colour-shaded map, but it turns out to be a considerable plain, made up of open agricultural land, copses, little lakes and wandering streams. Here the watershed between the regimes of the Elbe and the Danube is to be found not on the border but inside West German territory near Tirschenreuth, and the flat ground courses without a break from Cheb to Weiden, affording an easy access from the north.

THE BÖHMERWALD AND THE DANUBE VALLEY
VII US Corps (southern sector)
II West German Corps

THE BÖHMERWALD   South-east of the Weiden Gap the Czech border follows the range which carries the general name of the Böhmerwald ('Bohemian Woods'). This is one of the quieter areas of Germany. The humps of the border ridge extend endlessly across the horizon, and give way on the West German side to an agreeably undulating landscape of woods and verdant fields.

The Böhmerwald gains gradually in overall height towards the south-east, and reaches its greatest altitude about two-thirds of the way to the Austrian border at the peak of the Grosser Arber (1,456 metres), which in some years has a covering of snow as late as May. The ridge is interrupted by saddles and valleys, of which the three most important may be reached along roads radiating from Plžen (Pilsen), sixty kilometres inside Czechoslovakia:

- The E12 is one of the hillier passages. It crosses the frontier at Weidhaus and continues in the direction of Nuremberg, linking with the A93 autobahn at Wernberg-Köblitz. This axis of the E12 approximates to the operational boundary between the VII US Corps and the II West German Corps, which creates possibilities for discord and misunderstanding.
- The easiest avenue enters West Germany at Furth, and follows the fast Route 20 to the wide basin of Cham, from where a number of roads lead across or around the Bayerischer Wald to the Danube plain and Regensburg.
- The Czech Route 27 runs due south from Plzeň, passes the frontier at Železna Ruda, and becomes the narrow German

Route 11, skirting the Grosser Arber. This is probably the most easily blocked of the major entries.

A roundabout fourth route extends from Strakonice to Passau on the Danube, crossing into Bavaria near the Austrian border. For the sake of convenience we have ignored a large number of minor roads and tracks which might also serve military purposes.

The progress of the Warsaw Pact over the frontiers would certainly be delayed by timely tree-blowdown, but the border ridge is too narrow for a defence in depth, and the Americans and West Germans will probably put up their main resistance some way back from the frontier, taking advantage of the compartmentalised nature of the terrain.

To the north-west of the Cham basin a zonal defence might be based first on the Oberpfälzer Wald, then on the western slopes of the broad valley of the river Naab (about 40 metres wide, 1.5 metres deep) and finally on the deep woods of the Fränkische Alb. This last region is traversed by the potential anti-tank ditch formed by the Europa-Kanal Rhein–Main–Donau, which has been completed from the Main at Bamberg as far as Nuremberg, and which is in the process of being extended from there to the Danube at Kelheim. This great canal is one of the few works of German civil engineering which actually favour the defensive.

South-east of the Cham basin there are good defensive possibilities along the idyllic heights of the Bayerischer Wald, which run parallel with the main ridge of the Böhmerwald. The Danube closes up the rear, and the valley of the Regen stream acts as a forward boundary along the stretch between Regen town and Cham.

THE DANUBE VALLEY   In addition to watching the Böhmerwald, CENTAG must reckon with the possibility of a mass Warsaw Pact violation of Austrian territory, whereby Soviet and even Hungarian forces might push up the Danube and link up with Soviet and Czech troops breaking through from the north.

The defence of southern Bavaria is the business of the II West German Corps. Its 4th Mechanised Infantry Division stands watch in the lower Danube valley and along the foot of the Böhmerwald. The 8th Mountain Division guards the Alpine flank, and the 10th Armoured Division is held in reserve along the upper Danube, supported by the 56th Territorial Home Defence Brigade at Neuburg.

The military geography of this theatre is shaped to a great degree by the river lines. Before it leaves German territory the slate-green Danube already becomes a considerable river. In central Bavaria near Ingolstadt it measures 120 metres wide and 2.5 metres deep, and flows at half a metre per second. Downstream on the Austrian border at Passau it meets the Inn, and swells to an impressive 290 metres.

The course of the German Danube describes a shallow ∧, with the apex at Regensburg. Above this town the Danube may be called into service by NATO to help the defence of central Germany against attack from the south-east. Below Regensburg the Danube gives depth to the defence of the Böhmerwald, as already indicated, but it also invites an invasion by forces coming upriver from the direction of Austria. The Warsaw Pact will have its clearest run along the northern or left bank, along the narrow plain between the Böhmerwald and the river. This is a suitable passage for armour, as the 11th US Armoured Division showed in its dash for Passau on 26 April 1945, and the communications have been still further improved by the opening of the A3/E5 autobahn.

South of the Danube the Soviets are faced with the prospect of having to make the multiple crossings of the right-bank tributaries. The rivers and streams run in a general south-west to north-east direction, and their valleys are separated by low outlying spurs of the Alps, which reach down to the Danube plain like fingers.

The first and most formidable obstacle is the frontier river of the Inn, which is shorter than the Danube, but just as impressive in its other dimensions. The Inn forms a chain of lakes on either side of Braunau, and where it joins the Danube at Passau it is as wide as the senior river. The average velocity of the lower reaches of the Inn is about two metres per second, which is very daunting for amphibious vehicles and ferries, and inland on the German side the ground is heavily wooded, and broken by the long ridges which reach down from the Alps to the plain of the Danube. Upstream from Braunau the Inn turns away from the border, but the river Salzach offers a natural strategic extension south to the Alps. All of this suggests that it would be advantageous for the Germans to put up an initial defence very close to the Austrian border. It is most unfortunate that the opening of the A10 autobahn across the Austrian Alps has detracted from the security of the Inn–Salzach line (see p. 106). Arriving from this direction, Warsaw Pact forces now have the opportunity of reaching the West German road system on the corner of the frontier near Salzburg.

Further inside Bavaria the other major tributary, the Isar, has an obstacle value less than half that of the Inn, but like many of the smaller streams it confronts invaders with the danger and inconvenience of having to make formal river crossings. The Inn valley upstream near Rosenheim must be particularly valuable for arranging a hot reception for any Soviets who might be tempted to make a dash along the foot of the Alps from Salzburg.

CHAPTER 12

The Central European Neutrals – Austria, Switzerland and Liechtenstein

One of the great unmentionables in modern strategic debate is the existence of three neutral states which together stretch for 800 kilometres across southern Central Europe. This zone attained its full extent on 15 May 1955, when the multi-national Austrian State Treaty founded the modern Austrian Republic. On the grand strategic plane the new Warsaw Pact (see p. 96) at once gained an important advantage, for with the end of occupation status in Austria the West lost the direct overland connection between Italy and northern European NATO. The sixty-kilometre-deep corridor of the Austrian Tyrol now divided the forces in West Germany from those in Italy, and any attempt to restore the integrity would have involved NATO in forcing the passage of the Brenner Pass.

For NATO in Germany the existence of the Central European neutrals, and Austria in particular, aggravates the problems of holding the Danube and the upper Rhine, and effectively adds 170 kilometres to the already long frontage of CENTAG.

AUSTRIA

Area:	83,850 square kilometres
Population:	7,550,000
Army:	1 standing division, 8 mobile *Landwehr* brigades

Modern Austria is the much-contracted core of one of the great empires of old Europe. She is drawn out for 500 kilometres along an east–west axis, and her 2,635 kilometres of frontier are shared with six states. Three of them are neutral or non-aligned, namely Yugoslavia, Switzerland and the Principality of Liechtenstein. Two of the borders are with members of the Warsaw Pact – the 354 kilometres with Hungary and the 547 with Czechoslovakia. Two more are with NATO states. The Austrian frontier with Italy is 430 kilometres long, and that with West Germany measures a total of 784, including that strategically very important stretch running from the Böhmer-wald across the Danube from the Alps.

As a matter of policy the Austrians have given clear notice of the principles which govern their national defence.

The structure of the Austrian forces is the result of a compromise which was reached in 1971. The permanent alert force (*Bereitschafts-truppe*) represents something of the conservative military predilec-tion for a standing army, while the Social Democratic ideal of a pure citizen army is reflected by a militia (*Landwehr*) comprising a mobile force and locally anchored territorial units.

Most unfortunately, Austria still labours under the armaments restrictions imposed by Article 13 of the State Treaty. The Austrians can endure the thought of having to live without submarines, torpedoes or aquatic mines, all of which are solemnly listed in that document, but the prohibition of guided weapons has become much more crippling than could have been envisaged in 1955, when such devices were still in their infancy.

Air defence is weak. Not only are the air forces small and depen-dent on second-hand foreign fighters, but the absence of anti-aircraft guided missiles makes the ground forces vulnerable to air attack, and leaves the airfields without adequate protection. These air bases are situated at Aigen in the province of Salzburg, Hörsching in Upper Austria, Gresten and Wiener Neustadt in Lower Austria, Langle-barn near Vienna, and Zeltweig and Graz-Thalerhof in Styria.

The Austrian army is similarly denied the possession of anti-tank guided weapons. It must resort to anti-tank guns (old-fashioned in concept if not design), tracked tank destroyers (the *Kürassier*) and the expedient of mounting obsolescent tank turrets in static posi-tions. Several hundred turrets have already been emplaced (the estimates vary greatly), and the Austrians continue to buy up old tanks for the same purpose.

Military doctrine is based on the concept of Area Defence (*Raum-verteidigung*), a strategy of dissuasion which proclaims that Austria will exact a high entrance price for any violation of national territory. At the lowest level of military activity the Austrians will guard the borders and vital points in the interior against subversion and airborne attack. Localised incursions are to be met by concentrations of the mobile forces. A full-scale invasion will bring all the militia and reserve elements into action as well, according to procedures that were tested in exercises in 1976, 1977, 1979 and 1982.

We must now assess the relevance of Austria's defence policy for the balance between NATO and the Warsaw Pact. The first violation

Going

EXCELLENT

EASY

FAIRLY ROUGH

DIFFICULT

Natural borders

OPEN

DIFFICULT

PROTECTED

Adapted from Danspeckgruber 1984

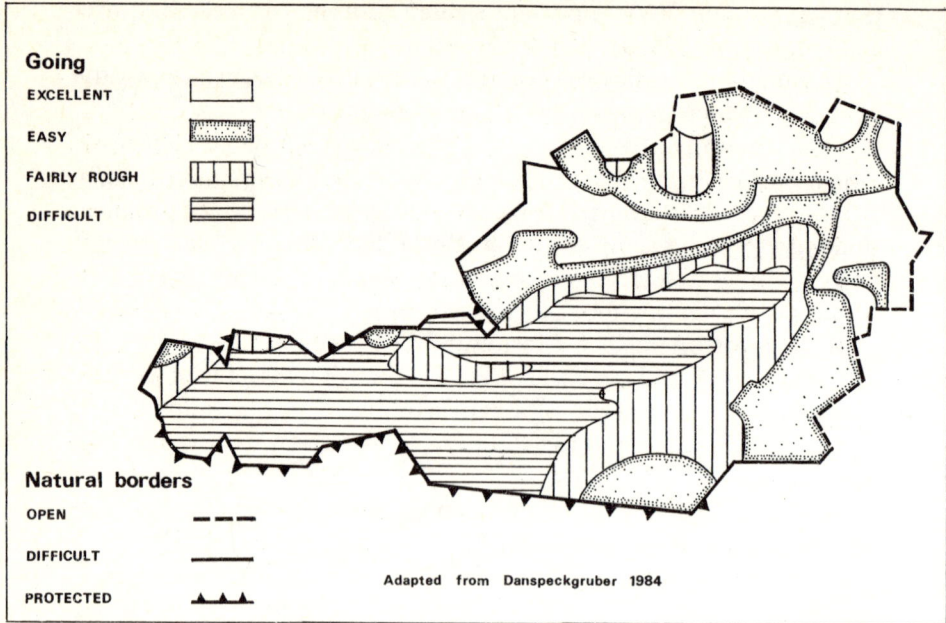

MAP 25   Austrian Geography – Schematic

of Austrian territory will come much more probably from the East
rather than NATO. If the Soviets were in need of a pretext they
might find an occasion in the Austrian interpretation of neutrality,
which is strict but humane, and not devoid of courage. The welfare
agencies have assumed a heavy commitment to receive refugee
Hungarians, Czechs, Poles, Soviet Jews and other unhappy peoples
from Eastern Europe, and Austrian forces stood ready to defend the
frontiers during the turmoils in Hungary in 1956 and Czechoslovakia
in 1968. Again Austrian public opinion was outraged when on 6
November 1984 Czech border guards shot dead an escapee inside
Austrian territory near Gmünd.

Some of the sharpness has gone out of the quarrel with Italy over
the status of the Germanic element in Alto Adige (the former
Austrian South Tyrol), thanks largely to the tactful dealings of the
Italian authorities. More potentially dangerous is the friction between the Slovenian minority and the Germanic nationalists of the
Freedom Party in the Austrian province of Carinthia, which lies next
to Yugoslavia.

Austria is spiritually aligned with the west, but in the face of
geographical realities her interpretation of Area Defence must of
necessity be a selective one, unfavourable to NATO.

Seventy-five per cent of the national territory is reckoned to be good defensive country, including the 45 per cent under forest. In winter the ice and snow augments the obstacle value of the ground, and from their reading of the Alpine campaigns against Italy (1915–18) the Austrians deduce that artificially induced avalanches could be made into a formidable weapon. In the springtime many of the valley floors are flooded by melt water, and the hillside meadows become difficult for armour.

Regrettably for NATO, some of the craggiest country faces Italy and West Germany, making what the Austrians themselves define as 'difficult terrain' and 'naturally protected frontiers' (Danspeckgruber, 1984, 722). The one notable exception is the floor of the Danube valley, and even here the NATO forces are badly placed, for they must divide their attention between the Austrian border and the Böhmerwald.

By way of contrast the frontiers with the Warsaw Pact are almost everywhere 'unprotected' and lead directly into 'excellent terrain' and 'easy going'. Vienna stands about one hour's drive from the Czech and Hungarian borders and Lower Austria as a whole must be considered virtually indefensible, along with most of Burgenland and south-eastern Styria. From this it is fair to conclude that in the event of an attack by the Soviet bloc the Austrian forces will withdraw into the Alps, leaving the invaders with a free run into NATO territories. Most obviously Soviet, Hungarian and Czech forces could invade Bavaria along the axis of the Danube (see p. 313). South-eastern Austria in the neighbourhood of Graz and Klagenfurt could just as easily becomes a corridor for Soviet and Hungarian divisions driving into Yugoslavia and Italy (see p. 106).

SWITZERLAND

Area:	41,288 square kilometres
Population:	6,513,000
Army:	12 field and mountain divisions, 17 frontier and fortress brigades

LIECHTENSTEIN

Area:	160 square kilometres
Population:	26,400
Army:	None

On occasion the most obvious truisms about a country enshrine a

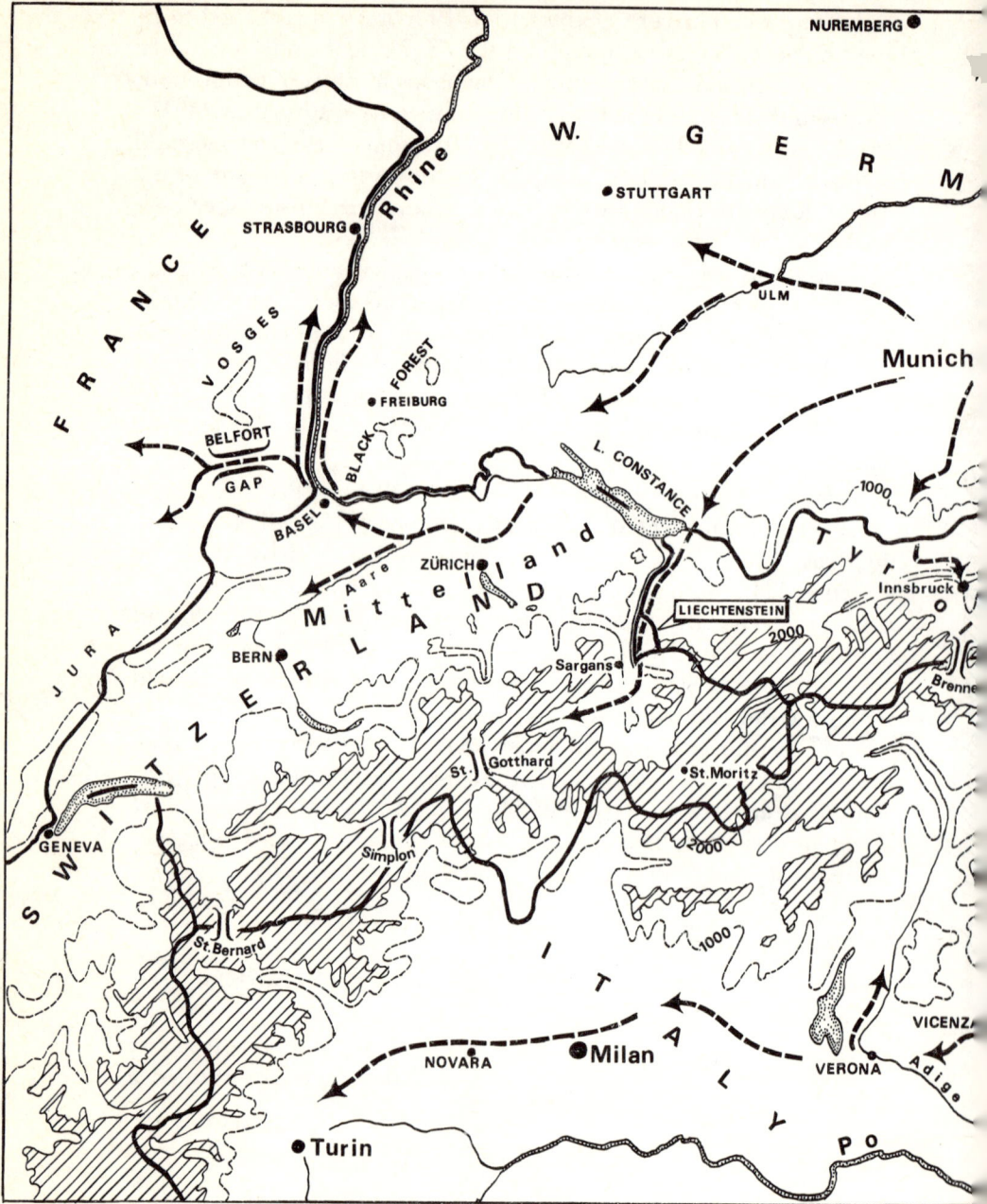

MAP 26   The Alpine Countries

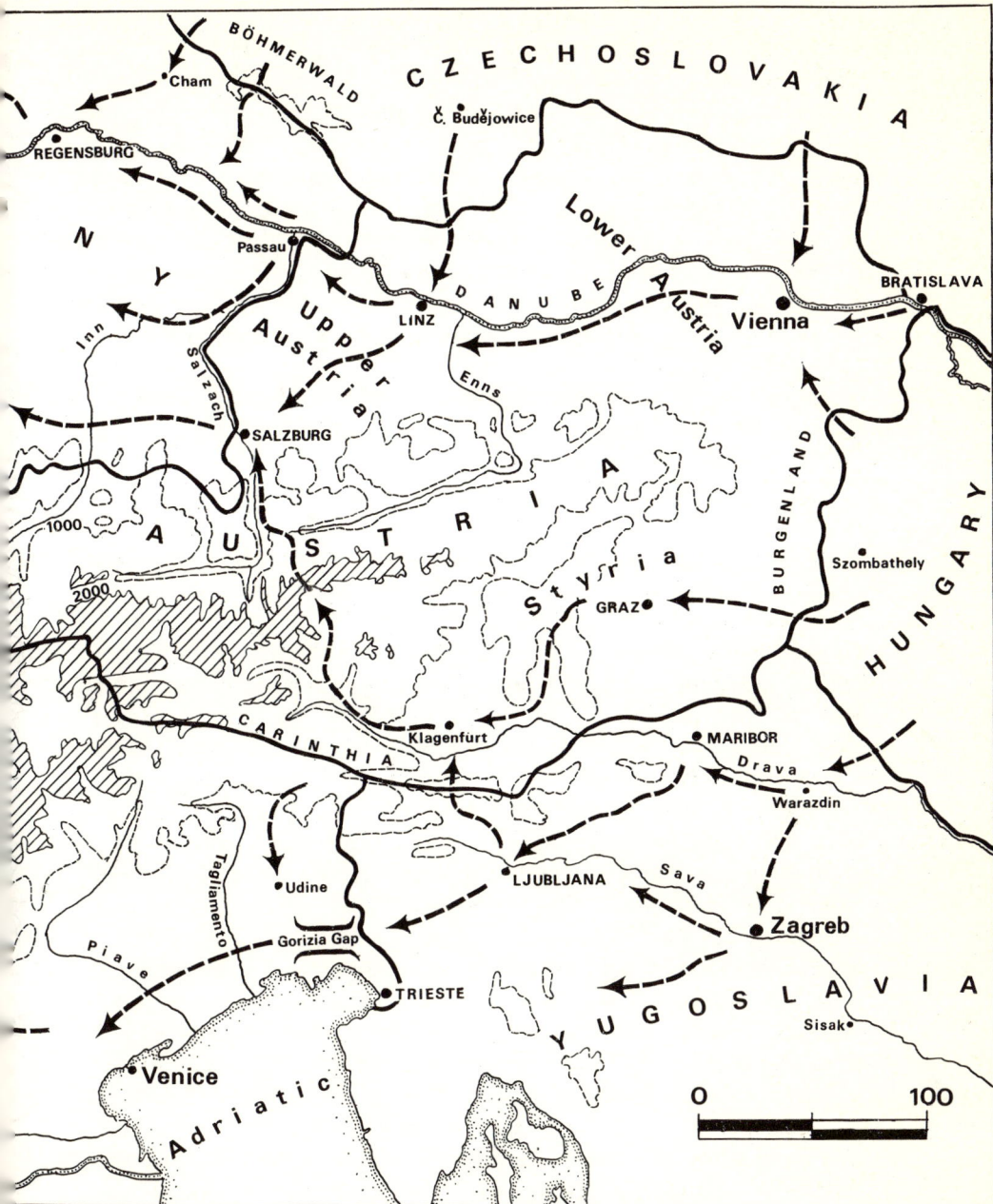

Map labels:

C Z E C H O S L O V A K I A

BÖHMERWALD

Cham

Č. Budějovice

REGENSBURG

Passau

Lower Austria

DANUBE

Austria

BRATISLAVA

LINZ

Vienna

Upper Austria

Inn

Salzach

Enns

SALZBURG

BURGENLAND

Szombathely

1000

A U S T R I A

Styria

GRAZ

HUNGARY

2000

CARINTHIA

Klagenfurt

MARIBOR

Drava

Warazdin

Tagliamento

Udine

LJUBLJANA

Sava

Zagreb

Piave

Gorizia Gap

TRIESTE

Y U G O S L A V I A

Sisak

Venice

Adriatic

0   100

number of the most important things you can say about it. Just as
Russia is a big and flat piece of ground, so Switzerland is a small but
very high one.

Switzerland measures just 200 by 300 kilometres, and yet this little
place supports monstrous peaks which rise beyond 4,000 metres, or
more than three times the highest summits of the Böhmerwald and
well into the Soviet category of 'high mountainous terrain'. The
principal passes (Simplon, St Gotthard, St Bernard) lie hard under
some of the most awesome mountains in Europe, and it is reckoned
that of the approximately 200 kilometres of the major north–south
roads more than half run through narrow valleys or tunnels or across
bridges.

Switzerland is an armed neutral *par excellence*. Her independence
derives from the defensive power of the geography, and from the fact
that the Swiss have long been one of the most heavily militarised
nations in the world. Tourists gain some inkling of what is going on
when they notice the crackle of rifle fire in the valleys, hear a piece of
rockface sliding upwards with a hissing noise, or see fighter planes
emerge from the bottom of a mountain like wasps from a nest.

Swiss law does not recognise the right of a citizen to be a
conscientious objector. The civil defence organisation comprises
400,000 personnel and provides shelter space for more than four-
fifths of the population. The standing military 'instructor' cadre is
tiny, yet the Swiss can mobilise a well-trained force of 625,000
citizen militia in a matter of hours. The number of main battle tanks
exceeds 800, which puts Switzerland in the European big league.
The rest of the armament is in the same impressive proportion.

The Swiss put much trust in engineered defences as an additional
force multiplier. Both the military and civil defence command
centres are installed underground, as are stores of every kind. Shelter
and servicing facilities for the entire complement of aircraft are
provided in mountainside caverns, and the airstrips are protected by
guns and missiles as well as by the lie of the ground, which will have
the effect of funnelling low-level attack along the axes of the valleys.

The number of terrain obstacles comes to about 4,000, if we take
in the prepared demolitions, emplaced minefields and readily available barricades. The permanent fortifications of the Swiss are the
most solid and highly developed of their kind in the world. These
works bristle with about 400 fortress guns and mortars, 600 anti-tank
guns, and 2,000 heavy machine guns, and are garrisoned by troops of
the specialised fortress and frontier brigades. The most elaborate
fortified complexes are to be found in the national redoubt in the

south of the country, in the regions of Sargans, the St Gotthard Pass and St Moritz. Since the early 1980s the permanent fortifications have been supplemented by a vast number of simple emplacements for anti-tank guided missiles, which indirectly underlines the ill fortune of the Austrians, who are denied the use of these vital weapons.

It would be wrong to exclude this remarkable country from consideration when we try to assess the balance of forces on the Central Front. The Swiss are firm in their policy of non-alignment, but they know that operations in great depth are a component of the 'Soviet Military Art', and they recognise the violation of Swiss neutrality by the forces of the Warsaw Pact is far more likely than intrusions by NATO. The specifically military threat comes in the shape of attacks to one side or another of Lake Constance.

The Swiss see the advance to the west of Lake Constance as part of a Soviet design to get around the southern flank of the Black Forest, and exploit down the Rhine or westwards into France. This sweep will bring the enemy through the fifty-kilometre-wide zone of the *Mittelland* in northern Switzerland. This is flat ground by Swiss standards, but 'low mountainous terrain' in the Soviet classification, rising to 1,000 metres, and broken by hillocks, forests, towns and fast-flowing rivers. The going is difficult for tanks, though by no means impossible, and in the event of a Soviet invasion this ground will almost certainly witness a duel between the Soviet armour and the three Swiss mechanised divisions.

The other avenue stretches east of Lake Constance by way of Austria, tiny Liechtenstein and the valley of the upper Rhine (Vorderrhein), which leads to the heart of the national redoubt. A powerful Soviet thrust in this direction does not threaten NATO immediately, but it might weaken the Swiss defence of the *Mittelland*, which is so important for NATO interests.

The neutrality of Switzerland is an awkward barrier to inter-NATO communications, but in other respects this robust little country must be counted as one of the assets of the Western world.

Conclusions

At the beginning of this book I suggested that the study of modern strategic affairs will gain from being pursued in the geographical and historical dimensions. I am more than ever convinced that this ambition is worthy of our best efforts, even if I do not advance any particular claims in favour of my own contribution.

NATO does not have many advantages, but one of them derives from being the sitting tenant on the ground. It seems scandalous that a precious asset of this order is so lightly regarded. Military men have done little to prepare the potential theatres of war for purposes of defence, or to open the eyes of their officers to their physical surroundings. Academic strategists, on the other hand, are capable of writing at great length about the 'Deep Attack', and other concepts, without devoting a single word to the question of where it is all supposed to be taking place. Here the proper study of military geography will serve as a corrective.

Historical judgments are every bit as relevant. They assist politicians and soldiers to identify national and strategic interests – helping them, for example, to determine what is and what is not worth defending *à outrance*, or to assess what a foreign power might have at stake in a particular part of the world.

On the operational side, history can still tell us something of interest even in this age of 'push-button warfare'. It would certainly be going too far to claim that the modern age is an 'historical period just like any other', if only because no single time is exactly like another one. But the later twentieth century has some decidedly old-fashioned aspects to it, and it is ripe for treatment by the historical method. As has been commonly observed, when rival forces possess nuclear arsenals of roughly equal power, the weapons cancel each other out, and the effects are to accentuate local struggles of a low-level kind on the peripheries, and open the possibility of at least a conventional phase in a general war betwen the parties. The machinery of grand strategy is certainly in danger of going out of control, but probably less so than in 1914, and at lower levels something of the human element has been restored to the conduct of military affairs, thanks to the way in which computers have helped to simplify the tactical information which is presented to commander, gunner or pilot.

It is a pity that the relevant historical information is not so readily forthcoming in a useful form. Here the academics must take the blame. Highbrow military history, of the sort which is debated at learned conferences, has ascended into rarefied altitudes of sociology and the like, and nowadays seldom descends into regions where it is possible to enquire why a particular valley or river crossing has figured so largely in operations over the centuries, and whether these considerations still hold good at the present time. Indeed, most professional historians appear to have renounced one of the greatest services that can be rendered by their trade, which is to dispel the facile historical generalisations which will otherwise hold the field, and point to the instances where an historical parallel does *not* obtain.

To ask an academic historian to engage in activity of this kind is to force him to leave a familiar environment. He must write in the knowledge that much of his work will have been overtaken by events before it appears in print – just as if he found out too late that Napoleon had returned from St Helena to overthrow the verdict of Waterloo. Many relevant facts are withheld from him, for good reasons of national security. He is accustomed to proceeding with circumspection, his every cautious step safeguarded by documentary evidence or the carefully worded generalisation: now he is summoned to venture far beyond the reach of his immediate academic competence, in fields where his ignorance and mistakes in matters of detail will provoke the scorn of the military professionals. The historian must now also write without the benefit of historical perspective, which is another way of saying that he will not always be able to distinguish what events or movements are going to be important in the long run – and historians are helped more than they generally appreciate by the cleaning-up process of hindsight, which so conveniently removes 'alternative futures' from their view.

My own response, as someone whose primary training was in history, has been on three levels:
– The mechanical and specific sides (the mountain passes and so on) come readily enough once you set your mind to it. Thus, by putting together considerations of policy, terrain, technology and history, you can arrive at a reasonably informed guess as to some of the options open to an invader on a theatre of war.

– In the realm of higher strategy I have become dimly aware of some of the forces which uphold the remarkable stability of the confrontation between NATO and the Warsaw Pact. Everybody will recognise the general concern to avoid nuclear war. Other common interests, perceived by some, if not always openly avowed, are in the continuing division of Germany, and the maintenance of the ghastly kind of peace imposed by the Soviet Union on wide areas of Central and Eastern Europe, where the national and tribal hatreds (which are far from extinguished) have engendered so many destructive conflicts in the more distant past. Here the academic is speaking.

– My third response is much more spontaneous and is probably shared with most Westerners of our time. Throwing the lectern aside I declare that I wish to be neither 'Red' nor 'dead', but alive and free. We should like to get along with the Soviet Union, but we find it difficult to do so when the forces of the Warsaw Pact so greatly exceed those needed for purposes of defence, when Soviet military doctrine bears so strongly marked an offensive character, and when the price of peace appears to be the happiness of so many of our contemporaries who live to the east of Brunswick.

Bibliography

ABBREVIATIONS

IDR *International Defense Review*, Geneva
NFN *Nato's Fifteen Nations*, Brussels
NSN *Nato's Sixteen Nations*, Brussels
RUSI *Journal of the Royal United Services Institute for Defence Studies*,
        London

Albright, D.E. (1984), 'On Eastern Europe: Security Implications for the
    USSR', *Parameters*, XIV, no. 2, Carlisle (Pa.).
Alford, J. (1977), 'Mobile Defence – The pervasive Myth: An Historical
    Investigation', PhD Thesis, University of London.
Artisien, P.F. (1985), 'Albania in the post-Hoxha Era', *The World Today*,
    XLI, no. 6, London.
Ascanio y Togores, R. (1983), 'The Spanish Army: Modernisation and
    Transfromation', *NSN*, Special Issue no. 1.
Bailey, A. (1983), *Along the Edge of the Forest: An Iron Curtain Journey*,
    London.
Bailey, J.B. (1984), 'The Case for Pre-placed Field Defenses', *IDR*, XVII,
    no. 7.
Barnaby, F. (1984), *Future War: Armed Conflict in the Next Decade*,
    London.
Baylis, J. (ed.) (1983), *Alternative Approaches to British Defence Policy*,
    London.
Baylis, J. (1984), *Anglo-American Defence Relations 1939–1984*, London.
Beetham, M. (1982), 'Air Power and the Royal Air Force: Today and the
    Future, *RUSI*, CXXVII, no. 4.
Belgrave, R. (1985), 'The Uncertainty of Energy Supplies in a Geopolitical
    Perspective', *International Affairs*, LXI, no.2, London.
Bertram, C. (ed.) (1979), *New Conventional Weapons and East–West
    Security*, London.
Bethge, A. (1982), 'The Role of the German Navy in the Northern Flank
    Area', *NFN*, Special Issue no. 2.
Bidwell, S. (1978), *World War 3*, London.
Biggs-Davison, J. (1981), 'Europe, NATO and Irish Neutrality', *NFN*,
    XXVII, no. 4.
Bildt, C. (1983), 'Sweden and the Submarines', *Survival*, XXV, no. 4,
    London.

Binieda, Z. (1981), 'The General Concept of a Theatre of Military Operations', trans. from *Polish Naval Review*, XII, Warsaw.

Boll, M.M. (1979), 'Turkey between East and West: The Regional Alternative', *The World Today*, September.

Boll, M.M. (1984), 'The Soviet–Bulgarian Alliance: From Subservience to Partnership', *Parameters*, XIV, no. 4, Carlisle (Pa.).

Bonds, R. (ed.) (1980), *The Soviet War Machine*, London.

Bonnart, F. (1982), 'The Extended Flank – Report on Turkey', *NFN*, XXVII, no. 2.

Booth, K. (1979), 'Superpower Naval Disengagement in the Mediterranean', *RUSI*, CXXIV, no. 2.

Boysen, H.M. (1983), 'Defence of the Islands and Coasts' (i.e. of Denmark), *NSN*, Special Issue no. 1.

Bracken, P. (1977), 'Urban Sprawl and NATO Defense', *Military Review*, LVII, no. 10, Fort Leavenworth.

Bradley, C.D. (1981), 'Wheels versus Tracks', *Armor*, XC, no. 3, Fort Knox.

Branson, R.V. (1976), 'Inflexibility in NATO's Flexible Response', *Military Review*, LVI, no. 1, Fort Leavenworth.

Brewik, R. (1982), 'Assuring the Security of Reinforcements to Norway', *NFN*, Special Issue no. 2.

Brown, N. (1983), 'Air Power in Central Europe', *The World Today*, October, London.

Burberry, J.W. (1978), 'Urbanized Terrain', *Military Review*, LVIII, no. 3, Fort Leavenworth.

Burrows, B., and Edwards, G. (1982), *The Defence of Western Europe*, London.

Cable, J. (1983), 'Surprise and the Single Scenario', *RUSI*, CXXVIII, no. 1.

Cable, J. (1985), *Diplomacy at Sea*, London.

Cairns, G. (1980), 'Developments in the United Kingdom Air Defence Region', *NFN*, XXV, no. 4.

Caligaris, L. (1983), 'Italian Defence Policy: Problems and Prospects', *Survival*, XXV, no. 2, London.

Campbell, C. (1982), *War Facts Now*, London.

Campbell, C. (1984), *Air Warfare: The Fourth Generation*, London.

Campbell, D. (1984), *The Unsinkable Aircraft Carrier: American Military Power in Britain*, London.

Canby, S.L. (1978), *Short (and Long) War Responses: Restructuring Border Defense, and Reserve Mobilization for Armored Warfare*, Santa Monica.

Capuzzo, U. (1983), 'Mountain Warfare on the North-East Frontier' (i.e. of Italy), *NATO's Sixteen Nations*, XVIII, no. 5, Special Issue no. 1, Brussels.

Carlson, A. (1981), 'Tanks in Urban Combat', *Armor*, XC, no. 2, Fort Knox.

Carver, M. (1983), 'Conventional Defence of Europe', *RUSI*, CXXVIII, no. 3.

Chaliand, G., and Rageau, J.P. (1983), *Atlas géographique*, Paris.

Chaplin, D. (1978), 'Russia and China: The forgotten Conflict', *British Army Review*, LX, London.

Chaplin, D. (1979), 'Norway – the northern Perimeter', *British Army Review*, LXII, London.

Chapman, J.W., Drifte, R., and Gow. F.T. (1983), *Japan's Quest for Comprehensive Security: Defence Diplomacy and Dependence*, London. Esp. for the discussion of 'strategic' minerals.

Clark, J.L. (1982), 'NATO, Neutrals and National Defence', *Survival*, XXIV, no. 6, London.

Coker, C. (1983), *US Military Power in the 1980s*, London.

Coker, C. (1984), *The Future of the Atlantic Alliance*, London.

Cottrell, A.J. (ed.) (1981), *Sea Power and Strategy in the Indian Ocean*, London.

Cousens, R.P. (1982), 'Light Infantry – a Renaissance?', *British Army Review*, LXXII, London.

Cowen, G. (1982), 'German Security Thinking Revisited', *RUSI*, CXXVII, no. 3.

Craufurd Price, W.H. (undated, *c.* 1914), *The Balkan Cockpit*, London.

Critchley, J. (1982), *The North Atlantic Alliance and the Soviet Union in the 1980s*, London.

Croker, F.P. (1984), 'The Defence of Northern Norway', *RUSI*, CXXIX, no. 4.

Cross, T. (1985), 'Forward Defence: A time for change?' *RUSI*, CXXX, no. 2.

Crowe, W.J. (1983), 'American Power: Support of NATO's Southern Flank', *RUSI*, CXXVIII, no. 1.

Däniker, G. (1984), 'The Swiss Model of Conventional Defence', *Armed Forces Journal*, CXXI, no. 12, Washington.

Danspeckgruber, W. (1984), 'The Defense of Austria', *IDR*, XVII, no. 6.

Defense Agency (Japanese) (1983), *Defense of Japan*, Tokyo.

Dinter, E., and Griffith, P. (1983), *Not Over by Christmas: NATO's Central Front in World War III*, Chichester.

Dixon, R.A. (1979), 'Winter Warfare by Any Other Name', *Military Review*, LIX, no. 3, Fort Leavenworth.

Donnelly, C.N. (1977), 'Fighting in Built-up Areas: A Soviet View – Part II', *RUSI*, CXXII, no. 3.

Dornan, J.E. (ed.) (1978), *The U.S. War Machine*, London.

Draper, S.E. (1984), 'Mobility/Countermobility in Winter Warfare', *Defence Update*, XLIV, Cologne.

Dukes, P. (1970). *The Emergence of the Super-powers: A Short Comparative History of the U.S.A. and the U.S.S.R.*, London.

Dunn, K.A. (1979), 'Limits upon Soviet military Power', *RUSI*, CXXIV, no. 4.

Dunnigan, J.F. (1982), *How to Make War: A Comprehensive Guide to Modern Warfare*, London.

Eberle, J. (1983), 'NATO's Treaty Limits – Safeguard or Straitjacket?', *NSN*, XXVIII, no. 7.

The Economist, 'Foreign Report' (periodical), London (consulted from 1978 onwards).

Engineer Studies Group, Department of the Army (1975), *Measuring Obstacle Effectiveness of Terrain*, Washington.

Epstein, J.M. (1984), *Measuring Military Power: The Soviet Air Threat to Europe*, London.

Erickson, J. (1976), 'The Northern Theatre (TVD): Soviet Capabilities and Concepts', *RUSI*, CXXI, no. 4.

Erickson, J. (*et al.*) (1983), *Organizing for War: The Soviet Military Establishment Viewed through the Prism of the Military District*, College Station (Texas).

Esposito, C.V. (1982), 'Armor Operations in Built-up Areas', *Armor*, XCI, no. 4, Fort Knox.

European Security Group (1983), *Strengthening Conventional Deterrence in Europe: Proposals for the 1980s,* London.

Eyre, K. (1981), 'Canada's Far Distant Flanks – Military Operations in the Arctic', *NFN*, XXVI, no. 2.

Farrar-Hockley, A. (1981), 'Defence in the Higher Latitudes', *NFN* XXVI, no. 2.

Farrar-Hockley, A. (1983), 'Dynamic Defence: The Northern Flanks', *RUSI*, CXXVIII, no. 4.

Fedder, E.H. (ed.) (1980), *Defense Politics of the Atlantic Alliance*, New York.

Flynn, G. (ed.) (1981), *The Internal Fabric of Western Security*, London.

Foot, P. (1981), *Improving Capabilities for Extra-European Contingencies: The British Contribution*, Aberdeen.

Foot, P. (1982), *Beyond the North Atlantic: The European Contribution,* Aberdeen.

Freemen, W.D. (1981), 'NATO Central Region Forward Defense', *National Security Affairs Issue Papers*, LXXXI–III, Washington.

Gans, D. (1980), 'Fighting Outnumbered and Win . . . Against What Odds?', *Military Review*, LX, no. 12, Fort Leavenworth.

Gething, M.J. (1981), 'Up the Sharp End – *Defence* Visits RAF Germany', *Defence*, XII, no. 11, Maidenhead.

Gibbs, G. (1983), 'The Iberian Atlantic Area', *Defence*, XIV, no. 2, Maidenhead.

Giovanni, G. (1982), 'Maintaining Naval Security in the Mediterranean', *NFN*, Special Issue no. 2.

Gomez, E. Munilla (1985), 'Spain and NATO: Problems of Military Integration, *IDR*, XVIII, no. 1.

Gomez Tardoso, P.A. (1980), 'Portugal', *NATO's Fifteen Nations*, Special Issue no. 1, Brussels.

Gormley, D.M. (1982), 'The Direction and Pace of Soviet Force Projection Capabilities', *Survival*, XXIV, no. 6, London.

Gray, C.S. (1977), *The Geopolitics of the Nuclear Era: Heartlands, Rimlands and the Technological Revolution*, New York.

Greenwood, D. (1985), *Britain's Defence Priorities*, London.

Gretton, M.P. (1979), 'Protecting New Frontiers on the Ocean Floor', *RUSI*, CXXIV, no. 1.

Gunston, B. (1985), *Air Superiority*, London.

Hagerup, N.J. (1975), 'Denmark and Danish Defence in NATO', *RUSI*, CXX, no. 2.

Hackett, J. (1982), *The Third World War: The Unknown Story*, London.

Hammond, D.S. (1983, 'Rubble as a Combat Multiplier', *Armor*, XCII, no. 4, Fort Knox.

Heitman, H.R. (1981), 'The Austrian Army', *Defence*, XII, no. 10, Maidenhead.

Henderson, N. (1982), *The Birth of NATO*, London.

Herlofsun, C.O. (1978), 'The Norwegian Navy', *NFN*, XXIII, Special Issue.

Heseltine, M. (1983), 'The United Kingdom's Strategic Interests and Priorities', *RUSI*, CXXVIII, no. 4.

Hill-Norton, P. (1978), *No Soft Options: The Politico-Military Realities of NATO*, London.

Hofsten, H. (1983), 'Sweden's Neutrality', *Defence*, XIV, no. 8, Maidenhead.

Holloway, D., and Sharp, J.M. (1984), *The Warsaw Pact: Alliance in Transition?*, London.

Hooton, T. (1983), 'NATO's Flanks – An Appreciation', *Defence,* XIV, no. 2, Maidenhead.

Howard, M. (1984), *The Causes of Wars and Other Essays*, London.

Howell, P. (1913), *The Campaign in Thrace*, London.

Hubatschek, Farwick (1978), *Entscheidung in Deutschland*, Berg-am-See.

Hulshof, J.H. (1984), 'Defence of the Approach Routes in the Eastern Atlantic', *NSN*, XXIX, no. 2.

Ingebrigtsen, E. (1983), 'Ground Defence of the North', *NSN*, Special Issue no. 1.

Isby, D.C., and Kamps, C. (1985), *Armies of NATO's Central Front*, London.

Jane's Defence Weekly, London.

Johnson, A.R. (1973), 'Yugoslav Total National Defence', *Survival,* XV, no. 2, London.

Johnson, A.R., Dean, R.W., and Alexiev, A. (1980), *East European Military Establishments: The Warsaw Pact Northern Tier*, New York.

Jordan, A.A., and Dickson, B. (1983), 'NATO's Global Challenge: The Threat from Soviet Expansion', *NSN*, XXVIII, no. 7.

Jukes, G. (1971), 'The Soviet Union and the Indian Ocean', *Survival*, XIII, no. 11.

Jungius, J. (1978), 'Maritime Aspects of the Northern Flank', *RUSI*, CXXIII, no. 4.

Kaplan, L.S., Clawson, R.W., and Luraghi, R. (eds) (1985), *NATO and the Mediterranean*, Wilmington (Delaware).

Karber, P.A. (1984), 'In Defense of Forward Defense', *Armed Forces Journal*, CXXI, no. 9, Washington.

Kasperson, R.E., and Minghi, J.V. (eds) (1970), *The Structure of Political Geography*, London. A very useful collection of geopolitical texts.

Kastenmayer, W. (1982), 'Reinforcements and Prepositioning', *NFN*, XXVII, no. 5.

Kemp, G. (1977), 'The New Strategic Map', *Survival*, XIX, no. 2.

Kidd, I. (1980), 'For Want of a Nail: The Logistics of the Alliance', in Myers (1980).

Klebusa, G.H. (1976), 'NATO: A View from the East', *Military Review*, LVI, no. 11, Fort Leavenworth.

Korb, L.J. (1982), 'US Military Power: Manpower and Logistics', *RUSI*, CXXVII, no. 4.

Krehbiel, C.C. (1980), 'Military Asymmetries in the Soviet–American Strategic Balance', *RUSI*, CXXV, no. 2.

Kuppermann, R.G., and Taylor, W.J. (1984), *Strategic Requirements of the Army to the Year 2000*, Lexington (Mass.).

Lange, N.F. (1982), 'Naval Control of the Danish Straits', *NFN*, Special Issue no. 2.

Leach, H. (1982), 'British Maritime Forces: The Future', *RUSI*, CXXVII, no. 3.

Leach, H. (1982), 'The Royal Navy in the Eastern Atlantic', *NFN*, Special Issue no. 2.

Leifer, M. (1983), 'The Security of Sea-Lanes in South-East Asia', *Survival*, XXV, no. 1, London.

Leifer, M. (ed.) (1985), *The Asian Balance of Power*, London.

Leighton, M.K. (1979), 'Greco-Turkish Friction: Changing Balance in the Eastern Mediterranean', *Conflict Studies*, CIX, London.

Leitão, A. de Sousa (1982), 'The Portuguese Navy and the Portuguese Strategic Triangle', *NFN*, Special Issue no. 2.

Leitão, A. de Sousa (1984), 'The Strategic Relevance of the Azores', *NSN*, XXIX, no. 2.

Lewis, W.J. (1982), *The Warsaw Pact: Arms, Doctrine and Strategy*, Washington.

Lofgren, S. (1984), 'Soviet Submarines against Sweden', *Strategic Review*, Winter 1984, Cambridge (Mass.).

Longworth, B. (1983), 'The Case for a Maritime Strategy', *Defence*, XIV, no. 2, Maidenhead.

Longworth, B. (1983), 'A Developing Flexible Strategy', *Defence,* XIV, no. 8, Maidenhead.

Longworth, B. (1984), 'Mine Countermeasures', *Defence*, XV, no. 1, Maidenhead.

Lopez, R. (1983), 'The AirLand Battle 2000 Controversy', *IDR*, XI.

McCaffrey, B.R. (1982), 'The Battle on the German Frontier', *Military Review*, LXII, no.3, Fort Leavenworth.

McKitrick, M.S. (1983), 'A Conventional Deterrent for NATO: An Alternative to the Nuclear Balance of Terror', *Parameters*, XIII, no. 1, (Carlisle, Pa.).

Maizière, U. de (1975), *Rational Deployment of Forces on the Central Front*, Paris.

Mako, W.P. (1983), *U.S. Ground Forces and the Defense of Central Europe*, Washington.

Mates, L. (1972), 'The Balkans and European Security', *Survival,* XIV, no. 2, London.

Maull, H.W. (1984), *Raw Materials, Energy and Western Society*, London.

Mauvillon, J. (1794), *Geschichte Ferdinands Herzogs von Braunschweig-Lüneburg*, 2 vols, Leipzig.

Mearsheimer, J.J. (1981–2), 'Maneuver, Mobile Defense, and the Central Front', *International Security*, VI, no. 3, Harvard.

Mellor, R.E. (1982), *The Soviet Union and its Geographical Problems*, London.

Millar, T.B. (1981), *The East–West Strategic Balance*, London.

Millar, T.B. (1983), 'The Far East in the Defence Equation', *NSN*, XVIII, no. 7.

Miller, D.M.O. (1980), 'Strategic Factors Affecting the Defence by NATO of Western Europe: A Reappraisal', *RUSI*, CXXV, no. 3.

Miller, D.M.O., Kennedy, W.V., Jordan, J., and Richardson, D. (1981), *East v. West: The Balance of Military Power*, London.

Ministry of Defence (Soviet) (1974), *Politicheskaya i voennaya Geografia*, Moscow.

Mlynar, Z. (1980), *Nightfrost in Prague*, New York.

Moorcraft, P.L. (1981), *Africa's Superpower* (i.e. South Africa), Johannesburg.

Moore, P. (1979), 'Macedonia: Perennial Balkan Apple of Discord', *The World Today*, October, London.

Myers, K.A. (ed.) (1980), *NATO: The Next Thirty Years*, London.

Newman, P.C. (1983), *True North: Not Strong and Free*, Toronto.

Nunn, S., and Bartlett, D.F. (Senators) (1977), *NATO and the New Soviet Threat. Report to the Committee on Armed Services. U.S. Senate*, Washington.

O'Connell, D.P. (1975), *The Influence of Law on Sea Power*, Manchester.

O'Connell, D.P. (1978), 'Transit Rights and Maritime Strategy', *RUSI*, CXXIII, no. 2.

Ollivant, S. (1984), 'Canada: How Powerful an Ally?', *Conflict Studies*, CLIX, London.

Ollivant, S. (1985), 'Arctic Challenge to NATO', *Conflict Studies*, CLXXII, London.

Ørvik, N. (1973), 'Defence against Help – A Strategy for Small States?', *Survival*, XV, no. 5, London.

Ørvik, N. (1984), 'Canadian Security and "Defence against Help" ', *Survival*, XXVI, no. 1, London.

O'Sullivan, P., and Miller, J.W. (1983), *The Geography of Warfare*, London.

Papas, N. (1982), 'The Importance of the Hellenic Navy', *NFN*, Special Issue no. 2.

Parker, G. (1983), *A Political Geography of Community Europe*, London.

Peltier, B.C., and Pearcy, G.E. (1966), *Military Geography*, Princeton.

Pengelly, P. (1983), 'AirLand Battle: A Hollow Charge?', *Defence Attaché*, no. 3, London.

Petraeus, D.H. (1985), 'Light Infantry in Europe', *Military Review*, LXIV, no. 2, Fort Leavenworth.

Poulsson, J.A. (1981), 'Operations on the Northern Flank of NATO', *NFN*, XXVI, no. 3.

Ranft, B., and Till, G. (1983), *The Sea in Soviet Strategy,* London.

Ratley, L.O. (1979), 'Von Manstein, "Fall Gelb" and NATO Options', *RUSI*, CXXIV, no. 1

Record, J. (1984), *Revising U.S. Military Strategy: Tailoring Means to Ends*, Washington.

Reed, R.F. (1983), *The US–Japan Alliance: Sharing the Burden of Defense*, Washington.

Rees, D. (1980), 'Afghanistan's Role in Soviet Strategy', *Conflict Studies*, CXVIII, London.

Rice, C. (1984), *The Soviet Union and the Czechoslovak Army*, Princeton.

Ries, T. (1984), 'Finland's Armed Forces, Isolated but Unbowed', *IDR*, XVII, no. 3, Geneva.

Ries, T. (1984), 'Soviet Submarines in Sweden. Psychological Warfare in the Nordic Region?', *IDR*, XVII, no. 6.

Rissanen, T.I. (1977), 'Finland, from a Geopolitical Perspective', *Military Review*, LVII, no. 10, Fort Leavenworth.

Roesch, O. (1980), 'Area Defence – Austria's Security', *NFN*, XXV, no. 3.

Rouarch, C. (1984), 'The Naval Mine', *IDR*, XVII, no. 9.

Rubin, F. (1983), 'Security Concerns of the USSR and the Other Warsaw Treaty Organisation Countries', *RUSI*, CXXVIII, no. 3.

Rys, S.L. (1983), *U.S. Military Power*, London.

Salmon, T.C. (1979), 'The Changing Nature of Irish Defence Policy', *The World Today*, November, London.

Salusbury, D.J. (1983), 'Spain: The Challenge for NATO', *RUSI*, CXXVIII, no. 3.

Sanchez-Gijon, A. (1981), 'Spain on the Threshold of the Atlantic Alliance', *NFN, XXVI*, no.3

Schemmer, B.F. (1984), 'The Pacific Naval Balance', *Armed Forces Journal*, CXXI, no. 9, Washington.

Schepe, G. (1983–4), 'Mountain Warfare in Europe', *NSN*, XXVIII, no. 8.

Schlimm, A. (1982), 'The Belgian Navy and Mine Countermeasures in the Channel', *NFN*, Special Issue no. 2.

Schroeter, H. (1978), 'The Allied Command Naval Forces Baltic Approaches', *NFN*, XXIII, Special Issue.

Schulze-Torge, U.J. (1985), 'Sowjetische Werften und ihre Kriegsschiff-Bauprogramme', *Österreichische Militärische Zeitschrift*, 1985, no. 2, Vienna.

Senger und Etterlin, F. (1981), 'Defence of Central Europe. The Challenge of the 1980s', *NFN*, Special Issue no. 2.

Sepulveda, F.L. (1984), 'Restructuring Spain's Defence Organization', *IDR*, XVII, no. 10.

Sharp, J. (1976), 'The Northern Flank', *RUSI*, CXXI, no. 4.

Shear, H.E. (1979), 'The Southern Flank of NATO', *NFN*, XXIII, no. 6.

Sim, R., and Anderson, J. (1980), 'The Caribbean Strategic Vacuum', *Conflict Studies*, CXXI, London.

Simpkin, R. (1982), 'Hammer, Anvil and Net', *British Army Review*, LXXII, London.

Singh, B. (1983), *The Indian Ocean and Security*, Patiala.

Singleton, F.B. (1978), 'Finland between East and West', *The World Today*, August.

Skinner, M. (1983), *U.S.A.F.E.: A Primer of Modern Air Combat in Europe*, London.

Sokolsky, J.J. (1982), 'NATO: Taking Canada More Seriously', *RUSI*, CXXVII, no. 4.

Special Committee of the Senate (Canadian) (1985), *Canada's Territorial Air Defence*, Ottawa.

Spiers, E. (1982), 'Conventional Defence: No Alternative to Trident', *RUSI*, CXXVII, no. 2.

Staudenmaier, W.O. (1980), 'Some Strategic Implications of Fighting Outnumbered on the NATO Battlefield', *Military Review*, LX, no. 5, Fort Leavenworth.

Steinke, R., and Vale, N. (eds) (1983), *Germany Debates Defence: The NATO Alliance at the Crossroads*, New York.

Strachan, H. (1984–5), 'Conventional Defence in Europe', *International Affairs*, LXI, no. 1, London

Suarez de la Hidalga, S. (1982), 'The Role of the Spanish Navy in the Atlantic and the Mediterranean', *NFN*, Special Issue no. 2.

Sutton, B.D. (*et al.*) (1984), 'New Directions in Conventional Defence', *Survival*, XXVI, no. 2, London.

Suvorov, V. (1981), *The Liberators – Inside the Soviet Army,* London.

Tanzer, M. (1984), *Race for Resources*, London.

Thompson, J.M. (1984), 'The Southern Flank and Out-of-area Operations', *RUSI*, CXXVIII, no. 4.

Till, G. (1982), *Maritime Strategy and the Nuclear Age*, London.

Tillson, J. (1978), *The Forward Defense of Europe*, Washington.

Tillson, J. (1981), 'The Forward Defense of Europe', *Military Review*, LXI, no. 5, Fort Leavenworth.

Train, H. (1982), 'Challenge at Sea: Naval Strategy for the 1980s', *NFN*, Special Issue no. 2.

Treverton, G.F. (1981), 'The Strategic Significance of the Iberian Peninsula', *NFN*, XVI, no. 3.

Treverton, G.F. (1983), 'Defence beyond Europe', *Survival*, XXV, no. 5.

Tümer, N. (1982), 'Naval Control of the Turkish Straits', *NFN*, Special Issue No. 2.

Turbiville, G.H. (1976), 'Warsaw Pact Forces in Hungary: A Key Element in Pact Contingency Planning', *RUSI*, CXXI, no. 4.

Tuzo, H. (1975), 'Northern Army Group and Its British Component', *RUSI*, CXX, no. 2.

Urban, M. (1985), *Soviet Land Warfare*, London.

Urquart, G.M. (1977), 'Canadian Defence Policy', *RUSI*, CXXII, no. 2.

Valley, B.L. (1983), 'Turkey and Its NATO Allies: Friends or Foes', *RUSI*, CXXVIII, no. 1.

Verdecchia, P. (1983), 'Italian Armor, Past, Present and Future', *Armor*, XCII, no. 3, Fort Knox.

Vigor, P.H. (1977), 'Fighting in Built-up Areas: A Soviet View – Part I', *RUSI*, CXXII, London.

Vigor, P.H. (1980), 'Doubts and Difficulties Confronting a Would-be Soviet Attacker', *RUSI*, CXXV, no. 2.

Vigor, P.H. (1983), *Soviet Blitzkrieg Theory*, London.

Villar, R. (1982), 'The Alternative Strategy', *RUSI*, CXXVII, no. 4.

Volgyes, I. (1982), *The Political Reliability of the Warsaw Pact Armies*, Durham (N.C.).

Wallin, L.D. (1979), *Doctrines, Technology and Future War: A Swedish View*, Stockholm.

Watt, C.I. (1983), 'The Influence of Terrain on Soviet Operational and Tactical Doctrine', Ph.D. thesis, University of London.

Wettern, D. (1978), 'Amphibious Warfare: The Northern Flank', *NFN*, XXIII, no. 2.

Wettern, D. (1984), 'Britain's Dilemma: A Naval Strategy but Few Ships', *Daily Telegraph*, 20 January 1984.

Whetten, L. (1984), 'Turkey's Role in the Atlantic Alliance', *Atlantic Review*, II, no. 3, London.

Whiteley, P. (1978), 'The Importance of the Northern Flank to NATO', *NFN*, XXIII, no. 2.

Whiteley, P. (1979), 'The Reinforcement of Europe', *NFN*, XXIV, no. 4.

Wiener, F. (1976), *Partisankampf am Balkan*, Vienna. Esp. for the review of Serbian military history.

Willmott, H.P. (1981), *Sea Warfare: Weapons, Tactics and Strategy*, Chichester.

Wyllie, J.H. (1984), *The Influence of British Arms: An Analysis of British Military Intervention since 1956*, London.

Ziemke, E.F. (1959), *The German Northern Theatre of Operations 1941–1945*, Washington.

Zoppo, C.E., and Zorgbibe, C. (eds) (1985), *On Geopolitics: Classical and Nuclear*, Dordrecht, Boston and Lancaster.

Index

Abbreviations are entered as they stand – thus NATO appears as 'NATO', and not as the 'North Atlantic Treaty Organisation'.